THE CORPORATION

Classic and Contemporary Readings
Edited by Max B.E. Clarkson

The term stakeholders defines a group much broader than a corporation's shareholders. It includes employees, customers, suppliers, and governments, and extends to anyone who benefits from the company. There is considerable debate, given that large multifunctional corporations are now the dominant form of economic organization worldwide, about how responsive and accountable companies should be to their stakeholders. This debate includes fundamental questions such as: Who should be considered stakeholders? Which stakeholder interests should a corporation take into account? How should stakeholder interests be balanced against shareholder objectives (such as profits)? What changes should be made to corporate governance to reflect these new interests?

This anthology is designed to sharpen the debate about the role and purpose of the corporation in society through the provision of seminal articles on the concept and recognition of stakeholders, and the integration of stakeholder interests into decision making. It provides a theoretical base for managerial action, and will assist researchers in planning further studies to shed light on the issues involved.

MAX B.E. CLARKSON is Director of the Clarkson Centre for Business Ethics, and Professor Emeritus in the Faculty of Management at the University of Toronto.

The Corporation and Its Stakeholders: Classic and Contemporary Readings

Edited by Max B.E. Clarkson

UNIVERSITY OF TORONTO PRESS
Toronto Buffalo London

© University of Toronto Press Incorporated 1998
Toronto Buffalo London

Printed in Canada

ISBN 0-8020-4300-3 (cloth)
ISBN 0-8020-8127-4 (paper)

Printed on acid-free paper.

Canadian Cataloguing in Publication Data

Main entry under title:

The corporation and its stakeholders : classic and contemporary readings

ISBN 0-8020-4300-3 (bound)   ISBN 0-8020-8127-4 (pbk.)

1. Corporations.   I. Clarkson, Max B.E.

HD27311.C67 1998   338.7'4   C97-932226-X

University of Toronto Press acknowledges the support of the Canada
Council for the Arts and the Ontario Arts Council for its publishing program.

Contents

Foreword vii

Clarkson, Max B.E., University of Toronto 1
  "Introduction"

Part 1: Shareholders and Stakeholders

Clark, J.M., University of Chicago 13
  "The Changing Basis of Economic Responsibility"
  The Journal of Political Economy (Vol. 24, #3, 1916) 209-229.

Dodd, E. Merrick, Harvard Law School 31
  "For Whom Are Corporate Managers Trustees?"
  Harvard Law Review (Vol. 45, #7, May 1932) 1145-63.

Blair, Margaret M., The Brookings Institution 47
  "Whose Interests Should Be Served?"
  Chap. 6 in *Ownership and Control: Rethinking Corporate Governance for the Twenty-First Century.* (Washington, D.C.: Brookings Institution, 1995) 202-234.

Carroll, Archie B., University of Georgia and
Juha Näsi, University of Jyväskylä 71
  "Understanding Stakeholder Thinking: Themes from a Finnish Conference." *Business Ethics — a European Review* (Vol. 6, #1, January 1997) 46-51.

Part 2: Morality, Ethics and Stakeholder Theory

Sen, Amartya, All Souls College, Oxford 83
  "The Moral Standing of the Market"
  Social Philosophy & Policy (Vol. 2, #2, 1985) 1-19.

Goodpaster, Kenneth E., University of St. Thomas 103
  "Business Ethics and Stakeholder Analysis."
  Business Ethics Quarterly (Vol. 1, #1, 1991) 53-73.

R. Edward Freeman, University of Virginia 125
"A Stakeholder Theory of the Modern Corporation." In *Ethical Theory and Business*, edited by Tom L. Beauchamp and Norman E. Bowie. (Englewood Cliff, N.J.: Prentice-Hall, 1994) 66-76.

Carroll, Archie B., University of Georgia 139
"Stakeholder Thinking in Three Models of Management Morality: A Perspective with Strategic Implications."
In *Understanding Stakeholder Thinking*, edited by Juha Näsi. (Helsinki, Finland: LSR - Publications, 1995) 47-74.

Part 3: *Stakeholder Theory and Management Performance*

Donaldson, T., Georgetown University
and L.E. Preston, University of Maryland 173
"The Stakeholder Theory of the Corporation: Concepts, Evidence and Implications." *Academy of Management Review* (Vol 20, #1, 1995) 65-91.

Jones, Thomas M., University of Washington 205
"Instrumental Stakeholder Theory: A Synthesis of Ethics and Economics." *Academy of Management Review* (Vol 20, #2, April 1995) 404-437.

Clarkson, Max B.E., University of Toronto 243
"A Stakeholder Framework for Analysing and Evaluating Corporate Social Performance." *Academy of Management Review* (Vol 20, #1, 1995) 92-117.

Mitchell, R. K., University of Victoria, B. R. Agle and
Donna J. Wood, University of Pittsburgh 275
"Toward a Theory of Stakeholder Identification and Salience: Defining the Principle of Who and What Really Counts."
Academy of Management Review (Vol 22, #4, 1997) 853-886.

Wood, Donna J., and R. E. Jones., University of Pittsburgh 315
"Stakeholder Mismatching: A Theoretical Problem in Empirical Research on Corporate Social Performance."
The International Journal of Organizational Analysis
(Vol. 3, #3, 1995) 229-267.

Foreword:
Redefining the Corporation

The Alfred P. Sloan Foundation, named for one of the founders of General Motors, has long had an interest in the role of the corporation as a central and characteristic institution of American society. This interest has intensified and broadened as US-based firms have penetrated foreign environments, foreign-based firms have become active in the US, and a global system of competition and interdependence has evolved. Within this new global setting, trends affecting the operations and status of all kinds of firms, both domestic and multinational, require analysis, and the potential effects of differences in policies, practices and governance structures among firms based in different national jurisdictions demand critical examination.

In 1995, a representative of the Foundation proposed that a small group of scholars interested in the status and future of the corporation establish an international network of scholars and practitioners in order to launch a program of research and discussion that might lead to new thinking and new knowledge in this area. The result of this initiative is the "Redefining the Corporation" Project, which has now established an e-mail network, created a website[1], and arranged several invitational seminars and open conference programs. A number of small research grants have been awarded to support individual empirical studies, and a larger "core project" involving careful study and comparison of a few large, multinational corporations has been started.

The purpose of all of this activity is to "redefine" the corporation as an entity within the economy, polity and society. The focus of this redefinition effort is the "stakeholder model" of the corporation, the concept of the corporation as a network involving multiple participants, and interests, each of which may make contributions and receive rewards as a result of a corporate activity. As Clarkson emphasizes in his Introduction, below, there has been an increasing amount of discussion, both public and academic, about the nature and purpose of the corporation in recent years, and it is apparent that the stakeholder model has gained considerable acceptance among both scholars and executives. However, neither the empirical evidence of stakeholder orientation, nor its operating and performance implications, have been fully explored.

The "Redefining the Corporation" Project begins with a simple proposition: *Corporations ARE what they DO*. The Project aims to examine the *nature* of the corporation from this perspective, raising questions such as the following:

> How are stakeholder interests manifested and recognized, and how does corporate management deal with them?
>
> Do corporations that profess and attempt to implement "stakeholder-orientation" policies actually behave any differently or achieve any different performance outcomes than others?
>
> Do differences in stakeholder orientation among firms based in different political jurisdictions have any effects on their global competitive interaction, success or failure?
>
> How do varying legal requirements interact with voluntary stakeholder-oriented policies and practices, and with what results?

These empirical questions are being raised against the background of a large theoretical and philosophical literature, and the idea of preparing a set of "benchmark" readings was conceived as a critical step in preparing for future work. Nominations for inclusion were solicited through the e-mail network, and Max Clarkson accepted the task of organizing the papers selected and preparing them for publication. Two papers are from earlier eras, and a rereading of these suggests that the problem of "redefining the corporation" has been with us for a very long time, and is likely to command attention for some years into the future.

Thomas Donaldson, University of Pennsylvania
Lee E. Preston, University of Maryland

---

[1] The "Redefining the Corporation Project" website address is http://www.mgmt.utoronto.ca/~stake/

The Corporation and Its Stakeholders: Classic and Contemporary Readings

Introduction by Max B.E. Clarkson

The Context

Our objective in publishing this book is to sharpen the terms of debate about the role and purpose of the corporation in society. Different beliefs about this important issue lie at the heart of continuing disagreements about corporate governance and the responsibilities of directors and officers towards stockholders and other stakeholders. These debates are not new, and are now occurring in all important parts of the world economy: North and South America, Europe, Russia and its former satellites, Japan and the rest of Asia.

Following the fall of the Berlin Wall and the collapse of the USSR, the world economy has experienced the consequences of freer trade, intensified competition with consequent pressures on labor costs and wage levels, and corporate restructuring or re-engineering, all coupled with unaccustomed levels of unemployment in many industrialized countries and massive urbanization in developing countries. New and widespread applications of technology and telecommunications have resulted in the questioning of many old and comfortable assumptions. The *status quo* has become an endangered concept everywhere.

It is not surprising therefore that serious questions are being raised about the belief, widely held in North America, that the purpose of the corporation in society is to maximize profits and financial value for the primary benefit of its shareholders, who are also assumed, mistakenly, to be the corporation's owners. Those who hold this belief about the primacy of shareholder value maintain that the interests of all other participants in the corporation's activities and operations are protected adequately by some kind of contractual arrangements, either explicit or, more likely, implicit.

The corporation consequently is described as a "nexus of contracts," each of which is assumed to satisfy fully and equitably the legitimate concerns of all interested parties. The protection afforded by corporations to employees, communities and other participants by these often implicit contracts was seen to be thin or non-existent during the 1980s, a period that witnessed the rapid growth of the market for corporate control, accompanied by the widespread use of high interest bonds to finance takeovers. The disposition of assets that resulted from many of these takeovers, borrowings and restructurings often caused major dislocations and losses for employees and communities. They had no recourse and certainly no comfort as they learned about the windfall profits accruing frequently to shareholders and officers who were favorably situated.

As takeover financing became more ambitious and the targets ever larger, obvious questions were asked, such as: "Whose interests are being served?" and "Whose interests *should* be served?" One answer was provided by the new "stakeholder statutes" that were adopted by a majority of the legislatures of the United States. In about thirty states there is now legislation that provides legal protection for boards of directors that decide to resist takeover offers which, in their judgment, are not in the best interests of such stakeholders as employees, suppliers, customers or the local community, even though a premium over market is being offered to the shareholders.

The Concept of Stakeholders

The use of the term "stakeholder" has become widespread relatively recently in the literature of management and corporate governance. In 1984 Freeman's *Strategic Management: A Stakeholder Approach* was published. Since then several hundred publications that are based on the stakeholder concept have appeared in the academic and popular press. As a figure of speech, "stakeholder" clearly appeals to those who seek to provide a broader and more inclusive vision of the role and purpose of the corporation in society than that of the advocates of "shareholder" primacy. The legal definitions of "shareholder" and "share" have evolved over many years, whereas "stakeholder" has only recently become used in a legal context and there is not yet general agreement about its meaning.

A "stake" can be defined as something of value, some form of capital, human, physical, or financial, that is at risk, either voluntarily or involuntarily. Stakeholders in a corporation are those persons or interests that have a stake, something to gain or lose as a result of its activities. Voluntary stakeholders are those who have chosen to take a stake and bear some form of risk in anticipation of some form of gain or increase in value, whether as a shareholder or investor, an employee, customer, or supplier.

Involuntary stakeholders are those that are, or may be, exposed unknowingly to risk and thus be harmed, or benefitted, as a consequence of the corporation's activities. Their stakes are not assumed willingly, but are consequential on the activities of others. Involuntary stakeholders, including governments, communities and the environment, are particularly subject to the risks and consequences of the failure of corporations to internalize all their costs. The heavy burden of costs that have been externalized becomes clearly evident when pollution, destruction or death are the consequences of a corporation's operations and activities.

The concept of "stakes as risk capital," either financial, physical, or human, enables us to distinguish between stakeholders—defined as those who bear some form of risk—and those who make claims on the organization, but bear no risk. These claimants cannot therefore be ignored by managers, but without some form of stake at risk they are not in the same category as stakeholders. Risk is the common thread or element underlying claims, ownership, interests, and legal or moral rights in a corporation and its activities. Stakes are always at risk. Risk, coupled with the prospect of reward, is the mainspring of capitalism. From this perspective the corporation can be defined as "a nexus of risks."

Risks must be managed. From the beginnings of commercial time, merchants and traders, manufacturers and bankers have found it essential to manage their relationships with those who had something at risk in order to satisfy the needs and expectations of governments and investors, of customers, employees, and suppliers. These essential elements of commercial survival and profitability are defined as "stakeholders." Stakeholder theory is grounded in the realities of management practice and behavior.

The use of the term "stakeholder," intuitively appealing as it may be, however, does not answer important questions about definition and classification. The authors of the papers in this book discuss and clarify such concepts as stakeholder management, stakeholder theory, stakeholder models, perspectives and approaches, stakeholder analysis and stakeholder synthesis. All attempt, in one way or another, to make the concepts surrounding stakeholder theory more useful to practicing managers and investors, to academic researchers and students of organizations.

The Contents of this Volume

The articles that have been reproduced in this volume were selected after soliciting suggestions from participants in the international colloquy, *Redefining the Corporation*. They are linked by some common themes that are expressed in the two "classic" readings, by Clark (1916) and Dodd (1932). Clark was concerned about what he defined as the "economics of irresponsibility" prevailing in business at that time. He went on to make the case for "an economics of responsibility, developed and embodied in our working business ethics."

The authors represented in this book all share Clark's concern about the "economics of irresponsibility," which today manifests itself as "finance theory" or the "theory of shareholder primacy," the widely held belief that the purpose of the corporation is to maximize profits for the primary benefit of its shareholders. When Clark and Dodd were writing, more than sixty years ago, stakeholder theory had not been developed. Its conceptual basis, however, is clearly evident in their work. The "great task" ahead, as defined then by Clark, was "to substitute an economics of responsibility for an economics of irresponsible conflict." The proponents of stakeholder theory and stakeholder management today are now attempting to complete Clark's "great task."

The selections from the stakeholder literature in this book have been arranged in three parts. Part 1, *Shareholders and Stakeholders*, demonstrates that the basic questions about the role and purpose of the corporation are not new. Several key issues in the debate were identified many years ago. This brief historical survey concludes by establishing the relationship between stakeholder theory and business ethics, which is discussed further in Part 2, *Morality, Ethics, and Stakeholder Theory*, together with issues concerning governance and strategic management. Part 3, *Stakeholder Theory and Management Performance*, focuses on the managerial implications of stakeholder theory and its practical application to the measurement of management performance.

Part 1. Shareholders and Stakeholders

Clark made the point in 1916 that "business economics separates business sharply off from the rest of life." He deplored the consequences of the attitude that "business is business," and predicted change because "we have begun to realize the many inappropriate values that are created and the many unpaid damages that are inflicted in the course of business exchanges." The "stakeholder statutes" of recent years represent one such change.

Dodd also shows that there is nothing new about the essentials of the stakeholder/stockholder debate, as he raises questions about the belief that the purpose of the corporation is "maximum stockholder profit." He quoted approvingly business leaders, including the then Dean of the Harvard Business School, who held that managers should be concerned "with the interests of employees, consumers, and the general public, as well as of the stockholders." Dodd believed that "a sense of social responsibility" would become "the appropriate attitude" and that "business ethics may thus tend to become in some degree those of a profession rather than of a trade."

Blair brings the historical record up to date in asking "Whose Interests Should be Served?". She confirms Dodd's prediction, stating that by "the late 1960s and early 1970s, corporate responsiveness to a broad range of stakeholders had become accepted business practice." In terms of the governance of corporations, she believes that stakeholders are "all those who truly have something invested and at risk in the enterprise," and argues that control rights should be distributed so as to ensure that one stakeholder group could not externalize costs and increase the value of its stake "by pushing costs and risks onto other stakeholders." She too rejects the "simplistic finance model" of the corporation, but wishes to "retain the compelling logic that private control of private property leads to the most efficient use of society's resources."

Carroll completes this brief historical survey by pointing out that the current roots of the stakeholder concept are to be found in the 1960s, in Scandinavia, at the Stanford Research Institute, and in the works of Ansoff. Carroll goes on to define the questions that a manager should answer to reach the corporation's objectives, satisfy stakeholders, and deal with them ethically. He views stakeholder theory as "undergirding business ethics."

Part 2. Morality, Ethics, and Stakeholder Theory

Sen discusses *The Moral Standing of the Market* and relates it to results. He underlines the inability of the market to address issues of inequality. He does not find persuasive arguments on behalf of the virtues of the market, and concludes with faint praise for the market mechanism, primarily because there is neither a superior nor practical alternative. It is precisely around this point —the inability of the market to deal with issues of inequality— that the stakeholder/stockholder debate revolves.

Goodpaster examines another aspect of the fundamental question: "How can a corporation, given its economic mission, be managed with appropriate attention to ethical concerns?" He explores the paradox of business without ethics, which he maintains is the consequence of strategic stakeholder synthesis, or of ethics without business, the consequence of a multi-fiduciary stakeholder synthesis. He proposes a third approach to stakeholder thinking, which is a result of understanding that the conscience of the corporation is a logical and moral extension of the consciences of its principals.

Freeman does not agree with Goodpaster, maintaining that "managers bear a fiduciary relationship to stakeholders." He argues that stakeholders have a right not to be treated as a means to the end of stockholder profit, and "therefore must participate in determining the future direction of the firm in which they have a stake." The purpose of the firm, he believes, must be redefined "to serve as a vehicle for coordinating stakeholder interests." The logical extensions of his arguments are proposals for changes in corporate governance such as stakeholder boards of directors, stakeholder bills of rights, and concomitant changes to corporate law.

Carroll shows how stakeholder thinking can be used to integrate ethics with strategic management. He describes, defines, and illustrates immoral, amoral, and moral strategic management. Those who are interested in applying stakeholder thinking at both strategic and operational levels will find Carroll's definitions useful and his illustrations relevant. He maintains that the stakeholder perspective provides a powerful framework for the description and analysis of the relationship between an organization and its environment. The use of this framework enables the manager to avoid the trap, identified long ago by Clark, of viewing the corporation as a purely economic enterprise that operates in a separate compartment in society called 'business' and is devoted solely to the maximization of shareholder profit.

Part 3. Stakeholder Theory and Management Performance

Donaldson and Preston have made an important contribution to the development of stakeholder theory by identifying its three different, but complementary, aspects: descriptive, instrumental, and normative. They conclude that these "three approaches to stakeholder theory, although quite different, are mutually supportive, and that the *normative* base serves as the critical underpinning for the theory in all its forms." This normative, or ethical, base, providing a strong foundation for most definitions of stakeholder theory, is clearly evident in the articles in this book, all the way back to Clark and Dodd. Some three generations have now passed since they criticized the theory of shareholder primacy and voiced their concerns about its moral inadequacy, its empirical inaccuracy, and its false dichotomy of business and society.

Donaldson and Preston confront these concerns by arguing that stakeholder theory can be normatively based on the evolving theory of property, now properly understood as a bundle of many rights, some of which may be limited. They underline the irony of this new and original approach, since "the traditional view has been that a focus on property rights justifies the dominance of shareowner interests."

They discuss the managerial implications of stakeholder theory, including the problem of defining stakes and stakeholders and the distinction between influencers and stakeholders. They conclude that "managers *should* acknowledge the validity of diverse stakeholder interests, and *should* attempt to respond to them within a mutually supportive framework, because that is a moral requirement for the legitimacy of the managerial function itself."

Jones also explores the managerial implications of stakeholder theory and advances several propositions for empirical testing. These propositions are based on his definition of the core theory as a subset of ethical principles (trust, trustworthiness, and cooperativeness) that can result in significant competitive advantage for a corporation. His propositions specify indicators of corporate performance that relate to issues concerning four stakeholder groups: shareholders, managers, employees, and suppliers. These propositions assert that firms adopting certain practices will outperform those that do the obverse.

These and other propositions demonstrate the practical application of stakeholder theory to predictions about, and the measurement of, indicators of corporate performance. Traditional accounting-based measures of corporate financial performance, firmly rooted in the past, are necessarily historical. Consequently they often fail when it comes to predicting future success or failure. Stakeholder theory and frameworks, however, provide an orderly and logical approach to identifying, analysing, and measuring those elements of corporate performance that are most likely to indicate future success or failure.

Performance is what counts. Corporations are what they do. Whether they are motivated by enlightened self-interest, common sense, high or low standards of ethical behavior are all questions that cannot be answered by any social scientist or empirical methodology available today. But performance can be defined, managed, measured and evaluated. For better or worse corporations manage their relationships with their customers and employees, with suppliers, communities and other stakeholders. Well managed corporations identify critical success factors, measure results, and evaluate and reward performance accordingly.

My own contribution to this volume provides a summary of conclusions about stakeholder management that are the result of a ten year research program into the performance of over seventy corporations. An analytical framework has been developed, together with a comprehensive guide to typical social and stakeholder issues. These are accompanied by definitions and detailed descriptions of the data that are required in order to evaluate a corporation's performance in managing its relationships with, and its responsibilities to, its stakeholders.

The identification, classification and definition of *stakeholders* and *non-stakeholders* have caused continuing debate during the development of stakeholder theory and its application to the management of corporations. "Who (or what) are the stakeholders of the firm? And to whom (or what) do managers pay attention?" are the important questions raised by Mitchell, Agle, and Wood. They build on the definitions put forward by several contributors to this book, and develop a method of stakeholder identification that is based on the importance of three major attributes of business relationships: power, urgency, and legitimacy. Using this valuable insight into the nature of stakeholder relationships, they develop a typology of stakeholders, together with propositions about the relative importance of different classes of stakeholders to managers of the firm.

They have produced two comprehensive summaries of scholarly work since 1963 related to key issues of stakeholder identification: (i) a chronology of answers to the question "Who is a stakeholder?"; and (ii) a listing of different rationales that have been advanced for identifying stakeholders. These thorough catalogues demonstrate clearly that building a new theory is a cooperative scholarly enterprise, particularly when the prevailing current theory, that of shareholder primacy, has attained doctrinal status.

Empirical data are simply not available to prove either the stakeholder or shareholder cases. Many attempts have been made to show that socially responsible corporate behavior is, or is not, correlated with financial or stock market performance. But as Wood and Jones show, in the concluding article of this book, there is no way to determine which stakeholders are relevant to which kind of measure of corporate performance. Investors and financial analysts are no longer satisfied that historical financial data can predict successful performance. Corporations are learning to manage performance by means of multiple measures, an approach that is being referred to as the 'balanced scorecard'. Scholars and practitioners therefore should beware of simplified assumptions about the relationship between success, however defined, and selected stakeholder measures or variables. The development of stakeholder theory is not dependent on trying to show that corporate virtue is necessarily rewarded by the stock market.

The Future of Stakeholder Theory and Management

Survival, as Charles Darwin told us long ago, depends not on strength or intelligence, but on adaptability to the environment. Stakeholder theory provides a logical and useful framework for analysing and describing the relationships between a corporation and its environment. This framework is grounded in the reality of the key elements of corporate success, which are its relationships with those people, interests, and groups that are essential for its survival. Without the continuing support and cooperation, over the long term, of employees, customers, shareholders, investors, suppliers, communities and governments, a corporation cannot continue as a profitable going concern.

Stakeholder management can be defined as the strategic planning and operating decisions necessary for a corporation to maintain an appropriate balance in the reasonable satisfaction of the diverse and often conflicting needs and expectations of its stakeholders. Implementing stakeholder management requires that corporations communicate openly and clearly with their stakeholders, particularly about relevant benefits and costs and about the severity and probability of harmful risks to which they may be or become exposed; that corporations do not externalize costs or engage in activities that can give rise to socially unacceptable risks or consequences; that they implement policies and use processes that internalize costs; and that they adopt modes of behavior that are transparent, accessible, and appropriate to the commitments, investments, and risks of all those who are involved.

From this perspective, therefore, the purpose of the corporation, as the converter into goods and services of the resources and stakes that are at risk, is to create wealth or value for all its stakeholders, without exposing them or others to involuntary harm or loss. In this way it would then be possible to perform the "great task" defined by Clark many years ago and develop "an economics of responsibility embodied in our business ethics."

I am greatly indebted for his careful editorial assistance to my colleague, Professor Leonard J. Brooks, Professor of Business Ethics and Accounting and Executive Director, The Clarkson Centre for Business Ethics, at the Joseph L. Rotman School of Management, University of Toronto; to Ms. Enola Stoyle for her skill in website publishing; to Ms. Carol Brady for her secretarial support; and to the members of the "Redefining the Corporation" Colloquy who made suggestions for articles to be published in this book.

M.B.E.C.

Part 1

Shareholders and Stakeholders

The Changing Basis of Economic Responsibility

J. Maurice Clark, University of Chicago

I. Forecast of the Argument

Twenty years ago an economist writing under this title would have been expected to deal chiefly or solely with the responsibility of the individual for his own economic destiny: his responsibility for paying his debts and keeping out of the poor-house. Economic responsibility meant self-reliance and self-dependence.[1] Today any treatment of the subject from such a limited standpoint would be an anachronism. The ideas of obligation which embody the actual relations of man to man in the twentieth century, and answer the needs of the twentieth century, are radically different from the ideas which dominated the nineteenth.

Some have failed to realize what the change means and have resisted it uncomprehendingly. Interdependence means no more to them than it did in the days when free exchange seemed adequate to organize the world, and enlist the far islands of the seas to furnish London breakfast tables. That was one kind of interdependence, marvelously far-reaching and marvelously effective—but not the interdependence that is putting its peculiar stamp on the life of the present generation.

Some have gone to the other extreme and have lost their old sense of personal accountability in an easy philosophy that lays the burdens on the impersonal state, and the blame on heredity and environment. But most of us have not gone so far as that. We do not want a state that shall prohibit all our vices, syndicate all our virtues, and render old-fashioned self-reliance obsolete, if indeed that were remotely possible! Instead, many men are honestly seeking to know what their obligations are in this new era, that they may meet them on their own initiative. More knowledge is wanted, that men may guide themselves. The modern prayer is not so much for strength as for wisdom.

In the economic world this issue is presented more clearly perhaps than anywhere else. We have inherited an economics of irresponsibility. We are in an economy of control with which our intellectual inheritance fits but awkwardly. To make control really tolerable we need something more; something which is still in its infancy. We need an economics of responsibility, developed and embodied in our working business ethics.

II. *The Swing of the Pendulum*

We have gone through a revolution of late in many realms of thought and policy. We have swung far away from narrow individualism toward a sense of solidarity and social-mindedness. In religion the dominant ideal is no longer a narrowly personal salvation granted from above as a reward of personal faith, but rather an attitude of love and service to one's fellows which are in themselves salvation. The old idea of free will is giving way to determinism, individualism to public control, personal responsibility to social responsibility.

This changed attitude shows itself in economic matters in a hundred ways. The common law treated industrial accidents as matters of personal responsibility and attempted to fix a personal blame. The results were intolerable. Something was wrong. Contrast the attitude of a system of compulsory compensation which blames nobody, and seems almost to take away all responsibility, distributing it between the state and the employer and treating the employer impersonally, as the representative of the industry. This policy expresses a new idea of responsibility.

Not long ago we were almost morbidly afraid to do anything to relieve distress, for fear of undermining people's independence and perpetuating the disease we aimed to cure. If these unfortunates could not quickly be put in a condition of doing for themselves there was danger in doing too much for them. Anything looking toward permanent assistance was a confession of failure in the present and an omen of evil to come. Meanwhile poverty continued to breed poverty. Now free meals for school children are becoming more and more common, the minimum wage in a mild form is being seriously tried out, and we seem to be on the threshold of similar experiments with old-age pensions, mothers' pensions, and insurance against unemployment.

The old-time lumber-gang boss or division superintendent promoted men or discharged them at will. He was responsible to his superior officer for getting results, and to his conscience, if he had one, for the rights and wrongs of his actions. Often he adopted a policy of rewards or punishments that were sudden, unexpected, and intentionally arbitrary, his object being to keep the men in proper awe of what might happen, and to keep them on their good behavior in little things: things so small in themselves that only the momentary impulse of an arbitrary autocrat would take any notice of them. It was every man's own lookout that the blow did not fall on his head. This system could work tolerably well in a young country, so rich in opportunity that most men could "fall on their feet" whatever happened and whenever and wherever they might be cast adrift.

But today the consequences are too serious to be treated thus cavalierly. Compare the situation of the modern official dealing with a strong union. He cannot discharge men without the possibility of having to face a committee of their fellow-laborers who will make him give an account of his actions. A group has assumed responsibility for its members and a new responsibility of an individual toward the group is being enforced. How shall the group, the union, have brought home to it its own responsibility to the larger group of which it is a part? That is the next chapter of the story, and the end is not yet written.

Unemployment used to be considered largely a matter of personal fitness and willingness to work; now it is spoken of as a disease of our economic system. Criminals and prostitutes used to be regarded quite simply as wicked people. Now they are quite as often looked upon as victims of the social order. In fact this explanation is so much in the air that it has become a habit, an unthinking reaction to anything and everything that goes wrong, and anyone and everyone who goes to pieces. There is little room to question that our habit of overworking this conveniently impersonal scapegoat is closely connected with what Miss Repplier has called our national "loss of nerve." It is all a most disquieting phase of the spread of deterministic ideas among people ready to absorb them one-sidedly.

But it is all part of a movement we cannot escape, with its successes and its failures, its inspiration for the man big enough to catch it, and its enervating effect on those without the vision. It is the product of new situations and new knowledge, and we must use the knowledge to make the best of the situations. We must take what it gives and fight to keep whatever of good it threatens to take away.

It is the product of many things, from psychology to life insurance and from bacteriology to large-scale manufacturing. The bottom facts are, first, that we are becoming interdependent in new and unforeseen ways, and, second, that we are finding out more about the remote causes of things, which we used to take for granted.

Psychology shows us our minds as products of inherited tendencies and the environment to which they react. This makes the living conditions of the slum responsible for the gangster's criminal tendencies and many lesser personal faults and failures. Mortality tables show us occupational environments as killing so many men out of a thousand every year, and statisticians correlate hot weather and suicide, and attempt to correlate crime and heredity.

Indeed, statistics, together with the mass-phenomena they measure, have been the instrument of a surprising deal of altered thinking. When we are looking at John Smith alone, we cannot tell just what he will do in a given situation or what a change in environment will do to him. He is still an independent personality and a law unto himself. But we can tell in advance what such a change will do to a thousand John Smiths. It may kill so and so many, or save so and so many alive, and we become accustomed to the idea that enfeebling environments have made so and so many criminals, and so and so many good-for-nothing idlers, who would otherwise have remained on the safe side of respectability and self-support. The environment has become responsible for John Smith.

But at the same time John Smith has become responsible for the environment. A knowledge of bacteria makes criminal neglect out of what were once matters of purely private concern, and the outcome is to make medicine more and more a matter of maintaining a healthful environment and hence a matter of public prevention rather than of private cure.

Man is ever in the presence of powers too strong for him to cope with, and never knows when they may reach out and take his life. Where the environment that threatens and the powers that kill are the environment and the powers of nature, he worships and watches his priming, learns to sleep lightly, to read footprints, and to know the signs of water. Where the environment is man-made and the powers are those of machinery, he ceases to worship, and he may begin instead to resent, to protest, and ultimately to revolt. Large-scale industry puts the laborer in surroundings, no more dangerous perhaps than the forest or desert which faced the old-time frontiersman, but surroundings which, dangers and all, are the work of human hands and human brains. All these things have given us new ideas of causes and effects, and these have given us new ideas of responsibility. We are finding out that many things' are not to be taken for granted as of old, because they are things over which someone can exercise control, and that means they are things for which someone is responsible.

III. Causation

If we try to trace the causes of anything fully, we are overwhelmed. Everything is a joint result of so many contributing causes that the whole universe may seem to have conspired to make one commuter miss the four-thirty train. So that when we talk about the "reason why," we never mean more than a few out of an infinite series of reasons. How do we go to work to pick out those few?

We are likely to look first at the cause that is closest to the event and gives the most obvious push or offers the most obvious resistance. The teacup broke because the maid dropped it. The workman lost his fingers through a moment of carelessness at his machine plane. The panic was precipitated because of such and such failures.

Of course we shall never get anywhere on any such superficial principle. And yet we cannot go wandering through the mazes of infinity looking far the ultimate and the fundamental. We have a purpose: to shape the world-or our little bit of it -"nearer to the heart's desire." We want to know two things: "Which are the causes that are really important in deciding the exact nature of the outcome?" These are the significant causes. Also, "Which are the causes over which we have some control and before which we do not stand entirely helpless?" These we may call the responsible causes.

The failure of such and such a bank may have precipitated the panic, but the panic would have arrived and run much the same course in any case. Sun-spots may cause crises, or they may be symptoms of something else which causes climatic changes and these may be a cause of crises, and statistics may support this with its most convincing proofs. But these climatic cycles are not the only things that disturb the smooth running of the machinery of production and consumption, and the essential thing seems to be that we have an industrial system in which misfits work cumulatively, regardless of the source from which the original disturbance arises. In a system of private production with enormous use of capital, involving the staking of industrial fortunes on a distant future, any irregularity is intensified in some quarters. An unexpected weakening of demand is felt more keenly by wholesalers than by retailers, since the retailer not only has sold fewer goods, but is allowing his stock to diminish. For the time being he buys even less than he sells. For the same reason the manufacturer feels the slackening of demand more keenly still, and the machine industries and construction industries most of all, since new construction is suspended and even maintenance is likely to be postponed. Those engaged in these industries can buy less, and this may lead to a slackening of demand for many products. Even in active times contractors may be squeezed by a rise in the price of their materials, and their profits turned to losses. Their failures, in turn, embarrass their creditors and may spread a feeling of panic to the whole financial community. The part played by banks in making both expansion and contraction cumulative is too well known to call for comment here.[2]

Compared to these qualities of our industrial organization the exact nature of the one most regular disturbance of production would seem to have little to say in determining the exact nature of the outcome. We should in all probability have panics without sun-spots or climatic cycles, but with a different industrial system sun-spots could come and go without producing anything like the present type of panic. Sun-spots may help us to predict the time of stress, but apart from this they are probably not the most significant cause for our purposes. Moreover, we cannot do anything about sun-spots, while we can change our credit system. Sunspots are therefore not a responsible cause of panics.

One of the greatest things that the progress of science and industry has done for us is to give us responsible causes of a social and environmental sort. We used to think we could change men more easily than their environment, and we preached thrift, industry, and all the economic virtues, and let the rest stand as "natural laws," unchangeable. Now we are finding that to chance the individual we must change his environment, and that preaching is not usually a big enough environmental change to get the desired results. We are coming to take a certain amount of human carelessness for granted and demanding safeguarded machinery and shortened hours with a view to securing an environment in which the natural weakness will be guarded against and the limited endurance not overtaxed.

When a man is discharged because he is not worth a living wage and the employer seeks another in his place his personal shortcomings are certainly the cause of his trouble, whatever we may think about the ultimate causes of his inefficiency. But when a railroad or an industrial corporation turns off thousands of men at a time because a cut of a certain per cent is deemed necessary or advisable, how does the case stand? It is still the least competent who go and their incompetence is the cause of their being the ones selected. But it is not absolute incompetence in this case, but relative incompetence: merely the fact that they are at the bottom of the list.

If some are absolutely incompetent, that is an evil to be remedied. But something tells us that no amount of personal effort and no amount of education or hygiene can hope to prevent 10 per cent of the men from being less efficient than the other 90 per cent. In such a case the incompetence of the men may well cease to be the responsible cause in our minds, and instead the industrial situation, under which an industry wants now 10 per cent more men and now 10 per cent less, may come to stand as the thing we try to change, the thing we hold responsible for the evil of unemployment.

Not that personal efficiency does not make a difference, but opinion is unfortunately divided between those who think that the laborer ought to try to solve the problem by improving his efficiency and those who think that this would only make matters worse and that if the men increase their capacity 10 per cent there will be fewer men needed. In this disagreement the economist takes the side of those who emphasize individual self-dependence and would hold the laborers to the duty of making the utmost of whatever capacities they have and whatever situation they may find available.

In this case as in all other cases anyone who thinks that individual responsibility is becoming less because collective responsibility is becoming greater is making a mistake somewhat like that of the dog in the fable,

J. Maurice Clark

who dropped his piece of meat to catch the other which he saw reflected in the water. For what is collective responsibility but personal responsibilities reflected in the social mirror? We need all the sense of responsibility we can arouse, of all kinds, organized and directed into the most intelligent and efficient channels, to make even moderately satisfactory headway with the increasingly complex problems that are piling up ahead of us.

The scope of personal responsibility is broader than ever before, not narrower. It is a false notion of the meaning of determinism which interprets it in such a way as to undermine the responsibility of the individual for his own choices. John Smith is still a law unto himself, whatever the statistics may tell us about the thousand. We cannot predict him, for the determining causes of his destiny lie partly in his own personality. The power over his environment of a man who does not know when he is beaten is the last thing we can afford to belittle or ignore. It is only too obvious what a difference it makes whether men who are free to act as they will, choose to act with courage, self-reliance, and generosity or not. The only way the environment can overcome man completely is by persuading him that it can do so.

And laying responsibility on the environment cannot take it off the shoulders of persons so long as the environment of each of us consists chiefly of the rest of us. The responsibility is harder to bring home to the subject, and the duties it imposes are harder to fulfill effectively, for "what is everybody's business is nobody's business." But that simply means that our first obligation is to organize machinery by which these most difficult of obligations can be first effectively brought home and, second, effectively performed. This means, again, that we are facing the difficult task of keeping the sense of obligation alive while delegating to specialists the bulk of the active work involved in meeting our obligations and fulfilling them.

But it is not alone by making us jointly responsible for the general social environment that our personal responsibilities are being broadened. We are coming to see that our everyday business dealings have more far-reaching effects than we have ever realized, and that the system of free contract is by itself quite inadequate to bring home the responsibility for these effects. We have begun to realize the many inappropriable values that are created and the many unpaid damages that are inflicted in the course of business exchanges. New possibilities at once of parasitism and of service are here revealed, and here at least is a field in which responsibility is being concentrated instead of diffused. Instead of unearned increments which come from a shadowy social environment, and wastes for which an impersonal "system" is responsible, we are making some beginnings at tracing these things home to the policies of particular enterprises and the doings of particular individuals. Unemployment is being traced partly to seasonal trades, as one of their unpaid costs of production.

IV. Responsibility and the Liberal Economics

By comparison with the scope of responsibility as it has been conceived and presented here the laissez-faire economics may well be characterized as the economics of irresponsibility, and the business system of free contract is also a system of irresponsibility when judged by the same standard. Of static theory we must simply say that while it does not deny social responsibilities it does to a large extent ignore them. Since its abstract premises leave out most of the facts on which they are based, they are left to be taken account of in other departments of the science. Liberal economics or business economics in general accomplishes much the same result by separating business sharply off from the rest of life.

"Business is business," and while men are unselfish and recognize many kinds of obligations to their fellows beyond the letter of the law, their unselfishness is not carried into business relations, and the extra-legal responsibilities are not business responsibilities, except such as have become so firmly established in business morals as to have the binding force of laws. In business, men do not render services without being paid such price as they are willing to accept nor undergo sacrifices except for a consideration which they deem sufficient. From this it may be concluded that both parties are better off for every business transaction, at least in their own minds at the moment, than if the transaction had not been made.

With this dangerously inadequate idea of bargaining and contract, and with the equally inadequate idea of business competition as a sort of Darwinian struggle for survival, constantly tending toward the natural selection, of the fit, it is small wonder if the business man is willingly convinced that in the struggle for financial success he is fulfilling the whole duty that society can reasonably impose upon his business hours. In other words, theory and practice combine to further an irresponsible attitude among leaders of industry and laborers alike.

Meanwhile the demand for control has grown with amazing speed, and in every direction experiments are being tried. This should properly be regarded as a recognition of special kinds of responsibility which the business economics leaves out of account and which the machinery of free contract furnishes no way of bringing home to the proper persons. But instead, this regulation is looked on by too many as a phase of the old irresponsible struggle, merely translated from the field of business into the field of politics. It is under suspicion as being mere irresponsible class legislation, and unfortunately the suspicion has some justification.

Hence employers often feel either contemptuous or deeply injured when laws begin to interfere with customary business practices, and when investigating committees ask prying questions which imply a demand for a righteousness that shall exceed the righteousness of the scribes and Pharisees. Business men with this point of view oppose the growth of public control with a resistance that is now adroit and now stubborn but nearly always powerful. The economics of control is at war with the economics of irresponsibility.

Beyond all the special issues of this struggle there stand out certain general questions of attitude and interpretation that are most real and most vital. Are these new policies of regulation to be regarded as exceptions to our general economic philosophy or are they an integral part of it? Are they special and disconnected cases or are they phases of one consistent program whose central features can be formulated? And above all, are they mere matters of political struggle and political compromise; matters to be temporarily settled by a show of hands, or of teeth, and perpetually unsettled again with every real or fancied change in the strength of the contending parties? Or are they matters of economic law, with a solid foundation in real relationships of cause and effect which no party in the many-sided struggle can permanently ignore? Do our economic regulations mean merely the creation and attempted enforcement of arbitrary requirements or do they mean the recognition and bringing home of existing and very real responsibilities? And, if the answer to this last be in the affirmative, is there a twilight zone of obligations not yet enforced by law or custom but no less real for that? If there is such a twilight zone, how shall we act toward it?

It is good and necessary that new proposals should be first treated as exceptions to economic theory, for they need to be settled on their merits, but it is not good that they should remain permanently unassimilated. It is good and necessary that they be urged by men intensely devoted, each to his special cause, but it is also good ultimately to absorb them all into a broadly constructive plan. It is good when political force breaks down stereotyped codes and precepts masquerading as "natural rights" and natural law, but it is not good to imagine that there are no laws to which men and groups of men are responsible other than the law of getting all they can.

The task of economic theory in these matters is clear, and the importance of this task is often too little realized. There are principles underlying our multifarious social policies—principles as general and far-reaching as those underlying the "theory of value and distribution." In fact, they are all phases of one process, social housekeeping. And until "free exchange" and "social reform" are both interpreted as governed by one consistent set of laws, they are not interpreted correctly. The crucial task of such a theory is to unify, to reveal those causes and consequences of things men do which transcend the scope of free exchange. These create responsibilities which, in turn, the policy of regulation is attempting to enforce. In a broad sense the great task of the theorist of our tremendously dynamic age is to substitute an economics of responsibility for the economics of irresponsible conflict. That is his part in furthering the growth of willing co-operation in the endless process of adapting our organization and industrial ways to the unforeseen needs and relationships which machinery and science are continually thrusting, upon us.

V. *Difficulties of Public Control*

Any system of regulation of private industry needs a well developed basis of agreement as to what in general the mutual obligations of the parties are, or else the system will not work. For without it confidence is lacking and as a result co-operation is crippled. It is expensive when the people distrust the leaders of industry and are in turn distrusted by them: it is only less expensive than trust misplaced. It is hard enough for those familiar with trade practices to adopt rules for their own observance; it becomes well-nigh impossible when the rules are passed by outsiders, themselves unfamiliar with the details of the situation, who are forced to interpret all advice from the interested parties in the light of those parties' interests and to suspect it of subtly aiming to thwart the ends of public policy. This is not a complete picture of our present situation, fortunately, but it is a true picture of one most exasperating phase of it, showing itself particularly, perhaps, in legislation on banking and on unfair competition.

Another weakness of regulation of private enterprise is, that while it consists largely in forbidding things, it often describes these things in terms of form, not of spirit and essential effect. The result is the widespread feeling that useful ways of doing business are being outlawed because they are capable of abuse.

Attempts to limit speculation and capitalization, for example, are so regarded, with how much or how little justice we need not stop here to inquire. All of this leads to a hostile public opinion on the part of a large and solid class, and against such a solid and sincere opinion laws cannot be profitably enforced. Indeed, regulation would not now be able to show its present record of success unless this hostile opinion had been to some extent convinced and won over to a belief in the need and the justice of control.

This attitude is in itself a clear recognition that the business economics is inadequate and needs revising, at least at certain points. But many fail to see what a far-reaching change of attitude is involved in this simple admission, though they may feel uneasily that there is a camel's head inside the tent. The conservative expects things to continue on the principle that "business is business," meaning that it is a self-regarding business, and that his only business obligations are those enforced by law and settled custom. They have been added to somewhat, but that is all, and wherever the law has not yet spoken there is no reason for taking any but the old irresponsible attitude. Further responsibilities there may be of a social or charitable sort, but not further business responsibilities.

This view might be more convincing if only every business transaction were a wholly isolated fact, concerning only one buyer and one seller at one moment of time, and having no possible effect on other people or on other transactions. Only if that were true, most of our existing body of business regulations would be wholly unnecessary, so that the question at issue would not be likely to arise at all. But to argue about modern industrial dealings as if they could be so insulated in their effects from all other relationships would seem to imply a certain lack of insight.

After what has been said already, it is only necessary to point out that, thanks largely to modern machinery and the complex organization that goes with it, every act has numberless effects on others, furthering or thwarting their purposes in ways often unknown to them personally, but known to someone nevertheless. These by-products may often be far more important in the aggregate than the one service or the one sacrifice over which a voluntary bargain happens to be struck. And thanks to science, the specialist can find out about these matters on which the man in the street could never by any possibility inform himself. And not only could he not inform himself, but he cannot even understand if he is told. Science has made available for society's use an amount of knowledge of what is happening to its members vastly greater than they can ever absorb individually and use individually in the daily course of looking out for their interests. No one who appreciates this fact can hold that a system of free contract normally protects all interests, and that every free business transaction is automatically self-supporting and productive for society as a whole.

Now we can expect the employer—a specialist—to watch his own business and to know what it is doing, though we could not expect the same man in his role of unspecialized consumer to watch with the same effectiveness every producer whose policies affect his welfare. And if men are responsible for the known results of their actions, business responsibilities must include the known results of business dealings, whether these have been recognized by law or not. Indeed, when they have passed into the statute books they are no longer responsibilities at all in the highest sense: of obligations which the individual must himself decide how to meet. The decision is made for him by government and he has only to obey or take the consequences. But where the law has not spoken, every man must decide on his own initiative.

Now if men are to follow this out in the simplest way, if they are merely to make good as nearly as possible all actual damage they cause, they will find themselves going far indeed before the task is accomplished. The ideal is to pay one's way, not to hurt others without compensation, to get value only for value given, and to leave the world in other respects just as one found it, or at least not to leave it the worse for one's presence.

In other words, it is a static idea of business we are discussing. But it is simply impossible for anyone to leave the world just as he found it, especially if he is one whose decisions have any importance. As Professor Veblen says: "Invention is the mother of necessity" in the most unexpected ways. The necessity for writing these words (if there be any such necessity) is a by-product of the mechanical inventions that gave us the industrial revolution and the subsequent vast "advances" in scientific production and large-scale industry. Every lumberman in the Mississippi Basin is jointly with others a cause of the new flood conditions that are inflicting so much damage and calling for so much expenditure of money and thought to devise methods of prevention. Some few have managed their property so as to avoid increasing the danger of floods; others have contributed to relief funds and studies in flood prevention. But whether they have met the responsibility or not, it is there.

To the extent that each of us is a factor in economic evolution, be it only that his presence adds one member to the population, he shares in all the increasing difficulties which economic evolution brings with it. He cannot do anything so far-reaching as building a house without affecting other people's property interests for better or for worse. Unless he affects them for the better he is pretty sure to affect them for the worse. And unless he leaves society stronger in its power to master the manifold troubles of modern industry he will leave it relatively weaker by just so much as those troubles have grown in size and complexity. Modern industry gives a new meaning to the text, "He that is not with me is against me," and is constantly showing, new ways in which, whether we like it or not, we are our brothers' keepers.

In many such matters, such as the policy of lumbermen toward the danger of floods that comes with deforestation, or the employer's attitude toward the unemployment that arises from the seasonal nature of his trade, the responsibility is one which we are not yet ready to crystallize into a legal obligation. Law and custom can at best never keep pace with the needs which they are made to meet, for the simple reason that the need must be there before it can be felt, and it must be felt in a substantial way to be worth making a law about, and felt for a long time and by a considerable number to give rise to a custom. These agencies which prescribe just how a man shall take upon himself the consequences of his acts can never cover more than a few of the more direct and the more obvious. By far the greater number must always remain in a sort of extra-legal borderland.

If they are neglected, the result may be evils which will ultimately call forth legislation of an experimental sort, ill-informed and inept perhaps, and usually not calculated to improve the morale of our attitude toward government. But if these matters are treated as public obligations by those most directly responsible, much of this friction and waste motion can be avoided. The interested parties may ultimately want a law to help control them, for the sake of controlling also the bolters in their own ranks. But it will be a law asked for by the governed, not imposed on them from outside.

We have become accustomed to the idea that nineteen men who want good conditions may be coerced by one competitor whose standard is more unscrupulous. They may actually be unable to do as they wish unless commanded by law. We have not always seen that this is a two-edged doctrine. It has been used to show how far regulation can go without transgressing the principle of industrial freedom and the natural right of the business man to run his enterprise as he sees fit. It has been used by the individualist to set limits on the sphere of government.

But surely the more significant thing about it is the fact that it takes for granted that competitive standards and standards of public good are not one and the same, whether the majority in the trade are awake to that fact or not. And it further takes for granted a widespread sense of responsibility on the part of a majority of business men, not limited to the letter of the law. If this sense of responsibility is to be a guide to legislation, it must go before the law and be independent of it.

This is one great reason why the state cannot afford to assume all responsibility for the outcome of the business system and leave individuals to look after their own interests with a single eye and a clear conscience. Some feel that the state has taken the responsibility, once for all, of a system in which individuals are supposed to look after their own interests and that while there may be abuses it does not fall on the individual to correct them. Moreover, they hold that the state is the only agency that can effectively bear the burdens and perform the tasks of correcting the miscarriages of free contract. Men who are under the compelling force of competition must seek their own interests foremost and all the time or go to the wall. If they try to correct abuses, to follow fairer tactics and leave off using competitive weapons that do damage, the general practice will not be changed, they will simply be forced out of business and their place will be taken by others less scrupulous.

We have seen that the state cannot well do all that this attitude would demand of it. Let us look at the idea further. It is possible that free contract would do more good than harm even in the hands of a wholly selfish and irresponsible population, though nowadays there is more and more evidence to the contrary. But there can be no doubt that enough harm would be done to offset much of the good, and it is quite possible that the strain of conflicting selfish interests might ultimately rack the system to pieces.

Indeed, this is just what the Socialists think is now happening before our unseeing eyes. What with the unmeasured wastes of competition where it remains active, the exploitation where competition has ceased to act, the parasitism which is so inextricably bound up with the guidance of sound production, and the disintegrating effects of the distrust and hostility that rule between large bodies of the population, roused by the sense that each is reckless of the interests of the others—with all these to combat it often seems that we need all the saving sense of public obligation we can possibly muster, merely to keep the machinery running at all.

It is often raised as a conclusive objection to Socialism that it relies on altruism, while the present system harnesses to our service the more reliable force of self-interest. The fact is that in this respect the contrast between the two systems is a matter of degree only. Socialistic industry would find many ways of enlisting and utilizing selfish motives, and we cannot say how great its demands on altruism would be without more extensive experiments than have yet been tried. But we do know that the present system also calls for a great deal of public spirit to make it run properly, and this fact is daily becoming more prominent, and is driven home afresh by every reading of the morning paper.

Suppose the state does take its chances of the harm which business selfishness can work, and with its eyes open sanctions a system which it knows to be capable of abuse. Does it thereby tacitly approve all abuses, or take for granted that men will commit as many (always inside the law) as they see fit? Does not its very act impliedly make every man responsible for the balance of good or harm that may come from his own efforts?

And as for the argument that private persons cannot do anything effective, there are three reasons why that is not conclusive: First, when we are speaking of human relationships,"impossible" is a relative term, and we may occasionally find ourselves forced to choose between two courses, both of which seemed impossible till one was forced upon us. Secondly, we have seen enough to realize fully the well-nigh fatal weakness of state action without a strong sense of responsibility in the people at large to make the way as easy as possible. Thirdly, private individuals can act collectively where one alone is helpless and get results which would be impossible for the official machinery of government.

Is it not probable that more could be done to check unfair competitive practices by trade organizations regulating their members and adjusting relations between each other's members than by any number of special laws and court decisions? If only we could trust such bodies to act truly in the public interest, and not merely to eliminate competition for their own benefit or to fortify a wastefully numerous class of middlemen against the competition of more direct and efficient methods!

VI. *Responsibility as an Actual Force*

And this brings us to the final point, which is that business responsibility beyond the law is not an ideal only but to a considerable extent a fact. Business men's associations are the very effective embodiment of it. The retailer and manufacturer take the responsibility for not short-circuiting the wholesaler, and in return the wholesaler does not "poach" on the retailer. This is responsibility to a group, enforced by mutual interests. All that is needed is to make it cover a larger group—to make it general.

The sense of general responsibility is a fact, also, though it is weaker than the tie that binds a class, a trade, or a profession. In proportion as it grows in strength we can rely on it more and more to guide public policy. Perhaps in some future century we may even venture to ask business men's advice on proposed laws for the prevention of unfair competition without the uneasy feeling that their only purpose in giving of their wisdom is to make the laws ineffective and keep things as they are.

With the idea generally accepted that "wealth is a trust" the next order of development is a gradually broadening revelation of how far the trusteeship extends. It most surely extends to the earning of the wealth as well as the spending of it. It extends to a sincere effort to make labor conditions as nearly right as possible in plants from which one draws dividends, and conditions of competition as fair and free from waste as they can be made.

In fact, one of the most serious objections to the present degree of concentration of wealth is that the largest capitalists are interested in so many industries that they cannot do by any of them what their position demands. They have undertaken, or have had thrust upon them, responsibilities utterly beyond their power to fulfill.

Still more effective in bringing about this result is the corporation, which holds out a standing invitation to every man of considerable means to split his investments with a view to greater safety. Sometimes this is carried so far as to defeat its own end. The eggs are in many baskets and the baskets cannot all be watched. But long before this point is reached the watching is reduced to the bare essentials necessary to knowing if the investment is profitable and safe. And when a man's familiarity with his own money-making enterprises—and every investment comes under this head—when his familiarity dwindles to the irreducible money-making minimum, something has evaporated, and that something is a social interest of incalculable importance. Private fortunes may be safer, but not without cost to the nation. Has the principle of limited liability been carried too far? If a moderate curtailment of that privilege should result in concentrating each man's investments in fewer enterprises, the commonwealth would be the gainer in a very real way.

From the same point of view one of the worst features of the internal organization of corporations is its wonderful aptitude for dividing responsibility, concealing it from outside observers and even from the members themselves, and making it thoroughly ineffective for other than "business" purposes. To an economics of irresponsibility this might appear as an incidental blemish; to an economics of responsibility it is one of the very roots of evil.

Many men would fulfill their responsibilities in a very different spirit if they were put before them in present and tangible shape: for example, if they had to bargain with their laborers directly. But it is an unusual stockholder who will so instruct his paid officials that they shall feel free to lessen dividends if necessary to make the industry truly a source of gain for the other participants, laborers, and others. And yet they usually have it in their power to make it either a source of gain or a source of net loss to those whom it affects by its operations.

VI. *Conclusion*

In conclusion: the world is familiar enough with the conception of social responsibilities. These do not need to be rediscovered in the year of our Lord 1916. But the fact that a large part of them are business responsibilities has not yet penetrated, and this fact does need to be brought home to a community in which business men and theoretical economics alike are still shadowed by the fading penumbra of laissez-faire. This issue is deeper and more far-reaching than anyone can realize who has not tried earnestly to understand the sources of the deep sense of injustice that animates the discontented classes. The trouble is not that the unfortunate are not helped, but that they are helped in the name of charity, regardless of whether they are victims of their own weakness or of the misfit grindings of our none-too-perfectly-adjusted industrial machine. To many the very word "charity" is as a red flag to a bull, and this will never be otherwise as long as so much that passes for charity is merely repairing the damage or salvaging the wreckage for which industry is the chief responsible cause; the same industry which distributes the dividends out of which charity funds so freely come.

The cry for "justice, not charity" may cover a deal of hysteria and wrong-mindedness, but it also has a solid basis in scientific fact, and the way to quench the hysteria is to investigate sanely just what that solid basis is. Such studies are the task of experts and specialists. All that is here attempted is to show the important place which such work has to fill in our scheme of social management and social interpretation, and to do whatever may be done to hasten by ever so little the growth of a broadened attitude toward the responsibilities of business relationships.

---

[1] Cf. Hadley, *Economics*, chap. ii. Cf. also Henry C. Adams, *The Relation of the State to Industrial Action*, pp. 80-85. Here the dominant note is reliance on free competition wherever free competition naturally prevails. Action by the state is urged, (1) to enable the majority in a trade to decide what the plane of their competition shall be, and (2) in the case of natural monopolies. The author announces the theory of responsibility as the keynote of this policy, using the term "responsibility" none too definitely, but in a strongly individualistic sense.

[2] For a full treatment of these and other causes contributing to crises, the reader is referred to W. C. Mitchell's *Business Cycles*.

Copyright © 1916 The University of Chicago.
All rights reserved. Reprinted with permission.

For Whom Are Corporate Managers Trustees?

E. Merrick Dodd Jr., Harvard Law School

An individual who carries on business for himself necessarily enters into business relations with a large number of persons who become either his customers or his creditors. Under a legal system based on private ownership and freedom of contract, he has no duty to conduct his business to any extent for the benefit of such persons; he conducts it solely for his own private gain and owes to those with whom he deals only the duty of carrying out such bargains as he may make with them.

If the owner employs an agent or agents to assist him in carrying on business, the situation is only slightly changed. The enterprise is still conducted for the sole benefit of the owner; the customers and creditors have contract rights against him and not normally against the agent even when the agent is the person who actually transacts business with them. The agent himself shares in the receipts of the enterprise only to the extent provided by his agreement. He, however, on his part owes something more than a contract duty toward his principal. He is a fiduciary who must loyally serve his principal's interests.

Substitute several owners for one and the picture is scarcely altered, except that insofar as the owners take part in the conduct of the enterprise, there is a fiduciary relation between owner and owner, as well as between employee and owner. Incorporate the enterprise, making the owners stockholders and some of them or persons selected by them directors, and—if we adopt the widely prevalent theory that the corporate entity is a fiction[1]—our picture is substantially unchanged. The business is still a private enterprise existing for the profit of its owners, who are now the stockholders. Its customers and creditors have contract rights, normally against the corporation but in reality against the stockholders, whose liability is limited to the assets used in the business.[2] The directors and other agents are fiduciaries carrying on the business in the sole interest of the stockholders. These latter have indeed lost much of their *de jure* and, if the enterprise is a large one, perhaps nearly all of their *de facto* control so that they may appear to be more like *cestuis que trust* than like partners. Nevertheless they are not strictly *cestuis que trust*, for it is the association of which they are members and not an individual acting as trustee for them that comes into contract relations with customers and creditors.

Stress the theory of the corporate entity and the picture is altered slightly, but more in form than in substance. The corporation as a distinct legal person is now conceived of as carrying on the business and making the contracts, and the directors and other agents are fiduciaries for it. The sole function of the corporation is, however, conceived to be the making of profit for its stockholder-members,[3] so that they are the ultimate beneficiaries of the business and of the activities of the persons by whom it is carried on.

Subject to this, from a practical standpoint, relatively minor controversy as to the emphasis to be placed upon the corporate entity,[4] it is undoubtedly the traditional view that a corporation is an association of stockholders formed for their private gain and to be managed by its board of directors solely with that end in view. Directors and managers of modern large corporations are granted all sorts of novel powers by present-day corporation statutes and charters, and are free from any substantial supervision by stockholders by reason of the difficulty which the modern stockholder has in discovering what is going on and taking effective measures even if he has discovered it. The fact that managers so empowered not infrequently act as though maximum stockholder profit was not the sole object of managerial activities has led some students of corporate problems, particularly Mr. A. A. Berle, to advocate an increased emphasis on the doctrine that managerial powers are held in trust for stockholders as sole beneficiaries of the corporate enterprise.[5]

The present writer is thoroughly in sympathy with Mr. Berle's efforts to establish a legal control which will more effectually prevent corporate managers from diverting profit into their own pockets from those of stockholders, and agrees with many of the specific rules which the latter deduces from his trusteeship principle.[6] He nevertheless believes that it is undesirable, even with the laudable purpose of giving stockholders much-needed protection against self-seeking managers, to give increased emphasis at the present time to the view that business corporations exist for the sole purpose of making profits for their stockholders. He believes that public opinion, which ultimately makes law, has made and is today making substantial strides in the direction of a view of the business corporation as an economic institution which has a social service as well as a profit-making function, that this view has already had some effect upon legal theory, and that it is likely to have a greatly increased effect upon the latter in the near future.

Several hundred years ago, when business enterprises were small affairs involving the activities of men rather than the employment of capital, our law took the position that business[7] is a public profession rather than a purely private matter, and that the business man, far from being free to obtain all the profits which his skill in bargaining might secure for him, owes a legal duty to give adequate service at reasonable rates. Although a growing belief in liberty of contract and in the efficacy of free competition to prevent extortion led to abandonment of this theory for business as a whole, the theory survived as the rule applicable to the carrier and the innkeeper. In recent years we have seen this carrier law expanded to include a variety of businesses classed as public utilities. Under modern conditions the conduct of such businesses normally involves the use of a substantial amount of property. This fact, together with the accidental circumstance that a passage from Lord Hale was quoted in one of the briefs in the leading case of *Munn v. Illinois*,[8] has led to a change in the conventional legal phraseology. Instead of talking, as the early judges talked, in terms of the duty of one engaged in business activities toward the public who are his customers, it has become the practice since *Munn v. Illinois*[9] to talk of the public duty of one who has devoted his property to public use, the conception being that property employed in certain kinds of business is devoted to public use while property employed in other kinds of business remains strictly private.

This approach to the problem has been justly criticized as attempting to draw an unreasonably clean-cut distinction between businesses which do not differ substantially, and as furnishing no intelligible criterion by which to distinguish those businesses which are private property from those which are property devoted to public use.[10] The phrase does, however, have the merit of emphasizing the fact that business is permitted and encouraged by the law primarily because it is of service to the community rather than because it is a source of profit to its owners. Accordingly, where it appears that unlimited private profit is incompatible with adequate service, the claim of those engaged therein that the business belongs to them in an unqualified sense and can be pursued in such manner as they choose need not be accepted by the legislature. Despite certain recent conservative decisions such as *Tyson v. Banton*,[11] it may well be that the law is approaching a point of view which will regard all business as affected with a public interest. If certain businesses then continue to be allowed unregulated profits, it will be as a matter of legislative policy because the lawmakers regard the competitive conditions under which such businesses are carried on as making regulation of profits unnecessary, and not because the owners of such enterprises have any constitutional right to have their property treated as private in the sense in which property held merely for personal use is private.

At any rate, there is no doubt that property employed in a business now classed as a public utility is private property only in a qualified sense. Such a utility as an interstate railroad must render adequate service, expand its facilities when called upon by public authority, charge only reasonable rates, and treat all customers alike even though profitable new business might be secured by making concessions to certain patrons.[12] In addition to such regulations of its rates and services, an interstate railroad is powerless to issue new securities even to its existing stockholders without the consent of an administrative board which is charged with the duty of considering primarily the bearing of securities issue upon the welfare of the traveling or shipping public rather than the desirability of the issue from the standpoint of the stockholders as owners.[13] Furthermore, the relations between such a railroad and its employees are no longer solely a matter of private bargaining but have of recent years been regulated, first by the Adamson Act,[14] a thinly disguised measure for increasing wages, and more recently, by an act creating a labor board with power to determine wages in case of a dispute, although without any weapon save an appeal to public opinion for the enforcement of its determinations.[15] Whether these labor regulations be regarded as designed to protect the public against possible interruptions of service due to strikes, or as derived from a partial recognition of the validity of the claims of labor as an integral part of the enterprise to a fair share of the receipts—fairness to be dependent on criteria which, however vague, are not wholly a matter of bargaining strength—it is plain that these regulations, like those previously referred to, involve important limitations on the right of stockholders and managers acting in their interests to treat the enterprise as the private property of the former.

The law applicable to interstate railroads has, moreover, recently broken away from the idea that each business enterprise is a wholly distinct entity owing no obligations to aid in the success of the industry as a whole. The Transportation Act of 1920 as construed by the United States Supreme Court in the *New England Divisions Case*[16] treats the railroads of the country as parts of a single system to such an extent as to justify the Interstate Commerce Commission in dividing the joint rates charged by connecting carriers between those carriers in such a way as to increase the resources of the weaker roads by giving them a disproportionately large share of the total.

Although this single system concept has thus far been confined to interstate railroads, the limitations on unqualified pursuit of private profit imposed by the more advanced states on other so-called public utilities such as gas, electric, and telephone companies, are substantially similar to those imposed by federal law upon interstate railroads.[17] Outside the public utility field there is in the present state of the law little or no attempt to curtail private property in the interest of the customer, it being generally assumed that competition furnishes him adequate protection.[18] On the other hand, the inequality of bargaining power between employer and employee—an inequality which the recent rise of the large corporation has greatly accentuated—has resulted in a considerable amount of legislation designed to protect the health and safety, and even to a slight extent the financial rewards, of the employee.[19]

Recent economic events suggest that the day may not be far distant when public opinion will demand a much greater degree of protection to the worker. There is a widespread and growing feeling that industry owes to its employees not merely the negative duties of refraining from overworking or injuring them, but the affirmative duty of providing them so far as possible with economic security. Concentration of control of industry in a relatively few hands[20] has encouraged the belief in the practicability of methods of economic planning by which such security can be achieved in much greater degree than at present. This belief is no longer confined to radical opponents of the capitalistic system; it has come to be shared by many conservatives who believe that capitalism is worth saving but that it can not permanently survive under modern conditions unless it treats the economic security of the worker as one of its obligations and is intelligently directed so as to attain that object.[21]

It is true that, as many advocates of industrial planning have pointed out, high wages and economic security for workers tend in the main to increase the profits of stockholders, inasmuch as they tend to increase consumption of the things which business corporations produce.[22] It can not, however, be successfully maintained that the sort of industrial planning which may be found desirable to protect the employee is necessarily under all circumstances in line with the interest of the stockholders of each individual corporation. If contemporary discussion of the need for a planned economic order ultimately results in a more stabilized system of production and employment, we may safely predict that this will involve some further modifications of the maximum-profit-for-the-stockholders-of-the-individual-company formula.

It may, however, be forcibly urged that all these and other past, present, and possible future limitations on the pursuit of stockholder profit in no way alter the theory that the sole function of directors and other corporate managers is to seek to obtain the maximum amount of profits for the stockholders as owners of the enterprise. Ownership of a modern railroad may today be hedged about with restrictions which make such ownership considerably less absolute than was the ownership of a cotton mill at the time when economic and legal theories of *laissez faire* were most completely accepted. Ownership in the cotton industry tomorrow may be even more restricted in some ways than is ownership in the railroad field today. Regulations imposed in the interest of employees, consumers, or others may increasingly limit the methods which managers of incorporated business enterprises may employ in seeking profits for their stockholders without in any way affecting the proposition that the sole function of such managers is to work for the best interests of the stockholders as their employers or beneficiaries.

If, however, as much recent writing suggests, we are undergoing a substantial chance in our public opinion with regard to the obligations of business to the community, it is natural to expect that this change of opinion will have some effect upon the attitude of those who manage business. If, therefore, the managers of modern businesses were also its owners, the development of a public opinion to the effect that business has responsibilities to its employees and its customers would, quite apart from any legal compulsion, tend to affect the conduct of the better type of business man. The principal object of legal compulsion might then be to keep those who failed to catch the new spirit up to the standards which their more enlightened competitors would desire to adopt voluntarily. Business might then become a profession of public service, not primarily because the law had made it such but because a public opinion shared in by business men themselves had brought about a professional attitude.[23]

Our present economic system, under which our more important business enterprises are owned by investors who take no part in carrying them on—absentee owners who in many cases have not even seen the property from which they derive their profits—alters the situation materially. That Stockholders who have no contact with business other than to derive dividends from it should become imbued with a professional spirit of public service is hardly thinkable. If incorporated business is to become professionalized, it is to the managers, not to the owners, that we must look for the accomplishment of this result.

If we may believe what some of our business leaders and students of business tell us, there is in fact a growing feeling not only that business has responsibilities to the community but that our corporate managers who control business should voluntarily and without waiting for legal compulsion manage it in such a way as to fulfill those responsibilities. Thus, even before the present depression had set many business men thinking about the place of business in society, one of our leading business executives, Mr. Owen D. Young, had expressed himself as follows as to his conception of what a business executive's attitude should be:

> "If there is one thing a lawyer[24] is taught it is knowledge of trusteeship and the sacredness of that position. Very soon he saw rising a notion that managers were no longer attorneys for stockholders: they were becoming trustees of an institution.

If you will pardon me for being personal, it makes a great difference in my attitude towards my job as an executive officer of the General Electric Company whether I am a trustee of the institution or an attorney for the investor. If I am a trustee, who are the beneficiaries of the trust? To whom do I owe my obligations?

My conception of it is this: That there are three groups of people who have an interest in that institution. One is the group of fifty-odd thousand people who have put their capital in the company, namely its stockholders. Another is a group of well toward one hundred thousand people who are putting their labor and their lives into the business of the company. The third group is of customers and the general public.

Customers have a right to demand that a concern so large shall not only do its business honestly and properly, but, further, that it shall meet its public obligations and perform its public duties—in a word, vast as it is, that it should be a good citizen.

Now, I conceive my trust first to be to see to it that the capital which is put into this concern is safe, honestly and wisely used, and paid a fair rate of return. Otherwise we cannot get capital. The worker will have no tools.

Second, that the people who put their labor and lives into this concern get fair wages, continuity of employment, and a recognition of their right to their jobs where they have educated themselves to highly skilled and specialized work.

Third, that the customers get a product which is as represented and that the price is such as is consistent with the obligations to the people who put their capital and labor in.

Last, that the public has a concern functioning in the public interest and performing its duties as a great and good citizen should.

I think what is right in business is influenced very largely by the growing sense of trusteeship which I have described. One no longer feels the obligation to take from labor for the benefit of capital, nor to take from the public for the benefit of both, but rather to administer wisely and fairly in the interest of all."[25]

More recently Mr. Young's colleague, President Swope of the General Electric Company, has put forward his plan for the stabilization of industry which is based on the idea that "organized industry should take the lead, recognizing its responsibility to its employees, to the public, and to its stockholders—rather than that democratic society should act through its government."[26] That industry as at present organized can take this lead only through the agency of the directors and corporate executives who manage it is obvious and is tacitly assumed by Mr. Swope. As Professor Beard has put it in commenting on the Swope plan, "Mr. Swope spoke as a man of affairs, as president of the General Electric Company. No academic taint condemned his utterance in advance; no suspicion of undue enthusiasm clouded his product. As priest-kings could lay down the law without question in primitive society, so a captain of industry in the United States could propose a new thing without encountering the scoffs of the wise or the jeers of the practical."[27] In his recent study of the situation which confronts American business today, Dean Donham of the Harvard Graduate School of Business Administration has stated the problem as follows: "How can we as business men, within the areas for which we are responsible, best meet the needs of the American people, most nearly approximate supplying their wants, maintain profits, handle problems of unemployment, face the Russian challenge, and at the same time aid Europe and contribute most to or disturb least the cause of international peace?"[28]

Answering this question he says, "The only way to defend capitalism is through leadership which accepts social responsibility and meets the sound needs of the great majority of our people. Such leadership will seek to form constructive plans framed not in the interest of capital or capitalism but in the interest of the American people as a whole.... The responsibility of capital for leadership is overwhelming. To a large extent in this industrial civilization of ours the potential leadership of the country is concentrated in industry."[29] Dean Donham does not explicitly state that leadership of industry is in the hands of those who do not own it but he is too well-informed an observer of modern business not to be thoroughly aware that such is the case. Assumption of social responsibility by industrial leadership necessarily means assumption of such responsibility by corporate managers.

The view that those who manage our business corporations should concern themselves with the interests of employees, consumers, and the general public, as well as of the stockholders, is thus advanced today by persons whose position in the business world is such as to give them great power of influencing both business opinion and public opinion generally. Little or no attempt seems to have been made, however, to consider how far such an attitude on the part of corporate manners is compatible with the legal duties which they owe the stockholder-owners as the elected representatives of the latter.

No doubt it is to a large extent true that an attempt by business managers to take into consideration the welfare of employees and consumers (and under modern industrial conditions the two classes are largely the same) will in the long run increase the profits of stockholders. As Dean Donham and others have demonstrated, it is the lack of a feeling of security on the part of those who are dependent on employment for their livelihood which is largely responsible for the present under-consumption which has so disastrous an effect upon business profits. If the social responsibility of business means merely a more enlightened view as to the ultimate advantage of the stockholder-owners, then obviously corporate managers may accept such social responsibility without any departure from the traditional view that their function is to seek to obtain the maximum amount of profits for their stockholders.

And yet one need not be unduly credulous to feel that there is more to this talk of social responsibility on the part of corporation manners than merely a more intelligent appreciation of what tends to the ultimate benefit of their stockholders. Modern large-scale industry has given to the managers of our principal corporations enormous power over the welfare of wage earners and consumers, particularly the former. Power over the lives of others tends to create on the part of those most worthy to exercise it a sense of responsibility. The manners, who along with the sub-ordinate employees are part of the group which is contributing to the success of the enterprise by day-to-day efforts, may easily come to feel as strong a community of interest with their fellow workers as with a group of investors whose only connection with the enterprise is that they or their predecessors in title invested money in it, perhaps in the rather remote past.[30] Moreover, the concept that the manners are merely, in Mr. Young's phrase, "attorneys for the investors" leads to the conclusion that if other classes who are affected by the corporation's activities need protection, that protection must be entrusted to other hands than those of the manners. Desire to retain their present powers accordingly encourages the latter to adopt and disseminate the view that they are guardians of all the interests which the corporation affects and not merely servants of its absentee owners.

Any clash between this point of view and the orthodox theory that the managers are elected by stockholder-owners to serve their interests exclusively has thus far been chiefly potential rather than actual. Judicial willingness—which has increased of late—to allow corporate directors a wide range of discretion as to what policies will best promote the interests of the stockholders, together with managerial disinclination to indulge a sense of social responsibility to a point where it is likely to injure the stockholder, has thus far prevented the issue from being frequently raised in clear-cut fashion in litigation.[31]

Nevertheless there are indications that even today corporation managers not infrequently use corporate funds in ways which suggest a social responsibility rather than an exclusively profit-making viewpoint. Take, for example, the matter of gifts by business corporations to local charities. The orthodox legal attitude toward such gifts is well stated in the following language of Lord Bowen: "Charity has no business to sit at boards of directors *quâ* charity. There is, however, a kind of charitable dealing which is for the interest of those who practise it, and to that extent and in that garb (I admit not a very philanthropic garb) charity may sit at the board, but for no other purpose."[32] Other courts have expressed substantially the same view, which is generally regarded as representing the law on the subject.[33] There is, however, another viewpoint which is undoubtedly becoming widely prevalent with laymen if not layers. Most local charities are designed to carry on relief work which, if not thus carried on, might be undertaken as public enterprise supported by taxation. As recent efforts to relieve unemployment indicate, one community may rely wholly on charitable contributions for what another community may undertake with public funds. Where taxation is the method used, corporate, like individual wealth, contributes. There is a widespread feeling that it should also contribute where the voluntary method is employed. Lists of contributory to such charitable enterprises as community chests and unemployment relief funds indicate that donations by corporations, even by those whose employees are unlikely to share in any great part in the funds, are becoming frequent.[34] Conceivably, a stockholder advantage may result thereby through the creation of good will, but the suggestion that charitable gifts increase the good will of a corporation as a business enterprise assumes that the public no longer wholeheartedly believes in the principle that corporations have no right to be charitable. The view that directors may within limits properly use corporate funds to support charities which are important to the welfare of the community in which the corporation does business probably comes much nearer representing the attitude of public opinion and the present corporate practice than does the traditional language of courts and lawyers. Nor are there wanting signs of the adoption of a more liberal attitude by legislatures[35] and judges.[36]

Such a view is difficult to justify if we insist on thinking of the business corporation as merely an aggregate of stockholders with directors and officers chosen by them as their trustees or agents. It is not for a trustee to be public-spirited with his beneficiary's property. But we are not bound to treat the corporation as a mere aggregate of stockholders. The traditional view of our law is that a corporation is a distinct legal entity. Unfortunately, its entity character has been thought of as something conferred upon it by the state which, by a mysterious rite called incorporation, magically produces "*e pluribus unum.*" The present vogue of legal realism breeds dissatisfaction with such legal mysteries and leads to insistence on viewing the corporation as it really is. So viewing it we may, as many do, insist that it is a mere aggregate of stockholders; but there is another of regarding it which has distinguished adherents.

According to this concept any organized group, particularly if its organization is of a permanent character, is a factual unit, "a body which from no fiction of law but from the very nature of things differs from the individuals of whom it is constituted."[37]

If the unity of the corporate body is real, then there is reality and not simply legal fiction in the proposition that the managers of the unit are fiduciaries for it and not merely for its individual members, that they are, in Mr. Young's phrase, trustees for an institution rather than attorneys for the stockholders. As previously stated, this entity approach will not substantially affect our results if we insist that the sole function for the entity is to seek maximum stockholder profit. But need we so assume?

We have seen that the law has already reached the point, particularly in the public utility field, where it compels business enterprises to recognize to some extent the interests of other persons besides their owners. We have seen further that the same trend of public opinion which may in some cases compel such recognition may in other cases encourage and approve it without compelling it. A sense of social responsibility toward employees, consumers, and the general public may thus come to be regarded as the appropriate attitude to be adopted by those who are engaged in business, with the result that those who own their own businesses and are free to do what they like may increasingly adopt such an attitude. Business ethics may thus tend to become in some degree those of a profession rather than of a trade.

Such a development of business ethics which goes beyond the requirements of law and beyond the dictates of enlightened self-interest is impossible in these days when most business is incorporated unless it can touch incorporated business enterprises as well as those conducted by individual owners. As a practical matter, this can happen only if the managers of such corporations have some degree of legal freedom to act upon such an attitude without waiting for the unanimous consent of the stockholders. That the duty of the managers is to employ the funds of the corporate institution which they manage solely for the purposes of their institution is indisputable. That that purpose, both factually and legally, is maximum stockholder profit has commonly been assumed by lawyers. That such is factually the purpose of the stockholders in creating the association may be granted. Nevertheless, the association, once it becomes a going concern, takes its place in a business world with certain ethical standards which appear to be developing in the direction of increased social responsibility. If we think of it as an institution which differs in the nature of things from the individuals who compose it, we may then readily conceive of it as a person, which, like other persons engaged in business, is affected not only by the laws which regulate business but by the attitude of public and business opinion as to the social obligations of business. If business is tending to become a profession, then a corporate person engaged in business is a professional even though its stockholders, who take no active part in the conduct of the business, may not be. Those through whom it acts may therefore employ its funds in a manner appropriate to a person practising a profession and imbued with a sense of social responsibility without thereby being guilty of a breach of trust.

It may well be that any substantial assumption of social responsibility by incorporated business through voluntary action on the part of its managers can not reasonably be expected. Experience may indicate that corporate managers are so closely identified with profit-seeking capital that we must look to other agencies to safe-guard the other interests involved, or that the competition of the socially irresponsible makes it impracticable for the more public-spirited managers to act as they would like to do, or that to expect managers to conduct an institution for the combined benefit of classes whose interests are largely conflicting is to impose upon them an impossible task and to endow them with dangerous powers. The question with which this article is concerned is not whether the voluntary acceptance of social responsibility by corporate managers is workable, but whether experiments in that direction run counter to fundamental principles of the law of business corporations.

The view that they do so rests upon two assumptions: that business is private property, and that the directors of an incorporated business are fiduciaries (directly if we disregard the corporate fiction, indirectly in any case) for the stockholder-owners. The first assumption is being rapidly undermined, so rapidly that decisions like those in *Tyson v. Bantob*[38] and *Adkins v. Children's Hospital*[39] can hardly long survive. Business—which is the economic organization of society—is private property only in a qualified sense, and society may properly demand that it be carried on in such a way as to safeguard the interests of those who deal with it either as employees or consumers even if the proprietary rights of its owners are thereby curtailed.

The legal recognition that there are other interests than those of the stockholders to be protected does not, as we have seen, necessarily give corporate managers the right to consider those interests, as it is possible to regard the managers as representatives of the stockholding interest only. Such a view means in practice that there are no human beings who are in a position where they can lawfully accept for incorporated business those social responsibilities which public opinion is coming to expect, and that these responsibilities must be imposed on corporations by legal compulsion. This makes the situation of incorporated business so anomalous that we are justified in demanding clear proof that it is a correct statement of the legal situation.

Clear proof is not forthcoming. Despite many attempts to dissolve the corporation into an aggregate of stockholders, our legal tradition is rather in favor of treating it as an institution directed by persons who are primarily fiduciaries for the institution rather than for its members. That lawyers have commonly assumed that the managers must conduct the institution with single-minded devotion to stockholder profit is true; but the assumption is based upon a particular view of the nature of the institution which we call a business corporation, which concept is in turn based upon a particular view of the nature of business as a purely private enterprise. If we recognize that the attitude of law and public opinion toward business is changing, we may then properly modify our ideas as to the nature of such a business institution as the corporation and hence as to the considerations which may properly influence the conduct of those who direct its activities.

---

[1] There has been a voluminous amount of legal writing of late years on the corporate personality. Among legal expressions of the view that the corporation is in essence merely an aggregate of its members, see Hohfeld, "The Individual Liability of Stockholders and the Conflict of Laws" (1909) 9 *Col. L. Rev.* 492, (1910) 10 *id.* 283, 520; Radin, "The Endless Problem of Corporate Personality" (1932) 32 *id.* 643. Compare also the tendency today to "disregard the corporate fiction" in a wide variety of situations.

[2] For an analysis of the legal duties of corporations as legal duties of their stockholders, see Hohfeld, *supra* note 1.

[3] For a vigorous assertion of this view see Dodge v. Ford Motor Co., 204 Mich. 459, 170 N. W. 668 (1919).

[4] The amount of emphasis which should be given to the corporate entity concept is unimportant for our present purpose if we assume that the sole function of the entity is to make profits for the stockholders. If the latter proposition be disputed, the entity concept may then, as indicated below, become important.

[5] See Berle. "Corporate Powers as Powers in Trust" (1931) 44 *Harv. L. Rev.* 1049.

[6] That directors are fiduciaries for their corporations is indisputable. That many of their powers, such as the power of declaring or passing dividends and the power of issuing new stock, may affect the individual interests of the stockholders rather than the corporate enterprise as a whole is obvious and has led to a growing, tendency, to treat directors as fiduciaries for stockholders as well as for the corporate entity. Thus a stockholder may under some circumstances compel the declaration of a dividend even though the corporate entity would not be injured by the failure to declare. Dodge v. Ford Motor Co., *supra* note 3; *In re* Brantman, 244 Fed. 101 (C.C.A. 2d. 1917). A stockholder may also enjoin the issue of new stock by directors where the purpose of the issue is to change the control of the enterprise, even though the issue may not injure the corporation and even though the stockholder may not under the circumstances have any contractual preemptive right to have the stock issued to him. Elliott v. Baker, 194 Mass. 518, 80 N.E. 450 (1907); Luther v. C. J. Luther Co., 118 Wis. 112, 94 N.W. 69 (1903); see Dunlay v. Avenue M. Garage & R. R., 253 N.Y. 274, 279, 170 N.E. 917, 919 (1930).

It may be questioned, however, whether some of the problems which Mr. Berle treats as fiduciary problems—*e.g.*, that relating to dividends on non-cumulative preferred stock—are not questions of contract rather than of fiduciary law. *Cf.* Wabash Ry. v. Barclay, 280 U.S. 197 (1930). A further controversy as to the fiduciary duties of management when management is vested not in directors but in a particular group of stockholders is beyond the scope of the present article. See Berle. *Studies in the Law of Corporation Finance* (1928) c. 3. But *cf.* Wood, "The Status of Management Stockholders" (1928). 38 *Yale. L. J.* 57.

[7] It has been asserted that the medieval like the modern law drew a distinction between those businesses which were public and those which were private. See I. Wyman, *Public Service Corporations* (1911) 5. It is reasonably clear, however, that this view involves reading modern conceptions into the early cases and that what those cases really indicate is that all business publicly carried on was regarded as public in character. See Adler, *Business Jurisprudence* (1914) 28 HARV L. Rev. 135. "The notion of a distinct category of business 'affected with a public interest,' employing property 'devoted to a public use,' rests upon historical error." Brandeis, J., dissenting, in New State Ice Co. v. Liebmann, 52 Sup. Ct. 371, 383 (1932).

[8] See Hamilton. "Affectation With Public Interest" (1930) 39 *Yale L. J.* 1089, 1095.

[9] 94 U.S. 113 (1877).

[10] See Hamilton, *supra* note 8; Brandeis, J., in New State Ice Co. v. Liebmann, 52 Sup. Ct. 371, 383 (1932).

[11] 273 U.S. 418 (1927): *cf.* New State Ice Co. v. Liebmann, 52 Sup. Ct. 371 (1932).

[12] See 41 STAT. 474, 483 (1920). 49 U.S.C. §§ I, 6 (1926).

[13] See 41 STAT. 494 (1920). 49 U.S.C. § 20a (1926).

[14] 39 STAT. 721 (1916). 45 U.S.C. 65 (1926). Held constitutional in Wilson v. New, 243 U. S. 332 (1917).

[15] 41 STAT. 469 (1920), 45 U. S. C. §§ 131-34 (1926).

[16] 261 U. S. 184 (1923) *Cf.* Dayton-Goose Creek Ry. v. United States, 263 U. S. 436 (1924); Fifteen Per Cent Case, 178 I.C.C. 539 (1951). (For modification of the order in that case. See U.S. Daily, Dec. 8 1931, at 2275.)

[17] See. *e.g.*, N.Y. PUB. SERV. COM. LAW. (1910) c.480.

[18] The United States Supreme Court, as indicated above, takes the position that charges to the consumer can not constitutionally be regulated unless the business is one which in the Court's opinion may properly be regarded as a public utility.

[19] Reasonable health and safety measures such as limitations of hours of service are accepted as proper exercises of the police power. Bunting v. Oregon, 243 U.S. 426 (1917). Minimum wage laws are deemed invalid. Adkins v. Children's Hospital, 261 U.S. 525 (1923). More limited wage regulations such as those compelling payment in cash have been upheld. Knoxville Iron Co. v. Harbison. 183 U.S. 13 (1901).

[20] The extent to which control of American industry is thus concentrated has recently been investigated. See LAIDLER, CONCENTRATION OF CONTROL IN AMERICAN INDUSTRY (1931).

[21] See, *e.g.*, Donham, *Business Adrift* (1931) *passim*; *The Swope Plan,* (Frederick editor, 1931); Address of Daniel Willard, President of Baltimore & Ohio R.R. in *America faces the future* (Beard editor, 1932) 29; Butler, "Unemployment", *id.* at 141.

[22] *E.g.*, Donham, *Business Adrift* 129-37; *The Swope Plan* 20.

[23] *Cf.* Brandeis, *Business—A Profession* (1925).

24 Mr. Young practised law for many years before he became a business executive.

25 Address of Owen D. Young. January, 1929. quoted in Sears, *The New Place of the Stockholder* (1929) 209. *Cf.* Wormser, *Frankenstein, Incorporated* (1931) c.8.

26 *The Swope Plan* 22.

27 *America Faces The Future* 186.

28 Donham, *Business Adrift* 28.

29 *Id.* at 105-06.

30 Some of our most successful industrial corporations have for years obtained all the additional capital which they needed out of surplus profits without any further issue of securities. See, *e.g.* The General Electric Co., *Moody's Manual of Investments, Industrial Securities* (1931) 971, indicating that the only outstanding bonds of that corporation were issued in 1902 and that no stock has been issued since 1920 except as a stock dividend or split-up.

31 It was raised in the case of Dodge v. Ford Motor Co., *supra* note 3, in which Mr. Ford's expressions of an intention to share profits with the public through a reduction in prices were relied upon as justifying a decree compelling the declaration of a dividend out of the large surplus of the company. Neither the language of the opinion nor the relief granted necessarily involves an unqualified acceptance of the maximum-profit-for-stockholders formula. The opinion states that "a business corporation is organized and carried on primarily for the profit of the stockholders" and that directors cannot lawfully "conduct the affairs of a corporation for the merely incidental benefit of shareholders and for the primary purpose of benefiting others." 204 Mic, at 507, 170 N.W. at 684. Despite testimony of Mr. Ford that he planned to expand the enterprise in the interest of consumers rather than of stockholders, the court was careful so to limit its decree as not to interfere seriously with the expansion program. Its avowed reason for so doing was that expansion might be made profitable despite Mr. Ford's expressed indifference to profit. One may suspect that it was also motivated, consciously or unconsciously, by a reluctance to prevent the growth of a socially important enterprise.

32 Hutton v. West Cork Ry., 23 Ch. D. 654, 673 (1883). "The law does not say that there are to be no cakes and ale, but there are to be no cakes and ale except such as are required for the benefit of the company." *Ibid.*

33 The present tendency is to take a liberal view of what gifts may reasonably be thought by the directors to be for the financial benefit of the corporation. *Cf.* Evans v. Brunner, Mond & Co., 90 L.J. Ch. 294 (1920); Armstrong Cork Co. H.A. Meldrum Co., 285 Fed. 58 (W.D.N.Y. 1922). Many of the recent cases on corporate gifts involve the deductibility of the gift from income under the federal income tax act as an "ordinary and necessary expense incurred in carrying on trade or business." Here also the modern cases take a liberal view of what may be to the business advantage of the company. *Cf.* Corning Glass Works v. Lucas. 37 F.(2d) 798 (App. D.C. 1929); American Rolling Mill Co. v. Commissioner of Int. Rev., 41 F.(2d) 314 (C.C.A. 6th, 1930); Forbes Lithograph Mfg. Co. v. White, 42 F.(2d) 287 (D. Mass. 1930).

34 For example, the New York Telephone Company is said to have spent $233,000 for charity during the past three years, including $130,000 for unemployment relief. The New York Public Service Commission had recently ruled that such must be charged against surplus and not to operating expenses. See (1932) 70 *New Republic* 219.

35 *Cf.* Tex. Acts 1917, c. 15, §§ i, 3; construed in James McCord Co. v. Citizens' Hotel Co., 287 S.W. 906 (Tex. Civ. App. 1926); N.Y. Laws 1931, Supp. c. 24, § 33.

36 Again, we see no reason why if a railroad company desires to foster, encourage and contribute to a charitable enterprise, or to one designed for the public weal and welfare it may not do so. Maitland, in 'Collected Essays' says: 'If the law allows men to form permanently organized groups, those groups will be, for common opinion, right-and-duty bearing units; and if the lawgiver will not openly treat them as such he will misrepresent, or, as the French say, he will "denature" the facts: in other words, he will make a mess and call it law.' We see no reason why a railroad corporation may not, to a reasonable extent, donate funds or services to aid in good works." *Per* Letton, J., in State *ex rel*. Sorensen v. Chicago, B.& Q. R. R.,112 Neb. 248, 255-56, 199 N, W. 534, 537 (1924).

37 Dicey, *Law and Public Opinion in England* (3d ed. 1920) 165. *Cf.* Laski, "The Personality of Associations" (1916) 29 *Harv. L. Rev.* 404. See also United Mine Workers v. Coronado Coal Co. 259 U.S. 344 (1922); Taff Vale Ry. v. Amalgamated Soc. of Ry. Servants, [1901] A.C. 426.

38 273 U.S. 418 (1927).

39 261 U.S. 525 (1923).

Copyright © 1932 by the Harvard Law Review Association. Reprinted with permission.

Whose Interests Should Corporations Serve?

Margaret M. Blair, The Brookings Institution

The finance and market myopia views of the central problem of corporate governance start from an assumption that the appropriate social purpose of corporations is to maximize shareholder return. They differ only over how best to achieve this goal. Finance model advocates believe that shareholder interests are best served by policies and actions that maximize share price in the short run because they accept the central maxim of finance theory: that the price of a share of stock today fully reflects the market's best estimate of the value of all future profits and growth that will accrue to that company. Thus they advocate an unfettered market for corporate control and other reforms that enhance the power of shareholders. Market myopia advocates, however, question whether today's stock price is a reliable enough guide to the future value and returns from the company's investments to be the exclusive focus of managerial attention. They fear that pressures from the financial markets impart a bias in managerial judgments against managing for the long term.

A third point of view is occasionally voiced in the corporate governance debates. This view has two distinct incarnations, but both versions start from the premise that corporations do not exist solely to provide returns to shareholders. Instead, they must serve a larger social purpose. The more familiar version of this idea holds that corporations should be "socially responsible" institutions, managed in the public interest. This idea was popular among consumer advocates, environmentalists, and social activists in the 1960s, 1970s, and early 1980s and was used in the 1980s by some corporate executives as an argument in support of policies that would inhibit takeovers or give companies more defenses against them. The idea never had much theoretical rigor to it, failed to give clear guidance to help managers and directors set priorities and decide among competing socially beneficial uses of corporate resources, and provided no obvious enforcement mechanism to ensure that corporations live up to their social obligations. As a result of these deficiencies, few academics, policymakers, or other proponents of corporate governance reforms still espouse this model.

Nonetheless, the idea that corporations should have some social purpose beyond maximizing returns to shareholders survives, and a new view about what this purpose should be is just beginning to emerge among the leading thinkers about corporate governance issues. It is that corporations exist to create wealth for society.[1] According to this view, the goal of corporate governance mechanisms and the responsibilities of corporate directors are to see that the firm maximizes wealth creation. In some instances this broad goal may be equivalent to maximizing returns to shareholders, but that will not always be the case.

To those who believe that corporations must serve some larger social purpose, governance reform proposals from the finance and market myopia camps might do damage to this larger social purpose if they tilt too strongly toward compelling corporate executives and their boards of directors to focus exclusively on maximizing shareholder returns.

Reconsidering an Old Question

Whether it is in the public interest for widely held corporations to be run exclusively for shareholders is an old question. Although seemingly forgotten by most advocates of the finance model, a major issue that Berle and Means originally raised was whether shareholders in widely held companies should be given the same legal rights and protections as owners of other kinds of property. Their answer was no. Because shareholders could not adequately undertake all the responsibilities that ownership of, say, real property normally implies, Berle and Means wrote, they should not necessarily be given all of the rights normally associated with ownership.

> The property owner who invests in a modern corporation so far surrenders his wealth to those in control of the corporation that he has exchanged the position of independent owner for one in which he may become merely recipient of the wages of capital.
>
> ...The owners of passive property, by surrendering control and responsibility over the active property, have surrendered the right that the corporation should be operated in their sole interest,—they have released the community from the obligation to protect them to the full extent implied in the doctrine of strict property rights. At the same time, the controlling groups, by means of the extension of corporate powers, have in their own interest broken the bars of tradition which require that the corporation be operated solely for the benefit of the owners of passive property.[2]

Nonetheless, Berle and Means were careful not to imply that corporate management should be free to run companies in their own interest.

> Eliminating the sole interest of the passive owner, however, does not necessarily lay a basis for the alternative claim that the new powers should be used in the interest of the controlling groups. The latter have not presented, in acts or words any acceptable defense of the proposition that these powers should be so used. No tradition supports that proposition. The control groups have, rather, cleared the way for the claims of a group far wider than either the owners or the control. They have placed the community in a position to demand that the modern corporation serve not alone the owners or the control but all society.[3]

Finance model advocates often cite Berle and Means as their most important intellectual ancestors, but, curiously, they have ignored or dismissed as trivial the key question of whose interests corporations should serve. Moreover, proponents of the finance model have so dominated the debate over corporate governance in recent years that those who might have raised the question have largely been silenced or have been driven to make circuitous arguments that soft-pedal or sidestep the question.[4] By the early 1990s, for example, it had become quite unfashionable for corporate executives to talk about their jobs in any terms other than maximizing shareholder value. Similarly, in his critique of the U.S. system of capital allocation and corporate governance, Michael Porter never explicitly challenges the notion that corporations should be driven by the goal of maximizing value for shareholders. Instead, he refers repeatedly to the "divergence of interests between owners and corporations" and the need to align the goals of investors with those "of the corporation" or to align the goals of management or employees with those "of the corporation."[5]

For these kinds of arguments to make sense, we must think carefully about who and what the corporation is, what goals it should have, and whose interests it should serve. These questions can be asked as legalistic or descriptive ones: What does the law say? Or they can be asked as questions of public policy: What *should* the law say?

What the Law Says

From its earliest evolution, corporate law has always been a bit schizophrenic about the right to form corporations.[6] On one hand, the right to incorporate was viewed as a simple extension of property rights and the freedoms of association and contract on the part of property owners. Under this "inherence" theory, the right to incorporate is inherent in the right to own property and write contracts. It follows that corporations should be legal extensions of their "owners" in the sense that they should have all the same rights and responsibilities as the individuals who own their equity.

The earliest corporations were "joint stock companies," which in the seventeenth and eighteenth centuries were set up for limited durations to accomplish specific tasks.[7] They were mechanisms for amassing capital to finance trading expeditions, for example, or to finance the construction of roads or canals. The joint stock companies were typically owned by a relatively small group of wealthy people who exercised close control over them.

But from the beginning, these joint stock companies and their successors, first the "trusts" (which were really holding companies), and, ultimately, modern corporations, required some sort of grant or charter from the state to exist.[8] These charters were granted in part because the projects to be undertaken were believed to be in the public interest. Under the "concession" theory, corporations owe their existence to a special concession from the state. This theory considers corporations to be separate entities from the owners of their equity, with a separate right to own and dispose of property, to enter into enforceable contracts, and to engage in business transactions. But their rights and responsibilities are defined and limited by the state and are not equivalent to those of the individuals who own their equity.

For complex historical reasons, the corporate form was used in the nineteenth century much more extensively in the United States than it was in other countries. So corporate law was more fully developed at an earlier date here than elsewhere. The earliest corporations were not granted perpetual life, nor were equity holders granted limited liability, but by the 1820s, most states had passed general incorporation acts that granted both of these features. By the middle of the 1800s, most states permitted the formation of corporations "for any legal purpose" and imposed no limitations on their accumulations of wealth and property. Thus, the right to form corporations became available to all individuals (a fact that supports the inherence view), but corporations themselves had characteristics that were not available to individuals and that only the state could grant (a fact that supports the concession view).

The 'Property Conception' of the Corporation

Before the rise of the large, multiunit, modern business enterprise in the late 1800s, "owners managed and managers owned," as professor Alfred D. Chandler, Jr., put it.[9] Although the notion existed that corporations were special entities with some public purpose aspects, there was no real question in the law about who should have control over corporations and in whose interest they should be run. William T. Allen, chancellor of the state of Delaware, notes that a leading corporation law treatise of the mid-1800s regarded corporations as "little more than limited partnerships, every member exercising through his vote an immediate control over the interests of the body."[10] He further notes that the law had not yet established with certainty that the state even had the right to impose taxes on corporations (separately from taxing their shareholders), and that shareholder liability was not limited to the extent that it is today.

The Pujo Committee report of 1913 detailed the loss of control by shareholders as corporations grew and shareholdings became more dispersed, but by 1919, the law still held that corporations were supposed to be run for the benefit of the stockholders.[11] That point was made crystal clear in a famous case before the Michigan Supreme Court, Dodge v. Ford Motor Co. The Dodge brothers had sued Ford Motor Co., complaining that Henry Ford suspended dividend payments, choosing instead to retain $58 million in profits to be used to expand the business and lower the price of its products. As shareholders, the Dodge brothers wanted Ford to pay out some of those accumulated profits instead and asserted that, because shareholders owned the enterprise, they could force directors to pay out the profits. The Michigan Supreme Court agreed:

> A business corporation is organized and carried on primarily for the profit of the stockholders. The powers of the directors are to be employed for that end. The discretion of directors is to be exercised in the choice of means to attain that end, and does not extend to a change in the end itself, to the reduction of profits, or to the nondistribution of profits among stockholders in order to devote them to other purposes.[12]

According to Allen, this decision is "as pure an example as exists" of what he calls the "property conception of the corporation." Allen's property conception, which conforms closely to my finance model, is based on an inherence view of the corporation, a view that in modern times has been associated with the "Chicago School" of law and economics (much of the theoretical basis and analytical techniques used to defend this position was largely developed at the University of Chicago). Central to the property conception is the treatment of the corporation as a "nexus of contracts," through which the various participants arrange to transact with each other.[13] In this conception, assets of the corporation are the property of the shareholders, and managers and boards of directors are viewed as agents of shareholders, with all the difficulties of enforcement associated with agency relationships, but with no legal obligations to any other stakeholders. Under this view, "the rights of creditors, employees, and others are strictly limited to statutory, contractual, and common law rights," Allen says.¹⁴

The 'Social Entity Conception'

The property conception of the corporation held sway in U.S. corporate law throughout the 1800s and early part of the 1900s. But with the separation of ownership from control, the development of sophisticated securities markets, and the emergence of a class of professional managers who viewed themselves as "trustees" of great institutions, a competing view began to take hold. "It was apparent to any thoughtful observer that the American corporation had ceased to be a private business device and had become an institution," Berle wrote in the preface to *The Modern Corporation and Private Property*.¹⁵ Similarly, historian Dow Votaw noted that "the buccaneers of the late nineteenth century gave way to the more statesmanlike professional managers of the twentieth. The aggressive, profit- and power-seeking individualist was replaced by the arbitrator and diplomat whose motivations included organization survival, professional reputation, and equitable balancing of interests, as well as profit-making. The modern corporation has been aptly described as a 'constellation of interests' rather than the instrument of the acquisitive individual."¹⁶

Allen calls this view the "social entity conception," noting that the purpose of the corporation is seen as "not individual but social." As he puts it:

> Contributors of capital (stockholders and bondholders) must be assured a rate of return sufficient to induce them to contribute their capital to the enterprise. But the corporation has other purposes of perhaps equal dignity: the satisfaction of consumer wants, the provision of meaningful employment opportunities and the making of a contribution to the public life of its communities. Resolving the often conflicting claims of these various corporate constituencies calls for judgment, indeed calls for wisdom, by the board of directors of the corporation. But in this view, no single constituency's interest may significantly exclude others from fair consideration by the board.¹⁷

This idea, of course, is a direct descendent of the point Berle and Means made in the conclusion to their work in 1932. To be sure, Berle was concerned about the potential for corporate managers to abuse the powers implied in this conception. "Now I submit," he wrote in a later essay, "that you cannot abandon emphasis on 'the view that business corporations exist for the sole purpose of making profits for their stockholders' until such time as you are prepared to offer a clear and reasonably enforceable scheme of responsibilities to someone else."[18]

Until the 1980s the social entity conception of the corporation was never given official legal sanction, although many social activists and several business leaders adopted the idea.[19] As the modern corporation grew in size and power after World War II, the central concern of legal scholars was not so much whether corporations should or should not be run primarily for shareholders, and certainly not whether the separation of ownership from control would make corporations inefficient or uncompetitive. Rather, the concern was about who should control the vast economic, political, and social power of these large and powerful wealth-generating machines and how that power should be restrained. "It is not enough that the great corporation be a paragon of efficiency and production," Votaw wrote in 1965, expressing a view quite typical of the era.

> The large corporations are the possessors of substantial amounts of this power, and properly so. Without it they could not perform the tasks society demands of them. In a free society, however, we cannot leave the subject there. Power, in either private or public hands, raises difficult questions: How much power? In whose hands? Power for what purposes? To whom are the wielders of power responsible? What assurances are there that the power will be used fairly and justly? and, Is there machinery by which the power and the method of its exercise can be made responsive to the needs of society?[20]

Votaw noted that the political legitimacy of the corporation was challenged during the Depression, when it appeared that this power was not being used responsibly. But then "the corporation... performed brilliantly during World War II" and "the performance of the corporate system since the war has also been very good, as a whole, [producing] rising prosperity and standards of living." As a result, he said, "issues of legitimacy moved into the background."[21]

Questions of legitimacy faded in part because corporations were assuming more and more responsibilities as social institutions. By the late 1960s and early 1970s, corporate responsiveness to a broad group of stakeholders had become accepted business practice (for pragmatic reasons if nothing else).[22] Consumer advocates and religious and political groups that wanted to influence corporate behavior bought token shareholdings so that they could introduce resolutions and vote on important corporate policies. They also staged boycotts and waged publicity campaigns. Although no corporation ever went so far as to, say, elect Ralph Nader to the board of directors, many of them created public affairs offices, added consumer hotlines, gave research grants to universities and other special research institutes, contributed to charity, agreed to divest from South Africa, and engaged much more directly in political dialogue. They also gave their employees paid leave to engage in public service activities and participated in community development programs. Wages were still rising rapidly during this period, and large corporations were increasing the noncash benefits they gave their employees, such as health insurance, pensions, education and training support, and vacation and sick leave. In addition to paying relatively high taxes, they also became significant supporters of public institutions such as theaters, parks, schools, museums, and hospitals. Most companies looked upon such "socially responsible" behavior as a way to improve the general business climate.

The law moved to accommodate the social entity view by protecting companies that engaged in such activities, even when these activities were clearly not directly related to maximizing profits for shareholders. The courts, for example, generally upheld corporations that had made donations to museums or hospitals or had otherwise expended corporate resources on community-enhancing activities against challenges from shareholders. By the 1970s, in fact, forty-eight states had passed laws "explicitly providing that chartered corporations could give to charities without specific charter provision."[23] A clever legal device was developed to justify these kinds of activities without conceding that directors did not have a primary duty to maximize wealth for shareholders. The courts held that, while it might divert shareholder wealth in the short run, responding to the needs and interests of other stakeholders was good for shareholders "in the long run," because the good health and well-being of the communities in which companies operate was considered important for business. "The law papered over the conflict in our conception of the corporation by invoking a murky distinction between long-term profit maximization and short-term profit maximization," Allen writes. "The long-term/short-term distinction preserves the form of the stockholders-oriented property theory, while permitting, in fact, a considerable degree of behavior consistent with a view that sees public corporations as owing social responsibilities to all affected by its operation."[24]

Breakdown of Accommodation

For nearly half a century, this practical accommodation in the law worked. These activities were seldom challenged by shareholders, but when they were, they were successfully defended as being beneficial to shareholders in the long run. And, until the 1970s, it appeared that shareholders were benefiting—along with employees and communities—from the broad social role that most large corporations played. An investment made in the Standard & Poor's composite companies in 1945 would have yielded a compound annual rate of return of 7.59 percent by 1972, compared to an average annual yield on high-rated corporate bonds during this same period of about 4.30 percent.[25]

The "in the long run" device for reconciling the goal of maximizing value for shareholders with a more broadly defined goal of social responsibility for corporations broke down in the 1980s for three reasons, according to Allen: the rise of global competition; internationalization of financial markets; and the emergence of the hostile takeover. To these a fourth should be added: the collapse in stock market returns in the 1970s, followed by the rise in the cost of capital in the early part of the 1980s.

The rise of global competition contributed to an irregular but steady erosion of corporate profitability in the post-War decades, especially in the manufacturing sector. Meanwhile, the investment options overseas were expanding, and, by the early 1980s the real return on bonds and other, safer investments in the United States had climbed to new heights. Together, these changed the expectations of the financial markets about the return that corporations should provide, and the resulting discontent among investors opened the way for hostile takeovers and leveraged restructuring.[26]

The emergence of tender offers and hostile takeovers shattered the uneasy "in the long run" legal device for reconciling the property conception and the social entity conception. To shareholders who had been offered an immediate 35 or 40 percent premium to tender their shares, the possibility that the company might perform better as an independent entity "in the long run" seemed irrelevant. Even in terms of evaluating more ordinary business decisions, the extraordinarily high cost of capital that prevailed in the 1980s greatly weakened the defense for expenditures that would show returns only in the long run. At discount rates of 10 to 15 percent, the return on investments of any kind, whether in new plants and equipment or in community relations, must be much higher and come in much faster than it must at discount rates of 5 to 10 percent.[27]

The legal response to the breakdown of the accommodation between shareholder wealth maximization and corporate social responsibility has not been completely worked out. Throughout the 1980s, for example, the American Law Institute worked to develop a new consensus statement on principles of corporate governance. Reflecting the political dominance of the "finance model," or "property conception" of that decade, early drafts were strident in tone, asserting that corporations should absolutely and unequivocally be treated as the property of shareholders, that the goal of the corporation should be to maximize value for shareholders, and that the well-being of shareholders should take precedence in every corporate decision. The tone was softened considerably in the final document, which states that the objective of corporations should be "the conduct of business activities with a view to enhancing corporate profit and shareholder gain." In so doing, the document said, corporations "may devote a reasonable amount of resources to public welfare, humanitarian, educational, and philanthropic purposes." Nonetheless, this document still insists that shareholder interests should dominate and that directors should consider nonshareholder constituencies only when "competing courses of action have comparable impact on shareholders."[28]

At the state level, the rejection of the strict property conception (at least in the context of takeovers) was much more explicit. At least twenty-seven states have passed laws since 1985 that specifically make it legal for (and in at least one state, require) directors to consider other interests in addition to shareholders when making major business decisions, mainly in deciding whether to accept or fight a tender offer. (Two states, Pennsylvania and Ohio, had such a law before 1985.)[29] Typically, these statutes require directors to consider the "best interests of the corporation" as a whole, and then identify a specific set of stakeholders, including employees, creditors, suppliers, and the community in general in addition to shareholders, whose interests are considered tied to the corporation. "States saw a different side of the rampant takeover activity—the social responsibility side—and began to question whether attaining takeover benefits for shareholders was as consistent with other important interests as economic and legal orthodoxy presumed," says law professor Alexander C. Gavis.[30]

Steven M. H. Wallman, an SEC commissioner who helped to draft the original "corporate constituency" law passed in Pennsylvania in 1983 and its amendment in 1990, defines the corporation's interest as "enhancing its ability to produce wealth indefinitely ... [including] both profit from today's activities and expected profit from tomorrow's activities."[31] This wealth-producing language is not in the statutes, but Wallman's subsequent explication of what it means for directors to act "in the interest of the corporation" suggests that these laws, if interpreted and applied as Wallman believes they should be, could provide a legal basis for a new conception of the proper goals of corporate governance.[32] Linking the interests of the various constituencies to the interest of the corporation, he asserts, "resolves much of the tension that would otherwise exist from competing and conflicting constituent demands."[33] Defining the interests of the corporation in terms of maximizing the wealth-producing potential of the enterprise as a whole also provides the beginning of a way to resolve the long-term, short-term conflict, as well as a basis for deciding which corporate constituencies matter under what circumstances.

Many legal scholars, policy analysts, and others have sharply criticized these corporate constituency laws. Their only application is in the takeover context, critics say (because the "business judgement rule" still applies in other contexts). In this context, their effect is to give corporate executives and directors carte blanche to do whatever they want, the critics say, because almost any decision can be justified on the grounds that it benefits or protects some constituency. Thus, finance model advocates and even some market myopia advocates disparage these laws as no more than knee-jerk reactions by state legislatures to try to protect management and workers in their states from the threat of hostile takeovers.

The state of Delaware, where more than half of the Standard & Poor's 500 corporations are incorporated, has not passed such a statute, but the decision of the Delaware Supreme Court in *Paramount Communications v. Time Inc.* in 1989 was widely interpreted as giving similar leeway to management of Delaware-chartered firms. It did so, however, by again invoking the "long-term/short-term" distinction rather than by directly addressing the question of whose interests should take precedence. In that case, the board of directors of Time Inc. thwarted a takeover bid by Paramount Communications by quickly executing a tender offer for Warner Communications. Paramount's initial cash offering price represented about a 40 percent premium over the price at which Time's stock had been trading just before Paramount's offer, and Paramount later raised the bid, with the higher bid representing a 60 percent premium. But for months (indeed, years) before the Paramount bid, Time had been negotiating a stock-for-stock merger with Warner Communications and had announced a merger plan a few months before the Paramount offer was made. The Delaware Supreme Court refused to stop Time from proceeding with the tender offer for Warner, even though, in taking that action, Time's board foreclosed any opportunity for Time shareholders to accept the Paramount offer or even to vote on the merger with Warner. "The fiduciary duty to manage a corporate enterprise includes the selection of a time frame for achievement of corporate goals," the court ruled. "That duty may not be delegated to the stockholders.... Directors are not obliged to abandon a deliberately conceived corporate plan for a short-term shareholder profit unless there is clearly no basis to sustain the corporate strategy."[34] Allen, who wrote the chancery court opinion in the case, later wrote that the ruling "might be interpreted as constituting implicit acknowledgement of the social entity conception."[35]

Four years later, in a case again involving Paramount Communications, the Delaware Supreme Court appeared to shift its stance again, this time toward placing more weight on getting the highest value for shareholders, regardless of the effect on management's carefully laid long-range strategic plans. In this case Paramount was negotiating a merger agreement with Viacom when Paramount CEO Martin Davis learned that QVC Network was interested in acquiring Paramount. In response, Paramount put together a deal with Viacom to exchange Paramount shares for a mix of Viacom stock and cash that was estimated to be worth about $70 per Paramount share, and that gave Viacom an option to buy 19.9 percent of the stock of Paramount if the Paramount-Viacom deal were canceled for any of a number of reasons, including an acquisition of Paramount by some other bidder. The options included several unusual features that would be highly disadvantageous to QVC if it proceeded with a tender offer. Nonetheless, QVC did proceed, offering $80 a share for 51 percent of Paramount's stock and filing suit to have the stock option agreement invalidated.

In contrast to its assessment of the facts in the earlier case, the Delaware Supreme Court ruled that Paramount was embarking on a plan to sell control of Paramount and that Paramount's board was therefore obligated to consider all offers in order to get the best price for the company. "The pending sale of control implicated in the Paramount-Viacom transaction required the Paramount Board to act on an informed basis to secure the best value reasonably available to the stockholders," the court ruled.[36]

Technically, the difference between these two cases hinged on whether the defendant directors (Time's board in the first case, and Paramount's board in the second) had put their companies up for sale when they announced merger plans. But in the first case, the court seemed to give directors considerable leeway to reject takeover bids in order to protect long-range strategic plans, and in the second case, the court seemed to sharply circumscribe the types of long-range plans that would be so protected. Thus it remains unclear whether directors of companies incorporated in Delaware can consider the effect of a takeover decision on stakeholders other than just shareholders.[37]

So far, no stakeholder has tested the limits of the "corporate constituency" laws by attempting to enforce his or her claim to consideration in the courts.[38] Unless and until these laws are overturned, however, they give formal legal sanction to the idea that corporations have social purposes in addition to providing profits for shareholders.

What Should the Law Say?

Although the law has still not resolved the issue unequivocally, the belief that the primary goal of corporate endeavors should be to maximize value for shareholders still dominates the public policy debates and has largely been accepted even by corporate executives who not long before tended to resist that idea.[39] Three theoretical arguments are typically given for why it is in society's interest that corporations should be run for shareholders and why shareholders, in turn, should be given control.

Shareholders as 'Owners'
The first of these arguments holds that shareholders should have the right to control corporate resources and ensure that they are used to their own benefit because they are the "owners." The right to control private property is an essential part of what it means to own something, and ownership rights are a vitally important social norm and important for efficiency reasons.

By now, that argument—that shareholders own the corporation, so therefore they should be able to exercise control over it—should have been put safely to rest. It is simply circular logic. Shareholders own equity, and the question is what control rights ought to accompany that kind of claim against the company. The de facto separation of equity ownership from control, Votaw noted, changed the whole legal concept of property, at least with respect to corporations.

> Property consists of a bundle of rights which the owner of property posesses with regard to some thing—rights to possess, use, dispose of, exclude others, and manage and control. The corporate concept divides this bundle of rights into several pieces. The stockholder gets the right to receive some of the fruits of the use of property, a fractional residual right in corporate property, and a very limited right of control. The rights to possess, use, and control the property go to the managers of the corporation.[40]

When property rights have been broken up in this way, trying to identify one party as the "owner" is neither meaningful nor useful. "To assume that we can know who property owners are, and to assume that once we have identified them their rights follow as a matter of course, is to assume what needs to be decided," Joseph William Singer wrote in an essay on whether steelworkers have any legitimate property rights in the plant where they work.[41]

Building on the idea of property as a bundle of rights, Thomas Donaldson and Lee E. Preston argue that the various property rights that societies grant are generally based on some underlying concept of justice, especially distributive justice. Notions of distributive justice, in turn, are based on some socially constructed notion of who has what moral interest in the use of the asset—for example, who has contributed what effort or made what sacrifice, who has what need, or who has made what prior agreement about the uses of the asset. In modern corporations, by definition, all stakeholders have some stake or moral interest in the affairs of corporations, Donaldson and Preston observe and conclude that "the normative principles that underly the contemporary pluralistic theory of property rights also provide the foundation for the stakeholder theory as well."[42]

Chapter 6 in *Ownership and Control: Rethinking Corporate Governance for the Twenty-first Century* (Brookings Institution, 1995) 202-234.

Management Accountability
The second argument for why it is in the public interest to operate corporations for shareholders holds that, as a normative matter, corporate executives should not be allowed to make arbitrary decisions to use other people's property for their own interest or even for what they believe to be in the public interest. Managers must be held accountable to someone. Diffusing this responsibility among many groups of stakeholders means, in practice, that managers are accountable to no one.

Ronald Coase has argued that, if property rights are clearly established and if all parties can contract freely over the use of resources, then those resources will be used efficiently.[43] According to Coase, it makes no difference (from an efficiency standpoint) whether the factory owner has the right to pollute or the townspeople have the right to clean air. If the property rights are clearly established, the various parties can write a contract in which the townspeople pay the factory owner not to pollute or the factory owner pays the townspeople for the right to pollute. In either case, the process of contracting will determine a socially optimal "price" for polluting, and the factory owner will end up spending the right amount on pollution abatement equipment.[44]

But even if one agreed in principle that clearly established property rights would be socially useful, establishing completely clear "property" rights in complex organizations such as corporations is impossible in practice, in part because the concept of "property" is so complex and multifaceted. The question is which of the many "control" rights should be assigned to shareholders, which given to other stakeholders, and which left to managers.

Nonetheless, if managers do not themselves bear the full costs of their decisions and if they are not held accountable to someone for something, they will be accountable to no one, and they will have few incentives to use resources under their control efficiently.

Versions of this argument were often heard in the debates of the late 1960s and early 1970s about the "social responsibilities" of business. In its simple version, it says that performance is easier to monitor if only one dimension of performance, such as profits (or, in their capitalized form, share value) is measured. In more sophisticated versions, the argument is concerned about private uses of power. As Friedrich A. Hayek puts it, "the tendency to allow and even to impel the corporations to use their resources for specific ends other than those of a long-run maximization of the return on the capital placed under their control ... tends to confer upon them undesirable and socially dangerous powers."[45]

The central point here is the need for mechanisms to ensure that management is accountable for its decisions. Managers should be held accountable precisely because they are managing assets that are not their own and because they do not personally bear all of the costs of their decisions. But this argument fails to make the case that the objective of managers should be to maximize share value; it therefore also fails to make the case that the shareholders should necessarily be given greater control rights.

The third public interest argument used to justify assigning control rights to shareholders is that shareholders are the residual claimants.[46] They receive the residual gain and bear the residual risk associated with the corporate enterprise, this argument goes, and they therefore have the best incentive to monitor. To the extent that this is true, maximizing value for shareholders is equivalent to maximizing the social value of corporations, and it follows that it would be socially optimal to give control rights to shareholders to ensure that share value is maximized.

At first glance, this argument would seem to be the same as saying that the shareholders should monitor because it is their money that is being managed. But saying that it is the shareholders' money does not resolve the underlying questions about the meaning of "ownership" in this case. Ronald Gilson and Mark Roe make the distinction clear: "Equity has governance rights because the holder of the residual profits interest has the best incentive to reduce agency costs; the right to control rests with those who stand to gain the most from efficient production."[47] Previously, Gilson had held that the "description of shareholders as the 'owners' ... derives ... from the need for those holding the residual interest in corporate profits to have the means to displace management which performs poorly.... This position is based on matters other than a preconception of the rights associated with 'ownership'; indeed, if the statute did not provide for shareholders, we would have to invent them."[48] This argument is the product of a long and somewhat arcane scholarly effort to explain large enterprises in a way consistent with neoclassical economic theory. In very simplified terms, the theory that has been developed goes as follows: Team production is often much more efficient than individual production. But, because it is sometimes hard to tell who is responsible for what portion of the output produced by teams, individual team members might try to shirk. Team production thus requires that someone serve as monitor to be sure that no one shirks. What keeps the monitor from shirking? The monitor enters into contracts with all of the other input providers to pay each of them according to their opportunity cost (that is, what they could get if they sold their services or materials to the next highest bidder), and the monitor receives all of the extra value created by the enterprise, over and above these costs. In other words, the monitor bears the residual risk and receives the residual gain.[49]

In a small, entrepreneurial firm, this monitor is the owner-manager. But who bears the residual risk and receives the residual gain in large, widely held corporations? Scholars who have worked on these questions of organizational theory have generally assumed that it is the shareholders.[50] From that assumption, they have argued that hierarchical decision-making and oversight by boards of directors were institutional arrangements developed as substitutes for direct monitoring by shareholders.[51] And, from that argument, they conclude that boards of directors should represent the interests of shareholders above all other competing interests.

In the idealized model of a corporation described by these scholars, institutional and legal arrangements that direct as much of the oversight and control responsibilities as possible to shareholders or to their representatives make impeccable sense. But shareholders were long ago granted limited liability, which, of course, shifted some of the residual risk onto creditors and others. Moreover, the risks that shareholders bear can largely be diversified away by holding the shares as part of a balanced portfolio. Finally, shareholders generally have unrestricted rights to sell their shares, which means that shareholders, perhaps more than any of the other stakeholders in firms, have the option to "exit" if they are dissatisfied with the performance of the firm. Thus, the notion that the shareholders bear all of the residual risk seems doubtful on its face.[52]

For it to be strictly true that shareholders receive all of the residual gain and bear all of the residual risk, the suppliers of all other inputs into the corporate enterprise would have to be compensated by means of "complete" contracts (that is, contracts that specify exactly what is to happen in all circumstances). These contracts would have to compensate other input providers at their social opportunity cost (including compensation for any explicit, predictable risk they were bearing). If such arrangements were, indeed, the norm, it would not make any difference to employees, lenders, materials and equipment suppliers, dealers, communities, or other stakeholders if a corporation suffered losses and had to go out of business. That is because the inputs supplied by these other parties could be readily redeployed at the same price or wages they had commanded in their service to the corporation or because the providers of these inputs were compensated in advance for any losses they might incur at such time.[53]

Curiously, although this assumption about the allocation of risk and rewards in the corporate enterprise would appear patently wrong, it is almost never challenged outright. In fact, among true believers in the finance model, this assumption is dogma. But labor economists have long noted that workers in large corporations, especially in certain industries, earn higher wages and benefits than do workers with comparable skills and comparable jobs who are self-employed or who work for small entrepreneurial firms.[54] This differential would suggest that some of the residual gains from team production in large corporations are being shared with workers. Neoclassical economists have argued that apparent labor market differentials can be explained by unmeasured differences in labor quality and working conditions. An alternative view is that firms may, in some circumstances, pay higher wages to improve motivation, morale, and job stability, to make recruiting easier, and to encourage employees to develop special skills that may be valuable only to that employer. In other words, the higher productivity justifies the cost of paying wages above the competitive rate. Either way, the residual gain from team production is being shared with workers. And, as the next chapter shows, sharing the residual gain with workers necessarily implies that these workers are sharing in the residual risk associated with the ability of the enterprise as a whole to continue to generate those gains.[55]

It is easy to see why the assumption that shareholders are the residual claimants is so important to those who maintain that shareholders should have control. If other stakeholders could be shown to share in the residual gains and risks, their interest in being able to exercise some control over corporations would be significantly legitimized.

Despite the empirical weakness of the assumption that shareholders receive all of the residual gain and bear all of the residual risk, the underlying point of the finance model argument is quite important—corporations are more likely to be managed in ways that maximize social value if those who monitor and control firms receive (at least some of) the residual gain and bear (some of) the residual risk, and, conversely, if those who share in the residual gains and risks are given the access and authority they need to monitor. Put more simply, corporate resources should be used to enhance the goals and serve the purposes of all those who truly have something invested and at risk in the enterprise. Those parties, in turn, should be given enough of the control rights to ensure that corporate resources are used to those ends. If control rights could be allocated in this way, all of the participants would have an incentive to see that the total size of the pie is maximized, and any one stakeholder group would have trouble increasing the value of its stake simply by pushing costs and risks onto other stakeholders.

In short, it is possible to reject the simplistic finance model or property conception of the corporation to the extent that it implies that directors' only duty is to maximize value for shareholders, and still retain the compelling logic that private control of private property leads to the most efficient use of society's resources. In the next chapter I argue that the view of corporations as wealth-creating machines, with a social purpose of maximizing wealth, provides a clear basis for thinking about how control rights to that machine should be allocated. My conclusions differ from those of most finance model advocates, however, because I make a much more general assumption about what the source of value creation is, and who it is that bears the risk and receives the gains in most corporations today.

The primitive model of corporations in which shareholders are seen as earning all the returns and bearing all the risk is a throwback to an earlier time when the typical corporation owned and operated a canal, a railroad, or a big manufacturing plant. Entrepreneurial investors put up the financial capital, which was used to build or buy the railroad, canal, or factory and to make initial payments to hired managers. The managers, in turn, arranged to buy raw materials and energy, hire labor, oversee production or manage the operations, and (in the case of the factory) ship the goods to market. The proceeds from the sale of those goods was used to meet payroll (including the manager's salary), pay taxes, buy more raw materials, keep the machinery in working order and pay off any loans, and all of these inputs were acquired at the going market rate. Anything left over after that was "profit," and it seemed reasonable and appropriate that the profits belonged to the initial investors (shareholders), who were the only parties with significant assets tied up and at risk in the enterprise. These assets consisted of some inventories and receivables, the entrepreneurial know-how of the owner-manager, and, most, the canal, the roadbed and railcars, or the factory.[56]

For enterprises that fit this model, it may be a reasonable approximation of the truth that the capital investments and the entrepreneurial efforts of the investor are the sources of the wealth and that shareholders capture all of that wealth and bear all the associated risk. For firms that look like this, corporate governance arrangements that provide for them to be run for shareholders and that accordingly give as much control to shareholders as possible, serve to encourage wealth creation by fostering and protecting investments in physical capital and entrepreneurial effort.

But in the 1990s, fewer and fewer publicly traded corporations actually look like the factory model. Much of the wealth-generating capacity of most modern firms is based on the skills and knowledge of the employees and the ability of the organization as a whole to put those skills to work for customers and clients. Even for manufacturing firms, physical plant and equipment make up a rapidly declining share of the assets, while a growing share consists of intangibles (some recognized on the books and given an accounting value, some not) such as patent rights, brand reputation, service capabilities, and the ability to innovate and get the next generation product to market in a timely manner.[57]

It is commonplace to hear chief executives of major corporations say "our wealth is in our people."[58] Although such lines are probably not taken seriously nearly as often as they are said, there are important economic reasons why they should be taken seriously. Moreover, the idea that the wealth of a corporation is in its people has important implications for corporate governance arrangements.

Margaret M. Blair is a Senior Fellow at the Brookings Institution.

1. A few of the leading lawyers and management specialists active in corporate governance reform issues have begun describing corporate goals in these terms. Drucker (1991a, p. 112) argues that institutional owners of German and Japanese companies "do not attempt to maximize shareholder value or the short-term interest of any one of the enterprise's 'stakeholders.' Rather they *maximize the wealth producing capacity of the enterprise* [emphasis in the original]." Similarly, Millstein (1992, p. 42) writes about the role that "knowledgeable and diligent ownership (relationship investing) can play in causing corporations to better *maximize their wealth producing capacity in the global economy* [emphasis added]."

2. Berle and Means (1932, pp. 3, 355).

3. Berle and Means (1932, pp. 355-56).

4. An exception was an essay by Epstein (1986, p. 3) that at least acknowledged the question. "Out of this bitter debate [the 1980s takeover battles] emerged a sharp divergence of views on the purpose of the corporation in the American system of capitalism. Whereas many shareholders thought of it in terms of its profitability, corporate management tended to define it in terms of service to the community, suggesting that their corporations were 'institutions,' much like museums or hospitals, that served a public interest as well as the private interest of shareholders." Epstein goes on to defend a view that companies should be run for shareholders and that shareholders should be given more control. Thus Epstein's piece supports my fundamental point about the dominance of the finance model.

5. See, for example, Porter (1992, p. 20).

6. The section that follows draws heavily on an article by William T. Allen, chancellor of the state of Delaware. See Allen (1992). I have credited Allen where I have taken his arguments directly. See also Votaw (1965, chap. 1) for an informative essay on the evolution of the corporate form.

7. The first joint stock company was formed in 1555, but the form was rarely used before the 1600s. See Votaw (1965, pp. 13-17).

8. The original trusts were voluntary associations of small companies that each agreed to turn their stock over to a common board of trustees, in exchange for trust certificates of equal value, so that the operations of the companies could be managed in common. Their purpose was to formalize the otherwise unenforceable agreements among companies to fix prices or control supply. The trust form came under attack by state and federal courts, and, in response, the state of New Jersey passed a generalized incorporation law permitting the formation of holding companies. The standard Oil Trust and the other well-known "trusts" of the late 1800s and early 1900s were actually holding companies. See Chandler (1977, pp. 318-20).

9. Chandler (1977, p. 9).

10. Allen (1992, p. 8).

11. *Report of the Committee Appointed Pursuant to House Resolution 429 and 504 to Investigate the Concentration of Control of Money and Credit,* House Report 1593, 62d Cong. 3d sess. Government Printing Office, 1913, as cited in Herman (1981, p. 7).

12. 204 Mich. 459, 170 N.W. 668 (1919), cited in Allen (1992, p. 10).

13. Jensen and Meckling (1976, pp. 305-60).

Chapter 6 in *Ownership and Control: Rethinking Corporate Governance for the Twenty-first Century* (Brookings Institution, 1995) 202-234.

14 Allen (1992, p. 10).

15 Berle and Means (1932, p. v).

16 Votaw (1965, p. 28).

17 Allen (1992, p. 15).

18 Berle (1932). The Berle essay was one of a series of essays in a scholarly debate between Berle and Professor E. Merrick Dodd. Despite his apparent interest in the idea of the corporation as a social institution as expressed in the conclusion to *The Modern Corporation and Private Property,* Berle argued that giving corporate executives too much power "might be unsafe, and in any case it hardly affords the soundest base on which to construct the economic commonwealth which industrialism seems to require." (p. 1372) Dodd, by contrast, argued that the law was moving in the direction of viewing the corporation as "an economic institution which has a social service as well as a profit-making function. " See Dodd (1932, p. 1148).

19 In 1946 Frank Abrams, then chairman of Standard Oil Company of New jersey, described the role of the modern manager as maintaining "an equitable and working balance among the claims of the various directly interested groups—stockholders, employees, customers, and the public at large." See Rostow (1960). In 1978 directors of Control Data Corp. gave formal recognition to the view of corporations as social entities in its proxy statement to shareholders, urging them to pass several amendments to the company's articles of incorporation that would require the board to consider the effect of any takeover proposal on the company's employees and other "stakeholders." "The Board is mindful and supportive ... of the growing concept that corporations have a social responsibility to a wide variety of societal segments which have a stake in the continued health of a given corporation," the proxy letter stated. See Control Data Corp. Proxy Statement, May 3, 1978, p. 4.

20 Votaw (1965, p. 87).

21 Votaw (1965, p. 102).

22 Accepted, at least, by most business leaders. Economists and legal scholars of the Chicago School railed against such behavior, however. For example, Milton Friedman wrote that "businessmen who talk this way are unwitting puppets of the intellectual forces that have been undermining the basis of a free society these past decades." See Milton Friedman, "The Social Responsibility of Business Is to Increase Its Profits," *New York Times Magazine*, September 13, 1970, p. 33.

23 See Herman (1981, footnote 40, p. 401). Herman cautions that "corporate largess for purposes not readily reconciled with profit-effectiveness is still subject to legal challenge." (p. 256)

24 Allen (1992, pp. 16-17).

25 These calculations are unadjusted for inflation. The difference between the return earned by bondholders and that earned by stockholders over the period may simply be an appropriate level of compensation for the additional risk borne by stockholders. There is no way to measure how much shareholders should be paid for risk. One can only measure how much more they, in fact, earned on high risk investments relative to lower risk investments. The point here is only that shareholders shared in the wealth creation by large corporations, as they should have. The end date for this analysis was not chosen at random. By 1974 the S&P 500 average had fallen by 24 percent, wiping out all of the gains it had seen in the previous ten years (and reminding investors that investing in stocks did entail some significant risks). This loss in value was not fully regained until 1980. Many observers believe this poor performance by the stock market in the 1970s helped set the stage for the battles for corporate control in the 1980s.

26. This hypothesis about the cause of highly leveraged corporate restructuring activity in the 1980s was first presented in Blair and Litan (1990) and is a major thesis of several essays in Blair (1993).

27. Based on a survey of 228 Fortune 1000 firms conducted in 1990 and 1991, Poterba and Summers (1991) estimate that corporate executives use an average real (inflation adjusted) "hurdle rate" of 12.2 percent to evaluate investments. More recently, the *Wall Street Journal* reported that corporations were setting very aggressive hurdles on return on investment—some as high as 20 percent—for capital spending planned for 1994. See Fred R. Bleakley, "As Capital Spending Grows, Firms Take a Hard Look at Returns From the Effort," *Wall Street Journal,* February 8, 1994, p. A2.

28. The American Law Institute (1994, pp. 55, 405).

29. See Wallman (1993) for a list of the states with corporate constituency laws.

30. Gavis (1990, p. 1461).

31. Wallman (1991, p. 170).

32. In private correspondence with the author September 7, 1993, Wallman took pains to distinguish his "wealth-producing notion" of the duty of boards and the role of corporations from the "social responsibility model."

33. Wallman (1991, p. 170).

34. See Supreme Court of the State of Delaware, *Paramount Communications, Inc. v. Time Inc.*, 571 A.2d 1140-1155 (Delaware 1990).

35. Allen (1992, p. 20).

36. See Supreme Court of Delaware, *Paramount Communications Inc. v. QVC Network Inc.,* 637 A.2d 34 (Del. 1994).

37. Takeover lawyer Martin Lipton says that the two cases "can be summarized as holding that under Delaware law the objective of the corporation is the *long-term* growth of shareholder value; assuming the board of directors has used due care (followed reasonable procedures) and did not have a conflict of interest, the board may prefer *long-term* goals over *short-term* goals except when the decision is to sell control of the corporation or to liquidate it in which case the board must use reasonable efforts to get the best value obtainable for the shareholders. Under this standard the board has the right to invest for the *long-term* in people, equipment, market share and financial structure even though the financial markets do not recognize (or overly discount) the future value and even though the board's strategy results in elimination of dividends and reduction in market price of the stock. Also under this standard, the board has the right to 'just say no' to a premium takeover bid. However, the board does remain subject to shareholder control and the shareholders have the right at least once a year to replace at least some of the directors who have followed a strategy or taken a position disliked by the shareholders." [Emphasis in original] Private correspondence with the author, April 5, 1994.

38. "Case law interpreting nonshareholder constituency statutes appears to be non-existent," says Gavis, who suggests that states with these laws have relatively little corporate activity in them. See Gavis (1990, p. 1446). But some of the laws include language intended to rule out, or at least discourage, such enforcement action. See Sommer (1991b, p. 46). Such provisions reinforce the view of some legal scholars and observers who believe that the statutes were intended to protect management, not to give other stakeholders access or standing to make specific claims against corporations.

Chapter 6 in *Ownership and Control: Rethinking Corporate Governance for the Twenty-first Century* (Brookings Institution, 1995) 202-234.

39 Lazonick (1992, pp. 467, 469) argues that corporate executives have been co-opted by this finance-oriented view because they have risen to the tops of their organizations in an era that rewarded financial market performance more than innovative activity or growth in market share and because their own compensation is now, more than ever, tied to stock price performance.

40 Votaw (1965, pp. 96-97).

41 Singer (1988, pp. 637-38).

42 Donaldson and Preston (1995).

43 Coase (1960, pp. 15-16).

44 The information requirements are quite severe for this hypothesis to hold, however, and the difficulties in enforcing contracts could easily be insurmountable.

45 Hayek (1985, p.100).

46 This is the cornerstone of the corporate governance arguments made by Easterbrook and Fischel (1991). Shareholders hold voting rights, as opposed to bondholders, management, or employees, they argue, because shareholders are the residual claimants on firm income and are therefore willing to pay most for voting rights. When a firm is in distress, shareholder incentives become skewed and other constituents receive voting rights. "The fact that voting rights flow to whichever group holds the residual claim at any given time strongly supports our analysis of the function of voting rights," they wrote (p.405). See also Easterbrook and Fischel (1983).

47 Gilson and Roe (1993, p. 887).

48 Gilson (1981, p. 34).

49 See Alchian and Demsetz (1972), who wrote the classic article that marked the beginning of the development of this view of corporations.

50 In nearly all of the finance literature and much of management and economics literature, shareholders are assumed, without question, to play this role. A few organizational theorists and labor economists interested in the problems introduced by firm-specific investments in human capital have come to appreciate that shareholders are generally not the only residual risk-bearers, and that the assumption that they are is not inconsequential. But the implications of this fact for efficient corporate governance have not yet been acknowledged or studied by finance theorists nor have they been formally acknowledged in the law.

51 Fama and Jensen (1983) made this argument in their now classic article.

52 Finance specialists have long understood that the value of a company's equity can be increased by shifting some of the risk onto debt holders. Wallman (1991, p. 178) provides an easy-to-understand example. In this case, maximizing value for the shareholders is clearly not equivalent to maximizing social value. But finance model advocates tend to assume away the implications of this insight for corporate governance by asserting that creditors can write contracts that prohibit the managers of the firm from shifting more risk onto them than they initially bargain for.

53 Fama and Jensen (1983, pp. 302-3) assert (but do not demonstrate empirically) that "the contract structures of most organizational forms limit the risks undertaken by most agents by specifying either fixed promised payoffs or incentive payoffs tied to specific measures of performance. The residual risk—the risk of the difference between stochastic inflows of resources and promised payments to agents—is borne by those who contract for the rights to the net cash flows.... Moreover, the contracts of most agents contain the implicit or explicit provision that, in exchange for the specified payoff, the agent agrees that the resources he provides can be used to satisfy the interests of residual claimants.... Having

most uncertainty borne by one group of agents, residual claimants, has survival value because it reduces the costs incurred to monitor contracts with other groups of agents. Contracts that direct decisions toward the interests of residual claimants also add to the survival value of organizations."

54 See, for example, Dunlop (1988, p.56).

55 This last point is probably not obvious, but it arises from the fact that the workers have made firm-specific investments in human capital as part of the process of wealth creation in the enterprise.

56 "How can residual-claimant, central-employer-owner demonstrate ability to pay the other hired inputs the promised amount in the event of a loss?" Alchian and Demsetz ask. "He can pay in advance, or he can commit wealth sufficient to cover negative residuals. The latter will take the form of machines, land, buildings, or raw materials committed to the firm." See Alchian and Demsetz (1972, p.791). Historians Galambos and Pratt (1988, p.20) note also that most of the technology that was the source of added value in early factories was embodied in the capital—the physical plant and equipment—and that the employer-owner was often an engineer who was largely responsible for technical decisions about plant design or addition of new equipment.

57 A rough measure of this is the share of the market value of assets accounted for by property, plant, and equipment (PP&E). I calculated these numbers using data on all manufacturing and mining firms listed in Compustat for which the relevant information was available. In 1982 PP&E accounted for 62.3 percent of the market value of mining and manufacturing firms; by 1991, PP&E accounted for only 37.9 percent of the market value.

58 A quick review of interviews with twelve CEOs (on many topics) in recent issues of the *Harvard Business Review* produced the following quotes: "Our employees aren't just agents for the company, they are the company,"—Robert F. McDermott, CEO of USAA. "A company is not bricks and mortar or money and finance. It's people;" and "profit is in the hands of employees,"—Frederick C. Crawford, CEO of TRW; "If the people on the front line really are the keys to our success, then the manager's job is to help those people that they serve. That goes against the traditional assumptions that the manager is in control,"—Robert Haas, CEO of Levi Strauss & Co.

Copyright © 1995, The Brookings Institution Press.
Reprinted with permission.

Understanding Stakeholder Thinking: Themes from a Finnish Conference

Archie B. Carroll, University of Georgia
Juha Näsi, University of Jyväskylä

Discussion and debate on stakeholder theory continues unabated, but not a lot of people know that it first began in Finland in the 1960s, as this report of a recent Conference there shows. Archie B. Carroll, the well-known writer on corporate social responsibility, is Robert W. Scherer Professor of Management at the University of Georgia, Athens, GA, USA (e-mail acarroll@uga.cc.uga.edu); and Juha Näsi is Professor of Management at the University of Jyväskylä, Jyväskylä, Finland.

The stakeholder concept, or stakeholder thinking, has become the most recent theory over the past decade to facilitate the undergirding of business ethics. Though the stakeholder concept found its roots in the works of Rhenman and Stymne (1965) in Sweden, the SRI Institute of Stanford University, and Ansoff (1965) in the United States, the concept entered its "popular era" over a decade ago with publication of Ed Freeman's *Strategic Management: A Stakeholder Approach* (1984).

Since that time the popularity of stakeholder thinking has grown exponentially as fields such as business ethics, business and society, corporate social performance and strategic management have perceived the usefulness of linking their current theory and concepts to stakeholder notions. In 1989 Archie Carroll extended the interest in stakeholder thinking by authoring a business and society textbook and subsequent editions using the stakeholder approach (1989, 1993, 1996). In 1994 Joseph Weiss authored a business ethics textbook employing the stakeholder framework. In 1994 a strategic management textbook by Harrison and St. John utilized the stakeholder concept. Scores of articles have been published advocating and using the stakeholder model as their underlying premise or theory (Carroll, 1994).

At least three international conferences on the stakeholder concept have been held in recent years. Two of these conferences were held at the University of Toronto in Canada in 1993 and 1994 and were organized by former business executive and now Professor Max Clarkson. The third conference, the subject of this article, was held in the summer of 1994 at the University of Jyväskylä in Finland. The conference was convened by Professor Juha Näsi. Eighteen papers were presented. Conference participants came primarily from European and Scandinavian countries. In addition to Näsi, three keynote speakers travelled from the United States: Steven Brenner (Portland State University), Archie Carroll (University of Georgia) and Ed Freeman (University of Virginia). In subsequent sections of this article we will summarize some of the themes of the keynote speakers.

Before reporting on the conference, it is useful to define some key terms. A stakeholder may be defined as any individual or group who affects or is affected by the organization and its processes, activities and functioning. Thus, relevant groups of interest to business organizations may seen as internal and external stakeholders. Internal stakeholders would encompass such groups as employees, owners and managers. External stakeholders would include consumers, competitors, government, social activist groups, the media, the natural environment and the community. Stakeholders might also be construed in categories such as primary vs. secondary, active vs. passive, economic vs. social, core vs. strategic vs. environmental.

Stakeholders are those individuals and groups which have a valid stake in the organization. This does not mean they are idle bystanders. Stakeholders have a legitimate interest, or stake, in what the firm is doing and how it is accomplishing its objectives. This interest or stake might be manifested as a legal or moral right, or claim, on the organization. Legal stakes are established by the accepted legal system extant in a country. Moral claims, by contrast, are justified based on some ethical or moral claim on the organization. Such a moral claim might be argued to be upon the basis of moral principles or philosophies such as the theories of rights, justice or utilitarianism.

Donaldson and Preston (1995) have argued that the stakeholder approach is useful for descriptive, normative and instrumental reasons. Thus the power of stakeholder thinking is extended beyond its usefulness in describing organization-environment relationships. Stakeholder thinking also helps managers engage in normative and instrumental decision making. That is, it helps mangers "do ethics" more effectively and provides a useful framework for strategic business decision making as well. These dual ethics and strategic dimensions have been discussed at length by Goodpaster (1991).

As managers embrace stakeholder thinking they are more able to integrate the ethical dimension effectively into business practice. Those groups "out there in society" with which executives must deal now become partners in the enterprise, with vested interests, or "stakes", in the ongoing practices and operations of the firm. These groups or "publics" as they were once referred to, are now correctly seen as stakeholders—individual and groups affected by and/or affecting the organization. Stakeholders are now perceived as "names and faces" with whom management must communicate, establish transactions and interact. Successful firms then become those which are best able to manage stakeholder relationships. Being seen as legitimate partners in the enterprise with both legitimacy and power, it is essential that stakeholders be factored into decision making in a significant way.

Five key questions may be asked by managers to capture the information essential for effective stakeholder management. Who are our stakeholders? What are their stakes? What opportunities and challenges do our stakeholders present to the firm? What responsibilities (economic, legal, ethical and philanthropic) does the organization have to its stakeholders? What strategies or actions should the firm take to best respond to stakeholder challenges and opportunities? (Carroll 1996). The successful stakeholder manager thus becomes that individual who can effectively respond to these questions in such a way that the firm's goals are reached and stakeholders are satisfied and dealt with ethically.

Against this backdrop of stakeholders, stakeholder thinking and stakeholder management we now proceed to describe briefly some of the major themes set forth by the keynote speakers at the "Understanding Stakeholder Thinking" conference which was held in Finland in the summer of 1994.

Stakeholder Thinking: The State of the Art

The stakeholder approach is often juxtaposed as an alternative to the stockholder theory of the firm. In his paper, R. Edward Freeman suggests that this juxtaposing relies on a particular approach to business theory that is prevalent today: the separation thesis. The idea of Freeman's paper is to propose why and how we should give up this thesis. The separation thesis says

> "The discourse of business and the discourse of ethics can be separated so that sentences like 'x is a business decision' have no moral content, and 'x is moral decision' have no business content."

This kind of idea has two realms—the one of business and the other of ethics—and it has spread all over the organizational world. According to

Freeman 'business' is identified with self-interest, rationality, stockholders, finance and economics, empirical science and being hard-headed and tough-minded. 'Ethics', then, is identified with altruism, feelings, stakeholders (others than stockholders), philosophy and religion, conceptual thinking and being woolly-headed and soft-hearted.

Freeman argues that it is time to give up this thesis. We urgently need a conceptual mechanism which does not clearly distinguish between the business and the ethical parts of a decision, Freeman argues. And it is stakeholder thinking that can provide useful help in constructing this new 'mixed world'.

As earlier stated Donaldson and Preston (1995) have articulated three uses of the stakeholder idea: normative, descriptive and instrumental. Freeman now adds a fourth use: metaphorical. Once the idea is seen as a metaphor, the conclusion will be that there are multiple theories depending on the stakeholder idea, not a single, 'pure' apparatus.

The next step in Freeman's logic is to define the concept and meaning of the normative core of a theory. This core is the set of ethical assumptions and presuppositions. For example, in terms of theories of value creation the normative core must contain sentences such as:

A) Corporations ought to be governed...
B) Mangers ought to act to...

The third point (C) is that any normative core is embedded in a series of background disciplines. Now, when picking up, for instance, three different perspectives, say, The Doctrine of Fair Contracts, Feminist Standpoint Theory and Ecological Principles we find three more or less different normative cores, each consisting of their own As, Bs and Cs. Freeman continues by outlining the Doctrine of Fair Contracts consisting of six principles constructed in the spirit of pragmatic liberalism and leaning on John Rawls, Richard Rorty and others. In the end of his paper, Freeman proposes no less than requisite changes in the enabling laws of the land. In addition, three principles to serve as constitutive elements of attempts to reform the law of corporations shall be managed in the interest of its stakeholders and that directors shall have a "duty of care" of the corporation, with full accountability to stakeholders.

The original point to Freeman is this: to see stakeholders as fully complex moral beings who are inseparable from the idea of business. The conclusion from this perspective seems to be that we need to strive diligently for, not one single stakeholder theory, but many often complicated theories organized around the stakeholder idea. To Freeman, namely, "the attempt to prescribe one and only one normative core and construct a stakeholder theory is at best a disguised attempt to smuggle a normative core past unsophisticated noses of other unsuspecting academics who are just happy to see the end of the stockholder theory".

Stakeholder Thinking in Three Models of Management Morality: A Perspective with Strategic Implications

Two notable arenas in which stakeholder thinking has proven especially valuable include business ethics and strategic management. In his paper Archie B. Carroll combines these aspects as he focuses on the applicability of stakeholder thinking in his three models of management morality.

The concept of corporate social responsibility (CSR) is Carroll's point of departure (see Carroll 1979, 1991, 1993):

Total Corporate Social Responsibility = Economic Responsibility + Legal Responsibility + Ethical Responsibility + Discretionary (Philanthropic) Responsibility

In this view, a CSR firm should strive to make a profit, obey the law, engage in ethical behaviour and be a good corporate citizen. Carroll then 'isolates' the ethical component of this CSR definition and sharpens his focus by defining three major ethical models. These models were initially described in other works (see Carroll 1987,1991).

The first model, immoral management, is characterized by those managers whose behaviour suggests an active opposition to what is deemed ethical, thus implying a real, conscious negation of what is right. At the opposite extreme, moral management is the paradigm for the 'good guys' who employ and adhere to ethical norms which reflect a high standard of right behaviour. And in the middle of the representatives of the third model, amoral managers are neither immoral nor moral, but are not sensitive to, or aware of, the fact that their everyday decisions may have deleterious effects on other parties (stakeholders) involved. These managers lack ethical perception or awareness.

Carroll then connects his three models with the CSR pattern, concluding that moral management takes all four CSR components into account, amoral management locates in the middle, whereas immoral management focuses significant consideration only on the economic responsibility. Then, analyzing the domains of three models as to their orientation towards four basic stakeholders categories, namely owners/shareholders, customers/consumers, employees and community, he concludes that the moral management model fully embraces stakeholder thinking, the amoral model partially accepts stakeholder thinking, whereas the immoral model rejects it.

As for scholars in business and society, Carroll argues that the stakeholder approach has been more completely embraced by those who have seen it as a way to rationalize ethical business behaviour than those who have seen it as a new paradigm for strategic management. And, by way of contrast, scholars in strategic management have been slow to acknowledge and use the stakeholder approach. However, in the conclusion of his paper, Carroll outlines and illustrates what immoral, amoral and moral strategic management could be.

The methodological point in Carroll's paper is to depict how powerful a way stakeholder thinking can be of visualizing organizations and their responsibilities. The theoretical conclusions, then, include that for normative as well as instrumental reasons the goal of organizations should be moral strategic management. To fulfill its socially responsible purposes management thinking tomorrow will need all three perspectives—the moral, the stakeholder and the strategic.

Stakeholder Theory of the Firm: Its Consistency with Current Management Techniques

Steven N. Brenner pursued two major goals in his paper. His first purpose was to introduce and explain one version—as he says—of the stakeholder theory, and, second, to consider whether current management techniques are consistent with that stakeholder theory as proposed.

Brenner expresses his own view of the essence of the stakeholder theory of the firm in six explicit propositions, the first four of which are based are based on earlier work by him and Cochran (1991) and Evan and Freeman (1998). Proposition 1 defines that firms/organizations must fulfill some set of their various stakeholders' needs in order to continue to exist. Proposition 2 says that one way for firms/organizations to understand the relevant needs of their stakeholders is to examine the values and interests of their stakeholders. Proposition 3 states that the management of firm/organizations involves structuring and implementing choice processes among various stakeholders and such choice processes are a function of stakeholder influence relationships and their values. And finally Proposition 4 argues that identification of an organization's stakeholders, their various values and interests, the relative importance of each value for each stakeholder, the relative influence of each stakeholder's value position, and the nature of the value trade off processes provides information useful for understanding the behaviour of and within the firm/organization.

Proposition 5, a new one, posits that the fulfillment of the necessary set of firm/organization/stakeholders' needs requires a balancing of those needs using economic, legal and moral criteria (similar to Carroll's CSR definition). Proposition 6 explicates that organizational management consistent with the stakeholder theory of the firm produces superior long-term results due to its explicit recognition of a broad set of stakeholder values and to its required use of economic, legal and moral criteria.

As the propositions suggest, Brenner sees the stakeholder theory as a rather analytical and rational approach. Interesting to notice is that this entirety includes not only descriptive, but also normative propositions.

Brenner then takes stakeholder theory and relates it to current management techniques by noting 'There is always a question with any theory—is it consistent with what happens in the real world?' He then selects six management techniques and compares them with four consistency criteria. These criteria are as follows. First, does the technique recognize the relevance of a diverse set of stakeholders? Second, is stakeholder value, interest or need fulfillment explicitly, or implicitly part of the management technique? Third does the technique's decisions require use of two or more of the three choice process criteria (economic, legal or moral)? And, fourth, does the technique entail balancing the interests of various stakeholders beyond just owners?

The six management techniques Brenner selected for analysis included codetermination, multifunctional teams, management by walking around, total quality management's customer focus, participatory management and capital budgeting analysis. After TQM came (in order): codetermination, management by walking around, multifunctional teams, participative management, and finally capital budgeting. His evaluation concluded that total quality management 'wins' and capital budgeting 'loses' in this comparison.

There are at least two major points in Brenner's paper. First, it builds on stakeholder theories' earlier writings, clarifying existing propositions further as well as defining new ones. This means potential conceptual progress for the theory. Second, in the areas of management it is natural and primary to test the theory against the real world requirements for suitability assessment. As a tentative test his speculation offers illustration and a basis for further analysis.

A Scandinavian Approach to Stakeholder Thinking: Its Theoretical and Practical Uses

A generally unknown fact is that stakeholder thinking had an early blooming era in Scandinavia, starting some thirty years ago. Juha Näsi's aim in his paper was to describe and analyze key elements of this thought in its evolution.

The founder of stakeholder thinking in Scandinavia was Eric Rhenman from Sweden. Although the idea, concept and applications appeared in half a dozen of Rhenman's works, the most explicit and complete articulation of the stakeholder approach, or 'theory' as they said, was presented in a book co-authored by Eric Rhenman and Bengt Stymne, *Företagsledning I en föränderlig värld* (*Corporate Management in a Changing World*), 1965.

Juha Näsi describes and interprets this theory through certain key words, namely the concepts of stakeholders, a firm, its goals and management. All these concepts together constitute a theory by which it is possible to explain how things take place in a firm. "Stakeholders in an organization are the individuals and groups who are depending on the firm in order to achieve their goals and on whom the firm is depending for its existence", Rhenman and Stymne assert. The firm, then, is a social and technical system where different stakeholders play a part.

Their theory was based on thoughts and ideas of such classic authors as Barnard, Cyert, March, Simon and Thompson. In addition, they underscored the potential of the systems perspective.

In the second part of his paper, Näsi describes the many and varied consequences and applications of this theory in his home country, Finland. Stakeholder thinking became widely used as an approach within university circles, first in teaching. To substantiate this Näsi examined all the annual curriculum documents over the period 1996-1980 concerning studies in 'Management' at the University of Tampera. The result was interesting: books on stakeholder theory were a compulsory part of basic studies for every management student from 1968 to 1980.

In scientific research, stakeholder thinking typically became used as a conceptual foundation and a theoretical framework. For example, Juha Näsi's own dissertation, "The Basis of Corporate Planning. Conceptual and Methodological Structures and their Background from the Point of View of the Philosophy of Science", in 1979 was explicitly based on stakeholder thinking.

The ideas of this approach quickly spread to Finnish business practice too. The first field of application was long-range planning, often introduced and implemented by an outside consultant. Planning guides with stakeholder ideology were also published. Another area of practice was that of annual reports. In Finland at that time it was common to include a social disclosure section in these reports. The stakeholder framework fast became the major tool for classifying types of social interaction in this task.

Obviously, it had been due to the unfortunate language barrier that the Scandinavian "group" in stakeholder thinking is not widely known. However, it has been Juha Näsi's aim to show that the written history of stakeholder thinking necessarily needs an important Scandinavian section.

Final Notes and Thoughts

All the important keynote papers had the important characteristic in common of being conceptual. As to the core of stakeholder thinking they try by conceptual analysis to define, analyse, speculate and challenge. They also reveal how broad a field stakeholder thinking covers. At the same time what appears is how little has been done in spite of the seeming longevity of this way of thinking.

Ed Freeman's paper had a philosophical tone. He wanted to challenge the conventional idea to juxtapose two propositions. By tools of argumentation he proceeded to suggest and recommend a new and rather radical way to see and think about ethics and organizations.

Archie Carroll's paper was exploratory. He combined three perspectives, namely the moral, the strategic and the stakeholder one. He outlined their relationships and tried to conclude the routes by which they may fit together. the result is one step toward a larger and clearer conceptual system than we used to have.

Steve Brenner, after explicating what he precisely means by the stakeholder theory, took a management technique view and showed how well stakeholder theory fits with some prevailing techniques. By comparative analysis against a set of criteria the result reveals—in addition to the comparative evaluation—that the stakeholder approach certainly seems to have a significant potential for use in management.

Juha Näsi draws a historical picture. He illustrates that the theory has existed for decades in Scandinavian use. It was popular among scholars and was used in business practice. Considerable useful research material and thinking has remained without further use, on account of language barriers.

In addition to these keynote presentations a wide range of themes on and around stakeholder thinking were presented and discussed at the conference. They varied from comprehensive papers such as matching functional thinking with the stakeholder approach to rather specific viewpoints relating stakeholderism to boards of directors, managers' cognitive cause mapping, commitment and quality system, to name just a few. Many papers related stakeholder thinking to business ethics. All the eighteen presentations together established convincing evidence that stakeholder thinking on the one hand will have a lot to say within the domain of management in the future, but on the other hand that this approach has much still to do in order to become a more sophisticated and crystal-clear theory.

Ansoff, Igor H. (1965) *Corporate Strategy*. New York: McGraw-Hill.

Brenner, Steven N. and Cochran, Paul. (1991) The Stakeholder Theory of the Firm: Implications for Business and Society Theory and Research. *Proceedings of the International Association for Business and Society*, 449-467.

Carroll, Archie B. (1979) A Three-Dimensional Conceptual Model of Corporate Social Performance. *Academy of Management Review,* 4: 497-505.

Carroll, Archie B. (1987) In Search of the Moral Manager. *Business Horizons,* March-April, 7-15.

Carroll, Archie B. (1989) *Business and Society: Ethics and Stakeholder Management.* Cincinnati: South-Western Publishing Co. Also see 2nd Edition, 1993 and 3rd Edition, 1996.

Carroll, Archie B. (1991) The Pyramid of Corporate Social Responsibility: Toward the Moral Management of Organizational Stakeholders. *Business Horizons,* July-August, Vol. 34, No. 4, 39-48.

Carroll, Archie B. (1994) Social Issues in Management Research: Expert's Views, Analysis and Commentary. *Business and Society,* Vol. 33, No. 1, April 5-29.

Clarkson, Max B.E. (1994) *Proceedings of the Second Toronto Conference on Stakeholder Theory.* Toronto: The Centre for Corporate Social Performance and Ethics, University of Toronto.

Donaldson, Thomas and Preston, Lee E. (1995) The Stakeholder Theory of the Corporation: Concepts, Evidence and Implications. *Academy of Management Review,* Vol. 20, No. 1, January, 65-91.

Evan, W.M. and Freeman, R. Edward. (1988) A Stakeholder of the Modern Corporation: Kantian Capitalism. In Beauchamp, T.L. and Bowie, N.E. (Ed.) *Ethical Theory and Business,* Englewood Cliffs: Prentice-Hall.

Freeman, R. Edward. (1984) *Strategic Management: A Stakeholder Approach.* Boston: Pitman.

Goodpaster, Kenneth E. (1991) Business Ethics and Stakeholder Analysis. *Business Ethics Quarterly,* 1(1), 53-74.

Harrison, Jeffrey S. and St. John, Caron H. (1994) *Strategic Management of Organizations and Stakeholders.* Minneapolis/St.Paul: West Publishing Co.

Rhenman, Eric and Stymne, Bengt. (1965) *Företagsledning I en föränderlig värld,* Stockholm: Aldus/Bonniers.

Toronto Conference, The. Reflections on Stakeholder Theory. (1994) *Business and Society,* Vol. 33, No. 1, April, 82-131.

Weiss, Joseph W. (1994) *Business Ethics: A Managerial, Stakeholder Approach.* Belmont, CA: Wadsworth, Inc.

Copyright © Blackwell Publishers Ltd., Oxford, United Kingdom, 1997. Reprinted with permission.

Part 2

Morality, Ethics and Stakeholder Theory

The Moral Standing of the Market

Amartya Sen, All Souls College, Oxford

How valuable is the market mechanism for practical morality? What is its moral standing? We can scarcely doubt that as individuals we do value tremendously the opportunity of using markets. Indeed, without access to markets most of us would perish, since we don't typically produce the things that we need to survive. If we could somehow survive without using markets it all, our quality of life would be rather abysmal. It is natural to feel that in institution that is so crucial to our well-being *must be* valuable. And since moral evaluation can hardly be indifferent to our interests and their fulfillment, it might appear that there is nothing much to discuss here. The market's moral standing "has to be" high.

However, the value to an individual of a particular institution when society has been organised around that institution must be distinguished from how the society—and even that person—might have fared had the society been organized differently. We, as individuals, are thoroughly dependent on the market (as things stand), but that does not tell us much about the value of the market *as an institution*. We have to consider alternative ways of doing the things that the market does. The assessment of an institution cannot be based on examining the predicament of an individual who is suddenly denied access to it, without having the opportunity of being in another social arrangement with other types of institutions.

A second difficulty in treating the question as straightforward arises from problems in formulating the nature of the choice that is being considered. When somebody questions the value of the market, he or she is typically not considering the alternative of having no market transactions *at all*. In fact, that is hard even to visualize. Markets, in the widest sense, enter into an enormous range of activities. Some social activities are formal market transactions; others are quite informal; and some have only a few market-type features. Those who rail against the market mechanism are not about to recommend the cessation of all such transactions. To see it as an "all or nothing" question is to miss the point of the criticism altogether. It is a question of "how-much," "how unrestrained," "how supplemented." Even the most ferocious critic of the market mechanism is unlikely to be looking for a world in which every person must produce every bit of the goods and services that he or she can consume. The question must be posed differently.

A third problem comes from a different direction. Insofar as the market mechanism is valued as an instrument, its moral value must ultimately derive from somewhere else. We cannot begin to assess the moral standing of the market mechanism without first asking, "To what intrinsically valuable things is the market mechanism instrumental?" We have to place the role of markets in a fuller moral context.

I shall take up the question of instrumentality in the next section, and then go on to the problem of integration.

The Consequent Good or the Antecedent Freedom?

Most defenses of the market are instrumental in terms of the goodness of the *results* achieved. It works "efficiently"; it serves our "interests"; it is "mutually beneficial"; it delivers "the goods"; it contributes to "utility"; it serves as the "invisible hand" by which man is led to promote an end which has no part of his intention.[2] On this view, the market is good because its results are. For example, Friedman and Friedman argue: "on the whole, market competition, when it is permitted to work, protects the consumer better than do alternative government mechanisms that have been increasingly superimposed on the market."[3] We need, of course, a criterion for judging the interests of the consumers and the relevance of these interests to the overall moral assessment of the market. We also need some methodology for interpreting the exact content of the Friedmans' claim before it can be properly assessed. But there can be little doubt that this approach to the value of the market mechanism—whatever its exact content and force—rests on assessing *results*.

Perhaps less obvious—but obvious enough—so is the claim that the market makes people "free to choose," a freedom that might be seen to be valuable in itself (whether or not it also helps in other ways, such as the protection of the interests of the consumers). The goal of "freedom to choose" provides an alternative (though not unrelated) basis for the assessment of markets by its results. "That is the basic difference between the market and a political agency. You are free to choose. There is no policeman to take the money out of your pocket to pay for something you do not want or to make you do something you do not want to do."[4] Whether the freedom to choose is *itself* a fundamental value—not only instrumentally so at some "higher level" of analysis—is a difficult question that need not be addressed in the present context.[5] The importance of the market, on this "free to choose" view, derives from the *more basic* value of that freedom (no matter how the value of that freedom is itself obtained).

But there is also a different possibility that must be considered. It could be the case that is what is at issue is not the value of the freedom to choose. People may be seen as having fundamental "rights," and the exercise of those rights may be seen as not requiring any justification at all. If the market is seen as being part and parcel of the exercise of such rights, then markets may be defended on the basis of antecedent rights, rather than in terms of the results, including freedom of choice, that they may achieve. To assert "that individuals have rights, and there are things no person or group may do to them (without violating their rights)"[6] would *imply* the freedom to make market transactions (given the way the rights referred to are characterized). The question of the consequences, in this procedure, arises later, *after* the right to transact (and thus to engage in market relations, in the broad sense) has already been given a stable moral status.

In this formulation, rights specific rules—of ownership, transfer, etc.—that have to be followed for making a person's actual "holdings" legitimate. The results of these rules are accepted precisely because they have resulted from following the right rules, not because the results judged as *outcomes* are in themselves good. The results (including serving the interests of consumers or even enjoying the "freedom to choose") may or may not, in fact, be judged to be good *as results*. But whatever the conclusion of that outcome analysis might be, the justification of the market, in this approach, is not based on the merits of the results. Indeed, it is apparent that there are consistency problems in an attempt to combine this approach with another that justifies actions (including, of course, transactions) in terms of preferring one "pattern" of outcomes over another, since that would "over-determine" the system.[7]

If this rights-based "procedural" view is accepted, then the traditional assessment of the merits and demerits of the market, in terms of the goodness of outcomes, would be quite misplaced. The moral necessity of having markets would follow from the status of rights and not from the efficiency or optimality of market outcomes. This approach, incidentally, involves the rejection of the way economists—the professional group most immediately concerned with the assessment of the role of markets—have typically examined the case for and against the market. In the economist's picture of "social welfare," rights are seen as purely institutional (typically legal) artifacts, without any importance of their own: rights are judged—in the typical welfare economic framework—in terms of how they fulfill or thwart people's interests.

The failure to consider the "procedural" approach at all is certainly an omission that deserves some comment. Robert Nozick's analysis represents one example of nonconsequentialist moral reasoning, and this type of reasoning must be seriously considered by welfare economists. Even if such reasoning is ultimately rejected, there is no question that that approach deserves the most serious consideration.

It is also worth noting in this context that the force of a rights-based procedural justification of market operations is independent of our understanding of empirical regularities in the real world, in a way that any consequentialist justification for market operations cannot be. For example, one could have a lively debate as to whether Friedman and Friedman are right about what they say on the relative merits of the market mechanism in safeguarding the interest of consumers, or whether, in fact, it is the case that "the freedom to choose" in any substantive sense is better guaranteed by the market mechanism than by some feasible alternations. If it is shown that the empirical relationships on which the consequentialist justifications depend are erroneous, then the case for the market mechanism, denied from such reasoning, would collapse.

The same applies to a moral assessment of the market based on the "freedom" resulting from it. If that freedom is shown to be "illusory,"[8] then the case for the market mechanism would be dis-established. That assessment would have to be thoroughly dependent on the truth of the causal hypotheses linking markets and the resulting freedom. Questions can be raised on the empirical acceptability of the presumed causal connection.

In contrast, one interesting feature of the *a priori* rights-based justification of market operations is that it is not contingent on the empirical regularities that hold in the real world. The results of market transactions may be good, but even if they are bad or unassessable, they are still legitimate because they are sanctioned by antecedent rights. This can be seen as giving the nonconsequentialist approach a "robustness" that the consequentialist approach lacks, especially since empirical regularities are hard to establish, and predictive theories in this field can be extremely flimsy.

On the other hand, this "robustness" and the immunity from empirical critiques are also plausible sources of skepticism about that ethical structure. Why must we accept the priority of these rights?[9] Do the rights of ownership and exchange have "foundational" status? Must we really accept the notion that some arrangements required by the recognition of these rights are morally acceptable irrespective of their consequences—however bad they might be? What if the consequences are totally disastrous?

The last is not only a matter of purely theoretical speculation. As I have tried to argue elsewhere,[10] many large famines—in which millions of people have perished from hunger and hunger-related diseases—have taken place (even in the recent past) without any overall decline in food availability at all, with no "natural cause" making the famines inescapable. People have been deprived of food precisely because of sudden and violent shifts in "entitlements," resulting from the exercise of rights that people "legitimately" have within the given legal system. Loss of employment and wage income have often led to starvation. Changes of relative prices have sometimes driven the losers to the wall. The legal systems in question differ, of course, from an *idealized* legal structure of the kind required by a theory of rights of the type we are examining, but, nevertheless, in many respects they have a good deal of similarity. In fact, it is easy to show that, with a system of rights justified independently of consequences, it is possible to have disasters of this kind occurring without anyone violating anyone else's rights at all. The contingency of ownership, as well as influences that determine transfers and terms of trade, can easily lead a particular occupation group into absolute deprivation, destitution, and decimation, without anything illegitimate and perverse having happened from a rights' perspective.

It is not irrelevant to ask the question: If such starvation and famine were to occur, must the results of the market operation be taken as "acceptable," simply because they have followed from people legitimately, exercising the rights they have? It is not easy to understand why rules of ownership, transfer, etc., should have such absolute priority over the life and death of millions of people.

In response to this it can, of course, be claimed that only in these extreme cases will it be right to override the requirements imposed by rights and their legitimate exercise. There could be a caveat that nullifies rights in these cases, but not in others.[11]

Robert Nozick himself keeps the question open as to whether "catastrophic moral horrors" should provide a ground for violating rights. There *is* a dilemma here. If disastrous consequences can be used as a ground for nullifying deep-seated rights, surely, that completely undermines the consequence-independent way of looking at rights. If disastrous consequences would be adequate to nullify any rights (even the most important ones), perhaps bad-but-not-so-disastrous consequences would be adequate to nullify other, less central, rights? Some of the rights related to the ownership and use of property may well be seen to be less "deep-seated" than some other rights, e.g., the personal-liberty rights with which civil libertarians have been, understandably, most concerned. Once rejection, based on consequential evaluation is admitted into the picture of moral reckoning, it is difficult to find an obvious stopping place for a theory of rights that is based on a purely procedural approach.

It is hard to argue that the value of the market can be divorced from the value of its results and achievements. This is not to say that the assessment of market operations, or the evaluation of the market mechanism, must be based only on *utility* consequences (defined in terms of satisfaction, desire fulfillment, etc.). For example, it is quite possible to take into account what the market mechanism in general, and specific market operations in particular, would do to such things as the freedom of the individuals in society. If being "free to choose" is regarded as an important part of a person's well-being (*or* regarded as morally important despite its not being a part of personal well-being), it would be perfectly sensible to include this in the assessment of the consequences of market operations. This would obviously be inadequate for producing a procedural moral system of the kind that Robert Nozick and others have tried to develop. But by taking freedom into account in our calculation of consequences, the force of their criticism of narrow consequential systems can be partly accommodated.

I have, in fact, tried to argue elsewhere that taking note of the fulfillment or violation of rights, and of the realization or nonrealization of freedom, in the assessment of social arrangements, does more justice to the *importance* of rights and freedoms than a purely constraint-based (e.g., Nozickian) system of rights and freedom can do.[12] This is not, as is often assumed, only a matter of the contrast between "negative" and "positive" freedom. Even if one ignores altogether "positive" freedom, and confines one's attention to assessing "negative" freedom, there is still a strong case for including the badness of violation of negative freedom in evaluating, consequent states. Given imperfect compliance, the violation of negative freedom of A by B can sensibly figure in C's calculation regarding what to do, and a consequence-sensitive system can deal with such links. It is inadequate to try to deal with negative freedom through constraints only, since them have no relevance to C's calculations if it is B who violates A's negative freedom, even if C could have helped to stop this violation.

It could be argued that the consequential way of taking note of rights may not be able to pay adequate attention to the "deontological" aspects of agent-relative action assessment. This might be thought to be particularly so for the special role of "negative" freedom. To this point some responses may be made, which I shall note here without elaboration or development. First, this is really a separate matter requiring *additional* structure,[13] and the correct starting point for "deontological" issues may not rights at all, but some notion of duty linked with the position-relativity (in particular, "doer relativity") of moral evaluation.[14] Second, such additional structure for personal morals may be quite consistent with a result-oriented assessment of institutions such as markets and property.

No matter how that additional deontological question is dealt with, the *valuation* of freedom—even of "negative" freedom—would demand a more consequence-sensitive approach, not reliant only on imposing constraints. Those who have argued that the traditional consequentialist approaches—most notably the utilitarian systems—take inadequate note of the importance of freedom, have not been, in my view, mistaken in this claim. But the failure arises not so much from the concentration on consequences, but from the way consequences are assessed. If utilitarianism is split into three distinct parts,[15] viz., "welfarism" (judging states of affairs only by utility information), "sum-ranking" (dealing with utility information by simply adding them), and "consequentialism" (judging actions, rules, etc., ultimately by the goodness of the states of affairs resulting from them), then the primary failing, it can be argued, arises from "welfarism."

This is, of course, a more general question, and one which see need not really take up in this paper. If it is accepted that the moral importance of the market mechanism and market operations has to be seen primarily in terms of its results, then the need to go more deeply into consequential systems has to be recognized. The value of the market instrument is, then, consequential, derivative, and contingent. To assess that value we have to understand the more fundamental social values of well-being, freedom, and justice.[16] We have to examine also the causal links between the institutional arrangements and the realization of the more fundamental values.

Optimality and Inequality

The assessment of the market mechanism in welfare economics has tended to rely—at least in recent decades—on the so-called "basic theorem of welfare economics."[17] Indeed, in the theory of welfare economics, the main rationale of the market mechanism has been typically viewed in the light of the dual relationship captured by this theorem.[18]

The first part of this "basic theorem," asserting that every competitive equilibrium is a Pareto optimum, has been called the "direct theorem." The other part, claiming that every Pareto optimum is a competitive equilibrium, may be called the "converse theorem." Both theorems are established by making a set of restrictive assumptions. The assumptions are not exactly the same in the two cases, but they have several requirements in common (e.g., the absence of externalities[19]).

The ethical force of the direct theorem in establishing the case for the market mechanism may be seen to be quite limited. A Pareto optimum does, of course, have the valuable property that not all the parties can be made better-off (in terms of utility) in any alternative feasible state. But it is easily seen that a situation can be Pareto optimal but nevertheless highly objectionable—indeed, possibly disastrous. If the utility of the deprived cannot be raised without cutting, into the utility of the rich, the situation can be Pareto optimal but truly awful.

There are two standard responses to this criticism of the relevance of the direct theorem. One is to argue that the criticism is based on making explicit or implicit use of "egalitarian" values, and many people would dispute whether such values have force. I have tried to address that issue elsewhere,[20] and this is perhaps not the occasion to go again into that old question. I shall have a little more to say on this in the next section, but for the moment I simply assert that indifference to the inequality of well-being requires some justification. The fact that equality is widely valued does not of course, establish its validity. But it does demand a response, and a presumption of this kind calls for some serious argument as to why in this case, inequality is acceptable. If the direct theorem is to be treated as one great ethical significance, we must be told more about the *general moral irrelevance* of inequality of well-being, *or* of the moral case for the particular inequalities that would contingently occur *in each case*.

The other counterargument suggests that we should shift our attention from the "direct theorem" to the "converse theorem." Given "welfarism," i.e., assuming that "social welfare" is a function of utility information only (and this seems to be the common assumption in welfare economics), it is plausible to argue that the best of the feasible social states must be *at least* Pareto optimal. Since, according to the "converse theorem," *every* Pareto-optimal feasible state is a perfectly competitive equilibrium, with respect some set of prices (and some initial distribution of resources), it follows that it is invariably "possible" to achieve the very best through some market mechanism (provided the market is perfectly competitive). The fact that some particular Pareto-optimal states may be morally revolting does not affect this argument one iota, since we could have chosen another—better—Pareto optimum (not this awful one) by having a different initial distribution of resources, and by relying on the perfectly competitive mechanism to take us to the appropriate social optimum. Not surprisingly, Debreu describes the converse theorem as a "deeper" result, and Koopmans notes that it is the converse theorem, rather than the direct theorem, which is "the central proposition of the 'new welfare economics'."[21]

The converse theorem is undoubtedly a major theorem in the literature of resources allocation. But to use it as a justification for the market mechanism requires further argumentation. The converse theorem points to the possibility that, if we get the initial distribution of resources right, we can reach the very best state of affairs through the competitive market mechanism *without requiring any political interference with the market mechanism.* That can certainly be seen as a conditional rejection of the necessity of a political mechanism.

On the other hand, *how* do we get the appropriate initial distribution of resources? The need for the redistribution of ownership is, of course, one of the central political issues that divides the "right" from the "left." Classical socialist arguments have been concerned primarily with the ownership of "means of production," and only secondarily with such questions as "externalities" and other "vices" with which the market mechanism cannot allegedly cope. If the real case for the market mechanism—through the highroad of the "converse theorem"—is dependent on a major revolution in the distribution of resource ownership, then the case for *laissez-faire* and for using the allegedly "non-political" route of the market mechanism is thoroughly undermined. The "converse theorem" belongs to the "revolutionist's handbook."

There is, in fact, a further difficulty, and this concerns the issue of incentives. Once the initial distribution is appropriate to the optimal outcome, the perfectly competitive outcome, if unique and globally stable,[22] will take us in the direction of the best state of affairs. However, in order to determine the *appropriate* initial distribution of resources (for optimality in terms of the values usually invoked in traditional welfare economics, including "equity"), one would need a great deal of information about each person's productivity, tastes, etc. It will not be in the interest of those who are likely to lose out in the process of redistribution to reveal these facts. The incentive to reveal information is absent in such a system, under the standard assumption of self-interested behavior.[23]

It would, thus, appear that while the converse theorem is intellectually much more attractive, it is not easy to translate it into a practical case for the market mechanism.[24] If the *information* regarding individuals is inadequate for determining what the initial distribution of resources should be, or if there is an absence of—or reluctance to use—a political mechanism that would *actually* redistribute resource-ownership and endowments appropriately, then the practical relevance of the converse theorem is severely limited. On the other hand, the direct theorem continues to apply without these qualifications (provided the other assumptions, such as the absence of externalities of particular kinds can be legitimately made.)[25] Indeed, for the "non-omniscient," or the "non-revolutionary" government, it is the direct theorem rather than the converse theorem that is of immediate interest in judging the market mechanism.

This, of course, does bring us back to the earlier question as to how good an outcome we might regard a Pareto optimum to be. If one is concerned about income distribution, or about inequalities of utility or well-being, it is very hard to settle just for "any Pareto-optimal state," without looking further.

This particular difficulty brings out an extraordinary aspect of the market mechanism that is often overlooked. It is that the specification of the market mechanism is an essentially *incomplete* specification of a social arrangement. Even with the purest, perfectly competitive market mechanism, we are not in a position to understand precisely what will happen until we know something more about the rest of the social arrangement, in particular the distribution of endowments and resource ownership. It is an extraordinarily ambitious program to judge one part of the social arrangement (the market mechanism) without assuming something specific about the other parts. It is not surprising, therefore, that our view of the market mechanism may well be thoroughly dependent on how the incomplete description of the social arrangement given by the market mechanism is completed by other substantive descriptions. For any moral approach that responds positively to equality of one kind or another (of well-being, or of resources),[26] the assessment of the market mechanism must be integrally related to the rest of the picture.[27]

I ought to mention, in this context, that there are a number of other "results" that are often cited in the literature dealing with the moral case for the market mechanism based on achievement assessment. For example, in dealing with the *effects* of property rights, reference is often made to Ronald Coase's theorem[28]—that the optimality of the outcome is independent of the initial distribution of property rights, provided certain assumptions (such as absence of transactions costs) are made. However, the result depends upon a very weak definition of "optimality," and the difficult issues discussed in the last few paragraphs are essentially not addressed.[29]

The only way of dealing with the problem of inequality in the outcome of market mechanism is to face that issue directly, rather than avoiding it, either by silence, or by some peculiar definition of "optimality." It might be the case that inequality of well-being or of resources is of no moral concern, but if so, that position has to be made and defended. It becomes, of course, particularly hard to defend that proposition when inequalities are so great that some people live in extreme misery, or indeed die of starvation or hunger. But even otherwise the question is far too important to be neglected.

The Producers' Rights to the Product

One other line of moral defense of the market mechanism (traced to different "foundational" values) raises the question of who is "producing" what, and argues for the right of the producer to enjoy the fruits. On this view, inequalities in the outcome are of no concern, unless they are out of line with the production contributions made by the different individuals. This approach does directly address the issue of inequality, suggesting a method of dealing with it which is based on the *right of the producer* rather than on the *right of the needy*. I examine that approach next by scrutinizing, a powerful exposition of it by P. T. Bauer.[30]

Bauer's attack on "the unholy grail of economic equality" has several features, but it includes *inter alia* what I have elsewhere called "the personal production view."[31] This issue is quite central to the moral assessment of the market mechanism. Bauer argues that "economic differences are largely the result of people's varied capacities and motivations." (p.19) Given this interpretation of economic differences, he sees little that is wrong with such inequality: "...it is by no means obvious why it should be unjust that those who produce more should enjoy higher income." (p.17)

Bauer argues that the high income of "the relatively prosperous or the owners of property" are "normally...*produced* by their recipients and the resources they own." (p.12, emphasis added) Given this "personal production view" of inequality, the moral assertion of the appropriateness of such an inequality can be seen as a variant of an "entitlement" argument. However, the entitlement reasoning here does not take the procedural form it takes in the system of Nozick and others, since the rights that people have, on Bauer's view, are not that of ownership, transfer, etc., but of actually getting what one has "produced." Bauer is concerned with results and not just with procedural rules of contract, etc.

In this respect, the entitlement reasoning of Bauer relates to a labor-entitlement system of the kind that one interpretation of the Marxian theory of "exploitation" leads to. According to that view, labor "produces" all the value of the output (or "nature" and labor do, with no "residual" left), and the entitlement of labor to get the output is related to the fact. Any "shortfall" reflects "exploitation."[32] In Bauer's system, the output is produced not only (nor, in any Lockean sense, "ultimately") by labor, but by the different factors of production (including capital). And the marginal productivity theory is given an interpretation of real contribution, as opposed to having only allocational usefulness in terms of counterfactual calculations.

It is not at all implausible to think that "the personal production view," if correct, can lead to some case for inequality, even though it would still have to compete with claims arising from other considerations, such as that of needs. If, for example, a person has himself produced—unaided by others—some food, and another person wants to snatch that food away from the first, then the case for the first person rather than the second having that food might well be seen to be strong. While this judgement may be countered with competing arguments for a different distribution (the stronger need of the second person, if that is the case), there is undoubtedly some plausibility in arguing that the fact that the first person has produced the good in question is a matter of moral relevance. Also, if there are no strong contrary arguments, i.e., if the second person's needs are not noticeably different from those of the first, the case for the first having the food on grounds of having "produced" it would seem to be quite strong, at least in terms of common-sense morality.

"The personal production view" is, however, rather difficult to sustain. If production is an interdependent process, involving the joint use of different resources, it is not generally possible to separate out which resource has produced how much of the total output. There is no obvious way of determining that "this part" of the output is due to resource 1, and "that part" due to resource 2, etc. The method of attribution according to "the marginal product" concentrates on the extra output that one incremental unit of the resource would produce, *given* the amounts of the other resources. This method of accounting can lead to problems of internal consistency, except under some special assumptions (in particular, constant returns to scale). But even if these assumptions are made, the relevance of the accounting to "the personal production view" is deeply problematic.

In fact, the marginalist calculus is not concerned with finding out who "actually" produced what. Marginal accounting, when consistent, has an important function in decision making regarding the use of resources, suggesting when it would be appropriate to apply an additional unit of resource, and when it would not. To read in that counterfactual marginal story one of "actual production"—who in fact produced what part of the total output—is to take the marginal calculus well beyond its logical limits.

For example, if it turns out that, using the marginalist calculus to evaluate factor contributions, yields the result that 40 percent of the output is due to labor, 40 percent due to machinery, and 20 percent due to management, that just tells us something about the respective relative values of the marginal contributions multiplied by the total amounts of the respective resources. It would not, of course, follow that any of these three factors of production could produce their respective shares unaided by the others. Indeed, the apportioning is not even one that is done by adding together the marginal contributions of all the respective units one after another, but rather goes by weighting the *entire* amount of the resource input by the marginal valuation of the counterfactual additional contribution of that resource *at the point of equilibrium*. Under the competitive distributive process, that is what will determine the relative shares of income, and in this sense, it has predictive value as well as allocational use. But "the personal production view" adds to this real use a spurious interpretation as to who has "produced" what. This comes, as it were, from nowhere, and it is essentially a fiction. It might, of course, be seen as a "convenient fiction," but that fiction is a whole lot more convenient for some than for others.

The problem becomes even more complicated when the comparison extends to incomes generated from the production of *different* goods, since the relative incomes would then depend on the relative prices of these products, introducing an additional element of arbitrariness into "the personal production view." The significance of the relative prices in terms of "productive contributions" would require a further fiction in translating the "marginal rates of transformation"—again, a set of counterfactual magnitudes—into a set of actual production weights.

There is the further problem that "the personal production view" applies only to resources, and to move from there to the contribution of the person *owning* the resources is a considerable jump. The right of the owners of productive resources to receive high income requires some justification of the moral relevance of ownership. It is not justified on the simple ground, to which Bauer refers, of the income-rights of "those *who* are more productive and contribute more to output." (p. 11; emphasis added) Once again, the traditional socialist literature has not been so concerned with disputing the productive contribution of different resources as it has been with disputing the right of the *owners* of productive resources to grab what the resources produce.

If this reasoning is correct, the problem of inequality raised in the context of the other defenses of the market mechanism is not disposed of by moving to "the personal production view." This is not because there is no intuitive appeal whatever to the idea that one ought to have a right to something one has produced "oneself." But (1) in a world of interdependent production, that condition is difficult to apply to resources; and (2) in a world of nonpersonal resources, it is difficult to translate it from resources to persons.

There are, of course, circumstances in which "the personal production view" might be very powerful. If, for example, we are asked to arbitrate between two children fighting over a wooden toy, which has been made unaided and with free wood by one of them, and if we know nothing more about the two children, then it would be not unreasonable to be swayed by the fact of "personal production."[33] Utilitarians (and many others) will claim that this appeal is entirely explainable by some instrumental reasoning. Whether this is so is unclear. What is clear, and cannot be doubted, is that there is a strong moral intuition in that direction. But no matter what this appeal arises from, the possibility of applying it to judging actual market outcomes is so restricted by the fact of interdependence and the contrast between owning and producing, that this approach may be of little use in practical reasoning.

Concluding Remarks

The moral standing of the market mechanism has to be related to results, and it is, thus, derivative and contingent. While it is important to examine the possibility that market operations might be justified on grounds of the exercise of peoples' "prior" rights (irrespective of consequences), the implausibility and the arbitrariness of that approach are difficult to avoid. I have argued for the alternative of assessing market operations in terms of achievements, but also for treating achievements much more widely than "welfarism" permits (including such factors as the importance of "freedom to choose"). This has the advantage of taking note of the moral force of some of the arguments presented by the "procedural" view, while making that force compete with other moral claims in the overall decision.

The second approach examined finds the moral standing of the market mechanism in the values of the outcomes. This is the standard approach in welfare economics, which then proceeds to take the more specialist form of judging the outcomes exclusively by the utilities generated. In terms of that general approach of "optimality," while a case could be made for saying some nice things about the market mechanism, it is hard to go beyond some highly tentative statements. The crucial issue turns out to be our assessment of inequality. The "direct theorem" ignores it. The "converse theorem" deals with it in a way that is self-defeating, insofar as the noninterventionist "moral" of the market mechanism is concerned.[34] Of course, we might refuse to judge the outcome in terms of utility information only. I have tried to argue elsewhere[35] against the "welfarist" method of evaluation of states of affairs. But the issue of inequality does have to be addressed, whether inequality is seen in terms of utilities, well-being, incomes, resources, or freedoms (including the real "freedom to choose").[36] The practice of avoiding this question through evasion or silence, on the one hand, or through peculiar definitions of "optimality," on the other, seems hard to defend.

The third approach that was examined is one based on "the personal production view." Despite the possible relevance and force of that moral consideration, it appears that this gives us very little help in morally assessing market mechanisms in a world with (1) interdependent production, and (2) owned impersonal resources.

The argument that is much harder to dismiss is one that claims little for the market mechanism except superiority over other *practical* alternatives. Samuel Brittan has argued that "too often the defects of real world market are compared with the hypothetical action of a benevolent and omniscient dictator (as frequently—in the more technical writing—for reasons of mathematical convenience as from any deeply held conviction)."[37] Indeed, it is not unfair to ask a critic of the market mechanism what precise system he would put forward *instead*, how well does it work, and how does it compare?

Once the issue is seen in this way, it is clear that the question of the moral standing of the market mechanism cannot be given the kind of simple answer that some of the approaches examined have tried to give. It might well be the case that many alternatives suggested as substitutes for the market mechanism would do worse than the market mechanism, even in terms of the criteria used by the advocates of the change. It is also possible that, in terms of the criteria put forward by defenders of the market mechanism, replacement of the market in many spheres by other procedures would do much better.

The Chinese produced chaos by trying to do away with some features of the market mechanism. At the same time, they did expand the positive freedoms of many. For example, despite a per capita GNP only a fraction (about a seventh) of Brazil's and Mexico's, China has succeeded, through an interventionist regime, in raising life expectancy beyond that of Brazil and Mexico. It is also higher than that of South Korea, a country with a much higher level of income and a much faster rate of growth (based on a market economy with an active government policy). If we look at actual achievements across the world, the picture is a divided one, and there are many conditional conclusions to be drawn based on such empirical comparisons.[38] The difficulties in making the comparisons arise partly from the problem of isolating empirical regularities, but also from the formidable complications in setting an adequate moral criterion in terms of which the instrumentality of the market mechanism and its rivals can be judged.

When all the qualifications have been put in, the market mechanism certainly has some instrumental moral relevance, related to its handling of information and incentives. The result-oriented and contingent nature of that relevance does not make the lessons unimportant. The defenders of the market mechanism have often seen in hesitant acknowledgments like this one a tendency to damn the market with "faint praise." But while faint praise is no doubt one method of damning, unjustified and ferocious praise is certainly another. The vigor of the defense of the market mechanism examined earlier in the paper is not matched by its ability to meet criticisms. It also distracts us from the contingent importance of the use of the market mechanism in many real circumstances, and tends to make us overlook the relevance of these lessons for practical reasoning. There *is* a case for *faint* praise—not any less, nor much more.

1.   I am most grateful to Allan Gibbard for his discussion of the paper following my presentation at Bowling Green on 21 September 1984. I have also benefited from the general discussion, including comments by Jules Coleman, Donald Regan, Alexander Rosenberg, and Hal Varian, and from later correspondence with Varian.

2.   The last phrase comes from Adam Smith, *The Wealth of Nations* (1776). Aside from indicating wherein the virtue of the market mechanism lies, it points to the fact that no individual participant in the process aims at *all* the results the market achieves. Friedrich von Hayek has seen in this a great new insight—indeed a great theory of "the result of human action but not of human design"—initiated allegedly by Adam Smith, "revived" by Carl Menger, and now enshrined by Hayek; see his *Studies in Philosophy; Politics, and Economics* (Chicago: University of Chicago Press, 1967), pp. 96-105. One has to be careful about what is being asserted here. It would be wrong to say that no one aims at *any* of the results achieved. In this model, each person is assumed to pursue, as far as is feasible, his own interest, and this pursuit is *fulfilled* by the market transaction. "The butcher, the brewer, or the baker" did not aim at "our dinner," but *we* presumably *did*. The fact that not *all* the results, nor the *pattern* of the results, was anyone's "design" seems to be an unremarkable fact. Surely, Adam Smith's main contribution, in this area of analysis, was to show how the results of different peoples "designs" are *coordinated and achieved* by the market. I have discussed this question, among other issues, in "The Profit Motive," *Lloyds Bank Review*, vol. 147 (1983).

3.   Milton and Rose Friedman, *Free to Choose* (London: Seeker and Warburg, 1980), p.222.

4.   *ibid.*, p. 223.

5.   See R. M. Hare, *Moral Thinking: Its Levels, Methods and Point* (Oxford: Clarendon Press, 1981), on "levels" of moral thinking, and on the distinction between the "intuitive" and the "critical." See also John Gray, *Mill on Liberty: A Defence* (London: Routledge, 1983).

6.   Robert Nozick, *Anarchy, State and Utopia* (Oxford: Blackwell, 1974), p. 1.

7.   Robert Nozick does point to (what he calls) "invisible-hand explanations" of the emergence of social institutions (such as markets), quoting Adam Smith *(ibid.*, p. 18). But, consistently with his own approach, he does not proceed to assess such institutions in terms of the goodness of interest-fulfilling outcomes.

8.   See, for example, the different analyses of this issue by, Z. Husami, "Marx on Distributive Justice," *Philosophy and Public Affairs*, vol. 7 (1978); H. Steiner, "Individual Liberty," *Proceedings of the Aristotelian Society*, vol. 74 (1974), G.A. Cohen, "Capitalism, Freedom and the Proletariat," A. Ryan, ed., *The Idea of Freedom: Essays in Honour of Isaiah Berlin* (Oxford: Clarendon Press, 1979); G. A. Cohen, "Illusions about Private Property and Freedom," I. Mepham and D. Rubens, eds., *Issues in Marxist Philosophy*, (Hassocks: Harvester Press, 1981); O. O'Neill, "The Most Extensive Liberty," *Proceedings of the Aristotelian Society,* vol. 79 (1979-80); and others. See also Gerald Dworkin, *et al.*, *Markets and Morals* (Washington: Hemisphere Publishing, 1977).

9.   Allan Gibbard, "Natural Property Rights," *Nous*, vol. 10 (1976). Gibbard examines the possible claim of "property rights" to be "grounded in principles of natural liberty," with or without John Locke's [John Locke, *The Second Treatise of Government* (1974)] qualification regarding the libertarian position, and shows why the claim is hard to justify.

10.   Amartya Sen, *Property and Famines: An Essay on Entitlement and Deprivation* (Oxford: Clarendon Press, and New York: Oxford University Press, 1981).

11.   Contrast the model of "alienable rights" in A. Gibbard, "A Pareto-Consistent Libertarian Claim," *Journal of Economic Theory*, vol. 7 (1974), in which rights have extreme sensitivity to the nature of the outcome. It is arguable that such a system of outcome sensitivity

may not be full justice to the procedural nature of rights, but on the other hand it is very hard to see why rights should continue to be not alienable at all even when the results of the exercise of right are plainly terrible. Some connections between outcomes and rights are discussed in my "Rights and Agency" *Philosophy and Public Affairs*, vol.11 (1982). See also D. H. Regan, "Against Evaluator Relativity: A Response to Sen," *Philosophy and Public Affairs,*. Vol. 12 (1983). and Amartya Sen, "Liberty and Social Choice," *Journal of Philosophy,* vol 80 (1983).

12   Amartya Sen, "Rights and Agency".

13   See my "Evaluator Relativity and Consequential Evaluation," *Philosophy and Public Affairs*, vol. 12 (1983). and "Well-being, Agency and Freedom: The Dewey Lectures 1984," *Journal of Philosophy*, vol. 82 (1985).

14   One way of seeing the problem of personal morality in this cape of context is in terms of a system of action evaluation that is consequence-sensitive, but not fully "consequentialist." Another way of dealing with it is to make the evaluation of states of affairs *position-relative* to the person doing the evaluation (including his or her own agency). There is, in fact, a case for such position-relativity on grounds of ethical cogency; or at least so I have tried to argue in "Rights and Agency"; see also the exchange between Donald Regan, "Against Evaluator Relativity," and A. K. Sen, "Evaluator Relativity and Consequential Evaluation," *Philosophy and Public Affairs*, vol. 12 (1983).

15   Discussed in Amartya Sen, "Utilitarianism and Welfarism," *Journal of Philosophy*, vol. 70 (1979).

16   On questions as to how these moral values may be interpreted, assessed and integrated, there are—not surprising—enormous differences; see for example K. J.Arrow, *Social Choice and Individual Values* (New York: Wiley, 1951); J. C. Harsanyi, "Cardinal Welfare, Individualistic Ethics, and Interpersonal Comparisons of Utility," *Journal of Political Economy*. vol. 61 (1955); and *Essays on Ethics, Social Behavior and Scientific Explanation* (Dordrecht: Reidel, 1976); I. M. D. Little, *A Critique of Welfare Economics* (Oxford: Clarendon Press, 2nd edition 1957); J. M. Buchanan and G. Tullock, *The Calculus of Consent* (Arm Arbor, MI: University of Michigan Press, 1962); J. Rawls, *A Theory of Justice* (Cambridge, MA: Harvard University Press, 1971); and "Kantian Constructivism in Moral Theory: The Dewey Lectures 1984" *Journal of Philosophy*, vol. 77 (1980); R. Dworkin, *Taking Rights Seriously* (London: Duckworth, 1977); and "What is Equality," *Philosophy and Public Affairs*, vol. 10 (1981). For related matters, see also H. Varian, "Distributive Justice, Welfare Economics and The Theory of Fairness," *Philosophy and Public Affairs*, vol. 4 (1975); G. Dworkin, et al, *Markets and Morals*; G. Calabresi and P. Bobbitt, Tragic Choices (New York: Norton, 1978); D. Usher, *The Economic Prerequisites to Democracy* (New York: Columbia University Press, 1981); J. Roemer, *A General Theory of Exploitation and Class* (Cambridge, MA: Harvard University Press, 1982); and "Equality of Talent," Working Paper 239, Economics Department, University of California, Davis, (1984); B. C. Frey, *Democratic Economic Policy,* (Oxford: Martin Robertson, 1983); A. M. McLeod, "Justice and the Market," *Canadian Journal of Philosophy*, vol. 13, (1983); P. K. Pattanaik and M. Salles, *Social Choice and Welfare* (Amsterdam: North-Holland, 1983). I have tried to discuss some of these issues in Amartya Sen, *Collective Choice and Social Welfare* (San Francisco: Holden-Day, 1970; republished, Amsterdam: North-Holland, 1979); "Equality of What?" in S. McMurrin, ed., Tanner *Lectures on Human Values*, vol. 1 (Cambridge: Cambridge University Press, 1980, reprinted in my *Choice, Welfare and Measurement* (Oxford: Blackwell: and Cambridge, MA: M.I.T. Press, 1982); "Rights and Agencies," *Philosophy and Public Affairs;* Well-being, Agency and Freedom: The Dewey Lectures 1984."

17 K. J. Arrow, "An Extension of the Basic Theorems of Classical Welfare Economics," in J. Neyman, ed., *Proceeding of the Second Berkeley Symposium on Mathematical Statistics and Probability* (Berkley, C.A: University of California Press, 1951); G. Debreu, Theory of Value (New York: Wiley, 1959); K.J. Arrow and F.H. Hahn, *General Competitive Analysis* (San Francisco: Holden-Day, 1971; republished, Amsterdam: North-Holland, 1979).

18 As Dorftnan, Samuelson and Solow put it: "More recently it has become Common to sum up all these in one brief and easily understood theorem which comprises everything of significance and provides the backbone of welfare economics. This fundamental theorem states 'every competitive equilibrium is a Pareto optimum; and every Pareto optimum is a competitive equilibrium.'" R. Dorfman, P. Samuelson and R. Solow, *Linear Programming and Economic Analysis* (New York: McGraw-Hill, 1958), pp. 409-410.

19 This assumption is not in fact fully needed for each of the results; see S. Winter, "A Simple Remark on the Second Optimality Theorem of Welfare Economics," *Journal of Economic Theory* vol. 1 (1969); and G.C. Archibald and D. Donaldson, "Non-paternalism and the Basic Theorems of Welfare Economics," *Canadian Journal of Economics*, vol.9 (1976). These further results indicate the presence of an asymmetry, in the required assumptions regarding "externalities," between the direct theorem and the converse theorem. Some other Properties (e.g., convexity) have very disparate relevance, indeed, to the two theorems (the direct theorem does not require any contexts assumption, whereas the convexity theorem certainly requires it in some form or other).

20 Amartya Sen, *On Economic Inequality* (Oxford: Clarendon Press; and New York: Nortoe 1973).

21 G. Debreu, *Theory of Value;* T.C. Koopmans, *Three Essays on the State of Economic Science* (New York: McGraw-Hill, 1957), pg.27.

22 Uniqueness and global stability, incidentally, are additional assumptions and no mean demands either. See Arrow and Hahn, *General Competitive Analysis*.

23 This problem of the incentive to reveal information has to be distinguished front the problem of international economy, to which the procedures for "decentralized resource allocation" are addressed (see, for example, E. Malinvaud, "Decentralized Procedures for Planning," in E. Malinvaud and M.O.I. Bacharach, eds., *Activity Analysis in the Theory of Growth and Planning* (London: Macmillan, 1967); G.M. Heal, *The Theory of Economic Planning* (Amsterdam: Horth-Holland, 1973); M. Weitzman, "Prices versus Quantities," *Review Economic Studies,* vol. 41 (1974); P. Dagsputa, *The Control of Resources* (Oxford: Blackwell. 1982). In such "decentralized" procedures, each agent acts as a member of a "team," and it is typically assumed that they have *shared objectives,* though disparate access to information. The problem of decentralizes resource allocation, when the agents have their own respective goals, which may conflict, has not been much studied in the literature, and will certainly not lead to simple and comforting results.

24 There are various "incentive compatible" mechanisms (see, for examples, T. Groves and J. Ledyard, "Optimal Allocation of Public Goods: A Solution to the 'Free Rider' Problem." *Econometrica*, vol. 45 (1977); J. Green and J.-J. Laffont, "Characterization of Satisfactory Mechanisms for the Revelation of Preferences for Public Goods, "*Econometrica,* vol. 45 (1977); P. Dagsputa, P. Hammond, and E. Maskin, "The Implementation of Social Choice Rules: Some General Results in Incentive Compatibility," *Review of Economic Studies*, vol. 46 (1979); which deal effectively with the problem of "the free rider" in terms of the incentive to *do* the right thing, *given* the initial distribution of resources, despite the presence of such problems as "public goods." These "solutions" are not, however, addressed to the problem of how to deal with the incentive to reveal information of a kind that would

permit the policy makers to make judgments about the right initial distribution of resources (in line with the distributional objectives of policy making). Nor do they address the problem of revelation of individual *judgments* to be combined in an "aggregate" judgment (e.g., to decide on equity). On the last, see A. Gibbard, "Manipulation of Voting Schemes: A General Result," *Econometrica*, vol. 41 (1973); M.A. Satterthwaite, "Strategy-Proofness and Arrow's Conditions: Existence and Correspondence Theorems for Voting Procedures and Social Welfare Functions," *Journal of Economic Theory*, vol. 10 (1975); P.K. Pattanaik, *Strategy and Group Choice* (Amsterdam: North-Holland, 1978); J.-J. Laffont, ed., *Aggregation and Revelation of Preferences*. (Amsterdam: North-Holland, 1979); H. Moulin, *The Strategy of Social Choice* (Amsterdam: North-Holland, 1983); B. Peleg, *Game Theoretic Analysis of Voting in Committees* (Cambridge: Cambridge University Press, 1984).

25 In fact, insofar as we value the market achievement not in terms of Pareto-optimality (i.e., reaching an "undominated" vector of utilities), but in terms of the corresponding notice of being "free to choose" (i.e., having an "undominated" n-tuple of individual freedoms to pursue *whatever* they decide to seek), the assumption of self-interested behavior can be also significantly relaxed.

26 See R. Dworkin, "What is Equality." See also J. Roemer, "Equality of Talent"; and H. Varian, "Dworkin on Equality of Resources," mimeographed, University of Michigan, Ann Arbor (1984).

27 There can, however, be useful *partial* criteria of judging achievements, e.g., whether the mechanism satisfies specific requirements of "horizontal equity" or "symmetry presentation." The market mechanism can be partially defended from these particular perspectives. See, for example, D. Schmeidler and K. Vind, "Fair Net Trade," *Econometrica*, vol. 40 (1972); H. Varian. "Equity, Envy and Efficiency," *Journal of Economic Theory*, vol. 9 (1974).

28 R. H. Coase, "The Problem of Social Cost," *Journal of Law and Economics,* vol. 3 (1960).

29 For different interpretations of what Coase's line of reasoning achieves, see J.M. Buchanan, *Freedom in Constitutional Contract* (College Station: Texas A & M University, 1977); and "Rights, Efficiency, and Exchange: The Irrelevance of Transactions Cost," mimeographed, Center for Study of Public Choice, George Mason University (1983); G. Calabresi and P. Bobbit, *Tragic Choices*; R. Cooter, "The Cost of Coase," *Journal of Legal Studies*, vol. 11 (l982); E.J. Green, "Equilibrium and Efficiency under Pure Entitlement Systems," in A.H. Meltzer ind T. Romer, eds., *Proceedings of the Conference on Political Economy*, vol. 2, Supplement to *Public Choice* (1982).

30 P. T. Bauer, *Equality, The Third World and Economic Delusion* (Cambridge, MA: Harvard University Press, 1981).

31 See Amartya Sen, "Just Desert." *New York Review of Books*, vol. 19 (March 4, 1982). Sec also: P.T. Bauer's rejoinder in the same journal, June 10, 1982; also P. T. Bauer, *Reality and Rhetoric: Studies in the Economics of Development* (London: Weidenfeld, 1984).

32 There are, of course, a great many difficulties in this way of seeing the Marxian system, as many contributions by Marxian economists have brought out. There is in fact, a strong case for seeing the relevance of Marxian exploitation theory from a perspective different from that of production entitlement. On these issues, see M. Morishima, *Marx's Economics* (Cambridge: Cambridge University Press, 1973); I. Steedman, *Marx after Sraffa* (London: NLB, 1977); G. A. Cohen, *Karl Marx's Theory of History* (Oxford: Clarendon Press, 1978); J. Elster, "Exploitation and the Theory of Justice." mimeographed, Historisk Institute, University of Oslo (1980); J. Roemer, *A General Theory of Exploitation and Class.*

[33] I have discussed this question in "Ethical Issues in Income Distribution: National and International," in S. Grassman and E. Lunberg, eds., *The World Economic Order: Past and Prospects* (London: Macmillan, 1981); reprinted in Amartya Sen, *Resources, Values and Development* (Oxford: Blackwell. and Cambridge, MA: Harvard University. Press, 1984).

[34] It is not surprising, in view of this, that the early contributions to the efficiency of the market mechanism came from socialist writers like O. Lange, "The Foundations of Economics," *Econometrica,* vol. 10 (1938); and A. P. Lerner, *The Economics of Control* (London: Macmillan, 1944).

[35] Amartya Sen, *Collective Choice and Social Welfare;* "Utilitarianism and Welfarism"; "Rights and Agency."

[36] On the last, see Amartya Sen, "Equality of What?"; Well-being, Agency and Freedom: The Dewey Lectures 1984.

[37] S. Brittan, *The Role and Limits of Government: Essays in Political Economy.* (London: Temple Smith, 1983); p.37. See also I. M. D. Little, *Economic Development: Theory, Policy and International Relations* (New York: Basic Books, 1982).

[38] The question is discussed in Amartya Sen, "Public Action and the Quality of Life in Developing Countries," *Oxford Bulletin of Economics and Statistics,* vol. 43 (1981); and "Development: Which Way Now?" *Economic Journal,* vol. 93 (1973).

Copyright © *Social Philosophy & Policy,* 1985.
Reprinted with permission.

Business Ethics and Stakeholder Analysis

Kenneth E. Goodpaster, University of St. Thomas

Abstract: Much has been written about stakeholder analysis as a process by which to introduce ethical values into management decision-making. This paper takes a critical look at the assumptions behind this idea, in an effort to understand better the meaning of ethical management decisions.

A distinction is made between stakeholder analysis and stakeholder synthesis. The two most natural kinds of stakeholder synthesis are then defined and discussed: strategic and multi-fiduciary. Paradoxically, the former appears to yield business without ethics and the latter appears to yield ethics without business. The paper concludes by suggesting that a third approach to stakeholder thinking needs to be developed, one that avoids the paradox just mentioned and that clarifies for managers (and directors) the legitimate role of ethical considerations in decision-making.

> So we must think through what management should be accountable for, and how and through whom its accountability can be discharged. The stockholders' interest, both short and long-term, is one of the areas. But it is only one.
>
> Peter Drucker, 1988
> Harvard Business Review

What is ethically responsible management? How can a corporation, given its economic mission, be managed with appropriate attention to ethical concerns? These are central questions in the field of business ethics. One approach to answering such questions that has become popular during the last two decades is loosely referred to as "stakeholder analysis." Ethically responsible management, it is often suggested, is management that includes careful attention not only to *stockholders but to stakeholders generally* in the decision-making process.

This suggestion about the ethical importance of stakeholder analysis contains an important kernel of truth, but it can also be misleading. Comparing the ethical relationship between managers and stockholders with their relationship to other stakeholders is, I will argue, almost as problematic as ignoring stakeholders (ethically) altogether presenting us with something of a "stakeholder paradox."

Definition

The term "stakeholder" appears to have been invented in the early 60s as a deliberate play on the word "stockholder" to signify that there are other parties having a "stake" in the decision-making of the modern, publicly-held corporation in addition to those holding equity positions. Professor R. Edward Freeman, in his book *Strategic Management: A Stakeholder Approach* (Pitman, 1984), defines the term as follows:

> A stakeholder in an organization is (by definition) any group or individual who can affect or is affected by the achievement of the organization's objectives. (46)

Examples of stakeholder groups (beyond stockholders) are employees, suppliers, customers, creditors, competitors, governments, and communities. *Exhibit 1* illustrates one way of picturing the conventional stakeholder groups along with the two principal channels through which they often affect the corporation, law and markets.

Another metaphor with which the term "stakeholder" is associated is that of a "player" in a game like poker. One with a "stake" in the game is one who plays and puts some economic value at risk.[1]

Much of what makes responsible decision-making difficult is understanding how there can be an ethical relationship between management and stakeholders that avoids being too weak (making stakeholders mere means to stockholders' ends) or too strong (making stakeholders quasi-stockholders in their own right). To give these issues life, a case example will help. So let us consider the case of General Motors and Poletown.

The Poletown Case[2]

In 1980, GM was facing a net loss in income, the first since 1921, due to intense foreign competition. Management realized that major capital expenditures would be required for the company to regain its competitive position and profitability. A $40 billion five year capital spending program was announced that included new, state-of-the-art assembly techniques aimed at smaller, fuel-efficient automobiles demanded by the market. Two aging assembly plants in Detroit were among the ones to be replaced. Their closure would eliminate 500 jobs. Detroit in 1980 was a city with a black majority, an unemployment rate of 18% overall and 30% for blacks, a rising public debt and a chronic budget deficit, despite high tax rates.

The site requirements for a new assembly plant included 500 acres, access to long-haul railroad and freeways, and proximity to suppliers for "just-in-time" inventory management. It needed to be ready to produce 1983 model year cars beginning in September 1982. The only site in Detroit meeting GM's requirements was heavily settled, covering a section of the Detroit neighborhood of Poletown. Of the 3,500 residents, half were black. The whites were mostly of Polish descent, retired or nearing retirement. An alternative "green field" site was available in another midwestern state.

Using the power of eminent domain, the Poletown area could be acquired and cleared for a new plant within the company's timetable, and the city government was eager to cooperate. Because of job retention in Detroit, the leadership of the United Auto Workers was also in favor of the idea. The Poletown Neighborhood Council strongly opposed the plan, but was willing to work with the city and GM.

The new plant would employ 6,150 workers and would cost GM $500 million wherever it was built. Obtaining and preparing the Poletown site would cost an additional $200 million, whereas alternative sites in the midwest were available for $65-80 million.

The interested parties were many—stockholders, customers, employees, suppliers, the Detroit community, the midwestern alternative, the Poletown neighborhood. The decision was difficult. GM management needed to consider its competitive situation, the extra costs of remaining in Detroit, the consequences to the city of leaving for another part of the midwest, and the implications for the residents of choosing the Poletown site if the decision was made to stay. The decision about whom to talk to and *how* was as puzzling as the decision about *what* to do and *why*.

I. *Stakeholder Analysis and Stakeholder Synthesis*

Ethical values enter management decision-making, it is often suggested, through the gate of stakeholder analysis. But the suggestion that introducing "stakeholder analysis" into business decisions is the same as introducing ethics into those decisions is questionable. To make this plain, let me first distinguish between two importantly different ideas: stakeholder analysis and stakeholder synthesis. I will then examine alternative kinds of stakeholder synthesis with attention to ethical content.

The decision-making process of an individual or a company can be seen in terms of a sequence of six steps to be followed after an issue or problem presents itself for resolutions.[3] For ease of reference and recall, I will name the sequence PASCAL, after the six letters in the name of the French philosopher-mathematician Blaise Pascal (1623-62), who once remarked in reference to ethical decision-making that "the heart has reasons the reason knows not of."

(1) PERCEPTION or fact-gathering about the options available and their short and long-term implications;
(2) ANALYSIS of these implications with specific attention to affected parties and to the decision-maker's goals, objectives, values, responsibilities, etc.;
(3) SYNTHESIS of this structured information according to whatever fundamental priorities obtain in the mindset of the decision-maker;
(4) CHOICE among the available options based on the synthesis;
(5) ACTION or implementation of the chosen option through a series of specific requests to specific individuals or groups, resource allocation, incentives, controls, and feedback;
(6) LEARNING from the outcome of the decision, resulting in either reinforcement or modification (for future decisions) of the way in which the above steps have been taken.

We might simplify this analysis, of course, to something like "input," "decision," and "output," but distinguishing interim steps can often be helpful. The main point is that the path from the presentation of a problem to its resolution must somehow involve gathering, processing, and acting on relevant information.

Now, by *stakeholder analysis* I simply mean a process that does not go beyond the first two steps mentioned above. That is, the affected parties caught up in, each available option are identified and the positive and negative impacts on each stakeholder are determined. But questions having to do with processing this information into a decision and implementing it are *left unanswered*. These steps are not part of the *analysis* but of the *synthesis, choice,* and *action*.

Stakeholder analysis may give the initial appearance of a decision-making process, but in fact it is only a *segment* of a decision-making process. It represents the preparatory or opening phase that awaits the crucial application of the moral (or nonmoral) values of the decision-maker. So, to be informed that an individual or an institution regularly makes stakeholder analysis part of decision-making or takes a "stakeholder approach" to management is to learn little or nothing about the ethical character of that individual or institution. It is to learn only that stakeholders are regularly identified *not why and for what purpose*. To be told that stakeholders are or must be "taken into account" is, so far, to be told very little. Stakeholder analysis is, as a practical matter, morally *neutral*. It is therefore a mistake to see it as a substitute for normative ethical thinking.[4]

What I shall call "stakeholder synthesis" goes further into the sequence of decision-making steps mentioned above to include actual decision-making and implementation (S,C,A). The critical point is that stakeholder synthesis offers *a pattern or channel by which to move from stakeholder identification to a practical response or resolution*. Here we begin to join stakeholder analysis to questions of substance. But we must now ask: What kind of substance? And how does it relate to *ethics*? The stakeholder idea, remember, is typically offered as a way of integrating *ethical* values into management decision-making. When and how does substance become *ethical* substance?

Strategic Stakeholder Synthesis
We can imagine decision-makers doing "stakeholder analysis" for different underlying reasons, not always having to do with ethics. A management team, for example, might be careful to take positive and (especially) negative stakeholder effects into account for no other reason than that offended stakeholders might resist or retaliate (e.g., through political action or opposition to necessary regulatory clearances). It might not be *ethical* concern for the stakeholders that motivates and guides such analysis, so much as concern about potential impediments to the achievement of strategic objectives. Thus positive and negative effects on relatively powerless stakeholders may be ignored or discounted in the synthesis, choice, and action phases of the decision process.[5]

In the Poletown case, General Motors might have done a stakeholder analysis using the following reasoning: our stockholders are the central stakeholders here, but other key stakeholders include our suppliers, old and new plant employees, the City of Detroit, and the residents of Poletown. These other stakeholders are not our direct concern as a corporation with an economic mission, but since they can influence our short or long-term strategic interests, they must be taken into account. Public relation's costs and benefits, for example, or concerns about union contracts or litigation might well have influenced the choice between staying in Detroit and going elsewhere.

I refer to this kind of stakeholder synthesis as "strategic" since stakeholders outside the stockholder group are viewed instrumentally, as factors potentially affecting the overarching goal of optimizing stockholder interests. They are taken into account in the decision-making process, but as external environmental forces, as potential sources of either good will or retaliation. "We" are the economic principals and management; "they" are significant players whose attitudes and future actions might affect our short-term or long-term success. We must respect them in the way one "respects" the weather—as a set of forces to be reckoned with.[6]

It should be emphasized that managers who adopt the strategic stakeholder approach are not necessarily *personally* indifferent to the plight of stakeholders who are "strategically unimportant." The point is that in their *role as managers*, with a fiduciary relationship that binds them as agents to principals, their basic outlook subordinates other stakeholder concerns to those of stockholders. Market and legal forces are relied upon to secure the interests of those whom strategic considerations might discount. This reliance can and does take different forms, depending on the emphasis given to market forces on the one hand and legal forces on the other. A more conservative, market-oriented view acknowledges the role of legal compliance as an environmental factor affecting strategic choice, but thinks stakeholder interests are best served by minimal interference from the public sector. Adam Smith's "invisible hand" is thought to be the most important guarantor of the common good in a competitive economy. A more liberal view sees the hand of government, through legislation and regulation, as essential for representing stakeholders that might otherwise not achieve "standing" in the strategic decision process.

What both conservatives and liberals have in common is the conviction that the fundamental orientation of management must be toward the interests of stockholders. Other stakeholders (customers, employees, suppliers, neighbors) enter the decision-making equation either directly as instrumental economic factors or indirectly as potential legal claimants. (See again *Exhibit 1*.) Both see law and regulation as providing a voice for stakeholders that goes beyond market dynamics. They differ about how much government regulation is socially and economically desirable.

During the Poletown controversy, GM managers as individuals may have cared deeply about the potential lost jobs in Detroit, or about the potential dislocation of Poletown residents. But in their role as agents for the owners (stockholders) they could only allow such considerations to "count" if they served GM's strategic interests (or perhaps as legal constraints on the decision).

Professor Freeman (1984, cited above) appears to adopt some form of strategic stakeholder synthesis. After presenting his definition of stakeholders, he remarks about its application to any group or individual "who can affect or is affected by" a company's achievement of its purposes. The "affect" part of the definition is not hard to understand; but Freeman clarifies the "affected by" part:

> The point of strategic management is in some sense to chart a direction for the firm. Groups which can affect that direction and its implementation must be considered in the strategic

management process. However, it is less obvious why those groups who are affected by the corporation" are stakeholders as well... I make the definition symmetric because of the changes which the firm has undergone in the past few years. Groups which 20 years ago had no effect on the actions of the firm, can affect it today, largely because of the actions of the firm which ignored the effects on these groups. Thus, by calling those affected groups "stakeholders," the ensuing strategic management model will be sensitive to future change... (46)

Freeman might have said "who can actually or potentially affect" the company, for the mind-set appears to be one in which attention to stakeholders is justified in terms of actual or potential impact on the company's achievement of its strategic purposes. Stakeholders (other than stockholders) are actual or potential means/obstacles to corporate objectives. A few pages later, Freeman writes:

From the standpoint of strategic management, or the achievement of organizational purpose, we need an inclusive definition. We must not leave out any group or individual who can affect or is affected by organizational purpose, *because that group may prevent our accomplishments.* (52) [Emphasis added.]

The essence of a strategic view of stakeholders is not that stakeholders are ignored, but that all but a special group (stockholders) are considered on the basis of their actual or potential influence on management's central mission. The basic normative principle is fiduciary responsibility (organizational prudence), supplemented by legal compliance.

Is the Substance Ethical?
The question we must ask in thinking about a strategic approach to stakeholder synthesis is this: Is it really an adequate rendering of the *ethical* component in managerial judgment? Unlike mere stakeholder *analysis*, this kind of synthesis does go beyond simply *identifying* stakeholders. It integrates the stakeholder information by using a single interest group (stockholders) as its basic normative touchstone. If this were formulated as an explicit rule or principle, it would have two parts and would read something like this: (1) Maximize the benefits and minimize the costs to the stockholder group, short and long-term, and (2) Pay close attention to the interests of other stakeholder groups that might potentially influence the achievement of (1). But while expanding the list of stakeholders may be a way of "enlightening" self-interest for the organization, is it really a way of introducing ethical values into business decision-making?

There are really two possible replies here. The first is that as an account of how ethics enters the managerial mind-set, the strategic stakeholder approach fails not because it is *im*moral; but because it is *non*moral. By most accounts of the nature of ethics, a strategic stakeholder synthesis would not qualify as an ethical synthesis, even though it does represent a substantive view. The point is simply that while there is nothing necessarily *wrong* with strategic reasoning about the consequences of one's actions for others, the kind of concern exhibited should not be confused with what most people regard as *moral* concern. Moral concern would avoid injury or unfairness to those affected by one's actions because it is wrong, regardless of the retaliatory potential of the aggrieved parties.[7]

The second reply does question the morality (vs. immorality) of strategic reasoning as the ultimate principle behind stakeholder analysis. It acknowledges that strategy, when placed in a highly effective legal and regulatory environment and given a time-horizon that is relatively long-term, may well avoid significant forms of anti-social behavior. But it asserts that as an operating principle for managers under time pressure in an imperfect legal and regulatory environment, strategic analysis is insufficient. In the Poletown case, certain stakeholders (e.g., the citizens of Detroit or the residents of Poletown) may have merited more *ethical* consideration than the strategic approach would have allowed. Some critics charged that GM only considered these stakeholders *to the extent that* serving their interests also served GM's interests, and that as a result, their interests were undermined.

Many, most notably Nobel Laureate Milton Friedman, believe that market and legal forces are adequate to translate or transmute ethical concerns into straightforward strategic concerns for management. He believes that in our economic and political system (democratic capitalism), direct concern for stakeholders (what Kant might have called "categorical" concern) is unnecessary, redundant, and inefficient, not to mention dishonest:

> In many cases, there is a strong temptation to rationalize actions as an exercise of "social responsibility." In the present climate of opinion, with its widespread aversion to "capitalism," "profits," the "soulless corporation" and so on, this is one way for a corporation to generate good will as a by-product of expenditures that are entirely justified in its own self-interest. If our institutions, and the attitudes of the public make it in their self-interest to cloak their actions in this way, I cannot summon much indignation to denounce them. At the same time, I can express admiration for those individual proprietors or owners of closely held corporations or stockholders of more broadly held corporations who disdain such tactics as approaching fraud.

Critics respond, however, that absent a pre-established harmony or linkage between organizational success and ethical success, some stakeholders, some of the time, will be affected a lot but will be able to affect in only a minor way the interests of the corporation. They add that in an increasingly global business environment, even the protections of law are fragmented by multiple jurisdictions.

At issue then is (1) defining ethical behavior partly in terms of the (nonstrategic) decision-making values *behind* it, and (2) recognizing that too much optimism about the correlation between strategic success and virtue runs the risk of tailoring the latter to suit the former.

Thus the move toward substance (from analysis to synthesis) in discussions of the stakeholder concept is not necessarily a move toward ethics. And it is natural to think that the reason has to do with the instrumental status accorded to stakeholder groups other than stockholders. If we were to treat all stakeholders by strict analogy with stockholders, would we have arrived at a more ethically satisfactory form of stakeholder synthesis? Let us now look at this alternative, what I shall call a "multi-fiduciary" approach.

Multi-Fiduciary Stakeholder Synthesis
In contrast to a strategic view of stakeholders, one can imagine a management team processing stakeholder information by giving the same care to the interests of, say, employees, customers, and local communities as to the economic interests of stockholders. This kind of substantive commitment to stakeholders might involve trading off the economic advantages of one group against those of another, e.g., in a plant closing decision. I shall refer to this way of integrating stakeholder analysis with decision-making as "multi-fiduciary" since all stakeholders are treated by management as having equally important interests, deserving joint "maximization" (or what Herbert Simon might call "satisficing").

Professor Freeman, quoted earlier, contemplates what I am calling the multi-fiduciary view at the end of his 1984 book under the heading *The Manager As Fiduciary To Stakeholders:*

> Perhaps the most important area of future research is the issue of whether or not a theory of management can be constructed that uses the stakeholder concept to enrich "managerial capitalism," that is, can the notion that managers bear a fiduciary relationship to stockholders or the owners of the firm, be replaced by a concept of management whereby the manager must act in the interests of the stakeholders in the organization? (249)

As we have seen, the strategic approach pays attention to stakeholders as to factors that might affect economic interests, so many market forces to which companies must pay attention for competitive reasons. They become actual or potential legal challenges to the company's exercise of economic rationality. The multi-fiduciary approach, on the other hand, views stakeholders apart from their instrumental, economic, or legal clout. It does not see them merely as what philosopher John Ladd once called "limiting operating conditions" on management attention.[8] On this view, the word "stakeholder" carries with it, by the deliberate modification of a single phoneme, a dramatic shift in managerial outlook. In 1954, famed management theorist Adolf Berle conceded a long-standing debate with Harvard law professor E. Merrick Dodd that looks in retrospect very much like a debate between what we are calling strategic and multi-fiduciary interpretations of stakeholder synthesis. Berle wrote:

> Twenty years ago, [I held] that corporate powers were powers in trust for shareholders while Professor Dodd argued that these powers were held in trust for the entire community. The argument has been settled (at least for the time being) squarely in favor of Professor Dodd's contention. (Quoted in Ruder, see below.)

The intuitive idea behind Dodd's view, and behind more recent formulations of it in terms of "multiple constituencies" and stakeholders, not just stockholders is that by expanding the list of those in whose trust corporate management must manage, we thereby introduce ethical responsibility into business decision-making.

In the context of the Poletown case, a multi-fiduciary approach by GM management might have identified the same stakeholders. But it would have considered the interests of employees, the city of Detroit, and the Poletown residents *alongside* stockholder interests, not solely in terms of how they might *influence* stockholder interests. This may or may not have entailed a different outcome. But it probably would have meant a different approach to the decision-making process in relation to the residents of Poletown (talking with them, for example).

We must now ask, as we did of the strategic approach: How satisfactory is multi-fiduciary stakeholder synthesis as a way of giving ethical substance to management decision-making? On the face of it, and in stark contrast to the strategic approach, it may seem that we have at last arrived at a truly moral view. But we should be cautious. For no sooner do we think we have found the proper interpretation of ethics in management than a major objection presents itself. And, yes, it appears to be a *moral* objection!

It can be argued that multi-fiduciary stakeholder analysis is simply incompatible with widely-held moral convictions about the special fiduciary obligations owed by management to stockholders. At the center of the objection is the belief that the obligations of agents to principals are stronger or different in kind from those of agents to third parties.

The Stakeholder Paradox

Managers who would pursue a multi-fiduciary stakeholder orientation for their companies must face resistance from those who believe that a strategic orientation is the only legitimate one for business to adopt, given the economic mission and legal constitution of the modern corporation. This may be disorienting since the word "illegitimate" has clear negative ethical connotations, and yet the multi-fiduciary approach is often defended on ethical grounds. I will refer to this anomalous situation as the *Stakeholder Paradox:*

> It seems essential, yet in some ways illegitimate, to orient corporate decisions by ethical values that go beyond strategic stakeholder considerations to multi-fiduciary ones.

I call this a paradox because it says there is an ethical problem whichever approach management takes. Ethics seems both to forbid and to demand a strategic, profit-maximizing mind-set. The argument behind the paradox focuses on management's *fiduciary* duty to the stockholder, essentially the duty to keep a profit-maximizing promise, and a concern that the "impartiality" of the multi-fiduciary approach simply cuts management loose from certain well-defined bonds of stockholder accountability. On this view, impartiality is thought to be a *betrayal of trust*.

Professor David S. Ruder, a former chairman of the Securities and Exchange Commission, once summarized the matter this way:

> Traditional fiduciary obligation theory insists that a corporate manager owes an obligation of care and loyalty to shareholders. If a public obligation theory unrelated to profit maximization becomes the law, the corporate manager who is not able to act in his own self interest without violating his fiduciary obligation, may nevertheless act in the public interest without violating that obligations.[9] (226).

Ruder continued:
Whether induced by government legislation, government pressure, or merely by enlightened attitudes of the corporation regarding its long range potential as a unit in society, corporate activities carried on in satisfaction of public obligations can be consistent

with profit maximization objectives. In contrast, justification of public obligations upon bold concepts of public need without corporate benefit will merely serve to reduce further the owner's influence on his corporation and to create additional demands for public participation in corporate management. (228-9)

Ruder's view appears to be that (a) multi-fiduciary stakeholder synthesis *need not* be used by management because the strategic approach is more accommodating than meets the eye; and (b) multi-fiduciary stakeholder synthesis should not be invoked by management because such a "bold" concept could threaten the private (vs. public) status of the corporation.

In response to (a), we saw earlier that there were reasonable questions about the tidy convergence of ethics and economic success. Respecting the interests and rights of the Poletown residents might really have meant incurring higher costs for GM (short-term as well as long-term).

Appeals to corporate self-interest, even long-term, might not always support ethical decisions. But even on those occasions where they will, we must wonder about the disposition to favor economic and legal reasoning "for the record." If Ruder means to suggest that business leaders can often *reformulate* or *re-present* their reasons for certain morally-grounded decisions in strategic terms having to do with profit maximization and obedience to law, he is perhaps correct. In the spirit of our earlier quote from Milton Friedman, we might not summon much indignation to denounce them. But why the fiction? Why not call a moral reason a moral reason?

This issue is not simply of academic interest. Managers must confront it in practice. In one major public company, the C.E.O. put significant resources behind an affirmative action program and included the following explanation in a memo to middle management:

> I am often asked why this is such a high priority at our company. There is, of course, the obvious answer that it is in our best interest to seek out and employ good people in all sectors of our society. And there is the answer that enlightened self-interest tells us that more and more of the younger people, whom we must attract as future employees, choose companies by their social records as much as by their business prospects. *But the one overriding reason for this emphasis is because it is right.* Because this company has always set for itself the objective of assuming social as well as business obligations. Because that's the kind of company we have been. And with your participation, that's the kind of company we'll continue to be.[10]

In this connection, Ruder reminds us of what Professor Berle observed over twenty-five years ago:

> The fact is that boards of directors or corporation executives are often faced with situations in which they quite humanly and simply consider that such and such is the decent thing to do and ought to be done... They apply the potential profits or public relations tests later on, a sort of left-handed justification in this curious free-market world where an obviously moral or decent or humane action has to be apologized for on the ground that, conceivably, you may somehow make money by it. *(Ibid.)*

The Problem of Boldness
What appears to lie at the foundation of Ruder's cautious view is a concern about the "boldness" of the multi-fiduciary concept [(b) above].[11] It is not that he thinks the strategic approach is always satisfactory; it is that the multi-fiduciary approach is, in his eyes, much worse. For it questions the special relationship between the manager as agent and the stockholder as principal.

Ruder suggests that what he calls a "public obligation" theory threatens the private status of the corporation. He believes that what we are calling multi-fiduciary stakeholder synthesis *dilutes* the fiduciary obligation to stockholders (by extending it to customers, employees, suppliers, etc.) and he sees this as a threat to the "privacy" of the private sector organization. If public obligations are understood on the model of public sector institutions with their multiple constituencies, Ruder thinks, the stockholders loses status.

There is something profoundly *right* about Ruder's line of argument here, I believe, and something profoundly *wrong*. What is right is his intuition that if we treat other stakeholders on the model of the fiduciary relationship between management and the stockholder, we will, in effect, make them into quasi-stockholders. We can do this, of course, if we choose to as a society. But we should be aware that it is a radical step indeed. For it blurs traditional goals in terms of entrepreneurial risk-taking, pushes decision-making towards paralysis because of the dilemmas posed by divided loyalties and, in the final analysis, represents nothing less than the conversion of the modern private corporation into a public institution and probably calls for a corresponding restructuring of corporate governance (e.g., representatives of each stakeholder group on the board of directors). Unless we believe that the social utility of a private sector has disappeared, not to mention its value for individual liberty and enterprise, we will be cautious about an interpretation of stakeholder synthesis that transforms the private sector into the public sector.

On the other hand, I believe Ruder is mistaken if he thinks that business ethics requires this kind of either/or: either a private sector with a strategic stakeholder synthesis (business without ethics) or the effective loss of the private sector with a multi-fiduciary stakeholder synthesis (ethics without business).

Recent debates over state laws protecting companies against hostile takeovers may illustrate Ruder's concern as well as the new challenge. According to one journalist, a recent Pennsylvania anti-takeover law

> does no less than redefine the fiduciary duty of corporate directors, enabling them to base decisions not merely on the interests of shareholders, but on the interests of customers, suppliers, employees and the community at large. Pennsylvania is saying that it is the corporation that directors are responsible to. Shareholders say they always thought they themselves were the corporation.

Echoing Ruder, one legal observer quoted by Elias (*ibid.*) commented with reference to this law that it "undermines and erodes free markets and property rights. From this perspective, this is an anticapitalist law. The management can take away property from the real owners."

In our terms, the state of Pennsylvania is charged with adopting a multifiduciary stakeholder approach in an effort to rectify deficiencies of the strategic approach which (presumably) corporate raiders hold.

The challenge that we are thus presented with is to develop an account of the moral responsibilities of management that (i) avoids surrendering the moral relationship between management and stakeholders as the strategic view does, while (ii) not transforming stakeholder obligations into fiduciary obligations (thus protecting the uniqueness of the principal-agent relationship between management and stockholder).

II. Toward a New Stakeholder Synthesis

We all remember the story of the well-intentioned Doctor Frankenstein. He sought to improve the human condition by designing a powerful, intelligent force for good in the community. Alas, when he flipped the switch, his creation turned out to be a monster rather than a marvel! Is the concept of the ethical corporation like a Frankenstein monster?

Taking business ethics seriously need not mean that management bears *additional* fiduciary relationships to third parties (nonstockholder constituencies) as multi-fiduciary stakeholder synthesis suggests. It may mean that there are morally significant *nonfiduciary* obligations to third parties surrounding any fiduciary relationship (See *Figure I.*) Such moral obligations may be owed by private individuals as well as private-sector

Figure 1: Direct Managerial Obligations

	Fiduciary	Non-fiduciary
Stockholders	●	
Other Stakeholders		●

organizations to those whose freedom and well-being is affected by their economic behavior. It is these very obligations in fact (the duty not to harm or coerce and duties not to lie, cheat, or steal) that are cited in regulatory, legislative, and judicial arguments for constraining profit-driven business activities. These obligations are not "hypothetical" or contingent or indirect, as they would be on the strategic model, wherein they are only subject to the corporation's interests being met. They are "categorical" or direct. They are not rooted in the *fiduciary* relationship, but in other relationships at least as deep.

It must be admitted in fairness to Ruder's argument that the jargon of "stakeholders" in discussions of business ethics can seem to threaten the notion of what corporate law refers to as the "undivided and unselfish loyalty" owed by managers and directors to stockholders. For this way of speaking can suggest a multiplication of management duties *of the same kind* as the duty to stockholders. What we must understand is that the responsibilities of management toward stockholders are of a piece with the obligations that *stockholders themselves* would be expected to honor in their own right. As an old Latin proverb has it, *nemo dat quod non habet*, which literally means "nobody gives what he doesn't have." Freely translating in this context we can say: No one can expect of an agent behavior that is ethically less responsible than what he would expect of himself. I cannot (ethically) *hire* done on my behalf what I would not (ethically) do myself. We might refer to this as the "Nemo Dat Principle" (NDP) and consider it a formal requirement of consistency in business ethics (and professional ethics generally):

> (NDP) Investors cannot expect of managers (more generally, principals cannot expect of their agents) behavior that would be inconsistent with the reasonable ethical expectations of the community.[13]

The NDP does not, of course, resolve in advance the many ethical challenges that managers must face. It only indicates that these challenges are of a piece with those that face us all. It offers a different kind of test (and so a different kind of stakeholder synthesis) that management (and institutional investors) might apply to policies and decisions.

The foundation of ethics in management—and the way out of the stakeholder paradox—lies in understanding that the conscience of the corporation is a logical and moral extension of the consciences of its principals. It is *not* an expansion of the *list* of principals, but a gloss on the principal-agent relationship itself. Whatever the structure of the principal-agent relationship, neither principal nor agent can ever claim that an agent has "moral immunity" from the basic obligations that would apply to any human being toward other members of the community.

Indeed, consistent with Ruder's belief, the introduction of moral reasoning (distinguished from multi-fiduciary stakeholder reasoning) into the framework of management thinking may *protect* rather than threaten private sector legitimacy. The conscientious corporation can maintain its private economic mission, but in the context of fundamental moral obligations owed by any member of society to others affected by that member's actions. Recognizing such obligations does *not* mean that an institution is a public institution. Private institutions, like private individuals, can be and are bound to respect moral obligations in the pursuit of private purposes.

Conceptually, then, we can make room for a moral posture toward stakeholders that is both *partial* (respecting the fiduciary relationship between managers and stockholders) and impartial (respecting the equally important non-fiduciary relationships between management and other stakeholders). As philosopher Thomas Nagel has said, "In the conduct of life, of all places, the rivalry between the view from within and the view from without must be taken seriously".[14]

Whether this conceptual room can be used *effectively* in the face of enormous pressures on contemporary managers and directors is another story, of course. For it is one thing to say that "giving standing to stakeholders" in managerial reasoning is conceptually coherent. It is something else to say that it is practically coherent.

Yet most of us, I submit, believe it. Most of us believe that management at General Motors *owed* it to the people of Detroit and to the people of Poletown to take their (nonfiduciary) interests very seriously, to seek creative solutions to the conflict, to do more than use or manipulate them in accordance with GM's needs only. We understand that managers and directors have a special obligation to provide a financial return to the stockholders, but we also understand that the word "special" in this context needs to be tempered by an appreciation of certain fundamental community norms that go beyond the demands of both laws and markets. There are certain class-action suits that stockholders ought not to win. For there is sometimes a moral defense.

Conclusion

The relationship between management and stockholders is ethically different in kind from the relationship between management and other parties (like employees, suppliers, customers, etc.), a fact that seems to go unnoticed by the multi-fiduciary approach. If it were not, the corporation would cease to be a private sector institution and what is now called business ethics would become a more radical critique of our economic system than is typically thought. On this point, Milton Friedman must be given a fair and serious hearing.

This does not mean, however, that "stakeholders" lack a morally significant relationship to management, as the strategic approach implies. It means only that the relationship in question is different from a fiduciary one. Management may never have promised customers, employees, suppliers, etc. a "return on investment," but management is nevertheless obliged to take seriously its extra-legal obligations not to injure, lie to or cheat these stakeholders *quite apart from* whether it is in the stockholders' interests.

As we think through the *proper* relationship of management to stakeholders, fundamental features of business life must undoubtedly be recognized: that corporations have a principally economic mission and competence; that fiduciary obligations to investors and general obligations to comply with the law cannot be set aside; and that abuses of economic power and disregard of corporate stewardship in the name of business ethics are possible.

But these things must be recognized as well: that corporations are not solely financial institutions; that fiduciary obligations go beyond short-term profit and are in any case subject to moral criteria in their execution; and that mere compliance with the law can be unduly limited and even unjust.

The *Stakeholder Paradox* can be avoided by a more thoughtful understanding of the nature of moral obligation and the limits it imposes on the principal-agent relationship. Once we understand that there is a practical "space" for identifying the ethical values shared by a corporation and its stockholders—a space that goes beyond strategic self-interest but stops short of impartiality—the hard work of filling that space can proceed.

This paper derives from a conference in Applied Ethics, *Moral Philosophy in the Public Domain,* held at the University of British Columbia, in June 1990. It will also appear in an anthology currently in preparation at the UBC Centre of Applied Ethics.

1. Strictly speaking the historical meaning of "stakeholder" in this context is someone who literally *holds* the stakes during play.
2. See Goodpaster and Piper, *Managerial Decision Making and Ethical Values,* Harvard Business School Publishing Division, 1989.
3. See Goodpaster, PASCAL: A Framework For Conscientious Decision Making (1989).
4. Actually, there are subtle ways in which even the stakeholder identification or inventory process might have *some* ethical content. The very process of *identifying* affected parties involves the use of the imagination in a way that can lead to a natural empathetic or caring response to those parties in the synthesis, choice and action phases of decision-making. This is a contingent connection, however, not a necessary one.
5. Note that including powerless stakeholders in the analysis phase may indicate whether the decision-maker cares about "affecting" them or "being affected by" them. Also, the inclusion of what might be called secondary stakeholders as advocates for primary stakeholders (e.g., local governments on behalf of certain citizen groups) may signal the values that will come into play in any synthesis.
6. It should he mentioned that some authors, most notably Kenneth R. Andrews in *The Concept of Corporate Strategy* (Irwin, Third Edition, 1987) employ a broader and more social definition of "strategic" decision-making than the one implied here.
7. Freeman writes: "Theoretically, "stakeholder" must he able to capture a broad range of groups and individuals, even though when we put the concept to practical tests we must be willing to ignore certain groups who will have little or no impact on the corporation at this point in time." (52-3)
8. Ladd observed in a now-famous essay entitled "Morality and the Ideal of Rationality in Formal Organizations" (*The Monist,* 54, 1970) that organizational "rationality" was defined solely in terms of economic objectives: "The interests and needs of the individuals concerned, as individuals, must be considered only insofar as they establish limiting operating conditions. Organizational rationality dictates that these interests and needs must not be considered in their own right or on their own merits. If we think of an organization as a machine, it is easy to see why we cannot reasonably expect it to have any moral obligations to people or for them to have any to it." (507)
9. Public Obligations of Private Corporations, *U. of Pennsylvania Law Review,* 114 (1965). Ruder recently (1989) reaffirmed the views in his 1965 article.
10. "Business Products Corporation—Part 1," HBS Case Services 9-377-077.

[11] "The Business Judgement Rule" gives broad latitude to officers and directors of corporations, but calls for reasoning on the basis of the long-term economic interest of the company. And corporate case law ordinarily allows exceptions to profit-maximization criteria only when there are actual or potential *legal* barriers, and limits charitable and humanitarian gifts by the logic of long term self-interest. The underlying rationale is accountability to investors. Recent work by the American Law Institute, however, suggests a rethinking of these matters. See *Exhibit 2*.

[12] (Christopher Elias, "Turning Up the Heat on the Top," *Insight,* July 23, 1990).

[13] We might consider the NDP in broader terms that would include the relationship between "client" and "professional" in other contexts, such as law, medicine, education, government, and religion, where normally the community's expectations are embodied in ethical standards.

[14] T. Nagel, *The View from Nowhere,* Oxford U. Press (1986), p. 163.

Reprinted with permission of the *Business Ethics Quarterly* and the author.

Exhibit 1: Business decision-making and ethical values

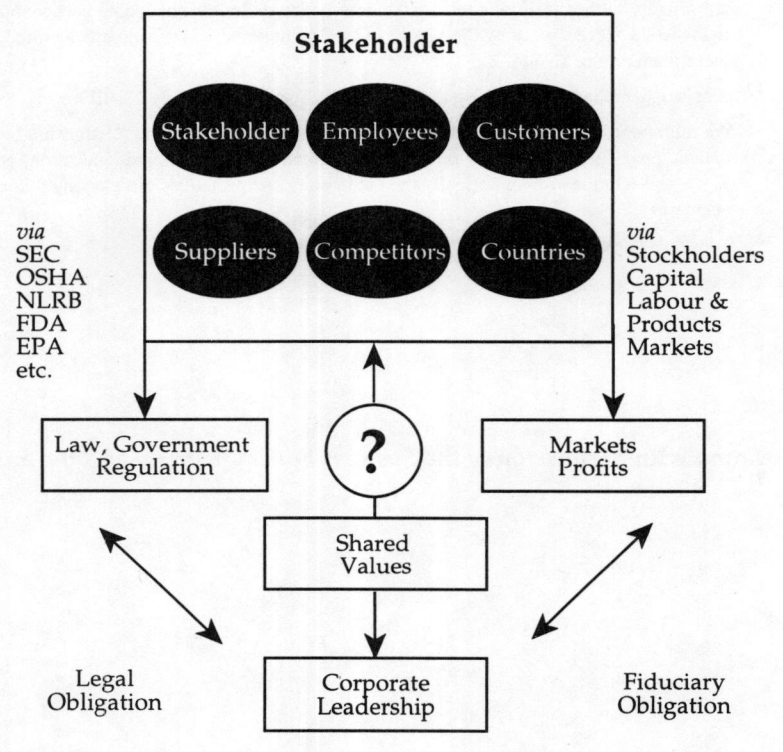

Exhibit 2

The American Law Institute

PRINCIPLES OF CORPORATE GOVERNANCE:
ANALYSIS AND RECOMMENDATIONS

Tentative Draft No. 2
(April 13, 1984)

Part II
THE OBJECTIVE AND CONDUCT OF THE BUSINESS CORPORATION

ANALYSIS AND RECOMMENDATION

§ 201. The Objective and Conduct of the Business Corporation

A business corporation should have as its objective the conduct of business activities with a view to enhancing corporate profit and shareholder gain, except that, whether or not corporate profit and shareholder gain are thereby enhanced, the corporation, in the conduct of its business

(a) is obliged, to the same extent as a natural person, to act within the boundaries set by law,

(b) may take into account ethical considerations that are reasonably regarded as appropriate to the responsible conduct of business, and

(c) may devote a reasonable amount of resources to public welfare, humanitarian, educational and philanthropic purposes.

A Stakeholder Theory of the Modern Corporation

R. Edward Freeman, *University of Virginia*

Introduction

> Corporations have ceased to be merely legal devices through which the private business transactions of individuals may be carried on. Though still much used for this purpose, the corporate form has acquired a larger significance. The corporation has, in fact, become both a method of property tenure and a means of organizing economic life. Grown to tremendous proportions, there may be said to have evolved a "corporate system"—which has attracted to itself a combination of attributes and powers, and has attained a degree of prominence entitling it to be dealt with as a major social institution.[1]

Despite these prophetic words of Berle and Means (1932), scholars and managers alike continue to hold sacred the view that managers bear a special relationship to the stockholders in the firm. Since stockholders own shares in the firm, they have certain rights and privileges, which must be granted to them by management, as well as by others. Sanctions, in the form of "the law of corporations," and other protective mechanisms in the form of social custom, accepted management practice, myth, and ritual, are thought to reinforce the assumption of the primacy of the stockholder.

The purpose of this paper is to pose several challenges to this assumption, from within the framework of managerial capitalism, and to suggest the bare bones of an alternative theory, *a stakeholder theory of the modern corporation*. I do not seek the demise of the modern corporation, either intellectually or in fact. Rather, I seek its transformation. In the words of Neurath, we shall attempt to "rebuild the ship, plank by plank, while it remains afloat."[2]

My thesis is that I can revitalize the concept of managerial capitalism by replacing the notion that managers have a duty to stockholders with the concept that managers bear a fiduciary relationship to stakeholders. Stakeholders are those groups who have a stake in or claim on the firm. Specifically I include suppliers, customers, employees, stockholders, and the local community, as well as management in its role as agent for these groups. I argue that the legal, economic, political, and moral challenges to the currently received theory of the firm, as a nexus of contracts among the owners of the factors of production and customers, require us to revise this concept. That is, each of these stakeholder groups has a right not to be treated as a means to some end, and therefore must participate in determining the future direction of the firm in which they have a stake.

The crux of my argument is that we must reconceptualize the firm around the following question: For whose benefit and at whose expense should the firm be managed? I shall set forth such a reconceptualization in the form of a *stakeholder theory of the firm*. I shall then critically examine the stakeholder view and its implications for the future of the capitalist system.

The Attack on Managerial Capitalism

The Legal Argument

The basic idea of managerial capitalism is that in return for controlling the firm, management vigorously pursues the interests of stockholders. Central to the managerial view of the firm is the idea that management can pursue market transactions with suppliers and customers in an unconstrained manner.

The law of corporations gives a less clearcut answer to the question: In whose interest and for whose benefit should the modern corporation be governed? While it says that the corporations should be run primarily in the interests of the stockholders in the firm, it says further that the corporation exists "in contemplation of the law" and has personality as a "legal person," limited liability for its actions, and immortality, since its existence transcends that of its members. Therefore, directors and other officers of the firm have a fiduciary obligation to stockholders in the sense that the "affairs of the corporation" must be conducted in the interest of the stockholders. And stockholders can theoretically bring suit against those directors and managers for doing otherwise. But since the corporation is a legal person, existing in contemplation of the law, managers of the corporation are constrained by law.

Until recently, this was no constraint at all. In this century, however, the law has evolved to effectively constrain the pursuit of stockholder interests at the expense of other claimants on the firm. It has, in effect, required that the claims of customers, suppliers, local communities, and employees be taken into consideration, though in general they are subordinated to the claims of stockholders.

For instance, the doctrine of "privity of contract," as articulated in *Winterbottom v. Wright* in 1842, has been eroded by recent developments in products liability law. Indeed, *Greenman v. Yuba Power* gives the manufacturer strict liability for damage caused by its products, even though the seller has exercised all possible care in the preparation and sale of the product and the consumer has not bought the product from nor entered into any contractual arrangement with the manufacturer. Caveat emptor has been replaced, in large part, with caveat venditor.[3] The Consumer Product Safety Commission has the power to enact product recalls, and in 1980 one U.S. automobile company recalled more cars than it built. Some industries are required to provide information to customers about a product's ingredients, whether or not the customers want and are willing to pay for this information.[4]

The same argument is applicable to management's dealings with employees. The National Labor Relations Act gave employees the right to unionize and to bargain in good faith. It set up the National Labor Relations Board to enforce these rights with management. The Equal Pay Act of 1963 and Title VII of the Civil Rights Act of 1964 constrain management from discrimination in hiring practices; these have been followed with the Age Discrimination in Employment Act of 1967.[5] The emergence of a body of administrative case law arising from labor-management disputes and the historic settling of discrimination claims with large employers such as AT&T have caused the emergence of a body of practice in the corporation that is consistent with the legal guarantee of the rights of the employees. The law has protected the due process rights of those employees who enter into collective bargaining agreements with management. As of the present, however, only 30 percent of the labor force are participating in such agreements; this has prompted one labor law scholar to propose a statutory law prohibiting dismissals of the 70 percent of the work force not protected.[6]

The law has also protected the interests of local communities. The Clean Air Act and Clean Water Act have constrained management from "spoiling the commons." In an historic case, *Marsh v. Alabama*, the Supreme Court ruled that a company-owned town was subject to the provisions of the U.S. Constitution, thereby guaranteeing the rights of local citizens and negating the "property rights" of the firm. Some states and municipalities have gone further and passed laws preventing firms from moving plants or limiting when and how plants can be closed. In sum, there is much current legal activity in this area to constrain management's pursuit of stockholders' interests at the expense of the local communities in which the firm operates.

I have argued that the result of such changes in the legal system can be viewed as giving some rights to those groups that have a claim on the firm, for example, customers, suppliers, employees, local communities, stockholders, and management. It raises the question, at the core of a theory of the firm: In whose interest and for whose benefit should the firm be managed? The answer proposed by managerial capitalism is clearly "the stockholders," but I have argued that the law has been progressively circumscribing this answer.

The Economic Argument
In its pure ideological form managerial capitalism seeks to maximize the interests of stockholders. In its perennial criticism of government regulation, management espouses the "invisible hand" doctrine. It contends that it creates the greatest good for the greatest number, and therefore government need not intervene. However, we know that externalities, moral hazards, and monopoly power exist in fact, whether or not they exist in theory. Further, some of the legal apparatus mentioned above has evolved to deal with just these issues.

The problem of the "tragedy of the commons" or the free-rider problem pervades the concept of public goods such as water and air. No one has an incentive to incur the cost of clean-up or the cost of nonpollution, since the marginal gain of one firm's action is small. Every firm reasons this way, and the result is pollution of water and air. Since the industrial revolution, firms have sought to internalize the benefits and externalize the costs of their actions. The cost must be borne by all, through taxation and regulation; hence we have the emergence of the environmental regulations of the 1970s.

Similarly, moral hazards arise when the purchaser of a good or service can pass along the cost of that good. There is no incentive to economize, on the part of either the producer or the consumer, and there is excessive use of the resources involved. The institutionalized practice of third-party payment in health care is a prime example.

Finally, we see the avoidance of competitive behavior on the part of firms, each seeking to monopolize a small portion of the market and not compete with one another. In a number of industries, oligopolies have emerged, and while there is questionable evidence that oligopolies are not the most efficient corporate form in some industries, suffice it to say that the potential for abuse of market power has again led to regulation of managerial activity. In the classic case, AT&T, arguably one of the great technological and managerial achievements of the century, was broken up into eight separate companies to prevent its abuse of monopoly power.

Externalities, moral hazards, and monopoly power have led to more external control on managerial capitalism. There are de facto constraints, due to these economic facts of life, on the ability of management to act in the interests of stockholders.

A Stakeholder Theory of the Firm

The Stakeholder Concept

Corporations have stakeholders, that is, groups and individuals who benefit from or are harmed by, and whose rights are violated or respected by, corporate actions. The concept of stakeholders is a generalization of the notion of stockholders, who themselves have some special claim on the firm. Just as stockholders have a right to demand certain actions by management, so do other stakeholders have a right to make claims. The exact nature of these claims is a difficult question that I shall address, but the logic is identical to that of the stockholder theory. Stakes require action of a certain sort, and conflicting stakes require methods of resolution.

Freeman and Reed (1983)[7] distinguish two senses of *stakeholder*. The "narrow definition" includes those groups who are vital to the survival and success of the corporation. The "wide-definition" includes any group or individual who can affect or is affected by the corporation. I shall begin with a modest aim: to articulate a stakeholder theory using the narrow definition.

Stakeholders in the Modern Corporation

Figure 1 depicts the stakeholders in a typical large corporation. The stakes of each are reciprocal, since each can affect the other in terms of harms and benefits as well as rights and duties. The stakes of each are not univocal and would vary by particular corporation. I merely set forth some general notions that seem to be common to many large firms.

Owners have financial stake in the corporation in the form of stocks, bonds, and so on, and they expect some kind of financial return from them. Either they have given money directly to the firm, or they have some historical claim made through a series of morally justified exchanges. The firm affects their livelihood or, if a substantial portion of their retirement income is in stocks or bonds, their ability to care for themselves when they can no longer work. Of course, the stakes of owners will differ by type of owner, preferences for money, moral preferences, and so on, as well as by type of firm. The owners of AT&T are quite different from the owners of Ford Motor Company, with stock of the former

Figure 1: A stakeholder model of the corporation

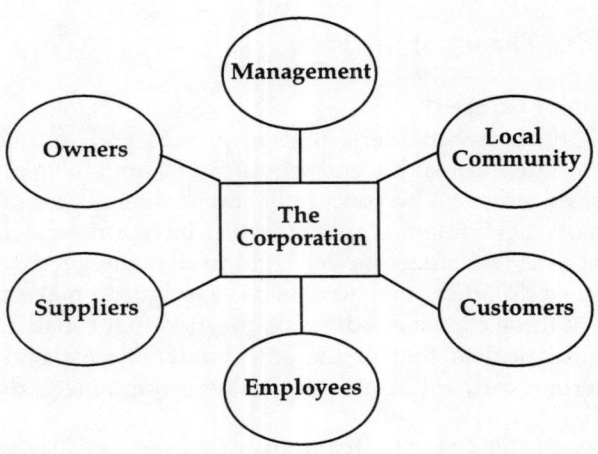

company being widely dispersed among 3 million stockholders and that of the latter being held by a small family group as well as by a large group of public stockholders.

Employees have their jobs and usually their livelihood at stake; they often have specialized skills for which there is usually no perfectly elastic market. In return for their labor, they expect security, wages, benefits, and meaningful work. In return for their loyalty, the corporation is expected to provide for them and carry them through difficult times. Employees are expected to follow the instructions of management most of the time, to speak favorably about the company, and to be responsible citizens in the local communities in which the company operates. Where they are used as means to an end, they must participate in decisions affecting such use. The evidence that such policies and values as described here lead to productive company-employee relationships is compelling. It is equally compelling to realize that the opportunities for "bad faith" on the part of both management and employees are enormous. "Mock participation" in quality circles, singing the company song, and wearing the company uniform solely to please management all lead to distrust and unproductive work.

Suppliers, interpreted in a stakeholder sense, are vital to the success of the firm, for raw materials will determine the final product's quality and price. In turn the firm is a customer of the supplier and is therefore vital to the success and survival of the supplier. When the firm treats the supplier as a valued member of the stakeholder network, rather than simply as a source of materials, the supplier will respond when the firm is in need. Chrysler traditionally had very close ties to its suppliers, even to the extent that led some to suspect the transfer of illegal payments. And when Chrysler was on the brink of disaster, the suppliers responded with price cuts, accepting late payments, financing, and so on. Supplier and company can rise and fall together. Of course, again, the particular supplier relationships will depend on a number of variables such as the number of suppliers and whether the supplies are finished goods or raw materials.

Customers exchange resources for the products of the firm and in return receive the benefits of the products. Customers provide the lifeblood of the firm in the form of revenue. Given the level of reinvestment of earnings in large corporations, customers indirectly pay for the development of new products and services. Peters and Waterman (1982)[8] have argued that being close to the customer leads to success with other stakeholders and that a distinguishing characteristic of some companies that have performed well is their emphasis on the customer. By paying attention to customers' needs, management automatically addresses the needs of suppliers and owners. Moreover, it seems that the ethic of customer service carries over to the community. Almost without fail the "excellent companies" in Peters and Waterman's study have good reputations in the community. I would argue that Peters and Waterman have found multiple applications of Kant's dictum, "Treat persons as ends unto themselves," and it should come as no surprise that persons respond to such respectful treatment, be they customers, suppliers, owners, employees, or members of the local community. The real surprise is the novelty of the application of Kant's rule in a theory of good management practice.

The local community grants the firm the right to build facilities and, in turn, it benefits from the tax base and economic and social contributions of the firm. In return for the provision of local services, the firm is expected to be a good citizen, as is any person, either "natural or artificial." The firm cannot expose the community to unreasonable hazards in the form of pollution, toxic waste, and so on. If for some reason the firm must leave a community, it is expected to work with local leaders to make the transition as smoothly as possible. Of course, the firm does not have perfect knowledge, but when it discovers some danger or runs afoul of new competition, it is expected to inform the local community and to work with the community to overcome any problem. When the firm mismanages its relationship with the local community, it is in the same position as a citizen who commits a crime. It has violated the implicit social contract with the community and should expect to be distrusted and ostracized. It should not be surprised when punitive measures are invoked.

I have not included "competitors" as stakeholders in the narrow sense, since strictly speaking they are not necessary for the survival and success of the firm; the stakeholder theory works equally well in monopoly contexts. However, competitors and government would be the first to be included in an extension of this basic theory. It is simply not true that the interests of competitors in an industry are always in conflict. There is no reason why trade associations and other multi-organizational groups cannot band together to solve common problems that have little to do with how to restrain trade. Implementation of stakeholder management principles, in the long run, mitigates the need for industrial policy and an increasing role for government intervention and regulation.

The Role of Management
Management plays a special role, for it too has a stake in the modern corporation. On the one hand, management's stake is like that of employees, with some kind of explicit or implicit employment contract. But, on the other hand, management has a duty of safeguarding the welfare of the abstract entity that is the corporation. In short, management, especially top management, must look after the health of the corporation, and this involves balancing the multiple claims of conflicting stakeholders. Owners want higher financial returns, while customers want more money spent on research and development. Employees want higher wages and better benefits, while the local community wants better parks and day-care facilities.

The task of management in today's corporation is akin to that of King Solomon. The stakeholder theory does not give primacy to one stakeholder group over another, though there will surely be times when one group will benefit at the expense of others. In general, however, management must keep the relationships among stakeholders in balance. When these relationships become imbalanced, the survival of the firm is in jeopardy.

When wages are too high and product quality is too low, customers leave, suppliers suffer, and owners sell their stocks and bonds, depressing the stock price and making it difficult to raise new capital at favorable rates. Note, however, that the reason for paying returns to owners is not that they "own" the firm, but that their support is necessary for the survival of the firm, and that they have a legitimate claim on the firm. Similar reasoning applies in turn to each stakeholder group.

A stakeholder theory of the firm must redefine the purpose of the firm. The stockholder theory claims that the purpose of the firm is to maximize the welfare of the stockholders, perhaps subject to some moral or social constraints, either because such maximization leads to the greatest good or because of property rights. The purpose of the firm is quite different in my view.

"The stakeholder theory" can be unpacked into a number of stakeholder theories, each of which has a "normative core," inextricably linked to the way that corporations should be governed and the way that managers should act. So, attempts to more fully define, or more carefully define, a stakeholder theory are misguided. Following Donaldson and Preston, I want to insist that the normative, descriptive, instrumental, and metaphorical (my addition to their framework) uses of 'stakeholder' are tied together in particular political constructions to yield a number of possible "stakeholder theories." "Stakeholder theory" is thus a genre of stories about how we could live. Let me be more specific.

A "normative core" of a theory is a set of sentences that includes among others, sentences like:

(1) Corporations ought to be governed...
(2) Managers ought to act to...

where we need arguments or further narratives which include business and moral terms to fill in the blanks. This normative core is not always reducible to a fundamental ground like the theory of property, but certain normative cores are consistent with modern understandings of property. Certain elaborations of the theory of private property plus the other institutions of political liberalism give rise to particular normative cores. But there are other institutions, other political conceptions of how society ought to be structured, so that there are different possible normative cores.

So, one normative core of a stakeholder theory might be a feminist standpoint one, rethinking how we would restructure "value-creating activity" along principles of caring and connection.[9] Another would be an ecological (or several ecological) normative cores. Mark Starik has argued that the very idea of a stakeholder theory of the *firm* ignores certain ecological necessities.[10] Exhibit 1 is suggestive of how these theories could be developed.

Exhibit 1:   *A reasonable pluralism*

	Corporations ought to be governed...	Managers ought to act...	The background disciplines of "value creation" are...
Doctrine of Fair Contracts	...in accordance with the six principles	...in the interests of stakeholders.	- business theories - theories that explain stakeholder behavior
Feminist Standpoint Theory	...in accordance with the principles of caring/connection and relationships.	...to maintain and care for relationships and networks of stakeholders.	- business theories - feminist theory - social science - understanding of networks
Ecological Principles	...in accordance with the principle of caring for the earth.	...to care for the earth.	- business theories - ecology - other

In the next section I shall sketch the normative core based on pragmatic liberalism. But, any normative core must address the questions in columns A or B, or explain why these questions may be irrelevant, as in the ecological view. In addition, each "theory," and I use the word hesitantly, must place the normative core within a more full-fledged account of how we could understand value-creating activity differently (column C). The only way to get on with this task is to see the stakeholder idea as a metaphor. The attempt to prescribe one and only one "normative core" and construct "a stakeholder theory" is at best a disguised attempt to smuggle a normative core past the unsophisticated noses of other unsuspecting academics who are just happy to see the end of the stockholder orthodoxy.

If we begin with the view that we can understand value-creation activity as a contractual process among those parties affected, and if for simplicity's sake we initially designate those parties as financiers, customers, suppliers, employees, and communities, then we can construct a normative core that reflects the liberal notions of autonomy, solidarity, and fairness as articulated by John Rawls, Richard Rorty, and others.[11] Notice that building these moral notions into the foundations of how we understand value creation and contracting requires that we eschew separating the "business" part of the process from the "ethical" part, and that we start with the presumption of equality among the contractors, rather than the presumption in favor of financier rights.

The normative core for this redesigned contractual theory will capture the liberal idea of fairness if it ensures a basic equality among stakeholders in terms of their moral rights as these are realized in the firm, and if it recognizes that inequalities among stakeholders are justified if they raise the level of the least well-off stakeholder. The liberal ideal of autonomy is captured by the realization that each stakeholder must be free to enter agreements that create value for themselves, and solidarity is realized by the recognition of the mutuality of stakeholder interests.

One way to understand fairness in this context is to claim *a la* Rawls that a contract is fair if parties to the contract would agree to it in ignorance of their actual stakes. Thus, a contract is like a fair bet, if each party is willing to turn the tables and accept the other side. What would a fair contract among corporate stakeholders look like? If we can articulate this ideal, a sort of corporate constitution, we could then ask whether actual corporations measure up to this standard, and we also begin to design corporate structures which are consistent with this Doctrine of Fair Contracts.

Imagine if you will, representative stakeholders trying to decide on "the rules of the game." Each is rational in a straightforward sense, looking out for its own self-interest. At least *ex ante*, stakeholders are the relevant parties since they will be materially affected. Stakeholders know how economic activity is organized and could be organized. They know general facts about the way the corporate world works. They know that in the real world there are or could be transaction costs, externalities, and positive costs of contracting. Suppose they are uncertain about what other social institutions exist, but they know the range of those institutions. They do not know if government exists to pick up the tab for any externalities, or if they will exist in the nightwatchman state of libertarian theory. They know success and failure stories of businesses around the world. In short, they are behind a Rawls-like veil of ignorance, and they do not know what stake each will have when the veil is lifted. What groundrules would they choose to guide them?

The first groundrule is "The Principle of Entry and Exit." Any contract that is the corporation must have clearly defined entry, exit, and renegotiation conditions, or at least it must have methods or processes for so defining these conditions. The logic is straightforward: each stakeholder must be able to determine when an agreement exists and has a chance of fulfillment. This is not to imply that contracts cannot contain contingent claims or other methods for resolving uncertainty, but rather that it must contain methods for determining whether or not it is valid.

The second groundrule I shall call "The Principle of Governance," and it says that the procedure for changing the rules of the game must be agreed upon by unanimous consent. Think about the consequences of a majority of stakeholders systematically "selling out" a minority. Each stakeholder, in ignorance of its actual role, would seek to avoid such a situation. In reality this principle translates into each stakeholder never giving up its right to participate in the governance of the corporation, or perhaps into the existence of stakeholder governing boards.

The third groundrule I shall call "The Principle of Externalities," and it says that if a contract between A and B imposes a cost on C, then C has the option to become a party to the contract, and the terms are renegotiated. Once again the rationality of this condition is clear. Each stakeholder will want insurance that it does not become C.

The fourth groundrule is "The Principle of Contracting Costs," and it says that all parties to the contract must share in the cost of contracting. Once again the logic is straightforward. Any one stakeholder can get stuck.

A fifth groundrule is "The Agency Principle" that says that any agent must serve the interests of all stakeholders. It must adjudicate conflicts within the bounds of the other principals. Once again the logic is clear. Agents for any one group would have a privileged place.

A sixth and final groundrule we might call, "The Principle of Limited Immortality." The corporation shall be managed as if it can continue to serve the interests of stakeholders through time. Stakeholders are uncertain about the future but, subject to exit conditions, they realize that the continued existence of the corporation is in their interest. Therefore, it would be rational to hire managers who are fiduciaries to their interest and the interest of the collective. If it turns out the "collective interest" is the empty set, then this principle simply collapses into the Agency Principle.

Thus, the Doctrine of Fair Contracts consists of these six groundrules or principles:

(1) The Principle of Entry and Exit
(2) The Principle of Governance
(3) The Principle of Externalities
(4) The Principle of Contracting Costs
(5) The Agency Principle
(6) The Principle of Limited Immortality

Think of these groundrules as a doctrine which would guide actual stakeholders in devising a corporate constitution or charter. Think of management as having the duty to act in accordance with some specific constitution or charter.

Obviously, if the Doctrine of Fair Contracts and its accompanying background narratives are to effect real change, there must be requisite changes in the enabling laws of the land. I propose the following three principles to serve as constitutive elements of attempts to reform the law of corporations.

The Stakeholder Enabling Principle
Corporations shall be managed in the interests of its stakeholders, defined as employees, financiers, customers, employees, and communities.

The Principle of Director Responsibility
Directors of the corporation shall have a duty of care to use reasonable judgment to define and direct the affairs of the corporation in accordance with the Stakeholder Enabling Principle.

The Principle of Stakeholder Recourse
Stakeholders may bring an action against the directors for failure to perform the required duty of care.

Obviously, there is more work to be done to spell out these principles in terms of model legislation. As they stand, they try to capture the intuitions that drive the liberal ideals. It is equally plain that corporate constitutions which meet a test like the doctrine of fair contracts are meant to enable directors and executives to manage the corporation in conjunction with these same liberal ideals.

Portions of this essay are contained in William E. Evan and R. Edward Freeman, "A Stakeholder Theory of the Modern Corporation: Kantian Capitalism" published in the third (1988) and fourth (1993) edition of this anthology and in R. Edward Freeman, "The Politics of Stakeholder Theory," *Business Ethics Quarterly*, 4 (1994), pp. 409-21. I am grateful to the editors of this volume for their editing of these two works. Used by permission.

R. Edward Freeman is the Elis and Signe Olsson Professor of Business Administration and Director of the Olsson Centre for Applied Ethics at the Darden School at the University of Virginia.

---

[1] Cf. A. Berle and G. Means, *The Modern Corporation and Private Property* (New York: Commerce Clearing House, 1932), 1. For a reassessment of Berle and Means' argument after 50 years, see *Journal of Law and Economics* 26 (June 1983), especially G. Stigler and C. Friedland, "The Literature of Economics: The Case of Berle and Means," 237-68; D. North, "Comment on Stigler and Friedland," 269-72; and G. Means, "Corporate Power in the Marketplace," 467-85.

2   The metaphor of rebuilding the ship while afloat is attributed to Neurath by W. Quine, *Word and Object* (Cambridge: Harvard University Press, 1960), and W. Quine and J. Ullian, *The Web of Belief* (New York: Random House, 1978). The point is that to keep the ship afloat during repairs we must replace a plank with one that will do a better job. Our argument is that stakeholder capitalism can so replace the current version of managerial capitalism.

3   See R. Charan and E. Freeman, "Planning for the Business Environment of the 1980s," *The Journal of Business Strategy* 1 (1980): 9-19, especially p. 15 for a brief account of the major developments in products liability law.

4   See S. Breyer, *Regulation and Its Reform* (Cambridge: Harvard University Press, 1983), 133, for an analysis of food additives.

5   See I. Millstein and S. Katsh, *The Limits of Corporate Power* (New York: Macmillan, 1981), Chapter 4.

6   Cf. C. Summers, "Protecting All Employees Against Unjust Dismissal," *Harvard Business Review* 58 (1980): 136, for a careful statement of the argument.

7   See E. Freeman and D. Reed, "Stockholders and Stakeholders: A New Perspective on Corporate Governance," in C. Huizinga, ed., *Corporate Governance: A Definitive Exploration of the Issues* (Los Angeles: UCLA Extension Press, 1983).

8   See T. Peters and R. Waterman, *In Search of Excellence* (New York: Harper and Row, 1982).

9   See, for instance, A. Wicks, D. Gilbert, and E. Freeman, "A Feminist Reinterpretation of the Stakeholder Concept," *Business Ethics Quarterly*, Vol. 4, No. 4, October 1994; and E. Freeman and J. Liedtka, "Corporate Social Responsibility: A Critical Approach," *Business Horizons*, Vol. 34, No. 4, July-August 1991, pp. 92-98.

10 At the Toronto workshop Mark Starik sketched how a theory would look if we took the environment to be a stakeholder. This fruitful line of work is one example of my main point about pluralism.

11 J. Rawls, *Political Liberalism*, New York: Columbia University Press, 1993; and R. Rorty, "The Priority of Democracy to Philosophy" in *Reading Rorty: Critical Responses to Philosophy and the Mirror of Nature (and Beyond)*, ed. Alan R. Malachowski, Cambridge, MA: Blackwell, 1990.

Reprinted with the permission of the author.

Stakeholder Thinking in Three Models of Management Morality: A Perspective with Strategic Implications

Archie B. Carroll, University of Georgia

The general theme of stakeholder thinking is an appropriate and effective way of articulating a whole host of concerns which surround the stakeholder concept or the stakeholder theory of the firm. More than anything else, it seems, the stakeholder concept envisions a way of thinking about organizations and managers' actions within and about organizations. More particularly, stakeholder thinking provides a concept for articulating, expressing, analysing and understanding managers in their relationships with individuals and groups "out there in the environment" known as stakeholders. At a broader level, stakeholder thinking helps us understand the business and society relationship.

Prior writings on stakeholder thinking have focused on theory development (Brenner and Cochran, 1991; Donaldson & Preston, 1994; Freeman, 1984), approaches for viewing groups with which management must interact (Goodpaster, 1991), operationalizing theory (Weber, 1992), strategies for managing stakeholders (Macmillan & Jones, 1986; Savage, Nix, Whitehead & Blair, 1991), assessing corporate social performance (Clarkson, 1991, 1994; Lamb, 1994), understanding management morality (Halme and Näsi, 1992), examining the stakeholder expectations of boards of directors (Huse, 1994), studying organizational justice (Husted, 1994), evaluating new ventures (Mitchell, 1994), investigating corporate governance and green values (Halme, Huse and Jystad, 1994), studying strategies in a conflict process (Näsi, Näsi and Savage, 1994), and understanding the business and society relationship (Carroll, 1993).

Two notable arenas in which stakeholder thinking has especially proven valuable include business ethics (or business morality) and strategic management (or strategic decision making). In the former, the theoretical perspective is often thought to be normative. In the latter, the perspective is often perceived to be instrumental. In each of these spheres stakeholder thinking has provided academics and managers alike with a useful, indeed a powerful, framework for description, analysis and prescription in the realm of organization-environment relationships.

This paper will focus on the applicability of stakeholder thinking in conceptualizing and understanding and extending what might be termed three models, types or patterns of management morality. At the same time, the strategic implications of these models of morality will be explored. The basic contours of these three models of management morality have been described in earlier works (Carroll, 1987, 1991). In this paper our goal is to develop these models more fully with a particular focus on the use of stakeholder thinking as an instrument by which these archetypes might be amplified and related to strategic management and strategic decision making.

In pursuing this objective, four major sections will follow. First, we will discuss corporate social responsibility (CSR) as a point of departure. Second, we will outline the basic characteristics of the three models of management morality. Third, we will examine ways in which stakeholder management as a special kind of stakeholder thinking provides a more robust understanding of the three morality types. Finally, we will examine strategic implications in the three models via stakeholder thinking. Through description and example, our purpose will be to demonstrate the utility of stakeholder thinking in grasping important ethics and strategy ideas for organizational management.

Corporate Social Responsibility as a Point of Departure

The concepts of corporate social responsibility, responsiveness and performance are essential ingredients or building blocks in developing our ideas in this discussion. Theodore Kreps articulated the view that individuals were concerned with the appraisal of businesses' social performance as early as the late 1930s. During that time, however, issues which were primarily economic in nature (employment, production, payrolls) were considered to be indicators of businesses' social contribution (Kreps, 1940). The modern era of social responsibility might be marked by Howard Bowen's 1953 volume, *Social Responsibilities of the Businessman*. (Apparently there were no business*women* in those days, or people did not acknowledge them). Like Kreps before him, Bowen even went so far as to suggest that *social audits* should be conducted—that is, evaluations of the performance of business from a social point of view (Carroll and Beiler, p.598).

From the 1950s to the 1970s many academics contributed to an evolving understanding of what social responsibility really meant (for example, Cheit, Davis & Blomstrom, McGuire, and Steiner). In 1975, S. Prakash Sethi set forth a useful three-state schema for classifying the adaptation of corporate behavior to social needs: social obligation, social responsibility and social responsiveness. Other notable contributors to CSR concepts during 1970s to early 1990s included Davis (1960), Ackerman and Bauer (1976), Backman (1975), Bowman and Haire (1975), Frederick (1978), Preston and Post (1975), Carroll (1979), Wartick and Cochran (1985) and Wood (1991).

In 1979 this author set forth a three dimensional corporate social performance model. The three dimensions or aspects of the model addressed major questions of concern to academics and managers alike: (1) What all is included in the concept of corporate social responsibility? (2) What are the social (or stakeholder) issues that organizations must address? and (3) What is or ought to be the organization's philosophy or mode of social responsiveness? (Carroll, 1979). Of concern here is the first dimension which sought to provide a basic definition of corporate social responsibility (CSR) by identifying the types or components of CSR which comprised the total CSR of business. The definition sought to embrace businesses' legitimate economic or profit-making function with responsibilities which extended beyond the basic economic role of the firm. Or, as Lerner and Fryxell (1994, p.60) observed, "Carroll's framework is significant in that it integrates economic obligations into CSR rather than treating them as antithetical."

The following comprehensive definition of CSR was set forth, therefore, in a partial effort to reconcile the business firm's economic orientation with its social orientation. The four-part definition or conceptualization contended that CSR embraced the notion that the corporation has not only economic obligations, but *legal, ethical* and *discretionary (philanthropic)* responsibilities as well (Carroll, 1979). In equation form, this definition postulated that:

Total Corporate Social Responsibility = Economic Responsibility + Legal Responsibility + Ethical Responsibility + Discretionary (Philanthropic) Responsibility

Other writings have provided more elaborate discussions of each of these four components (see for example, Carroll, 1979, 1991, 1993). We should add for purposes of this discussion that all of the four kinds of responsibilities, though not mutually exclusive, are vital components to achieving a comprehensive concept of CSR. It is particularly important to note that the ethical component, which we will discuss more fully later is viewed as one distinct element while at the same time we understand that each of the other three components also are infused or embedded with ethical issues or overtones.

A brief explanation of each of the definition's four components of CSR is in order. *Economic responsibilities* refer to businesses' fundamental call to be a profit making enterprise. Though it may seem odd to think of this as a "social" responsibility, this is, in effect what it is. First and foremost, the capitalistic system calls for business to be an economic institution. Profit making is an essential ingredient of a free enterprise economy. One of the major problems managers and academics alike have had in understanding and accepting CSR is that economic and social functions and roles are often viewed as hostile to one another rather than complementary (Carroll, 1993). Figure 1 presents some attributes and examples of businesses' economic as well as its' legal, ethical and discretionary (or philanthropic) responsibilities.

Just as society has sanctioned our economic system by permitting business to assume the economic role of producing goods and services and selling them at a profit, it has also laid down certain ground rules—laws—under which business is expected to pursue its fundamental economic role. *Legal responsibilities,* therefore, reflect a view of "codified ethics" in the sense that they embody basic notions of fairness or business righteousness.

Ethical responsibilities embrace those activities, practices or behaviors that are expected (in a positive sense) or prohibited (in a negative sense) by societal members though they are not codified into laws. Ethical responsibilities embrace the range of norms, standards or expectations of behavior that reflect a concern for what consumers, employees, shareholders and the community regard as fair, right, just, or in keeping with the respect for or protection of stakeholders' moral rights (Carroll, 1991, 39-48). Figure 1 summarizes some of businesses' legal and ethical responsibilities.

Discretionary/Philanthropic responsibilities include businesses' obligation to engage in social activities that are not mandated, not required by law and not generally expected of business in an ethical sense. The subtle distinction between ethical and discretionary/philanthropic responsibilities is that the latter are not expected with the same degree of force in a moral or ethical sense. In other words, if a firm did not give philanthropically to the extent that certain stakeholder groups expected of it, the stakeholders would not likely label the firm as unethical or immoral. The philanthropic responsibility does not carry with it the same degree of moral mandate as does the ethical responsibility of business. Figure 1 summarizes some examples of the discretionary responsibility category.

Figure 1: CSR components and their societal, managerial and normative attributes

Component of CSR	Societal Expectation	Illustrative Business Behavior/Decisions	Normative Prescription
Economic Responsibility	REQUIRED of business by society	Maximize sales revenue Minimize costs Make wise strategic decisions Be attentive to dividend policy	Be Profitable
Legal Responsibility	REQUIRED of business by society	Be responsive to international, federal, state and local laws, regulations and codes Environmental laws Consumer laws Employee laws	Obey the Law
Ethical Responsibility	EXPECTED of business by society	Avoid questionable practices Respond to "spirit" of laws Assume law is a "floor" on behavior: Operate at a level above that required Assert ethical leadership	Be Ethical
Discretionary/ Philanthropic Responsibility	DESIRED of business by society	Corporate contributions/philanthropy Community/education programs Executive loan programs Employee volunteerism	Be a Good Corporate Citizen

In summary, the total CSR of business entails the simultaneous fulfillment of the business firm's economic, legal, ethical and discretionary/philanthropic responsibilities as expected by society and moral reasoning at a point in time. Stated in more pragmatic or positive terms, the CSR firm should strive to make a profit, obey the law, engage in ethical behavior and be a good corporate citizen.

Though this four-part construct of CSR was not conceptualized as a stakeholder view of CSR in 1979 when it was first presented (i.e., Ed Freeman had not yet popularized the stakeholder concept), it is clearly reflective of stakeholder thinking when one considers the stakeholders implicitly addressed and affected in each of the four components. Figure 2 illustrates how each of the four CSR components, in actuality, is concerned with a different prioritization of stakeholders.

Figure 2: *A stakeholder view of corporate social responsibility (CSR)*

CSR Component	Stakeholder group addressed and affected				
	Owners	Consumers	Employees	Community	Others
CSR: Economic	1	4	2	3	5
CSR: Legal	3	2	1	4	5
CSR: Ethical	4	1	2	3	5
CSR: Philanthropic	3	4	2	1	5

Numbers in cells suggest the prioritization of stakeholders addressed and affected within each CSR Component. Numbers are illustrative only.

Implicit in Figure 2 is the idea that each stakeholder group has a "bottom line" that is affected by the corporation's social performance in each component of the CSR definition. For the firm as a whole, this perspective suggests that business faces many different "bottom lines," not just the financial one that is so often singularly identified.

Our goal in this first section has been to set forth a basic view or understanding of CSR that will serve as a "building block" in our discussion. Of particular significance is the ethical responsibility which establishes the foundation for our further examination of moral management models. These models, it should be stressed, are imbedded in a view of CSR which establishes the context and legitimacy of their expression. In the next section we will present three models of management morality and relate them to the definition of CSR thus far developed.

Three Types of Management Morality

The purpose of developing three models of management morality at this juncture is to establish a basis upon which we might expound upon the linkages between the firm's ethical responsibilities and its major stakeholder groups. In addition, it is desirable to illustrate how the three ethical models, or types, view the CSR components previously described. In this section "isolating" the ethical component of our CSR definition and discussing it more fully in terms of different perspectives in which it might be viewed.

Traditionally, major business ethics principles have been utilized as an approach to conceptualizing the topic. Principles such as rights, justice and utilitarianism have been used as the springboard for evaluating company and managerial actions and decisions as being either "ethical" or "unethical." We will take an alternative approach here and describe three models or types of ethical or moral behavior which we believe serve as exemplars to grasp the reality of management practices. These three models were initially described in other works (Carroll, 1987, 1991).

It is common in business ethics literature to think of the terms "ethics" and "morality" as essentially synonymous in the organizational context, though subtle distinctions could be drawn between them. For practical purposes, however, such distinctions are seldom made. Using the language of business morality for purposes of denominating these three models or types, we would argue that there are three major ethical types or approaches—immoral management, amoral management and moral management.

Though we use these terms to describe different types of managers or management, it is tempting to make the intuitive leap that is often made and to categorize organizations as a whole with these same descriptors. We must be cautious doing this, however, for seldom do we encounter an entire organization that is so completely infused with one of these pure moral types that we can justify such a generalization. Furthermore, theorists have long observed that it is people within organization's that act or behave and not the organizations per se.

In our study of managers, managerial behavior and organizations, we have come to the conclusion that it is often an oversimplification to think of behavior or decisions in either—or terms such as moral or immoral. For this reason we are proposing that a third category—amoral—is necessary and at this point these three types or models will be briefly profiled. We will take the two extreme types first for they are easier to describe.

Immoral Management
Immoral management is characterized by those managers whose decisions, actions or behavior suggest an active opposition to what is deemed ethical or right. The decisions of immoral managers are discordant with accepted principles of ethical behavior. These behaviors or decisions suggest or imply an active negation of what is moral. These managers are focused on their own personal success or their organization's success to the exclusion of consideration for other stakeholders. These managers see ethics and law as barriers or impediments they must overcome to accomplish their goals (Carroll, 1987).

In the U.S. during the late 1980s, the Savings and Loan Association debacle dominated the news. Within that context, Charles Keating was thought by many to personify the immoral manager. The federal government argued that Keating recklessly and fraudulently ran California's Lincoln Savings into the ground, reaping $34 million for himself and his family. Regarding Keating's actions, a major accounting firm said: "Seldom in our experience as accountants have we experienced a more egregious example of the misapplication of generally accepted accounting principles" (Forbes, 1989).

Another major scandal which might be classified as immoral management involved the Phar-Mor drugstore chain in the U.S. One lawyer who served as counsel to the examiner in what eventually became the Phar-Mor bankruptcy case, said that the examiner's report revealed a compelling case of fraud and corruption (Williger, 1994). It was revealed that Phar-Mor executives kept two sets of records—an official ledger that they sometimes manipulated with false entries and another where they kept track of the false entries. It now appears that losses to Phar-Mor stemming from internal fraud has reached $1 billion. The case involved embezzlement and other forms of fraud by top management (Stern, 1994). The fraud led to bankruptcy resulting in the billion dollar loss to shareholders and the forced layoff of thousands of employees.

Moral Management
At the opposite extreme from the immoral management model is the moral management model. If the immoral managers are the paradigm for the "bad guys," then moral managers are exemplars for the "good guys". Moral managers employ and adhere to ethical norms which reflect a high standard of right behavior. Moral managers not only conform to accepted and high levels of professional conduct, they also frequently exhibit ethical leadership. Moral managers strive towards profits also, but their pursuit of profits is done within the confines of sound legal and ethical precepts such as justice, due process and the protection of stakeholders' rights. Moral managers comply both with the letter and the spirit of laws. The law is seen as a minimum or floor on ethical behavior. Moral managers strive to operate well above and beyond what law mandates. Sound moral principles such as justice, rights, utilitarianism and the Golden Rule are employed to guide decision making and conduct (Carroll, 1987).

A couple of examples of moral management are useful. When McCullough Corporation withdrew from the national Chain Saw Manufacturer's Association because the association fought mandatory safety standards for the dangerous saws, this was moral management. McCullough knew its industry's products were dangerous and had put chain brakes on its saws years before even though it was not required by law to do so. Ethical leadership of this kind manifests moral management.

Another well known case of moral management occurred when Merck and Co. invested millions of dollars to develop a treatment for river blindness, a Third World disease affecting almost 18 million people. Seeing that no government or aid organization was agreeing to buy the drug. Merck pledged to supply the drug free forever. Merck's recognition that no effective mechanism existed to distribute the drug led to their decision to go far beyond industry practice and organize a committee to oversee the distribution (Business Enterprise Trust, 1994).

Amoral Management
Amoral managers are neither immoral nor moral but are not sensitive to or aware of the fact that their everyday business decisions may have deleterious effects on other stakeholders. These managers lack ethical perception or awareness. That is, they go through their organizational lives not thinking that their actions have an ethical dimension. Or, they may just be careless or insensitive to the implications of their actions on stakeholders. These managers may be well intentioned, but they do not see that their business decisions and actions may be hurting those with whom they transact business or interact. Typically their orientation is towards the letter of the law as their ethical guide. We have been describing a sub-category of amorality known as unintentional amoral managers. There is also another group we may call intentional amoral managers. These managers simply think that ethical considerations are for our private lives, not for business. They believe that business activity resides outside the sphere to which moral judgments apply. Though most amoral managers today are unintentional, there may still exist a few who simply do not see a role for ethics in business or management decision making (Carroll, 1987).

Examples of unintentional amorality abound. When police departments stipulated that applicants must be 5'10" and weigh 180 pounds to qualify for positions, they just did not think about the adverse impact their policy would have on women and some ethnic groups who, on average, do not attain that height and weight. The liquor, beer, and cigarette industries provide other examples. They did not anticipate that their products would create serious moral issues: alcoholism, drunk driving deaths, lung cancer, deteriorating health, and offensive secondary smoke. Finally, when McDonald's initially decided to use polystyrene containers for food packaging it just did not adequately consider the environmental impact that would be caused. McDonald's surely does not intentionally create a solid waste disposal problem, but one major consequence of its business is just that. To its credit, the company has responded to complaints by replacing the polystyrene packaging with paper products. Such a decision manifests movement from the amoral to the moral category. Amorality, like immorality, is basically antithetical to stakeholder thinking.

Moral Models and CSR
Now that the three models of management morality have been described, we would like to identify how each of the three types regard the four components of the CSR definition presented in the previous section. Figure 3 suggests one view of how the three moral types might regard the importance of the CSR components.

Figure 3: Three models of management morality and their views on CSR

	Components of the CSR definition			
Models of management morality	Economic responsibility	Legal responsibility	Ethical responsibility	Philanthropic responsibility
Immoral Management	✓✓✓	✓		✓
Amoral Management	✓✓✓	✓✓	✓	✓
Moral Management	✓✓✓	✓✓✓	✓✓✓	✓✓✓

Weighting code:
✓ = token consideration (appearances only)
✓✓ = moderate consideration
✓✓✓ = significant consideration

It is clear from Figure 3, that the moral management model completely fulfills the definition of CSR while the amoral management type only minimally or moderately fulfills the CSR definition. The immoral management model simply does not live up to anyone's definition of CSR. If we relate this discussion back to Figure 2, we can conclude that immoral managers care only about owner stakeholders (or, if the truth were known, themselves). Amoral managers care about owners, or themselves as agents of the owners, primarily, with only moderate consideration given to their legal responsibilities to consumers and employees. The community and others are afforded only token consideration. Moral managers give significant consideration to the entire gamut of stakeholders.

In the next section we will describe more fully how the three moral management models or types regard the potential levels of stakeholder management and provide specific insights as to how they would likely value the major stakeholders of the firm.

Stakeholder Management and the Moral Models
As we transition from discussing "stakeholders" or the "stakeholder approach" to a more applied concept known as "stakeholder management", it should be clarified at the outset about the purpose to which this applied term will be put. In Freeman's *Strategic Management: A Stakeholder*

Approach (1984) one is left with the distinct impression that the concepts are introduced primarily for the benefit of improving the organization's *strategic* management, for that was the theme of his book. Though values and societal issues are introduced and made a part of the strategic management process, the stakeholder approach is not advanced specifically as a perspective on managing ethically.

At this point it should be emphasized that stakeholder thinking or stakeholder management is useful for *just* managing strategically (akin to Goodpaster's strategic approach), *just* managing ethically (akin to Goodpaster's multifiduciary view) or, ideally, *both* (akin to Goodpaster's stakeholder synthesis view, 1991). In this section, we will take Freeman's concept of "stakeholder management capability" (SMC) which he presents more as a management tool and discuss how it is imbued with ethical implications by relating it to the three moral management models presented earlier. The objective will be to describe briefly the levels of SMC, identify Starik's elaborations of Freeman's three levels and to discuss the moral management model which best fits with each level.

Freeman's three levels of stakeholder management capability include the following: (1) the "rational" level, (2) the "process" level, and (3) the "transactional" level. Freeman states that these three levels parallel Graham Allison's (1971) three levels of organizational analysis (Allison, 1971). He further argues that the firm that fulfills all three levels has high or superior SMC whereas the firm that only fulfills level one has low or inferior SMC (Freeman, pp. 53-74). Thus, to transition from level one to level three is tantamount to improving upon one's stakeholder management, or stakeholder thinking.

Level one—the rational level. At the rational level, the organization identifies its stakeholders and their stakes. The appropriate question at this level is "who are our stakeholders and what are their stakes?" A "stakeholder map" is often used to identify those groups and individuals who can affect and are affected by the achievement of the organization's purposes. The typical organization today would enumerate among its stakeholders such groups as customers, employees, owners, suppliers, competitors, government, the media and a host of special interest groups. The identification of stakeholders might run its course from generic groups (customers, employees, owners) to a more specific identification of sub-groups with specific "names and faces." Stakeholder attributes such as "nature/type of stake" and "power" might also be identified at level one. It could well be argued that most business organizations today have achieved level one SMC though many of these will not have closely examined nature of stake (legitimacy) or power. Stakeholder initiatives today in business are often driven by management's perception of the "urgency" (a purely pragmatic perspective) of the needed response. As will be argued later, it is doubtful that Immoral Managers have even taken the time to achieve level one status.

Level two—the process level. Since many large, complex organizations have institutionalized processes for accomplishing tasks, we should not be surprised that some of these processes are targeted towards managing stakeholders better. Strategically-oriented processes might include portfolio analysis or strategic review processes where firms are striving to decide what businesses they should be in. Stakeholder-oriented processes might include such approaches as environmental scanning (to include futures research, scenario building trend analysis), issues management or crisis management. These processes are often "housed" in such departments as corporate public affairs, external affairs or public relations. Quite typically these processes entail no actual interactions with stakeholder groups but, rather, are geared toward gathering information which the organization might deem useful in its strategic management processes. It could be suggested that organizations which operate at level two tend to be populated with Amoral Managers just seeking to do a better job of fulfilling their financial mission.

Level three—the transactional level. At this third level of SMC, Freeman argues that we reach the "bottom line" for stakeholder management, that set of transactions or interactions managers have with stakeholders. Another key issue at this level are the resources the organization allocates to interact with each group. It is clear at this level that organizations which are truly "stakeholder serving" are characterized by frequent, high-quality interactions with their stakeholders. Starik (1990) posits that Freeman's third level is predicated upon communication effectiveness and that such communication efforts must be characterized by proactiveness, interactiveness, genuineness, frequency satisfaction and resource adequacy.

Our position here would be that this is the level which most frequently would be populated by Moral Managers. Figure 4 portrays our discussion in this section by suggesting an alignment among Freeman's SMC levels, Starik's stakeholder management components and Carroll's three moral models.

Some brief discussion of Figure 4 is useful. In the Immoral Management model, it is clear that no kind of meaningful stakeholder recognition has taken place. In the Immoral Management model, the firm and its managers are self absorbed. Immoral manager's motives are selfish. Management cares only about its or the company's gain. The goal is profitability and success at any price. Legal requirements, which to the average manager might be perceived as "moral minimums" are seen as barriers that management must overcome to accomplish what it wants. The strategy here is to exploit opportunities for corporate gain and to cut corners when it appears useful. Quite often the orientation of immoral managers is "what's in it for me?" with the organization itself frequently assuming second-class status to the personal gains of the managers.

Figure 4: A suggested alignment of Freeman's, Starick's and Carroll's stakeholder and moral management concepts

Freeman's (1984) SMC Level	Starik's (1990) Stakeholder Management Components	Carroll's (1987) Models of Moral Management
No recognition of stakeholders		Immoral Management
Level 1 "Rational" Level	Familiarization Comprehensiveness	Amoral Management
Level 2 "Process" Level	Planning Integrativeness	
Level 3 "Transactional" Level	Communication Proactiveness Interactiveness Genuineness Frequency Satisfaction Resource Adequacy	Moral Management

Two additional examples of the immoral management approach are in order. A recent (1994) indictment has named five former Honda Motor Co. executives with taking kickbacks and bribes from dealers and regional advertising associations. Of the $10 million allegedly paid or given to the former executives, $2.5 million came from an advertising kickback scam during 1991 and 1992. According to the indictment, dealers were trying to ensure delivery of the much-in-demand vehicles by offering Rolex watches, $1,000 suits and leases on a Mercedes-Benz 500 SL. In the process, the defendants allegedly bilked Honda and the regional dealer ad associations out of discretionary funds earmarked for supplemental marketing (Horton, 1994). If found guilty of these charges, these executives truly represent ideal examples of immoral management wherein no recognition of stakeholders took place.

A second example of the immoral management model comes from the recent disclosure (1994) that executives at Brown and Williamson Tobacco Co. knew 30 years ago that nicotine was addictive and that cigarettes were a cause of lung cancer. Company documents apparently show that in 1963 executives debated whether to disclose research that showed that the cigarettes cause lung cancer and some heart problems (Shapiro, 1994). In both the Honda case and the Brown and Williamson case it is evident that the managers involved did not recognize or acknowledge any stakeholders beyond themselves.

In Figure 4 we see Freeman's "rational level" of SMC interpreted by Starik as "familiarization comprehensiveness." Though we cannot say with perfect certainty that this corresponds with amoral management, it is easy to speculate that this would be the case. Managers who go through the motions of identifying stakeholders and then take no moral action based upon this information are conveying at least an image of moral neutrality. The same argument could be made for level two, the process level, if no moral action is taken based upon information acquired. One gets the impression that some organizations set up processes for gathering information about stakeholder group's issues and needs but then do not act upon the information gathered. Stakeholder intelligence is often perceived as just "background information about the environment" and not as specific rationales for driving decision making.

What often occurs among amoral managers is a rationalization of what the organization is doing. A rationalization process, however, may actually become a denial of stakeholders' needs or sensitivities. A case in point occurred when Backer Spielvogel Bates, a French advertising agency, used a naked and blindfolded young girl in a European glossy advertisement for Puiforcat, a cutlery, glass and jewelry shop. Critics claimed the ad raised the question of exploitation of children as children have been used heavily as marketing tools in recent years. The copywriter of the ad defended the ad claiming that it was just a very stylized image—not a question of skin and flesh, just lines that are very symbolic and pure. One observer stated that the ad just reflected creative people trying to be different rather than any kind of overt attempt to exploit a young woman's body. But, a psychologist at Aston University observed that there is a pressing danger in intellectualizing such images—giving them quasi-artistic status that dulls our natural sensitivities (Hall, 1991). Thus, if we say it is "art" it must be all right. To the amoral manager, there is a tendency to see "art" rather than "exploitation", and, consequently, an openness to stakeholder critics might be shut out rather than studied and treated as an important social issue with ethical ramifications. In the U.S., a similar kind of amoral posture might be taking place by MTV with its "Beavis and Butthead" cartoon show which some say may have led to two Ohio incidents in which kids started fires after watching the show. The cartoon features two teenage boys, Beavis and Butthead, who comment on rock videos, sniff paint thinner, torture animals, harass girls and set things on fire for amusement (Scott, 1993). To be sure, not all level one and two SMC organizations fall prey to amoral management, but it is most likely to occur at these levels.

Finally, the moral management category deserves further illustration particularly as it entails activating the transactional level mentioned in the previous discussion and in Figure 4. In the moral management model, ethical leadership is manifested by organizational representatives. Managers in this model enter into dialogues with stakeholder groups as they design or engineer their organizations actions and decisions. These executives prefer to operate at a level of moral sensitivity and awareness that resides well above what the law mandates (Carroll, 1987). Moral executives systematically employ principles such as honesty, integrity, loyalty, promise-keeping, trustworthiness, fairness, personal accountability and concern and respect for others (Josephson Institute of Ethics, 1989). Moral managers are likely to be found in what Pastin would refer to as "high-ethics" firms where a major operating principle is that executives are "at ease interacting with diverse internal and external stakeholder groups" (Pastin, 1986).

An illustration of moral managers operating at the transactional level is described by Paine in discussing Nova Care, a large company, which provides rehabilitation services to hospitals and nursing homes in the U.S. (Paine. 1994). In 1988, the company, concluded that its future was in jeopardy. Mutual distrust among employees and management and turnover among clinicians, therapists and other employees had escalated to 57% per year. Customers were defecting and the stock market price of its stock was in a slump. Nova Care brought in another firm, In Speech, to help it diagnose its problem. It was finally decided that they had been observing symptoms of the problem and that the real problem was a lack of common values and aspirations. It was concluded that there was a significant "disconnect" between the values of the therapists and clinicians, who were oriented towards the delivery of high-quality health care, and management's obsession with financial success of the firm.

John Foster, CEO, concluded there was a strong need for a common frame of reference and language to bring about a unity of communication among the divergent groups. With the help of consultants, interviews and focus groups with customers, managers and health-care professionals, an employee task force created and proposed a vision statement for the company. Hundreds of other employees suggested revisions to their draft. Company executives then developed a statement of the company's fundamental beliefs and guiding purposes which would become the framework for management goals, decisions and conduct. The company's core beliefs were summarized in four key values: respect for the individual, service to the customer, pursuit of excellence and commitment to personal integrity. In addition, a number of structural and operational changes were introduced into the company. Many Nova Care employees have said that the values initiative and the process by which it was developed and implemented played a crucial role in the company's 1990 turn-around (Paine, 1994).

A useful way to conclude our section on stakeholder management (or thinking) and the three models of management morality is to set forth a series of descriptive statements which purport to characterize how each moral model would view or be oriented towards four key stakeholder groups: owner/shareholders, customers, employees and the local community. It is anticipated that these specific descriptions will provide for a richer and fuller appreciation of how stakeholder thinking is a vital attribute of management morality. Figures 5-8 adapted from Carroll (1991), profile these perspectives.

Figure 5: Three moral management models and their orientation toward owner/shareholder stakeholders

Model of management morality	Orientation toward owner/shareholder stakeholders
Immoral Management	Shareholders are minimally treated and given short shrift. Focus is on maximizing positions of executive groups—maximizing executive compensation, perks, benefits. Golden parachutes are more important than returns to shareholders. Managers maximize their positions without shareholders being made aware. Concealment from shareholders is the operating procedure. Self-interest of management group is the order of the day.
Amoral Management	No special thought is given to shareholders; they are there and must be minimally accommodated. Profit focus of the business is their reward. No thought is given to ethical consequences of decisions for any stakeholder group, including owners. Communication is limited to that required by law.
Moral Management	Shareholders' interest (short- and long-term) is a central factor. The best way to be ethical to shareholders is to treat all stakeholder claimants in a fair and ethical manner. To protect shareholders, an ethics committee of the board is created. Code of ethics is established, promulgated, and made a living document to protect shareholders' and others' interests.

Figure 6: Three moral management models and their orientation toward customer (consumer) stakeholders

Model of management morality	Orientation toward customer stakeholders
Immoral Management	Customers are viewed as opportunities to be exploited for personal or organizational gain. Ethical standards in dealings do not prevail; indeed, an active intent to cheat, deceive, and/or mislead is present. In all marketing decisions—advertising, pricing, packaging, distribution—customer is taken advantage of to the fullest extent.
Amoral Management	Management does not think through the ethical consequences of its decisions and actions. It simply makes decisions with profitability within the letter of the law as a guide. Management is not focused on what is fair from perspective of customer. Focus is on management's rights. No consideration is given to ethical implications of interactions with customers.
Moral Management	Customer is viewed as equal partner in transaction. Customer brings needs/expectations to the exchange transaction and is treated fairly. Managerial focus is on giving customer fair value, full information, fair guarantee, and satisfaction. Consumer rights are liberally interpreted and honored.

Figure 7: Three moral management models and their orientation toward employee stakeholders

Model of management morality	Orientation toward employee stakeholders
Immoral Management	Employees are viewed as factors of production to be used, exploited, manipulated for gain of individual manager or company. No concern is shown for employees' needs/rights/expectations. Short-term focus. Coercive, controlling, alienating.
Amoral Management	Employees are treated as law requires. Attempts to motivate focus on increasing productivity rather than satisfying employees' growing maturity needs. Employees still seen as factors of production but remunerative approach used. Organization sees self-interest in treating employees with minimal respect. Organization structure, pay incentives, rewards all geared toward short and long-term productivity.
Moral Management	Employees are a human resource that must be treated with dignity and respect. Goal is to use a leadership style such as factors of consultative/participative that will result in mutual confidence and trust. Commitment is a recurring theme. Employees' rights to due process, privacy, freedom of speech, and safety are maximally considered in all decisions. Management seeks out fair dealings with employees.

Figure 8: Three moral management models and their orientation toward community stakeholders

Model of management morality	Orientation toward community stakeholders
Immoral Management	Exploits community to fullest extent; pollutes the environment. Plant or business closings take fullest advantage of community. Actively disregards community needs. Takes fullest advantage of community resources without giving anything in return. Violates zoning and other ordinances whenever it can for its own advantage.
Amoral Management	Does not take community or its resources into account in management decision making. Community factors are assumed to be irrelevant to business decisions. Community, like employees, is a factor of production. Legal considerations are followed, but nothing more. Deals minimally with community, its people, community activity, local government.
Moral Management	Sees vital community as a goal to be actively pursued. Seeks to be a leading citizen and to motivate others to do likewise. Gets actively involved and helps institutions that need help—schools, recreational groups, philanthropic groups. Leadership position in environment, education, culture/arts, volunteerism, and general community affairs. Firm engages in strategic philanthropy. Management sees community goals and company goals as mutually interdependent.

One added distinction about the moral management models and stakeholder thinking should be introduced at this juncture. This is the observation that stakeholder theory may be viewed according to several different perspectives which focus on the purpose or use of the theory or way of thinking. Donaldson and Preston (1994) have argued that stakeholder theory may be descriptive/empirical, instrumental or normative. In the descriptive/empirical category, the focus is on describing and explaining specific corporate characteristics and behavior. It could be said that this paper is a good example of the descriptive approach to stakeholder theory. Through describing management's attributes in the three moral management models, we gain a better understanding of their relationships to stakeholder thinking. Instrumental uses of stakeholder theory refers to the linkages between stakeholder thinking and the achievement of traditional corporate objectives such as profitability and growth. A normative perspective or use of stakeholder theory would focus on some underlying moral or philosophical justification for using the stakeholder perspective—such as it is "the right thing to do" because stakeholders merit significant consideration in management's decisions.

Donaldson and Preston posit that the ultimate justification for the stakeholder theory is to be found in its normative base.

If we link these views of stakeholder theory to our current discussion, we find some useful connections. With respect to the immoral management model we would be forced to conclude that these managers reject stakeholder theory and thus find no use for it in terms of descriptive/empirical, instrumental or normative justification. By contrast, we could argue that amoral managers accept an extremely narrow view of stakeholder thinking and primarily adopt an instrumental usage of the approach. Finally, in the moral managers we find an enthusiastic embracing of the wide view of stakeholders, to include all legitimate stakeholders, and an adoption of a normative combined with instrumental posture with respect to stakeholder thinking. Among moral managers we would like see a normative view prevailing—that is, stakeholders will be maximally considered because they possess intrinsic worth in and of themselves; that is, they are *ends* not *means*. Figure 9 recapitulates these relationships.

Figure 9: The moral management models and acceptance of stakeholder thinking (SHT)

Model of management morality	Acceptance of stakeholder thinking (SHT)	Stakeholder thinking embraced
Immoral Management	SHT Rejected; Management is self-absorbed	SHT Rejected, not deemed useful. Accepts profit maximization model but does not really pursue it.
Amoral Management	SHT Accepted: Narrow View (minimum number of Shs considered)	Instrumental View of SHT prevails
Moral Management	SHT Enthusiastically Embraced: Wider View (maximum number of Shs considered)	Normative View of SHT prevails

Strategic Implications of Moral Models and Stakeholder Thinking

In the decade since Freeman popularized the stakeholder concept, it is this writer's view that the approach has been more completely embraced by those who have seen it as a way to revitalize ethical business behavior than by those who have seen it as a new paradigm for strategic management. To be sure, this distinction between stakeholder thinking as a worldview of "ethics" versus "strategy" is somewhat artificial and is drawn primarily for purposes of contrast, but it does provide for a useful distinction for purposes of discussion. In the academic world, scholars in business and society, social issues in management and business ethics have enthusiastically embraced stakeholder thinking for it so effectively captures many of the attributes of interest for these teachers, researchers and thinkers. Papers, articles, textbooks, symposia, frameworks, models, and approaches by these academics are replete with stakeholder thinking and theory. Indeed, two major invitational conferences on stakeholder theory have been convened by Max Clarkson and the Centre for Corporate Social Performance and Ethics at The University of Toronto in 1993 and 1994. Reflections on the 1993 Toronto Conference have been published in *Business and Society*, the journal of IABS, the International Association for Business and Society (Toronto Conference, 1994).

By way of contrast, scholars in strategic management have been slow to acknowledge and use stakeholder thinking. The "language" of stakeholders has begun to appear in some strategic management literature and one wishes to be encouraged by this. In 1994 a strategic management textbook was published by Harrison and St. John which as part of its title purports to advocate a stakeholder perspective: *Strategic Management of Organizations and Stakeholders*. The instrumental value of stakeholder thinking will doubtless draw strategic management scholars into using it more in the future. What is particularly encouraging, however, is the notion of employing stakeholder thinking to integrate both financial and ethical dimensions into corporate and managerial decision making and performance. Linking stakeholder theory to an expanded view of corporate social responsibility, such as that presented in the four part model of CSR, provides a useful basis for integrating the firm's concern for itself (economic responsibility) with its concern for society (legal, ethical and discretionary/philanthropic responsibilities). We might call this an Integrative View of stakeholder thinking.

Freeman, in 1984, also popularized the concept of "enterprise level strategy" as an overarching strategy emphasis on the firm's role in society. Enterprise level strategy, though earlier discussed by Ansoff and Hofer, both strategic management scholars, did not provide the basis for its popular appeal as did Freeman. As alluded to earlier, Freeman's presentation of the stakeholder approach as a way to manage strategically, ironically did not catch on as much among strategy academics as it did among business and society/business ethics scholars. Only now, a decade later, with a few exceptions, do we begin to see serious consideration of stakeholders by strategic management academics.

As for management practitioners, it is more difficult to judge the extent to which they have truly embraced stakeholder thinking. They increasingly adopt the language of stakeholders and, frequently operate at Level Two—the process level of SMC—but it is rare to see Level Three "transactional level" thinking and the accompanying moral management model. As a footnote to this statement, however, it must be observed that with global competitiveness and the need for and use of the "total quality" movement, we are likely to see more examples of higher order stakeholder and moral thinking in the years to come.

As we focus our attention on the strategic implications of stakeholder thinking and models of management morality, it is helpful to briefly comment on strategic management and strategic thinking. Strategic management refers to the overall management process that seeks to align a firm with its environment. A basic way in which the firm relates to its environment is through the products and services it produces and the markets in which it chooses to participate. Strategic management can also be seen as a kind of overall organizational management by the firm's top-level executives. In this sense it represents the overall leadership function in which the sense of direction of the organization is decided upon and implemented. Both these positions are steeped in the literature of strategic management.

Top managements must address many issues as a firm is positioning itself relative to its environment. The more traditional issues involve product/market decisions—the principal decision thrust of most organizations. Other decisions relate to production, finance, marketing, human resource management, research and development, competition and so on. Anytime there is a social or ethical facet to these decisions, organizations have an opportunity for stakeholder thinking (especially of the normative perspective) to enter the picture and inform decision making. Sound corporate public policy would suggest that this be the case.

To be sure, top managements have a choice to make which might reflect quite divergent views of stakeholder thinking, CSR and management morality. It would be argued here that business for both instrumental and normative reasons would best be advised to reject the view of CSR and stakeholder thinking that focuses on the firm alone to the exclusion of other stakeholders. The desired posture, it would seem, would be to totally embrace CSR in its full definition, stakeholder thinking at the highest level and to pattern itself after the attributes of moral management. It would be implicit in stakeholder theory that these be our objectives.

Linking our concepts of management morality with notions of strategic management, we propose three models of moral strategic management: immoral strategic management, amoral strategic management and immoral strategic management. Each will be briefly described and illustrated.

Immoral Strategic Management (ISM)

ISM possesses all the attributes of immoral management previously described but focuses on the strategic as opposed to operational levels of the organization. Specifically, product/market choices and top management level decisions are corrupted by an exclusive focus on management or corporate gain to the exclusion of all other considerations. Likewise, strategic management processes exclude the desirability and usefulness of stakeholder thinking.

To the example of Phar-Mor presented earlier, which depicted ISM, we can easily add several others. The case of Beech-Nut Nutrition Corporation is worthy of mention. A couple years after joining the company, the CEO (a strategic manager) found evidence suggesting that the company was purchasing adulterated apple juice concentrate and then passing, it off as "100 % pure" apple Juice to its customers. It turns out the suppliers were shipping nothing more than sugar water and chemicals to Beech-Nut. Rather than destroying the poor quality inventory, the CEO, pressured by a desire to turn the ailing company around, apparently took what he might have viewed as an "amoral" posture (business is business?) and took no action. Several years later, the Food and Drug Administration (FDA) investigated the company. The company eventually pleaded guilty to selling adulterated and misbranded juice. Two years later, with two criminal trials behind it, the CEO pleaded guilty to ten counts of mislabeling, resulting in losses to the firm of an estimated $25 million (Paine, 1994).

The Beech-Nut case clearly involved a strategic decision regarding a product being sold to the customer, but the company focused exclusively on its own profitability goal (economic responsibility) to the exclusion of the customer stakeholders (legal and ethical responsibilities). The CEO may have thought he was adopting an amoral posture but, in fact, he was engaging in an illegal action (selling adulterated, misbranded juice) and putting his firm at risk of criminal liability.

The issue of immoral strategic management not only affects individual companies but may affect entire industries as well. In the early to mid-1980s, serious questions were being raised about the all-terrain vehicles (ATVs) industry. The three wheeled, small motorized vehicles with balloon tires were being increasingly linked to injuries and deaths, particularly of children. Critics labelled the vehicles "death machines" and essentially called them immoral products. The ATV makers, firms such as Honda, Kawasaki, Suzuki, and Yamaha, defended their product saying, that they were being singled out unfairly and that "gross misuse" by a small minority of riders was really the problem. Intervention by the U.S. Consumer Product Safety Commission (CPSC) led to studies, hearings, lawsuits and an eventual settlement with the ATV industry to ban the three wheeled versions, which were unstable, to prominently notify consumers of the dangers of ATVs and for dealers to provide "hands on" training to purchasers. One could argue that the ATV industry had adopted an amoral management posture, but the statistics linking the ATVs to injuries and deaths suggests an immoral management strategy. Without the intervention of the CPSC, it is up to question whether the industry would have taken action.

A more recent example of an industry facing charges and perceptions of an immoral strategy is the tobacco industry, especially in the U.S. Not only is the industry facing lawsuits, smoking bans and smoking-cessation campaigns, but new charges allege that the major tobacco firms have suppressed information on nicotine addition, manipulated levels of nicotine in cigarettes, concealed nicotine's addictive effects and asserted through broad claims in their advertising that it was not addictive. The immorality of tobacco products companies is summed up by some in the saying: "tobacco is the only product which if used according to its intended purposes, will kill you." Whether tobacco products will continue to be permitted to be legal or not however, is under increase continues to be debated. Their marketing strategy, however, is under increasing attack also. In particular, there is growing evidence that cigarette ads influence children and teens to smoke. One cannot help but mention R.J. Reynold's character, Joe Camel, as a typical example of a firm's attempt to market the product to youthful markets. Already two-thirds of Americans—including almost half of smokers—want the U.S. government to impose greater restrictions on cigarette advertising (Colford and Teinowitz, 1994).

Other examples of immoral strategic decisions are likely found when one examines the following companies and their experiences with the indicated products: GM and its Corvair motorcar, A.H. Robins and its Dalkon Shield IUD device, Firestone and its ill-fated 500 radial tires, Manville and its asbestos, Eli Lilly and its drug Orafex, Ford and its Pinto motorcar, and GE and its PCBs, just to mention a few (Mokhiber, 1988).

Amoral Strategic Management (ASM)
ASM possesses all the attributes of amoral management previously described but also focuses on the strategic levels of decision making. Amoral strategic management sometimes gets confused with ISM. As in the ATV and tobacco cases presented above, the two can sometimes be

difficult to distinguish from one another. In ASM, we give management more credit and assume, sometimes mistakenly, that it did not know that what it was doing was wrong or unfair. In the business ethics environment of the 1990s, it will be more challenging to defend management actions as amoral rather than immoral. Nevertheless, there are still cases where outright immorality does not fairly characterize the strategy and for which a description of amorality is more fitting. A good example of ASM is in the situation where top management was well intended but through negligence or not carefully considering its actions or effects on stakeholders, people are hurt or taken advantage of.

A useful illustration of amoral strategic management involves the 1992 case of Sears. Roebuck & Co. and its automotive service business. Paine (1994) describes how consumers and attorney generals in 40 states had accused the company of misleading consumers and selling them unneeded parts and services. In the face of declining, revenues and shrinking, market share, Sear's executives put into place new goals, quotas and incentives for auto center service personnel. Service employees were given product-specific and service-specific quotas—sell so many brake jobs, batteries, front-end alignments—or face consequences such as reduced working hours or transfers. Some employees spoke of the "pressure" they felt to generate business. Though Sear's executives did not set out to defraud customers, they put into place a commission system that led to Sear's employees feeling pressure to sell products and services that consumers did not need. Soon after the complaints against Sears occurred, CEO Edward Brennan acknowledged that management had created an environment in which mistakes were made, though no intent to deceive consumers existed. Fortunately, Sears eliminated its quota system as a partial remedy to the problem (Paine, 1994).

The Sear's case is a classic example of Amoral Strategic Management—a well intended company falling into questionable practices because it just did not think ethically. The company just did not think through the impacts that its strategic decisions would have on important stakeholders.

Moral Strategic Management (MSM)

MSM possesses all the attributes of moral management described previously. MSM is characterized by moral decision making and leadership taking place at the strategic level of the organization. Moral Strategic Management is characterized by its executives living in their organizational worlds by sound ethical standards. MSM executives do not just avoid unethical behavior. They assume positions of ethical leadership and develop and implement policies and programs that manifest ethical leadership in all their strategic roles and decisions. If ethical leadership is commonplace among this executive group, it follows that maximum consideration of stakeholders is paramount. These executives operate at Level 3—the "transactional" level—in their stakeholder relationships.

To be sure, moral strategic management strives to ensure that the company does not produce goods and services that are at odds with high ethical standards. Since most companies fare well on this criterion, however, it does not turn out to be the key discriminating factor differentiating moral from amoral and immoral managements. However, the moral issue may have played some role in American Brand's recent decision to sell its American Tobacco division to Britain's B.A.T. Industries *(The Economist*, April 30, 1994, p. 75). In the social investing industry it is evident that corporate strategic decisions to avoid certain kinds of industries is viewed as an important "screen" for socially responsible or ethical investors. Some ethical mutual funds, for example, screen out investments in firms in industries such as tobacco, alcohol, gambling, nuclear power, and defense. These kinds of screens are quite crude, however, and do not represent broadly held values regarding the ethics of various industries.

Another key indicator of moral strategic management entails the actual performance of a company on a specific social or ethical issue. Issues which involve ethical questions include such areas as the firm's minority recruitment and affirmative action record, its environmental protection record, its employee safety record, and so on. Some publications, such as *Fortune* magazine keep scorecards on certain categories of firm performance. We discover that *Fortune*, for example, publishes an Environmental Scorecard on which its "ten leaders" are recognized *(Fortune*, 1993, p. 119). There we find that AT&T, Apple Computer, Church & Dwight, Clorox and Digital Equipment rank in *Fortune's* top ten. AT&T was recognized for lowering air emissions 81% and cutting waste disposal in half; Apple Computer developed a technology that eliminated the need for CFC-based solvents to clean circuit boards; Church & Dwight markets technologies that use baking soda to treat lead in drinking water; Clorox reduced its toxic releases to the lowest of the majors in the cosmetic and soap industry; and, Digital Equipment developed innovative ways to reduce manufactured waste.

Beyond considering specific arenas of performance to identify MSM, one might examine what companies are doing to promote sound ethics or to advocate high moral standards in their organizational policies and practices. Several examples illustrate this manifestation of moral strategic management, often observed in the strategy implementation stage.

Robert Haas, chairman and CEO of Levi Strauss & Co. says that his firm is "integrating ethics and other corporate values (such as empowerment and diversity) into every aspect of our business—from our human-resources programs to our vendor relationships" (Haas, 1994). To deal with the fact that the company operates in many countries and diverse cultures, in early 1992 the firm developed and adopted a set of global sourcing guidelines that established standards for their contractors to meet to ensure that their practices were compatible with Levi's values. The guidelines were developed by a working group made up of 15 employees from a broad section of the company. The working group researched the views of key stakeholder groups, using an ethical decision making model which set out a process for making decisions by taking into consideration all stakeholders' issues.

Outside directors on the board of GM recently developed a "magna carta for directors" which is intended to spell out the way things ought to be if directors are going to do their job—make management accountable to shareholders. The "magna carta" is a six-page, 28-point document designed to ensure the board's independence (Dobrzynski. 1994). In addition, in February of 1994, GM became the first U.S. automaker to endorse the CERES Principles (formerly the Valdez Principles). GM also committed to publish an annual report on environmental performance *(Business Ethics,* May/June, 1994, p. 11).

In Dayton, Ohio, Children's Medical Center (CMC) recently created an Ethics Advisory Committee. After six months of work, the committee produced a CMC Ethics Handbook which set forth a statement of ethical principles, an outline of operating procedures for a new Ethics Development System and practical guidelines for moral practices at CMC. The committee also attended ethics training, seminars (Business Ethics, September/October, 1993. 30).

For some time now, companies have been integrating their philanthropy with their corporate strategies. The whole area now referred to as "strategic philanthropy" provides one excellent example of how moral strategic management is being manifested. Strategic philanthropy is an approach by which corporate giving or philanthropic endeavors of a firm are designed in such a way that best fits with the firm's overall mission goals or objectives. Strategic philanthropy is an approach wherein managers can help others while at the same time help themselves. Craig Smith observes: "... philanthropic and business units have joined forces to develop giving strategies that increase their name recognition among consumers, boost employee productivity, reduce R&D costs, overcome regulatory obstacles, and foster synergy among business units." (Smith, 1994). Some U.S. companies have carried their strategic philanthropy to the point of promoting social causes. Examples of this social activism include General Mills (fighting hunger), Bank of America (community and economic development), and McGraw Hill Publishers (promoting literacy). Strategic philanthropy, of course, addresses the discretionary/philanthropic component of the four-part CSR model.

There are a multitude of ways that managers can exert moral strategic management. More than anything else, management needs to create an organizational climate that will foster moral decision making on the part of all managers and employees. Tangible actions such as missions and values statements, codes of conduct, policies, ethics committees, ethics officers, whistle blowing mechanisms, and ethics training are all desirable components of an ethics initiative. Decision making processes that enhance the firm's ability to yield ethical due process to stakeholders is vital. Beyond these, management leadership in thought, word and action are essential.

Recently, Paine (1994) has submitted that firms have two basic strategic options for pursuing ethics management: a compliance strategy and an integrity strategy. There are many parallels between these two and amoral strategic management and moral strategic management. Her compliance strategy focuses on the prevention of criminal misconduct (which would be consistent with amorality). Her integrity strategy has as its objective the enablement of responsible conduct. Clearly, this latter theme would be quite similar to moral strategic management.

Other examples of moral strategic management may be found in the recently published volume, *Companies With a Conscience: Intimate Portraits of Twelve Firms That Make a Difference* (Scott and Rothman, 1994).

Conclusion

Stakeholder thinking is a powerful way of visualizing organizations and their social responsibilities. Addressing the needs and expectations of diverse stakeholders such as owners, employees, consumers, the community and the environment necessitates a broad and encompassing concept of corporate social responsibility. Therefore, a four-part construct of CSR was set forth as a springboard or point of departure for our discussion. This four-part model embraced businesses' economic, legal, ethical and philanthropic responsibilities.

Focusing on the ethics component of the definition, we next set forth three models or types of management morality: immoral management, amoral management and moral management. One goal was to set up templates or basepoints against which managements might compare and contrast their own decision making perspectives. Another objective was to link the moral types to our concept of CSR and to explore how stakeholder thinking provided us with a more robust understanding of social responsibility and business morality. An underlying agenda to this discussion was highlighting the amoral management type which is frequently not identified as a dangerous problem in organizations and to expose its features, characteristics and downside consequences.

We concluded by extending the moral management models into strategic forms which parallel the basic three types. Thus, immoral strategic management, amoral strategic management and moral strategic management were defined, described and illustrated. Stakeholder thinking and concepts played a vital role in explicating these models. The models provide us with a glimpse of the nexus between strategic decision making and management morality and serve as a constant reminder that an integrative view of stakeholder thinking is essential. This integrative view necessitates the melding of strategic and moral considerations much akin to the quest Freeman and Gilbert pursued in their *Corporate Strategy and the Search for Ethics* (1988). Our conclusion here would be that for normative as well as instrumental reasons the goal of organizations should be moral strategic management. When one examines the annals of corporate strategy, the immoral and amoral forms simply do not stand out as success stories when examined from a stakeholder perspective. The moral model serves as an exemplar of the socially responsible firm and the stakeholder serving enterprise. To pursue less is to suboptimize all that organizations today have the capacity to achieve.

Archie B. Carroll is Professor of Management and the holder of the Robert W. Sherer Chair of Management and Corporate Public Affairs at the University of Georgia.

Ackerman, R.W. and Bauer, R.A. (1976) *Corporate Social Responsiveness.* Reston. VA: Reston Publishing Co.

Allison, Graham. (1971) *Essence of Decision.* Boston: Little Brown.

Atlanta Journal. (1994) "Honda Bribery Case Brings Guilty Pleas." March 15. D5.

Backman, J. (1975) *Social Responsibility and Accountability.* New York: NYU Press.

Bowen, H.R. (1953) *Social Responsibilities of the Businessman.* New, York: Harper & Row.

Bowman, E.H. and M. Haire. (1975) "A Strategic Posture Toward Corporate Social Responsibility." *California Management Review* 18(2): 49-58.

Brenner, Steven N. and Philip Cochran. (1991) "The Stakeholder Theory of the Firm: Implications for Business and Society Theory and Research." IABS 1991 Proceedings, 449-466.

Business Enterprise Trust. (1994) The Business Enterprise Awards - 1991 Recipients (unpublished announcement).
Business Ethics. (1994) "GM Turns Green." May-June, 11.
Business Ethics. (1993) "Developing Ethical Work Cultures at Home and Abroad." September October, 30-31.
Business Ethics. (1993) "A Powerful Prescription: Merck & Co." November-December, 1993, 29.
Carroll, Archie B. (1979) "A Three-Dimensional Conceptual Model of Corporate Social Performance." *Academy of Management Review,* 4: 497-505.
Carroll, Archie B. (1993) *Business and Society: Ethics and Stakeholder Management, 2nd Ed.* Cincinnati, OH: South-Western Publishing Co.
Carroll, Archie B. (1987) "In Search of the Moral Manager." *Business Horizons,* 30: March-April, 7-15.
Carroll, Archie B. (1991) "The Pyramid of Corporate Social Responsibility: Toward the Moral Management of Organizational Stakeholders." *Business Horizons,* 34: July-August, 39-48.
Carroll, Archie B. and George W. Beiler. (1975) "Landmarks in the Evolution of the Social Audit." *Academy of Management Journal,* September: 589-599.
Cheit, E.F. (1964) *The Business Establishment.* New York: Wiley.
Clarkson, Max B.E. (1991) "Defining, Evaluating, and Managing Corporate Social Performance: The Stakeholder Management Model." *Research in Corporate Social Performance and Policy,* Vol. 12: 331-358.
Clarkson, Max B.E. (1994) "A Stakeholder Framework for Analyzing and Evaluating Corporate Social Performance." *Academy of Management Review.* Forthcoming.
Colford, Steven W. and Ira Teinowitz. (1994) "Teen Smoking and Ads Linked." *Advertising Age,* February 21, 1.
Davis, Keith. (1960) "Can Business Afford to Ignore Social Responsibilities?" *California Management Review* 2: 70-76.
Davis, Keith and R.L. Blomstrom. (1966) *Business and Its Environment.* New York: McGraw-Hill.
Dobrzynski, Judith H. (1994) "At GM, A Magna Carta for Directors." *Business Week,* April 4.37.
Donaldson, Thomas and Lee E. Preston. (1994) "The Stakeholder Theory of the Corporation: Concepts, Evidence, Implications." *Academy of Management Review.* Forthcoming.
Economist . (1994). "The Tobacco Industry: The Last Drag?" April 30, 1994, 75.
Forbes. (1989) "Good Timing, Charlie." November 27: 140-144.
Fortune. (1994) "Environmental Scorecard: The Ten Leaders." July 26. 1993, 119.

Frederick, W.C. (1978) "From CSR, to CSR2: The Maturing, of Business and Society Thought." Working Paper No. 279, Graduate School of Business, University of Pittsburgh.

Freeman, R. Edward. (1984) *Strategic Management: A Stakeholder Approach.* Boston: Pitman.

Freeman, R. Edward and Daniel R. Gilbert. (1988) *Corporate Strategy and the Search for Ethics.* Englewood Cliffs, NJ: Prentice-Hall.

Goodpaster, Kenneth E. (1991) "Business Ethics and Stakeholder Analysis." *Business Ethics Quarterly* 1: 53-73.

Haas, Robert D. (1994) "Ethics in the Trenches." *Across the Board,* May 12-13.

Hall, Dinah. (1991) "A guilty picture of innocence?" *The (London) Times,* April 8:12.

Halme, Minna and Juha Näsi. (1992) "Stakeholder Pressure Against Immoral Management: A Case Study of a Company's Destruction." IABS 1992 Proceedings, 276-284.

Halme, Minna. Morten Huse and Per Jystad. (1994) "Corporate Governance and Green Values: A Nordic Sample." IABS 1994 Proceedings, 511-516.

Harrison, Jeffrey S. and Caron H. St. John. (1994) *Strategic Management of Organizational Stakeholders: Theory and Cases.* Minneapolis/St. Paul: West Publishing Co.

Horton, Cleveland. (1994) "Feds Claim $2.5M 'Hondagate' Ad Scam." *Advertising Age,* March 21, 3.

Huse, Morten. (1994) "Stakeholder Expectations from Boards of Directors: An Empirical Examination." IABS 1994 Proceedings. 351-356.

Husted, Bryan. (1994) "Organizational Justice and the Management of Stakeholder Relations." IABS 1994 Proceedings. 20-25.

Josephson Institute of Ethics. (1989) *Ethics: Easier Said Than Done.* Vol. 2, No. 1.

Kreps, Theodore J. (1940) "Measurement of the Social Performance of Business." Monograph No. 7. Washington. DC: U.S. Government Printing Office.

Lamb, William B. (1994) "Measuring Corporate Social Performance: A Stakeholder Approach." IABS 1994 Proceedings, 247-252.

Lemer, Linda D. and Geraid E. Fryxell. (1994) "CEO Stakeholder Attitudes and Corporate Social Activity in the Fortune 500." *Business and Society* 33(1): 58-81.

MacMillan, Ian C. and Patricia E. Jones. (1986) *Strategy Formulation: Power and Politics.* St. Paul: West Publishing Co.

Millei., Krystal. (1994) "Former Honda Executives Plead Guilty to Charges Tied to Bribes from Dealers." *Wall Street Journal,* March 15, A4.

Mitchell, Ronald K. (1994) "Stakeholder Theory and Liabilities of Newness in New Ventures." IABS 1994 Proceedings, 345-350.

Mokliiber, Russell. (1988) *Corporate Crime and Violence*. San Francisco: Sierra Club Books.

Näsi, Juha, Salme Näsi and Grant T. Savage. (1994) "A Stubborn Entrepreneur Under the Pressure of a Union and the Courts: An Analysis of Stakeholder Strategies in a Conflict Process." IABS 1994 Proceedings, 228-233.

Näsi, Juha. (1991) *Arenas of Strategic Thinking*. Helsinki. Finland: Foundation for Economic Education.

Paine, Lynn Sharp. (1994) "Managing for Organizational Integrity." *Harvard Business Review*, March-April. 106-117.

Pastin, Mark. (1986) *The Hard Problems of Management: Gaining the Ethics Edge*. San Francisco: Jossey-Bass.

Preston, Lee and James Post. (1975) *Private Management and Public Responsibility*. Englewood Cliffs. NJ: Prentice-Hall.

Savage, Grant, T.W. Nix, C.J. Whitehead and J.D. Blair. (1991) "Strategies for Assessing and Managing Organizational Stakeholders." *Academy of Management Executive* 2: 61-75.

Scott, Mary and Howard Rothman. (1994) *Companies With a Conscience: Intimate Portraits of Twelve Firms That Make a Difference*. New York: Carol Publishing Group.

Scott, Jeffrey. (1993) "Heh, heh-heh, heh-heh, heh-heh: Beavis and Butt-head's last laugh?" *The Atlanta Journal*. October 12, C3.

Sethi, S. Prakash. (1975) "Dimensions of Corporate Social Responsibility." *California Management Review* 17(3): 58-64.

Shapiro, Eben. (1994) "Tobacco Firms May Face New Pressure With Disclosure of Executive's Memo." *Wall Street Journal*. May 9, 5.

Smith, Craig. (1994) "The New, Corporate Philanthropy." *Harvard Business Review*. May-June, 105-116.

Starik. Mark. (1990) Stakeholder Management and Firm Performance: Reputational and Financial Relationship to U.S. Electric Utility Consumer-Related Strategies. Unpublished PhD dissertation. University of Georgia.

Steiner, George. (1975) *Business and Society, 2nd Ed*. New York: McGraw-Hill.

Toronto Conference: Reflections of Stakeholder Theory. (1994) *Business and Society* 33(1): 82-131.

Wartick, Steven L. and Philip L. Cochran. (1985) "The Evolution of the Corporate Social Performance Model." *Academy of Management Review* 10: 765-766.

Weber, James. (1992) "Operationalizing the Stakeholder Theory of the Firm: Establishing Classification Schemes for the Matrix Dimension." IABS 1992 Proceedings. 200-215.

Williger, Stephen D. (1994) "Phar-Mor—A Lesson in Fraud." *Wall Street Journal*, March 28, A12.

Wood, Donna J. (1991) "Corporate Social Performance revisited." *Academy of Management Review*, October: 691-718.

Reprinted with the permission of the Foundation for Economic Education, Helsinki, Finland.

Part 3

Stakeholder Theory and Management Performance

The Stakeholder Theory of the Corporation: Concepts, Evidence and Implications

Tom Donaldson, Georgetown University
Lee E. Preston, University of Maryland

Abstract: The stakeholder theory has been advanced and justified in the management literature on the basis of its descriptive accuracy, instrumental power, and normative validity. These three aspects of the theory, although interrelated, are quite distinct; they involve different types of evidence and argument and have different implications. In this article, we examine these three aspects of the theory and critique and integrate important contributions to the literature related to each. We conclude that the three aspects of stakeholder theory are mutually supportive and that the normative base of the theory—which includes the modern theory of property rights—is fundamental.

If the unity of the corporate body is real, then there is reality and not simply legal fiction in the proposition that the managers of the unit are fiduciaries for it and not merely for its individual members, that they are... trustees for an institution [with multiple constituents] rather than attorneys for the stockholders.

E. Merrick Dodd, Jr.
Harvard Law Review, 1932

The idea that corporations have *stakeholders* has now become commonplace in the management literature, both academic and professional. Since the publication of Freeman's landmark book, *Strategic Management: A Stakeholder Approach* (1984), about a dozen books and more than 100 articles with primary emphasis on the stakeholder concept have appeared. (Significant recent examples include books by Alkhafaji, 1989; Anderson, 1989; and Brummer, 1991; and articles by Brenner & Cochran,

1991; Clarkson, 1991; Goodpaster, 1991; Hill & Jones, 1992; and Wood, 1991a,b; plus numerous papers by Freeman and various collaborators, individually cited.) *Stakeholder management* is the central theme of at least one important recent business and society text (Carroll, 1989), and a diagram purporting to represent the *stakeholder model* has become a standard element of "Introduction to Management" lectures and writings.

Unfortunately, anyone looking into this large and evolving literature with a critical eye will observe that the concepts *stakeholder, stakeholder model, stakeholder management,* and *stakeholder theory* are explained and used by various authors in very different ways and supported (or critiqued) with diverse and often contradictory evidence and arguments. Moreover, this diversity and its implications are rarely discussed—and possibly not even recognized. (The blurred character of the stakeholder concept is also emphasized by Brummer, 1991.) The purpose of this article is to point out some of the more important distinctions, problems, and implications associated with the stakeholder concept, as well as to clarify and justify its essential content and significance.

In the following section we contrast the stakeholder model of the corporation with the conventional input-output model of the firm and summarize our central thesis. We next present the three aspects of stakeholder theory—descriptive/empirical, instrumental, and normative—found in the literature and clarify the critical differences among them. We then raise the issue of justification: Why would anyone accept the stakeholder theory over alternative conceptions of the corporation? In subsequent sections, we present and evaluate the underlying evidence and arguments justifying the theory from the perspective of descriptive, instrumental, and normative justifications. We conclude that the three approaches to stakeholder theory, although quite different, are mutually supportive and that the *normative* base serves as the critical underpinning for the theory in all its forms.

The Central Theses

We summarize our central theses here:

Thesis 1: The stakeholder theory is unarguably **descriptive**. It presents a model describing what the corporation is. It describes the corporation as a constellation of co-operative and competitive interests possessing intrinsic value. Aspects of this model may be tested for descriptive accuracy: Is this model more descriptively accurate than rival models? Moreover, do observers and participants, in fact, see the corporation this way? The model can also serve as a framework for testing any empirical claims, including instrumental predictions, relevant to the stakeholder concept (but not for testing the concept's normative base).

Thesis 2: The stakeholder theory is also **instrumental**. It establishes a framework for examining the connections, if any, between the practice of stakeholder management and the achievement of various corporate performance goals. The principal focus of interest here has been the proposition that corporations practicing stakeholder management will, other things being equal, be relatively successful in conventional performance terms (profitability, stability, growth, etc.).

Thesis 3: Although Theses 1 and 2 are significant aspects of the stakeholder theory, its fundamental basis is **normative** and involves acceptance of the following ideas:

> (a) Stakeholders are persons or groups with legitimate interests in procedural and/or substantive aspects of corporate activity. Stakeholders are identified by **their** interests in the corporation, whether the corporation has any corresponding functional interest in **them**.
>
> (b) The interests of all stakeholders are of **intrinsic value.** That is, each group of stakeholders merits consideration for its own sake and not merely because of its ability to further the interests of some other group, such as the shareowners.

Thesis 4: The stakeholder theory is **managerial** in the broad sense of that term. It does not simply describe existing situations or predict cause-effect relationships; it also recommends attitudes, structures, and practices that, taken together, constitute stakeholder management. Stakeholder management requires, as its key attribute, simultaneous attention to the legitimate interests of all appropriate stakeholders, both in the establishment of organizational structures and general policies and in case-by-case decision making. This requirement holds for anyone managing or affecting corporate policies, including not only professional managers, but shareowners, the government, and others. Stakeholder theory does not necessarily presume that managers are the only rightful locus of corporate control and governance. Nor does the requirement of simultaneous attention to stakeholder interests resolve the longstanding problem of identifying stakeholders and evaluating their legitimate "stakes" in the corporation. The theory does not imply that all stakeholders (however they may be identified) should be equally involved in all processes and decisions.

The distinction between a stakeholder conception of the corporation and a conventional input-output perspective is highlighted by the contrasting models displayed in Figures 1 and 2. In Figure 1, investors, employees, and suppliers are depicted as contributing inputs, which the "black box" of the firm transforms into outputs for the benefit of customers. To be sure, each contributor of inputs expects to receive appropriate compensation, but the liberal economics, or "Adam Smith" interpretation, of this model in long-run equilibrium is that input contributors, at the margin, receive only "normal" or "market competitive" benefits (i.e., the benefits that they would obtain from some alternative use of their resources and time). Individual contributors who are particularly advantaged, such as possessors of scarce locations or skills, will, of course, receive "rents," but the rewards of the marginal contributors will only be "normal." As a result of competition throughout the system, the bulk of the benefits will go to the customers. (There is, of course, a

Figure 1: Contrasting models of the corporation:
Input-output model

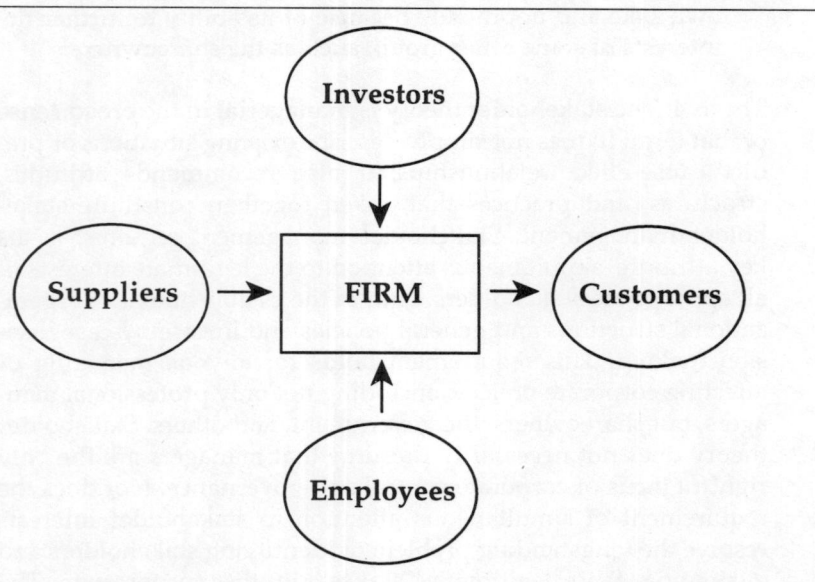

Marxist-capitalist version of this model in which both the customer and the investor arrows are reversed, and the object of the game is merely to produce benefits for the investors. This interpretation now seems to be confined almost exclusively to the field of finance.)

The stakeholder model (Figure 2) contrasts explicitly with the input-output model in all its variations. Stakeholder analysts argue that *all* persons or groups with legitimate interests participating in an enterprise do so to obtain benefits and that there is no prima facie priority of one set of interests and benefits over another. Hence, the arrows between the firm and its stakeholder constituents run in both directions. All stakeholder relationships are depicted in the same size and shape and are equidistant from the "black box" of the firm in the center. The distinctive features of this conception, as contrasted with conventional input-output conceptions, will become apparent as our analysis proceeds.

This summary of the stakeholder theory and our discussion throughout this article refer specifically to the theory's application to the investor-owned corporation. Although stakeholder concepts have been applied in

Figure 2: Contrasting models of the corporation: The stakeholder model

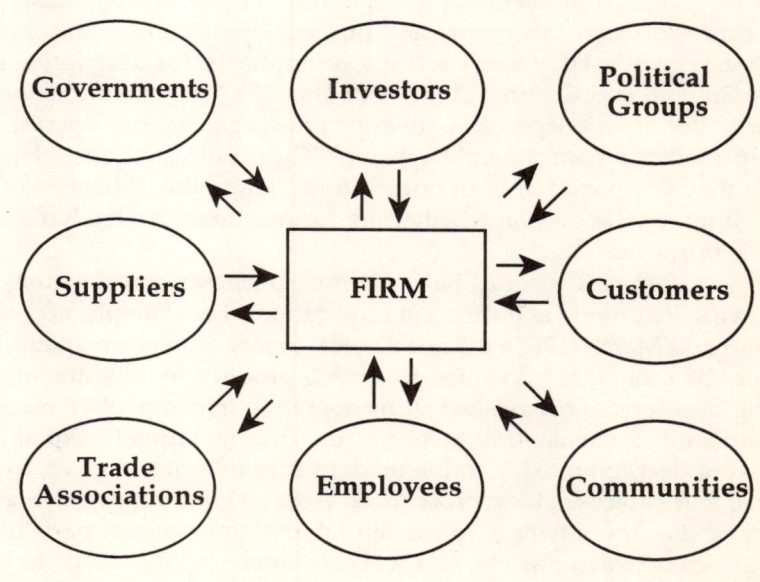

other settings (e.g., government agencies and social programs), these situations are fundamentally different, and simultaneous discussion of a variety of possible stakeholder relationships leads, in our view, to confusion rather than clarification. The critical corporate stakeholder issues, both in theory and in practice, involve evidentiary considerations and conceptual issues (e.g., the meaning of property rights) unique to the corporate setting.

It is also worth noting at the outset that the extent to which the stakeholder theory is understood to represent a controversial or challenging approach to conventional views varies greatly among market capitalist economies. These differences are highlighted in a recent issue of *The Economist* (1993: 52):

> In America, for instance, shareholders have a comparatively big say in the running of the enterprises they own; workers... have much less influence. In many European countries, shareholders have less say and workers more... [I]n Japan... managers have been left alone to run their companies as they see fit—namely for the benefit of employees and of allied companies, as much as for shareholders.

Alternative Aspects of Stakeholder Theory: Descriptive/Empirical, Instrumental, and Normative

One of the central problems in the evolution of stakeholder theory has been confusion about its nature and purpose. For example, stakeholder theory has been used, either explicitly or implicitly, for descriptive purposes. Brenner and Cochran (1991: 452) offered a "stakeholder theory of the firm" for "two purposes: to describe how organizations operate and to help predict organizational behavior." They contrasted this "theory," which they developed only in outline form, with other "theories of the firm," but they did not ask whether the various theories cited have comparable purposes.

In fact, different theories have different purposes and therefore different validity criteria and different implications. For example, according to Cyert and March (1963), the neoclassical theory of the firm attempts to explain the economic principles governing production, investment, and pricing decisions of established firms operating in competitive markets. In contrast, their behavioral theory of the firm attempts to explain the process of decision making in the modern firm in terms of goals, expectations, and choice-making procedures. Aoki's (1984) cooperative game theory of the firm attempts to explain internal governance, particularly the balance between owners' and workers' interests. In contrast to all of these contributions, transaction cost theory attempts to explain why firms exist (i.e., why economic activities are coordinated through formal organizations rather than simply through market contacts) (Coase, 1937; Williamson & Winter, 1991). (Although all of these theories are put forward as "positive" or "scientific" conceptions, there is a tendency for them to be used for normative purposes as well.)

The stakeholder theory differs from these and other "theories of the firm" in fundamental ways. The stakeholder theory is intended both to explain and to guide the structure and operation of the established corporation (the "going concern" in John R. Commons' famous phrase). Toward that end it views the corporation as an organizational entity through which numerous and diverse participants accomplish multiple, and not always entirely congruent, purposes. The stakeholder theory is general and comprehensive, but it is not empty; it goes well beyond the descriptive observation that "organizations have stakeholders." Unfortunately, much of what passes for stakeholder theory in the literature is implicit rather than explicit, which is one reason why diverse and sometimes confusing uses of the stakeholder concept have not attracted more attention.

The stakeholder theory can be, and has been, presented and used in a number of ways that are quite distinct and involve very different methodologies, types of evidence, and criteria of appraisal. Three types of uses are critical to our analysis.

Descriptive/Empirical

The theory is used to describe, and sometimes to explain, specific corporate characteristics and behaviors. For example, stakeholder theory has been used to describe (a) the nature of the firm (Brenner & Cochran, 1991), (b) the way managers think about managing (Brenner & Molander, 1977), (c) how board members think about the interests of corporate constituencies (Wang & Dewhirst, 1992), and (d) how some corporations are actually managed (Clarkson, 1991; Halal, 1990; Kreiner & Bhambri, 1991).

Instrumental

The theory, in conjunction with descriptive/empirical data where available, is used to identify the connections, or lack of connections, between stakeholder management and the achievement of traditional corporate objectives (e.g., profitability, growth). Many recent instrumental studies of corporate social responsibility, all of which make explicit or implicit reference to stakeholder perspectives, use conventional statistical methodologies (Aupperle, Carroll, & Hatfield, 1985; Barton, Hill, & Sundaram, 1989; Cochran & Wood, 1984; Cornell & Shapiro, 1987; McGuire, Sundgren, & Schneeweis, 1983; Preston & Sapienza, 1990; Preston, Sapienza, & Miller, 1991). Other studies are based on direct observation and interviews (Kotter & Heskett, 1992; O'Toole, 1985; see also, O'Toole, 1991). Whatever their methodologies, these studies have tended to generate "implications" suggesting that adherence to stakeholder principles and practices achieves conventional corporate performance objectives as well or better than rival approaches. Kotter and Heskett (1992) specifically observed that such highly successful companies as Hewlett-Packard, Wal-Mart, and Dayton Hudson—although very diverse in other ways—share a stakeholder perspective. Kotter and Heskett (1992: 59) wrote that "[a]lmost all [their] managers care strongly about people who have a stake in the business—customers, employees, stockholders, suppliers, etc."

Normative
The theory is used to interpret the function of the corporation, including the identification of moral or philosophical guidelines for the operation and management of corporations. Normative concerns dominated the classic stakeholder theory statements from the beginning (Dodd, 1932), and this tradition has been continued in the most recent versions (Carroll, 1989; Kuhn & Shriver, 1991; Marcus, 1993). Even Friedman's (1970) famous attack on the concept of corporate social responsibility was cast in normative terms.

Contrasting/Combining Approaches
Each of these uses of stakeholder theory is of some value, but the values differ in each use. The *descriptive* aspect of stakeholder theory reflects and explains past, present, and future states of affairs of corporations and their stakeholders. Simple description is common and desirable in the exploration of new areas and usually expands to generate explanatory and predictive propositions. (All such activities shall be called *descriptive* for our purposes.) *Instrumental* uses of stakeholder theory make a connection between stakeholder approaches and commonly desired objectives such as profitability. Instrumental uses usually stop short of exploring specific links between cause (i.e., stakeholder management) and effect (i.e., corporate performance) in detail, but such linkage is certainly implicit. The much-quoted Stanford Research Institute's (SRI) definition of stakeholders as "those groups without whose support the organization would cease to exist" (SRI, 1963; quoted in Freeman, 1984: 31) clearly implies that corporate managers must induce constructive contributions from their stakeholders to accomplish their own desired results (e.g., perpetuation of the organization, profitability, stability, growth).

In *normative* uses, the correspondence between the theory and the observed facts of corporate life is not a significant issue, nor is the association between stakeholder management and conventional performance measures a critical test. Instead, a normative theory attempts to interpret the function of, and offer guidance about, the investor-owned corporation on the basis of some underlying moral or philosophical principles. Although both normative and instrumental analyses may be "prescriptive" (i.e., they may express or imply more or less appropriate choices on the part of decision makers), they rest on entirely different bases. An instrumental approach is essentially hypothetical; it says, in effect, "If you want to achieve (avoid) results X, Y, or Z, then adopt (don't adopt) principles and practices A, B, or C." The normative approach, in contrast, is not hypothetical but categorical; it says, in effect, "Do (Don't do) this because it is the right (wrong) thing to do." Much of the stakeholder literature, including the contributions of both proponents and critics, is clearly normative, although the fundamental normative principles involved are often unexamined.

A striking characteristic of the stakeholder literature is that diverse theoretical approaches are often combined without acknowledgement. Indeed, the temptation to seek a three-in-one theory—or at least to slide easily from one theoretical base to another—is strong. Clarkson (1991: 349), for example, asserted an explicit connection among all three when he concluded that his stakeholder management model represents a new framework for "describing, evaluating, and managing corporate social performance."

All three types of theory are also to be found in the work of Freeman, whom many regard as the leading contributor to the stakeholder literature. In his original treatise, he asserted that changing events create a descriptive fit for the theory:

> Just as the separation of the owner-manager-employee required a rethinking of the concept of control and private property as analyzed by Berle and Means (1932), so does the emergence of numerous stakeholder groups and new strategic issues require a rethinking of our traditional picture of the firm... We must redraw the picture in a way that accounts for the changes. (1984: 24)

At the same time, he also endorsed the theory's *instrumental basis*. We should, he noted, "explore the logic of this concept in practical terms, i.e., in terms of how organizations can succeed in the current and future business environment" (1984: 25). Instrumental concerns are also reflected in Freeman's extensive discussion of stakeholder management implementation techniques, both in his 1984 treatise and in other papers (Freeman & Gilbert, 1987; Freeman & Reed, 1983). In a later work, however, Evan and Freeman (1988: 97) justified stakeholder theory on normative grounds, specifically its power to satisfy the moral rights of individuals. They asserted that the theory of the firm must be reconceptualized "along essentially Kantian lines." This means each stakeholder group has a right to be treated as an end in itself, and not as means to some other end, "and therefore must participate in determining the future direction of the firm in which [it has] a stake."

The muddling of theoretical bases and objectives, although often understandable, has led to less rigorous thinking and analysis than the stakeholder concept requires. To see the significance of the distinctions among descriptive, instrumental, and normative uses of the stakeholder concept, consider the current controversy over the special privileges of top managers in large corporations, particularly in connection with mergers and acquisitions. There is considerable evidence that in the burst of large corporate takeovers during the 1980s, share values typically rose for acquired firms and fell for acquiring firms. Many observers have speculated that self-serving managerial activity accounts for both results (Jensen, 1989; Weidenbaum & Vogt, 1987). The acquired firms gain in value because, prior to the takeover, they were burdened by inefficient, self-serving managers, and the acquiring firms lose in value because the impetus for the acquisition was not return on investment for owners but ego gratification and career advancement for their top managers. If this analysis is accurate, and if managers' nests are often feathered in other ways (e.g., salaries, bonuses) at the expense of shareowners, then it is descriptively true that managers' interests have priority over those of other stakeholders, including shareowners. But we cannot move directly from an *is* claim—the de facto priority of managers' interests—to an *ought* claim in either instrumental or normative contexts. Moreover, even if it were true that higher paid managers did, in fact, achieve higher levels of profitability (thus meeting instrumental criteria), it would still not follow that higher pay/profit results were normatively justifiable. (Witness the near-universal condemnation of the income/profit achievements of the 19th-century robber barons.)

The Problem of Justification

The underlying epistemological issue in the stakeholder literature is the problem of justification: Why should the stakeholder theory be accepted or preferred over alternative conceptions? Until this question is addressed, the distinctions among empirical, instrumental, and normative approaches can be papered over. Moreover, the answer to this question must be related to the distinct purpose that the theory is intended to serve. That is, reasons to accept the stakeholder theory as a descriptive account of how managers behave, or of how the business world is constituted, are different from reasons to accept the stakeholder theory as a guide for managerial behavior, and so on.

The stakeholder theory is justified in the literature, explicitly or implicitly, in ways that correspond directly to the three approaches to the theory set out in the previous section: descriptive, instrumental, and normative. Descriptive justifications attempt to show that the concepts embedded in the theory correspond to observed reality. Instrumental justifications point to evidence of the connection between stakeholder management and corporate performance. Normative justifications appeal to underlying concepts such as individual or group "rights," "social contract," or utilitarianism. (Brummer's recent survey of this literature ignores descriptive issues but emphasizes "power and performance," i.e., instrumental, and "deontological," i.e., normative, arguments; cf. Brummer, 1991.)

In our view, the three aspects of the stakeholder theory are nested within each other, as suggested by Figure 3. The external shell of the theory is its descriptive aspect; the theory presents and explains relationships that are observed in the external world. The theory's descriptive accuracy is supported, at the second level, by its instrumental and predictive value; *if* certain practices are carried out, *then* certain results will be obtained. The central core of the theory is, however, normative. The descriptive accuracy of the theory presumes the truth of the core normative conception, insofar as it presumes that managers and other agents act as *if* all stakeholders' interests have intrinsic value. In turn, recognition of

Figure 3: Three aspects of stakeholder theory

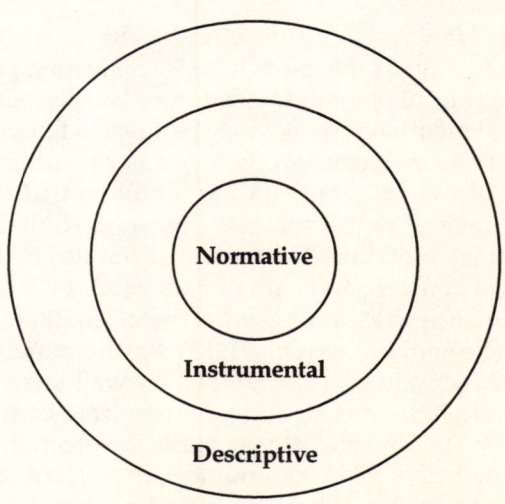

these ultimate moral values and obligations gives stakeholder management its fundamental normative base. In the following sections, we survey the evidence and argument involved in each of these approaches to the justification of the stakeholder theory.

Descriptive Justifications

There is ample descriptive evidence, some of which has already been cited, that many managers believe themselves, or are believed by others, to be practicing stakeholder management. Indeed, as early as the mid 1960s, Raymond Baumhart's (1968) survey of upper-level managers revealed that about 80 percent regarded it as unethical management behavior to focus solely in the interest of shareowners and not in the interest of employees and customers. Since then, other surveys asking similar questions about the stakeholder sensitivity of managers have returned similar results (Brenner & Molander, 1977; Posner & Schmidt. 1984). Ongoing empirical studies by both Clarkson (1991) and Halal (1990) attempt to distinguish firms that practice stakeholder management from those that do not, and both investigators found significant numbers of firms in the first category. Managers may not make explicit reference to "stakeholder theory," but the vast majority of them apparently adhere in practice to one of the central tenets of the stakeholder theory, namely, that their role is to satisfy a wider set of stakeholders, not simply the shareowners. (Note, however, that the 171 managers surveyed by Alkhafaji, 1989, did not believe that the corporate governance roles of any stakeholders, including shareowners, should be increased. Perhaps not surprisingly, they strongly favored increased dominance of corporate governance by management).

Another kind of descriptive justification for the stakeholder theory stems from the role it plays as the implicit basis for existing practices and institutions, including legal opinion and statutory law. Recent court decisions and new legislation have weakened the so-called "business judgment rule," which vests management with exclusive authority over the conduct of a company's affairs only on the condition that the financial welfare of stockholders is single-mindedly pursued (Chirelstein, 1974: 60). At last count, at least 29 states have adopted statutes that extend the range of permissible concern by boards of directors to a host of non-shareowner constituencies, including employees, creditors, suppliers, customers, and local communities (Orts, 1992). Furthermore, courts have tended to support these statutes. For example, the well-known Delaware Supreme Court decision in Unocal, although requiring corporate directors to show that a "reasonable" threat exists before fighting hostile takeover offers, nonetheless allowed a number of concerns to affect the determination of such "reasonableness," including "the impact [of the takeover] on 'constituencies' other than shareholders (i.e., creditors, customers, employees, and perhaps even the community generally)" (*Unocal Corp. v. Mesa Petroleum Co.*, 1985). In a more recent Delaware case, *Paramount Communications, Inc. v. Time, Inc.* (1990), the Unocal rationale was expanded to allow directors to include factors such as long-range business plans and a corporation's "culture." In one of the most dramatic challenges to the ownership rights of hostile acquirers, the Supreme Court of the United States upheld an Indiana statute that in the Court's own words "condition[s] acquisition of control of a corporation on approval of a majority of the pre-existing disinterested shareholders" (emphasis added) (*CTCS Corp. v. Dynamics Corp. of America*, 1987).

As Orts noted, this trend toward stakeholder law is not solely a U.S. phenomenon and is reflected in the existing and emerging laws of many developed countries. The so-called codetermination laws of Germany require employee representation on second-tier boards of directors. The Companies Act of Great Britain mandates that company directors shall include the interests of employees in their decision making (*Companies Act*, 1980). The new "harmonization" laws of the European Community (EC) will, when approved, include provisions permitting corporations to take into account the interests of creditors, customers, potential investors, and employees (Orts, 1992). Finally, the well-known corporate governance model in Japan—through both law and custom—presumes that Japanese corporations exist within a tightly connected and interrelated set of stakeholders, including suppliers, customers, lending institutions, and friendly corporations.

Another series of legal developments in the U.S. asserts the interests of third-party stakeholders—specifically, unsuccessful job applicants—in business operations. Title VII of the Civil Rights Act of 1964 explicitly makes it a violation of law for an employer "to fail or refuse to hire... any individual" on the basis of discriminatory criteria (42 U.S.C. §§2000e-2a(l) & (2), 1982). This legislation has become the focus of numerous legal complaints and some substantial settlements. In a class action suit involving Potomac Electric Power Co., Washington, DC, complainants charged that the company had hired far fewer Blacks from its applicant pool than would have been expected on statistical grounds. The judge certified a "class" of more than 7,000 unsuccessful Black applicants, most of whom will be eligible for compensation out of a $38.4 million settlement pool (which is also available to employees experiencing discrimination) (*The Washington Post*, 21 February 1993).

Both of these sets of legal developments reinforce our initial statement that stakeholders are defined by *their* legitimate interest in the corporation, rather than simply by the corporation's interest in *them*. But neither the legal developments nor the management survey results provide definitive epistemological justification for the stakeholder theory. Managers adopting the stakeholder approach may be relieved to learn that they are not alone, and indeed that they are conforming to the latest management or legal trends, but both the survey results and legal developments are, at bottom, simply facts. They do not constitute the basis for the stakeholder (or any other) theory of management. Indeed, even if the stakeholder concept is implicit in current legal trends (a proposition that is not universally accepted), one cannot derive a stakeholder theory of management from a stakeholder theory of law any more than one can derive a "tort" theory of management from the tort theory of law.

The hazards of using purely descriptive data, whether jurisprudential or otherwise, as justification for a broad theory are well known. There is the problem of the so-called "naturalistic fallacy," moving from *is* to *ought* or from *describe* to *evaluate*, without the necessary intervening analysis and explanation (Moore, 1959/1903: 15-16). Then, again, there is the simple problem of hasty generalization. By the logic of descriptive justification, if new surveys showed that managers were abandoning stakeholder orientations, or if the legal support for broad stakeholder interests were to weaken, the theory would be invalidated. But this observation offers a significant clue about the nature of the theory itself, because few if any of its adherents would be likely to abandon it, even if current legal or managerial trends were to shift. This suggests that the descriptive support for the stakeholder theory, as well as the critiques of this support to be found in the literature, are of limited significance and that the most important issues for stakeholder theory lie elsewhere.

Instrumental Justifications

Because the descriptive approach to grounding a stakeholder theory is inadequate, justifications based on a connection between stakeholder strategies and organizational performance should be examined. Consider, for example, the simple hypothesis that corporations whose managers adopt stakeholder principles and practices will perform better financially than those that do not. This hypothesis has never been tested directly, and its testing involves some formidable challenges. (Clarkson's ongoing work is the only significant effort of this type known to us; cf. Clarkson, Deck, & Shiner, 1992.) The view that stakeholder management and favorable performance go hand in hand has, however, become commonplace in the management literature, both professional and academic. The earliest direct statement is probably that of General Robert E. Wood, then-CEO of Sears, in 1950: "All I can say is that if the other three parties named above [customers, employees, community] are properly taken care of, the stockholder will benefit in the long pull" (quoted in Worthy, 1984: 64). A recent effort to introduce practicing managers to the stakeholder concept and to improve their ability to implement stakeholder management practices is the work by Savage, Nix, Whitehead, and Blair (1991). Brummer (1991) cited not only Freeman (1989) but also Ackoff; Manning; Maslow; Peters and Waterman; Starling; Sturdivant; and others in support of stakeholder theory's instrumental base.

Unfortunately, the large body of literature dealing with the connections, if any, between various aspects of corporate social performance or ethics, on one hand, and conventional financial and market performance indicators, on the other, does not translate easily into a stakeholder theory context. Whatever value the social/financial performance studies may have on their own merits, most of them do not include reliable indicators of the stakeholder management (i.e., the independent variable) side of the relationship. There is some evidence, based on analysis of the *Fortune* corporate reputation surveys, that the satisfaction of multiple stakeholders need not be a zero sum game (i.e., that benefits to one stakeholder group need not come entirely at the expense of another) (Preston & Sapienza, 1990). As previously noted, Kotter and Heskett's (1992) case studies of a small number of high-performance companies indicated that the managers of those companies tend to emphasize the interests of all major stakeholder groups in their decision making. However, there is as yet no compelling empirical evidence that the optimal strategy for maximizing a firm's conventional financial and market performance is stakeholder management.

Analytical Arguments
Even without empirical verification, however, stakeholder management can be linked to conventional concepts of organizational success through analytical argument. The main focus of this effort in the recent literature builds on established concepts of principal-agent relations (Jensen & Mechling, 1976) and the firm as a nexus of contracts (Williamson & Winter, 1991). Agency theory and firm-as-contract theory, although arising from different sources, are closely related and share a common emphasis: efficiency. (They also share the terminology and methodology of the new transaction cost literature; cf. Williamson, 1985.) Agency theorists argue that corporations are structured to minimize the costs of getting some participants (the agents) to do what other participants (the principals) desire. Firm-as-contract theorists argue that participants agree to cooperate with each other within organizations (i.e., through contracts), rather than simply deal with each other through the market, to minimize the costs of search, coordination, insecurity, etc.

Hill and Jones (1992: 132, 134) are responsible for the most ambitious attempt to integrate the stakeholder concept with agency theory (see also, Sharplin & Phelps, 1989). These authors enlarged the standard principal agent paradigm of financial economics, which emphasizes the relationship between shareowners and managers, to create "stakeholder-agency theory," which constitutes, in their view, "a generalized theory of agency." According to this conception, managers "can be seen as the agents of [all] other stakeholders." They noted that stakeholders differ among themselves with respect to (a) the *importance* (to them) of their stake in the firm and (b) their *power* vis-à-vis the managers. They also noted that there is considerable friction within the stakeholder-agent negotiation process—some of it because of some participants' ability to retard equilibrating adjustments that are unfavorable to themselves. They therefore argued that there is no reason to assume that stakeholder-agent relationships are in equilibrium at any particular time. (This contrasts sharply with the "perfect markets" hypothesis favored in the finance literature.) In their view, the process, direction, and speed of adaptation in stakeholder-agent relationships, rather than the equilibrium set of contributions and rewards, should be the primary focus of analysis. This brief summary cannot do justice to their rich conception, but the key point for current purposes is that the stakeholders are drawn into relationships with the managers to accomplish organizational tasks as efficiently as possible; hence, the stakeholder model is linked instrumentally to organizational performance.

A similar theme emerges from the firm-as-contract analysis of Freeman and Evan (1990; see also Evan & Freeman, 1988). They recommended integrating the stakeholder concept with the Coasian view of the firm-as-contract and a Williamson-style analysis of transaction costs to "conceptualize the firm as a set of multilateral contracts over time." According to Freeman and Evan,

> Managers administer contracts among employees, owners, suppliers, customers, and the community. Since each of these groups can invest in asset specific transactions which affect the other groups, methods of conflict resolution, or safeguards must be found. (1990: 352)

They emphasized that all parties have an equal right to bargain and, therefore, that a minimal condition for the acceptance of such multipartite arrangements by each contracting party is a notion of "fair contract," i.e., governance rules that "ensure that the interests of all parties are at least taken into consideration" (1990: 35 Once again, the stakeholder model (and its implementation through a set of acceptable implicit contracts) is seen as essential to successful organizational performance.

The stakeholder interpretations of both agency theory and firm-as-contract theory give special attention to the differential position and special role of managers vis-à-vis all other stakeholders. Hill and Jones (1992: 140) emphasized "information asymmetry" between managers and other stakeholders and contrasted the concentration of resource control by managers with the diffusion of control within stakeholder groups in which there may be no mechanism to gain command over a significant portion of the group's total resources. Evan and Freeman (1993: 102-103) asserted that "management has a duty of safeguarding the welfare of the abstract entity that is the corporation" and of balancing the conflicting claims of multiple stakeholders to achieve this goal. They further declared:

> A stakeholder theory of the firm must redefine the purpose of the firm.... The very purpose of the firm is, in our view, to serve as a vehicle for coordinating stakeholder interests. (102-103)

According to this perspective, success in satisfying multiple stakeholder interests—rather than in meeting conventional economic and financial criteria—would constitute the ultimate test of corporate performance.

But how will multiple and diverse stakeholders be assured that their interests are being coordinated in ways that lead to the most favorable possible results for themselves (i.e., the most favorable results consistent with the requirements of other stakeholders)? Hill and Jones (1992: 140-143) stressed the importance of (a) monitoring devices that have the effect of reducing information asymmetry (e.g., public reporting requirements) and (b) enforcement mechanisms, including law, "exit" (the possibility, or credible threat, of withdrawal from the relationship), and "voice." Freeman and Evan (1993) emphasized the notion of fairness. Going beyond the notion of "fair contracting," they recommended that the criterion of "fairness" in stakeholder bargains be a Rawlsian "veil of ignorance." Under a "veil of ignorance," parties to a bargain agree upon a set of possible outcomes prior to determining which outcome will be received by which party (e.g., one person cuts the cake, another takes the first slice) (Rawls, 1971, cited in Freeman & Evan, 1990: 352-353).

Both pairs of analysts, Hill and Jones and Freeman and Evan, placed greater emphasis on the process of multiple-stakeholder coordination than on the specific agreements/bargains. Both groups stressed that mutual and voluntary acceptability of bargains by all contracting stakeholders is the necessary criterion for efficient contracts. Both neglected the roles of potential stakeholders not conspicuously involved in explicit or implicit contracts with the firm. The two pairs of authors differed slightly in one respect: Hill and Jones saw the network of relationships as consisting of separate implicit contracts between each stakeholder group and "management" (as a central node). whereas Freeman and Evan ultimately viewed the firm "as a series of multilateral contracts among [all] stakeholders" (1990: 354).

Weaknesses of Instrumental Justifications

Perhaps the most important similarity between these two independent attempts to justify the stakeholder model lies in the fact that although they draw initially on the conceptual apparatus of instrumental or efficiency-based theories (i.e., principal-agent relations and "firm-as-contract" theory), they ultimately rely upon noninstrumental or normative arguments. This shift is less conspicuous in the case of Hill and Jones, who implied that monitoring and enforcement mechanisms will be sufficient to curb opportunistic behavior by managers at the expense of other stakeholders. The authors would no doubt agree, however, that the ultimate success of stakeholder-agency theory would require a fundamental shift in managerial objectives away from shareowners and toward the interests of all stakeholders; such a shift would necessarily involve normative, rather than purely instrumental, considerations. Freeman and Evan's recourse to a Rawlsian concept of "fairness" as the ultimate criterion for stakeholder bargains is an overt elevation of normative criteria over instrumental ones. No theorist, including Rawls, has ever maintained that bargains reached on the basis of a "veil of ignorance" would maximize efficiency. By elevating the fairness principle to a central role, Freeman and Evan shifted their attention from ordinary economic contracts of the sort envisaged by Coase, Williamson, and the mainstream agency theorists, which are governed by individual efficiency considerations. Instead, they emphasized what have been called "heuristic" or "social" contracts that rest upon broad normative principles governing human conduct (Donaldson & Dunfee, In press, 1994).

It should come as no surprise that stakeholder theory cannot be fully justified by instrumental considerations. The empirical evidence is inadequate, and the analytical arguments, although of considerable substance, ultimately rest on more than purely instrumental grounds. This conclusion carries an important implication: Although those who use the stakeholder concept often cite its consistency with the pursuit of conventional corporate performance objectives (and there is no notable evidence of its inconsistency), few of them would abandon the concept if it turned out to be only as *equally* efficacious as other conceptions. O'Toole (1991: 18-19), for example, examined a case in which the economic consequences of stakeholder versus conventional management "ended up neutral"; he stressed that "it is the *moral consequences* that are at issue" and described stakeholder analysis as "the sine quo non of business virtue" (emphasis in the original).

Normative Justifications

The normative basis for stakeholder theory involves its connection with more fundamental and better-accepted philosophical concepts. The normative assumptions of traditional economic theory are too feeble to support stakeholder theory, and the concept of a free market populated with free and rational preference seekers, however correct and important, is compatible with both stakeholder and nonstakeholder perspectives. Of course, the two normative propositions stated at the beginning of this article—that stakeholders are identified by *their* interest in the affairs of the corporation and that the interests of all stakeholders have intrinsic value— can be viewed as axiomatic principles that require no further justification. Unfortunately, this approach provides no basis for responding to critics who reject these propositions out of hand.

One way to construct a normative foundation for the stakeholder model is to examine its principal competitor, the model of *management* control in the interests of shareowners, as represented by the business judgment rule. As noted in previous sections, there is considerable criticism of this model on descriptive grounds. Pejovich (1990: 58) noted that in the modern corporation (as opposed to the owner-managed firm) the rights of shareowners are "attenuated" by the dispersion of ownership and by high agency costs; he stressed that "the *economic system*," not "the *legal system*," is responsible for this "attenuation of the right of ownership" (emphasis in original). Many direct observers (e.g., Geneen & Moscow, 1984; Pickens, 1987) have questioned managers' devotion to shareowner welfare, and survey results such as those of Alkhafaji (1989) and Posner and Schmidt (1992) provide statistical support for these perceptions.

But the management serving the shareowners model (i.e., the principal-agent model in its standard financial economics form) is not only descriptively inaccurate; careful analysis reveals that it is normatively unacceptable as well. Changes in state incorporation laws to reflect a "constituency" perspective have been mentioned. The normative basis for these changes in current mainstream legal thinking is articulated in the recent American Law Institute report, *Principles of Corporate Governance* (1992). The relevant portion of this document begins by affirming the central corporate objective of "enhancing corporate profit and shareholder gain," but it immediately introduces qualifications: "Even if corporate profit and shareholder gain are not thereby enhanced," the corporation *must* abide by law and *may* "take into account ethical considerations" and engage in philanthropy (Sec.2.01(a)(b); 1992: 69). The accompanying commentary explicitly affirmed the stakeholder concept:

> The modern corporation by its nature creates interdependencies with a variety of groups with whom the corporation has a legitimate concern, such as employees, customers, suppliers, and members of the communities in which the corporation operates. (1992: 72)

The commentary further noted that response to social and ethical considerations is often consistent with long-run (if not short-run) increases in profit and value, but it continues:

> Nevertheless, observation suggests that corporate decisions are not infrequently made on the basis of ethical consideration even when doing so would not enhance corporate profit or shareholder gain. *Such behavior is not only appropriate, but desirable. Corporate officials are not less morally obliged than any other citizens to take ethical considerations into account, and it would be unwise social policy to preclude them from doing so...* [The text] does not impose a legal obligation to take ethical considerations into account. However, the absence of a legal obligation to follow ethical principles does not mean that corporate decisionmakers are not subject to the same ethical considerations as other members of society. (American Law Institute, 1992: 80-82, emphasis added).

Formal Analysis: Theory of Property

To go beyond this practical rejection of the "management serving the shareowners" model, more formal normative-justifications of stakeholder theory might be based either on broad theories of philosophical ethics, such as utilitarianism, or on narrower "middle-level" theories derived from the notion that a "social contract" exists between corporations and society. A comprehensive survey of this terrain would go far beyond the scope of this article, and much of it has been recently traversed by others (Brummer, 1991; Freeman, 1991; see also, Donaldson, 1982). Here, we offer a brief sketch of a normative basis for the stakeholder theory that combines several different philosophical approaches and that is, we believe, original in the literature. We argue that the stakeholder theory can be normatively based on the evolving theory of property.

There is a subtle irony in proposing that the stakeholder model can be justified on the basis of the theory of property, because the traditional view has been that a focus on property rights justifies the dominance of shareowners' interests. Indeed, the fact that property rights are the critical base for conventional shareowner-dominance views makes it all the more significant that the current trend of thinking with respect to the philosophy of property runs in the opposite direction. In fact, this trend—as presented in the now-classic contributions of Coase (1960) and Honore (1961) and in more recent works by Becker (1978, 1992a,b,c) and Munzer (1992)—runs strongly counter to the conception that private property exclusively enshrines the interests of owners.

Considerable agreement now exists as to the theoretical definition of property as a "bundle" of many rights, some of which may be limited. More than 30 years ago, Coase (1960: 44) chided economists for adhering to a simplistic concept of ownership:

> We may speak of a person owning land... but what the landowner in fact possesses is the right to carry out a circumscribed list of actions. The rights of a land-owner are not unlimited... [This] would be true under any system of law. A system in which the rights of individuals were unlimited would be one in which there were no rights to acquire.

Honore (1961) specifically included the notion of restrictions against harmful uses within the definition of property itself. Pejovich (1990: 27-28), probably the most conservative economic theorist working in this area, emphasized that "property rights are relations between individuals" and thus "it is wrong to separate human rights from property rights"; he further noted that "the right of ownership is not an unrestricted right."

The notion that property rights are embedded in human rights and that restrictions against harmful uses are intrinsic to the property rights concept clearly brings the interests of others (i.e., of non-owner stakeholders) into the picture. Of course, *which* uses of property should be restricted and *which* persons should count as stakeholders remain unspecified. Simply bringing nonowner stakeholders into the conception of property does not provide by itself justification for stakeholder arguments assigning managerial responsibilities toward specific groups, such as employees and customers. The important point, however, is that the contemporary theoretical concept of private property clearly does not ascribe unlimited rights to owners and hence does not support the popular claim that the responsibility of managers is to act solely as agents for the shareowners. (The necessary compromise between individual property rights and other considerations is highlighted in the "takings" issue—i.e., modified to protect the interests of others or society in general. For a survey of current views on this complex matter, see Mercuro, 1992.)

These comments examine the scope of property rights, but it is also relevant to examine their *source* (i.e., What basic principles determine *who* should get [and be allowed to keep] *what* in society?). Unless property rights are regarded as simple, self-evident moral conceptions, they must be based on more fundamental ideas of distributive justice. The main contending theories of distributive justice include Utilitarianism, Libertarianism, and social contract theory (Becker, 1992). The battle among competing theories of distributive justice is most often a battle over which characteristics highlighted by the theories—such as need, ability, effort, and mutual agreement—are most relevant for determining fair distributions of wealth, income, etc. (The role of theories of justice within organizations is attracting considerable current attention; cf. Greenberg, 1987.)

For example, when the characteristic of need (a feature highlighted by Utilitarianism) is the criterion, the resulting theory of property places formidable demands upon property owners to mitigate their self-interest in favor of enhancing the interests (i.e., meeting the needs) of others. When *ability or effort* (features highlighted by Libertarianism) is the criterion, the resulting theory leaves property owners freer to use their resources (acquired, it is assumed, as a result of ability and effort) as they see fit. Social contract theory places primary emphasis on expressed or implied understandings among individuals and groups as to appropriate distributions and uses of property.

Many of the most respected contemporary analysts of property rights reject the notion that any *single* theory of distributive justice is universally applicable. Indeed, it seems counterintuitive that any one principle could account for all aspects of the complex bundle of rights and responsibilities that constitutes "property." Beginning with Becker's (1978) analysis, the trend is toward theories that are pluralistic, allowing more than one fundamental principle to play a role (Becker, 1992a; see also, Munzer, 1992). But if a pluralistic theory of property rights is accepted, then the connection between the theory of property and the stakeholder theory becomes explicit. All critical characteristics underlying the classic theories of distributive justice are present among the stakeholders of a corporation, as they are conventionally conceived and presented in contemporary stakeholder theory. For example, the "stake" of long-term employees who have worked to build and maintain a successful business operation is essentially based on effort. The stake of people living in the surrounding community may be based on their need, say, for clean air or the maintenance of their civic infrastructure. Customer stakes are based on the satisfactions and protections implicitly promised in the market offer, and so on. One need not make the more radical assertion that such stakes constitute formal or legal property rights, although some forceful critics of current corporate governance arrangements appear to hold this view (Nader & Green, 1973). All that is necessary is to show that such characteristics, which are the same as those giving rise to fundamental concepts of property rights, give various groups a moral interest, commonly referred to as a "stake," in the affairs of the corporation. Thus, the normative principles that underlie the contemporary pluralistic theory of property rights also provide the foundation for the stakeholder theory as well.

Managerial Implications

A full discussion of the managerial implications of this analysis would require much more discussion. As a summary, the two points we emphasize are (a) the recognition of specific stakeholders and their stakes by managers and other stakeholders and (b) the role of managers and the *management function,* as distinct from the *persons* involved, within the stakeholder model. These two issues are intimately intertwined.

It is the responsibility of managers, and the management function, to select activities and direct resources to obtain benefits for legitimate stakeholders. The question is, Who are the legitimate stakeholders? Some answers in the literature are, in our view, too narrow; others are too broad. The firm-as-contract view holds that legitimate stakeholders are identified by the existence of a contract, expressed or implied, between them and the firm. Direct input contributors are included, but environmental interests such as communities are also believed to have at least loose quasi-contracts (and, of course, sometimes very specific ones) with their business constituents.

We believe that the firm-as-contract perspective, although correct, is incomplete as a description of the corporation. For example, many business relationships with "communities" are so vague as to pass beyond even the broadest conception of "contract." The plant-closing controversy of the last couple of decades clearly shows that some communities had come to expect—and sometimes were able to enforce—stakeholder claims that some firms clearly did not recognize. As another example, potential job applicants, unknown to the firm, nevertheless have a stake in being considered for a job (but not necessarily to *get* a job). Lacking any connection to the firm, these potential employees are difficult to view as participating in the firm by reason of a *contract*, either implied or explicit. (We do not mean, however, to rule out possible relevance of so-called social contracts to such situations; cf. Donaldson & Dunfee, 1994b.) Stakeholders are identified through the actual or potential harms and benefits that they experience or anticipate experiencing as a result of the firm's actions or inactions. In practice, and in addition to legal requirements, appraisal of the legitimacy of such expectations is an important function of management, often in concert with other already recognized stakeholders.

Excessive breadth in the identification of stakeholders has arisen from a tendency to adopt definitions such as "anything influencing or influenced by" the firm (Freeman, 1984, quoting with approval Thompson, 1967). This definition opens the stakeholder set to actors that form part of the firm's environment—and that, indeed, may have some impact on its activities—but that have no specific stake in the firm itself. That is, they stand to gain no particular benefit from the firm's successful operation. The two types of interests that have cropped up most frequently in this connection are (a) competitors and (b) the media. Competitors were introduced as factors that have "an influence on managerial autonomy" in Dill's (1958) article, which is appropriately cited in the literature as a precursor of stakeholder analysis. However, neither the term stakeholder nor the notion of a *stake* (i.e., potential benefit) was explicitly introduced in Dill's analysis. In any event, in the normal course of events, competitors do not seek benefits from the focal firm's success; on the contrary, they may stand to lose whatever the focal firm gains. Competitive firms may, of course, join in common collaborative activities (e.g., through trade associations), but here the shared (noncompetitive) interests account for the stakeholder relationship. The notion that the media should be routinely recognized as stakeholders was originally introduced by Freeman (1984), but it seems to have been eliminated (without explicit explanation) from his later writings. It is essential to draw a clear distinction between influencers and stakeholders: some actors in the enterprise (e.g., large investors) may be both, but some recognizable stakeholders (e.g., the job applicants) have no influence, and some influencers (e.g., the media) have no stakes.

The role of managers within the stakeholder framework described in the literature is also contradictory. Aoki (1984), for example, recognized only investors and employees as significant stakeholders and saw managers as essentially "referees" between these two stakeholder groups. He acknowledged neither (a) the essential role of management in the identification of stakeholders nor (b) the fact that managers are, themselves, stakeholders—and, indeed, a very privileged class of stakeholders—in the enterprise. Williamson (1985) is almost alone among academic analysts in emphasizing the fact that the managers of a firm are one of its most important and powerful constituencies and that—wittingly or unwittingly—they are extremely likely to practice opportunistic and self-aggrandizing behavior.

This last point is absolutely critical for our argument, and recognition of it confirms our most important proposition: that the stakeholder theory is fundamentally normative. We observed at the close of our discussion of instrumental justifications that the instrumental case for stakeholder management cannot be satisfactorily proved. Here we restate that observation and add that the ultimate managerial implication of the stakeholder theory is that managers *should* acknowledge the validity of diverse stakeholder interests and *should* attempt to respond to them within a mutually supportive framework, because that is a moral requirement for the legitimacy of the management function.

It is feared by some that a shift from the traditional shareowner orientation to a stakeholder orientation will make it more difficult to detect and discipline self-serving behavior by managers, who may always claim to be serving some broad set of stakeholder interests while they increase their powers and emoluments. Indeed, Orts (1992: 123) saw this as the "greatest danger" of the new "constituency statutes" for corporate governance, although he nevertheless supported the constituency approach.

Our response to this fear is twofold: First, the conventional model of the corporation, in both legal and managerial forms, has failed to discipline self-serving managerial behavior. In this era of multimillion dollar CEO compensation packages that continue to increase even when profits and wages decline (Bok, 1993), it is difficult to conceive of managers having greater scope for self-serving behavior than they have already. Second, the stakeholder model we have advanced here entails comprehensive restrictions on such behavior. Indeed, its very foundation prohibits any undue attention to the interests of any single constituency. To be sure, it remains to implement in law the sanctions, rules, and precedents that support the stakeholder conception of the corporation; in short, it remains to develop the legal version of the stakeholder model. (See, for example, Eisenberg's [1976] attempt to restructure the legal model of the corporation.) Yet over time, statutory and common law are almost certainly capable of achieving arrangements that encourage a broader, stakeholder conception of management—one which eschews single-minded subservience to shareowners' interests—while at the same time restraining the moral hazard of self-serving managers.

Conclusion

We have argued that the stakeholder theory is "managerial" and recommends the attitudes, structures, and practices that, taken together, constitute a *stakeholder* management philosophy. The theory goes beyond the purely descriptive observation that "organizations have stakeholders," which, although true, carries no direct managerial implications. Furthermore, the notion that stakeholder management contributes to successful economic performance, although widely believed (and not patently inaccurate), is insufficient to stand alone as a basis for the stakeholder theory. Indeed, the most thoughtful analyses of why stakeholder management might be casually related to corporate performance ultimately resort to normative arguments in support of their views. For these reasons, we believe that the ultimate justification for the stakeholder theory is to be found in its normative base. The plain truth is that the most prominent alternative to the stakeholder theory (i.e., the "management serving the shareowners" theory) is morally untenable. The theory of property rights, which is commonly supposed to support the conventional view, in fact—in its modern and pluralistic form—supports the stakeholder theory instead.

Thomas Donaldson is the John F. Connelly Professor of Business Ethics in the School of Business at Georgetown University. He is also an adjunct professor in the Department of Philosophy and a senior research fellow at the Kennedy Institute of Ethics. His current research focuses on the intersection between social contract and stakeholder theories of ethics, especially in the context of international business.

Lee E. Preston received his Ph.D. from Harvard University. He is a professor of business and public policy in the College of Business and Management at the University of Maryland. His current research interests include international business-government relations.

The development of this article benefited greatly from discussions held at the Conference on Stakeholder Theory at the University of Toronto, May 1993, and from the specific comments of many people, including Professors Aupperle, Carroll, Clarkson, Halal, Freeman, Jones, and Sethi.

Alkhafaji. A.F. 1989. *A stakeholder approach to corporate governance: Managing in a dynamic environment.* New York: Quorum Books.

American Law Institute. 1992. *Principles of corporate governance: Analysis and recommendations.* (Proposed final draft, March 31. 1992). Philadelphia, PA: Author.

Anderson, J.W., Jr. 1989. *Corporate social responsibility.* New York: Quorum Books.

Aoki, M. 1984. *The co-operative game theory of the firm.* Oxford: Clarendon Press.

Aupperle, K.E., Carroll, A. B., & Hatfield, J.D. 1985. An empirical examination of the relationship between corporate social responsibility and profitability. *Academy of Management Journal,* 28(2): 446-463.

Barton, S.L., Hill, N.C., & Sundaram, S. 1989. An empirical test of stakeholder theory predictions of capital structure. *Financial Management.* 18(1): 36-44.

Baumhart, R. 1968. *An honest profit: What businessmen say about ethics in business.* New York: Holt, Rinehart and Winston.

Becker, L. C. 1978. *Property rights.* London: Routledge & Kegan Paul.

Becker, L.C. 1992a. Property. In L.D. Becker & C.B. Becker (Eds.), *Encyclopedia of ethics,* vol. 2: 1023-1027. New York: Garland.

Becker. L.C. 1992b. Places for pluralism. *Ethics.* 102: 707-719.

Becker, L.C. 1992c. Too much property. *Philosophy and Public Affairs,* 21: 196-206.

Berle, A., & Means, G. 1932. *Private property and the modern corporation.* New York: Macmillan.

Bok, D. 1993. *The cost of talent: How executives and professionals are paid and how it affects America.* New York: Free Press.

Brenner, S. N., & Cochran, P. 1991. *The stakeholder theory of the firm: Implications for business and society theory and research.* Paper presented at the annual meeting of the International Association for Business and Society, Sundance, UT.

Brenner, S. N., & Molander, E. A. 1977. Is the ethics of business changing? *Harvard Business Review,* 58(1): 54- 65.

Brummer, 1. 1. 1991. *Corporate responsibility and legitimacy: An interdisciplinary analysis.* New York: Greenwood Press.

Carroll. A.B. 1989. *Business and society: Ethics and stakeholder management.* Cincinnati, OH: South-Western.

Chirelstein, M.A. 1974. Corporate law reform. In J.W. McKie (Ed.), *Social responsibility and the business predicament:* 41-78. Washington. DC: The Brookings Institution.

Civil Rights Act. Title VII; 42 USC §§ 2000e-2a(l) & (2), 1982.

Clarkson, M.B.E. 1991. Defining, evaluating, and managing corporate social performance: A stakeholder management model. In J.E. Post (Ed.), *Research in corporate social performance and policy:* 331-358. Greenwich, CT: JAI Press.

Clarkson, M. B. E., Deck, M. C., & Shiner, N. I. 1992. *The stakeholder management model in practice.* Paper presented at the annual meeting of the Academy of Management. Las Vegas, NV.

Coase, R.H. 1937. The nature of the firm. In O.E. Williamson & S.G. Winter (Eds.), *The nature of the firm: Origins, evolution, and development:* 18-33. New York: Oxford University Press.

Coase. R.H. 1960. The problem of social cost. *Journal of Law and Economics,* 3: 1-44.

Cochran, P. L., & Wood, R. A. 1984. Corporate social responsibility and financial performance. *Academy of Management Journal,* 27(1): 42-56.

Companies Act, 1980, Great Britain.

Cornell, B., & Shapiro, A.C. 1987. Corporate stakeholders and corporate finance. *Financial Management,* 16: 5-14.

CTS Corp. v. Dynamics Corp. of America. 1987. U.S. Supr., 481. 69, 87.

Cyert, R. M., & March, J.G. 1963. *A behavioral theory of the firm.* Englewood Cliffs. NJ: Prentice Hall.

Dill. W.R. 1958. Environment as an influence on managerial autonomy. *Administrative Science Quarterly,* 2: 409-443.

Dodd, E.M., Jr. 1932. For whom are corporate managers trustees? *Harvard Law Review,* 45: 1145-1163.

Donaldson, T. 1982. *Corporations and morality.* Englewood Cliffs, NJ: Prentice Hall.

Donaldson, T., & Dunfee. T.W. 1994. Towards a unified conception of business ethics: Integrative social contracts theory. *Academy of Management Review,* 19: 252-284.

Donaldson, T., & Dunfee, T. W. In press. Integrative social contracts theory: A communitarian conception of economic ethics. *Economics and Philosophy.*

The Economist. 1992. [Corporate governance special section] September 11: 52-62.

Eisenberg, M.A. 1976. *The structure of the corporation: A legal analysis.* Toronto: Little, Brown.

Evan, W.M., & Freeman, R.E. 1988. A stakeholder theory of the modern corporation: Kantian capitalism. In T. Beauchamp & N. Bowie (Eds.), *Ethical theory and business:* 75-93. Englewood Cliffs. NJ: Prentice Hall.

Freeman, R.E. 1984. *Strategic management: A stakeholder approach.* Boston: Pitman.

Freeman, R.E. (Ed.). 1991. *Business ethics: The state of the art*. New York: Oxford University Press.

Freeman, R. E., & Evan, W. M. 1990. Corporate governance: A stakeholder interpretation. *The Journal of Behavioral Economics*. 19(4): 337-359.

Freeman, R. E., & Gilbert, D.R., Jr. 1987. Managing stakeholder relationships. In S.P. Sethi & C.M. Falbe (Eds.), *Business and society*: 397-423. Lexington, MA: Lexington Books.

Freeman. R. E., & Reed, D. L. 1983. Stockholders and stakeholders: A new perspective on corporate governance. *California Management Review*, 25(3): 88-106.

Friedman, M. 1970. The social responsibility of business is to increase its profits. *New York Times Magazine,* September 13: 32-33, 122, 126.

Geneen, H., & Moscow, A. 1984. *Managing.* Garden City, NY: Doubleday.

Goodpaster, K.E. 1991. Business ethics and stakeholder analysis. *Business Ethics Quarterly,* 1(1): 53-73.

Greenberg, 1. 1987. A taxonomy of organizational justice theories. *Academy of Management Review*, 12: 9-22.

Halal, W.E. 1990. The new management: Business and social institutions in the information age. *Business in the Contemporary World*, 2(2): 41-54.

Hill, C.W.L., & Jones, T. M. 1992. Stakeholder-agency theory. *Journal of Management Studies,* 29: 131-154.

Honore. A.M. 1961. Ownership. In A. G. Guest (Ed.), *Oxford essays in jurisprudence:* 107-147. Oxford: Clarendon Press.

Jensen, M.C. 1989. Eclipse of the public corporation. *Harvard Business Review,* 67(5): 61- 74.

Jensen, M.C., & Mechling, W. 1976. Theory of the firm: Managerial behavior, agency costs, and capital structure. *Journal of Financial Economics*, 3(October): 305-360.

Kotter, J., & Heskett, J. 1992. *Corporate culture and performance.* New York: Free Press.

Kreiner, P. & Bambri, A. 1991. Influence and information in organization-stakeholder relationships. In J.E. Post (Ed.), *Research in corporate social performance and policy,* vol. 12: 3-36. Greenwich, CT: JAI Press.

Kuhn, J.W., & Shriver, D.W., Jr. 1991. *Beyond success: Corporations and their critics in the 1990s.* New York: Oxford University Press.

Marcus. A.A. 1993. *Business and society: Ethics, government and the world economy.* Homewood, IL: Irwin.

McGuire. J.B., Sundgren, A., & Schneeweis, T. 1988. Corporate social responsibility and firm financial performance. *Academy of Management Journal*. 31: 354-372.

Mercuro, N. (Ed.). 1992. *Taking property and just compensation.* Boston: Kluwer.

Moore, G.E. 1959. *Principia ethica*. Cambridge, England: Cambridge University Press. (Original work published 1903)

Munzer, S.R. 1992. *A theory of property*. New York: Cambridge University Press.

Nader, R., & Green, M.J. (Eds.). 1973. *Corporate power in America*. New York: Grossman.

Orts, E.W. 1992. Beyond shareholders: Interpreting corporate constituency statutes. *The George Washington Law Review*, 61(1): 14-135.

O'Toole. J. 1985. *Vanguard management*. Garden City, NY: Doubleday.

O'Toole. J. 1991. Do good, do well: The business enterprise trust awards. *California Management Review*, 33(3): 9-24.

Paramount Communications, Inc. v. Time, Inc. 1990. Del. Supr., 571 A. 2d 1140.

Pejovich, S. 1990. *The economics of property rights: Towards a theory of comparative systems*. Dordrecht, The Netherlands: Kluwer Academic Publishers.

Pickens, T.B. 1987. *Boone*. Boston: Houghton Mifflin.

Posner, B.Z., & Schmidt. W.H. 1984. Values and the American manager. *California Management Review*, 26(3): 202-216.

Preston, L.E., & Sapienza, H.J. 1990. Stakeholder management and corporate performance *Journal of Behavioral Economics*, 19: 361-375.

Preston, L.E., Sapienza, H. I., & Miller, R. D. 1991. Stakeholders, shareholders, managers: Who gains what from corporate performance? In A. Etzioni & P.R. Lawrence (Eds.), *Social economics: Toward a new synthesis:* 149-65. Armonk, NY: M. E. Sharpe.

Rawis, J. 1971. *A theory of justice*. Cambridge, MA: Harvard University Press.

Savage, G.T., Nix. T.W., Whitehead, C.J., & Blair, J.D. 1991. Strategy for assessing and managing organizational stakeholders. *Academy of Management Executive*, 5(2): 61-75.

Sharplin, A., & Phelps, L.D. 1989. A stakeholder apologetic for management. *Business and Professional Ethics Journal*, 8(2): 41-53.

Thompson, J. 1967. *Organizations in action*. New York: McGraw-Hill.

Unocal Corp. v. Mesa Petroleum Co. 1985. Del. Supr., 493 A. 2d 946.

Wang, J., & Dewhirst, H.D. 1992. Boards of directors and stakeholder orientation. *Journal of Business Ethics*. 11: 115-123.

Washington Post. 1993. Pepco bias suit heads for 38 million settlement. February 21: Al.

Weidenbaum. M., & Vogt, S. 1987. Takeovers and stockholders: Winners and losers. *California Management Review*, 29(4): 157-168.

Williamson, O.E. 1985. *The economic institutions of capitalism*. New York: Free Press.

Williamson, O.E., & Winter, S. G. (Eds.). 1991. *The nature of the firm: Origins, evolution, and development.* New York: Oxford University Press.

Wood, D.J. 1991a. Corporate social performance revisited. *Academy of Management Review,* 16: 691-718.

Wood, D.J. 1991b. Social issues in management: Theory and research in corporate social performance. *Journal of Management,* 17: 383-405.

Worthy, J. C. 1984. *Shaping an American institution: Robert E. Wood and Sears, Roebuck.* Urbana: University of Illinois.

Copyright © *Academy of Management Review,* 1995.
Reprinted with permission from the Academy of Management.

Instrumental Stakeholder Theory: A Synthesis of Ethics and Economics

Thomas M. Jones, University of Washington

> This article is intended to enhance the position of stakeholder theory as an integrating theme for the business and society field. It offers an instrumental theory of stakeholder management based on a synthesis of the stakeholder concept, economic theory, behavioral science, and ethics. The core theory—that a subset of ethical principles (trust, trustworthiness, and cooperativeness) can result in significant competitive advantage—is supplemented by nine research propositions along with some research and policy implications.

Even before Preston (1975) issued an intellectual call-to-arms, scholars in the field of inquiry called *business and society* sought a paradigm or an integrating framework for topics thought to be central to the discipline. Various models—*corporate social performance, social control of business, and stakeholder*—have been advanced as part of this search. This article attempts to advance the case for using the stakeholder model as an integrating theme for the field by proposing a formal *instrumental theory* of stakeholder management. The theory represents a *synthesis* of the stakeholder concept, economic theory, insights from behavioral science, and ethics. The argument begins with a brief history of the search for a paradigm in the business and society field followed by a discussion of the stakeholder model as theory. Assumptions that underlie the theory are then offered along with discussions of the nature of contracting, efficient contracting, and the role of ethics in efficient contracting. An argument is presented for corporate morality as an analog to individual morality. At this point, the instrumental stakeholder theory is formally presented, followed by several research propositions. Implications and extensions of the theory and a brief conclusion complete the article.

The Quest for a Business and Society Paradigm

Although the business and society field has had at least a nominal presence at numerous business schools for over two decades and has experienced considerable growth since then in terms of faculty membership in academic organizations and numbers of outlets for scholarly articles, it has been plagued by the lack of a widely accepted paradigm or integrating framework. Preston (1975) crystallized the views of many scholars in the field when he challenged them to develop such a paradigm. Carroll (1979) provided an initial impetus for these efforts by proposing that *corporate social performance* could serve as an integrating theme for the field. Jones (1982) offered a *social control of business* framework as an (implicit) alternative to Carroll's proposal. Jones's model appeared to be a mirror image of Carroll's model because it was focused on the firm from a vantage point that was largely external to the firm, whereas the corporate social performance model was focused directly on the firm. It seems that Carroll's view has been more widely accepted because other scholars subsequently have developed and refined his central ideas in the management literature. Major works by Wartick and Cochran (1985) and Wood (1991a. 1991b) exemplify this development. Tellingly, Wood's (1991a) recent exposition of the corporate social performance theme is thought by business and society scholars to be more likely (by a wide margin) than other recent works to influence scholarship in the field in the coming years (Carroll, 1994).

The corporate social performance model may have to share the intellectual limelight, however. The *stakeholder* model, introduced by Freeman (1984), has spawned several attempts to integrate the field, including works by Jones, Hill, and Kelley (1989). Brenner and Cochran (1991), and Hill and Jones (1992), each of which purports to be "a stakeholder theory of the firm." Work by Clarkson, Deck, and Shiner (1992) and Preston and Sapienza (1990) also has addressed the stakeholder concept, albeit from an empirical perspective. Development of the stakeholder model was also the central theme of two "miniconferences" held in Toronto in 1993 and 1994.

A problem common to all three models advanced thus far, however, is that they offer no testable theory. The *social control of business* model (Jones, 1982) consists only of a framework that ties together major themes in the field. The *corporate social performance model*, although rich in detail and thorough in coverage in its current version (Wood, 1991a), offers no formal theory. Similarly, the stakeholder model leaves theory largely implicit. This article is intended to further develop the *stakeholder* model by offering an instrumental theory of stakeholder management. In the process, additional insights also may be drawn for the corporate social performance model.

The Stakeholder Model as a Theory

Pioneering work in the area of stakeholder management was provided by Freeman (1984), who outlined and developed the basic features of the concept in a book entitled *Strategic Management: A Stakeholder Approach*. Freeman's work, even though it formally recognizes the importance of corporate constituents in addition to shareholders, leaves the status of the stakeholder concept as theory unclear. Donaldson and Preston (1995) argued that stakeholder theory explicitly or implicitly contains theory of three different types—descriptive/empirical, instrumental, and normative. *Descriptive/empirical* formulations of the theory are intended to describe and/or explain how firms or their managers actually behave. *Instrumental* theory purports to describe what will happen if managers or firms behave in certain ways. *Normative* theory is concerned with the moral propriety of the behavior of firms and/or their managers. Briefly summarized, descriptive/empirical, instrumental, and normative theories address the questions: what happens? what happens if? and what should happen?, respectively.

Donaldson and Preston pointed out that Freeman, individually and with various colleagues (Evan & Freeman, 1993; Freeman & Gilbert, 1987; Freeman & Reed, 1983), has incorporated all three types of theory into the stakeholder concept. Proponents of stakeholder theory strive to describe what managers actually do with respect to stakeholder relationships, what would happen if managers adhered to stakeholder management principles, and what managers should do vis-à-vis dealing with firm stakeholders. Donaldson and Preston (1995) concluded that normative concerns underpin stakeholder theory in all of its forms. Although quality scholarship on the normative facets of stakeholder theory is indeed needed, instrumental and descriptive/empirical aspects need attention as well. Thus, this article focuses on the instrumental realm.

It should be noted that the term *instrumental* theory is used here in a manner that differs from its historical usage. Traditionally, in the philosophy of science literature, instrumental theories were deemed useful for explaining certain phenomena *regardless of their truth or falsehood* (Angeles, 1992). In short, they worked, albeit (perhaps) for the wrong reasons. The theories themselves were used as instruments to achieve some ends. The usage of instrumental theory employed in this article follows that used by Donaldson and Preston (1995), which appears to be original. For these authors, instrumental theory establishes (theoretical) connections between certain practices and certain end states. There is no assumption that the practices will be followed or that the end states are desirable. In instrumental theory, statements are hypothetical—if X, *then* Y or *if* you want Y, *then* do X. In this sense, X is an instrument for achieving Y. The truth or falsehood of instrumental theories of this latter type is an important issue.

Assumptions: Stakeholders and Economic Theory

Before any theory of stakeholder management can be advanced in a convincing manner, certain assumptions must be made regarding the economic and social conditions that provide context for the model. Assumptions appropriate for the purpose of this article have been drawn mainly from economic theory and the stakeholder concept. Collectively, they give a picture of the firm and its relationship to its environment.

The firm is characterized by relationships with many groups and individuals ("stakeholders"), each with (a) the power to affect the firm's performance and/or (b) a stake in the firm's performance (Freeman, 1984). In many cases, both conditions apply. Stakeholders include, but are not limited to, shareholders.

The contract is an appropriate metaphor for the relationships between the firm and its stakeholders (Eisenhardt, 1989). Ample precedent exists for a broad definition of "contract" (Dunfee, 1991; Jensen & Meckling, 1976; Ross, 1973; Williamson, 1984, 1985). Contracts can take the form of exchanges, transactions, or the delegation of decision-making authority, as well as formal legal documents.

The firm can thus be seen as a *"nexus of contracts"* (Jensen &Meckling, 1976) between itself and its stakeholders.

Top corporate managers, because they (a) contract with all other stakeholders either directly or indirectly through their agents and (b) have "strategic position" (Herman, 1981) regarding key decisions of the firm, can be considered the *contracting agents* for the firm. The firm is thus recast as a nexus of contracts between its top managers and its stakeholders.

This last assumption is somewhat controversial. At one level, controversy still exists as to who "controls" the large corporation (Berle & Means, 1932; Domhoff, 1967; Jones, 1979; Larner, 1970; Zeitlin, 1974). Herman's (1981) concept of "strategic position" renders the argument largely moot for the purposes of this article, however. He argues that managers make the vast majority of important decisions on behalf of the firm, even though shareholders may be able to wrest control from them under extreme circumstances by gaining control of the board of directors. (Top management and the board of directors are distinct entities, although their memberships often overlap, sometimes extensively.) In terms of shareholders being able to influence managerial decisions, the point is readily conceded. Indeed, the definition of "stakeholder" (above) explicitly recognizes the *influence* of individuals and groups on firm (managerial) decision making.

A second controversy arises regarding the firm's managers as contracting agents for the firm instead of as a class of stakeholders. Williamson (1984) explored this dilemma in a discussion of representation on the board of directors, but he did not resolve it. Although he said that "our understanding of the contract between firm and manager is complicated by the fact that managers apparently write their own contracts with one hand and sign them with the other. Also, management is often encouraged, for good reason, to think of itself and the firm as one" (1984: 1216). Williamson subsequently discussed contracting between the "firm and its managers" as if they were separate entities.

In this article, top managers and the firm will be considered as a single entity. Although top managers are technically stakeholders, their primary role is one of contracting on behalf of the firm (directly or indirectly) with other stakeholders as well as with themselves. Top managers are at the center of a "hub and spoke" stakeholder model of the firm because they contract with all other stakeholders. Relationships between or among nonmanagement stakeholder groups surely exist as well; in some cases, memberships in these groups may overlap. However, in this article, the focus is on the bilateral relationships between managers and stakeholders. Further, the term *stakeholder* applies not only to groups easily characterized by words such as *customers or employees* but also to subgroups of customers (e.g., buyers of over-the-counter medicine and buyers of shampoo) and employees (e.g., shopworkers and middle managers) who may have distinct (and competing) interests. Terms like *customers* and *employees* are used here for heuristic purposes only.

> *Markets* are characterized by a *tendency toward equilibrium*, as postulated by the Austrian school (Jacobson, 1992; Kirzner, 1979), not equilibrium, as assumed in neoclassical microeconomics.

This market assumption is critical. Equilibrium in markets would imply that inefficient contracting mechanisms and power differentials between the contracting parties could not exist. Efficient markets would drive out inefficient contracts, leaving only those in which neither party had significant discretion. If, instead, markets *tend toward* equilibrium, the pressure to contract efficiently will be less intense. Where market discipline is less sure and less swift, a rough sorting out of efficient and inefficient contracts will occur, but only over longer time periods. There will be a *tendency toward* efficient contracting, but inefficient contracts may endure over significant periods of time. Similarly, power differentials between contracting parties certainly exist, perhaps for several years.

No behavioral assumption is made. Because the theory that is advanced in this article is instrumental, the descriptive outcomes predicted by the theory are *contingent* on certain behaviors. According to the theory, *if* certain types of behavior occur, certain (favorable) outcomes become more probable; it does not assume that the desirable behaviors *will* occur.

Collectively these assumptions describe the relationship between the modern corporation and its environment.

1. Firms have relationships, called contracts, with many stakeholders.
2. Firms are run by professional managers.
3. Firms exist in markets in which competitive pressures do influence behavior but do not necessarily penalize moderately inefficient behavior.

Despite the fact that some firms have few stakeholders, some firms are run by their stockholders, and some markets are highly competitive and swiftly and surely punish inefficient behavior, these assumptions are an adequate general description of the modern corporate economy. Taken together, they create the context for development of an instrumental stakeholder theory of firm behavior.

The Nature of Contracting

As discussed previously, the relationships between corporate stakeholders and the firm's top managers can be described using the contract as a metaphor. These contracts vary greatly in terms of degree of formality and extent of specificity. Some contracts, say between a firm and it's neighboring community, are relatively vague and informal; certainly, no documents exist to describe these contracts. Contracts of this type have been called *relational contracts* by Macneil (1978) and Williamson (1985). At the other end of the spectrum are formal and specific contracts; the contract between a firm and its bondholders is an example. Contracting between the firm and its stakeholders also can vary in the frequency and regularity of the transactions or exchanges. At one extreme are continuous and ongoing relationships like those between managers and employees. The other extreme could be represented by an isolated parts order to a vendor that the firm normally does not deal with. Contracts that represent repeated or ongoing transactions are constantly being reaffirmed or reinterpreted. For such contracts that are also formal, the terms *honored* or *broken* can be substituted for *reaffirmed* and *reinterpreted*, respectively.

The nature of the contracts I have outlined has been described by economists using three basic theoretical frameworks—agency theory

(Jensen & Meckling, 1976; Ross, 1973), transaction cost economics (Coase, 1937; Williamson, 1975), and team production (Alchian & Demsetz, 1972). Each theory applies to certain types of contracts, but all have common threads.

Agency theory applies to relationships in which "one party (the principal) delegates work to another (the agent), who performs that work" (Eisenhardt, 1989: 58). In Mitnick's (1982) abbreviated terminology, the agent "acts for" the principal. Two problems exist in agency relationships. First, the agent and the principal have conflicting goals, and it is difficult and/or expensive for the principal to verify the agent's activities. Second, the principal and the agent have different propensities to accept risk. The central question of agency theory becomes: What type of contracts best suit agency relationships of various types (Eisenhardt, 1989)? Some contracts focus on the agent's *behavior*, and others focus on outcomes of interest to the principal. Contracts are thought to be efficient if they minimize the sum of the following agency costs:

1. *Monitoring costs* borne by the principal to reduce agent actions that would harm the interests of the principal
2. *Bonding costs* borne by the agent to guarantee that the agent will not take actions to harm the interests of the principal
3. *A residual loss* incurred because monitoring and bonding may not fully align agent behavior and principal interests (Jensen & Meckling, 1976).

Several mechanisms exist to either monitor or bond the behavior of agents. I will discuss some of these mechanisms in a later section.

There exist two general types of reasons for agent failure to adequately pursue the interests of the principal. *Moral hazard* exists due to a lack of effort (shirking) on the part of the agent. Stated differently, the principal cannot adequately verify the agent's effort. *Adverse selection* exists when the agent misrepresents his or her ability or, more generally, does not behave in the manner preferred by the principal (Eisenhardt, 1989). Agency costs are incurred in order to reduce or eliminate the effects of moral hazard and adverse selection.

Proponents of *transaction cost economics* share many of the assumptions of agency theory but focus on the *boundaries* between contracting parties rather than the contracts per se. Transaction costs stem from the need to negotiate, monitor, and enforce the implicit and explicit contracts required to bring resources together and utilize them efficiently. Williamson (1975) used transaction costs as the focal variable in the determination of the choice between contracting externally (markets) or internally (hierarchies). The choice, in Williamson's theory, is dictated by relative efficiency in transaction costs; that is, cheaper forms will drive out costlier forms. Transaction costs are significant and variable for two reasons. First, the seller of a resource has more information about it than does the buyer and may opportunistically misrepresent its value, either in terms of quality or, in the case of labor resources, its (his/her) propensity to shirk. Transaction costs, borne under these circumstances in order to reduce uncertainty in evaluating these resources, include (a) search costs, (b) negotiating costs, (c) monitoring costs, (d) enforcement costs, and (e) a residual loss.

A second source of transaction costs is the hold-up problem (Williamson, 1985). Hold-up problems impede investments in specialization, which would reduce production costs by increasing productivity. Investments in specialization (a) have increased value to specialized users (relative to less specialized resources) and (b) have reduced value to alternative users. Thus, if producer A invests in a specialized resource (an asset or a skill) of value to consumer B, the resource is of high value to B but of lower value to consumers C, D, E, and F. (The term *consumer* applies to consumer of the resource, which may mean industrial or commercial consumer.) This value differential exposes A to hold-up by B because B knows that A cannot easily sell his or her resources elsewhere. Therefore, producer A may be reluctant or unwilling to make specialized investments for B for fear of B's reneging on pricing agreements. Thus, the hold-up problem results in either (a) reduced investment in specialization or (b) expensive investments in preventing hold-up. The latter category includes the making of credible commitments, "exchanging hostages," and the negotiating, monitoring, and enforcing of contracts—in short, transaction costs (Williamson, 1975, 1985). Williamson (1975) argued that transaction costs often can be reduced through the use of hierarchy (merging consumer and producer), although hierarchies have governance costs that cannot be ignored.

Team production also can be described in terms of contracts and, thus, contracting problems can be illuminated using theories of team production. Team production problems arise in situations in which each individual team member's contribution to team output cannot be measured precisely (Alchian & Demsetz, 1972). The team's output, although clearly a function of each individual member's input, cannot be accurately attributed to each individual in proportion to the individual's input. If rewards to team members are in proportion to *team* output, not *individual* output, which by definition cannot be measured, team members will have an incentive to shirk on the job. That is, individuals can receive rewards disproportionate to their efforts by contributing less than they are capable of contributing. This phenomenon is similar to the well-documented "free rider" problem in economics and to problems of collective action (Olson, 1965). Further, if the problem is reversed by viewing the individual's contribution to collective output as the individual's consumption of collective resources, it bears a striking resemblance to Hardin's (1968) "tragedy of the commons" (Aram, 1989) and might be dubbed the *team consumption* problem. Regardless of which perspective one takes on the team production/consumption problem, one conclusion is clear: someone must bear the costs of the divergence of individual and team goals. These costs may take the form of reduced team production (the logical limit being no production) or costs incurred to monitor the behavior of team members.

The contracting problems described here under the headings of agency theory, transaction cost economics, and team production theory have some common threads. Problems of agents pursuing their own interests at the expense of principals, sellers of resources misrepresenting their value to consumers, consumers of resources "holding-up" their producers, and team members "free riding" all involve manifestations of *opportunism* on the part of one party to a contract. The *opportunist*, defined by Williamson (1975) as one who pursues self-interest "with guile," takes advantage of a situation in which he or she has power, however temporary, over the other contracting party or parties. Costs are incurred either because the opportunist succeeds or because one or more parties to the contract spends resources to reduce opportunism. Further, because costs are involved, markets reward those who are able to contract efficiently by reducing these costs and penalize those who contract inefficiently. It follows that, all else being equal, efficient contracting will result in competitive advantage.

Efficient Contracting

Efficient contracting has been the subject of much theorizing and empirical testing in financial economics for several years and is increasingly becoming a focal point of research in organization theory (Eisenhardt, 1988, 1989). This theory and research, in which opportunism is a behavioral assumption, focuses on such devices as interest-aligning mechanisms, incentive structures, monitoring mechanisms, and governing structures that will reduce opportunism to an "efficient" level for which the costs of further reductions outweigh the benefits. In the agency relationship between shareholders (principals) and managers (agents), for example, it is efficient for shareholders to allow the managers certain on-the-job consumption (e.g., high salaries and perquisites) because it is costly for thousands of dispersed shareholders to monitor and discipline their behavior. The extent of this consumption will be limited by interest-aligning mechanisms such as stock options, monitoring mechanisms such as boards of directors, and incentive structures such as performance bonuses. In addition, external governing structures such as regulation of information disclosure also may be employed. These devices, which are costly, assume opportunistic behavior and attempt to reduce it or link it to desirable ends.

There is another way to reduce opportunistic behavior, however—the voluntary adoption of standards of behavior that limit or eliminate it. Economists and moral philosophers since Adam Smith have observed that competitive market economies operate far better where shared values of honesty and integrity prevail than where they do not. North argued that "the absence of some degree of individual restraint from maximizing behavior would render the political or economic institution nonviable" (1981: 19). In another context, he claimed that "Strong moral and ethical codes of a society are the cement of social stability which makes an economic system viable" (North, 1981: 47).

An excellent summary explanation of the relationship between morals and economic efficiency at the microlevel is provided by Noreen (1988). He recalled the "market for lemons" (Akerlof, 1970), wherein the absence of reliable information about individual used cars on the part of potential auto buyers can result in substantial inefficiencies. If defect-free used cars of a certain vintage are worth $5,000 and similar cars with an average number of defects are worth $3,000, and if potential buyers of such cars cannot tell which cars have below average (or above average) defects, two behaviors will result. First, owners of cars in better than average condition will not bring them to market because they will not receive full value for them, if the market price is $3,000. Second, if "good" used cars are not offered for sale, only "average" to "poor" cars will be sold. Soon buyers will discover that the average value of cars offered for sale is lower than $3,000 and the prices will drop, eliminating the potential sale of formerly average cars and dropping the price further. Soon only the worst cars ("lemons") will be offered for sale. If the cost to repair the lemons exceeds $5,000, the market collapses entirely. Note that both sellers and buyers are harmed by this "adverse selection" problem. Potential sellers cannot sell except by accepting less than their cars are worth; (potential) buyers either will pay more than the cars are worth or will not buy a car at all. Many transactions that would benefit both parties, thereby promoting efficiency, will not take place. Solutions to this problem, a thorough inspection by a mechanic, for example, are themselves costly (Noreen, 1988). In short, the absence of reliable information and the presence of opportunism result in the malfunctioning or collapse of markets, to everyone's detriment.

At the macrolevel, opportunism burdens the economy and society-at-large with substantial "dead-weight losses" (Noreen, 1988). Prominent among these costs are economic regulation, social regulation, legal services related to contracting and postcontracting litigation, and whatever social malaise attends a lack of trust in society. The costs of denying monopolies their monopoly profits, cartel members the fruits of their collusion, and of deterring potential price fixers, are considerable. Also significant are the costs of reducing environmental degradation, raising workplace safety standards, reducing discrimination in employment, protecting employee pensions, and safely disposing of toxic wastes. Further, the psychological toll of an opportunistic culture on individuals in society may be significant; lives are made more complicated, and thus more difficult, by opportunism. In addition, the sense of injustice that results from instances in which opportunists "get away with it" can also be corrosive. Thus, the macrolevel effects of opportunism and attempts to curb it are likely to be pervasive and expensive. It follows that reduced opportunism, through the voluntary adoption of such shared values as honesty and integrity, aids the development of smoothly functioning, efficient markets (Noreen, 1988). Contracting and transacting possibilities expand. Monitoring and policing costs decline, although the need for some monitoring will remain in order to control opportunism that persists in the system.

An important question remains, however: Is it possible to enhance the functioning of markets through "enlightened self-interest" as opposed to the voluntary adoption of ethical standards in economic dealings? Game theory, in the form of the prisoner's dilemma (Figure 1), sheds some light on this question.

In any single play of the prisoner's dilemma, both players have incentives to choose D, the noncooperative strategy. If both do so, both will end up with a payoff of—3. However, as Axelrod (1984) has shown, in situations in which the same players engage each other repeatedly, the optimal strategy is "tit for tat." The decision rule for tit for tat is that one cooperates on the first play and then duplicates his or her opponent's previous move on all subsequent plays. If one's opponent cooperates on play number 4, one cooperates on play number 5. and so on. Axelrod's (1984) computer simulation of tournament strategies (designed by prominent game theorists) showed tit for tat to produce higher payoffs than all other strategies. The tit for tat strategy tended to induce a regime of mutual cooperation, often quite quickly. Axelrod's evaluation of the simulation is that a winning (and therefore-self-interested) strategy involves initial trust, provocability, and forgiveness (1984).

Figure 1: Prisoner's dilemma payoff matrix

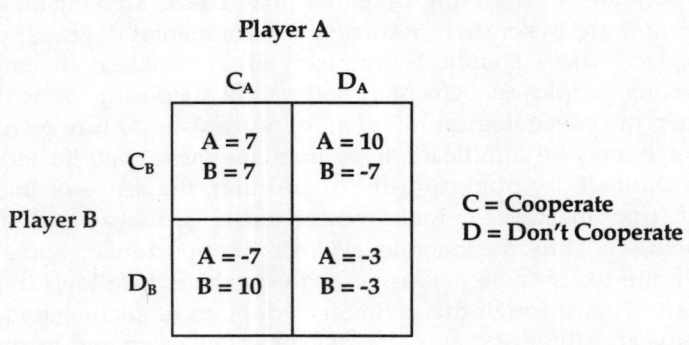

Actual human beings, as subjects in behavioral experiments, also settle into a mutually cooperative mode in repeat plays of the prisoner's dilemma game, albeit often only after several instances of noncooperation on the part of one or both players. Eventually, the poor outcomes resulting from noncooperative strategies induce most subjects to cooperate (Pruitt & Kimmel, 1977). Thus, human beings can be induced to make choices that are efficient in the long term, even though short-term self-interest would seem to dictate inefficient solutions.

It should be noted that the phenomenon described above and represented by a prisoner's dilemma game can be applied in all three instances in which opportunism is a problem—principal/agent relationships, transaction cost relationships, and team production relationships. Noreen's (1988) argument that shared values help reduce agency costs, summarized previously, was intended to apply to agency relationships, but it applies equally well to transaction cost economizing and team production. Regarding transaction costs, two implications are apparent. First, such costs can be reduced through mutual cooperation. If the seller accurately represents the value of his or her resource and the buyer trusts the seller to do so, an efficient transaction will take place. No incentive-aligning mechanisms are required and no costs are incurred for searching, negotiating, monitoring, or enforcing. In addition, investments in specialization will be facilitated when a producer ("A" in the above example) cooperatively makes specialized investments in the production of a resource and the consumer of the resource ("B" above) cooperates by not "holding-up" producer A after A has made specialized investments. Mutual cooperation, therefore, reduces transaction costs.

The benefits of mutual cooperation to team production efforts are readily apparent. Teams produce more efficiently when none of their members "shirks" or "free rides." If team members can be induced to cooperate fully in team efforts without any need to monitor their behavior, monitoring costs are served, and net team output will expand. Other costs of reducing opportunism also can be avoided by cooperative behavior on the part of team members.

Further, the benefits of cooperative strategies, when mutually adopted, obtain whether the prisoner's dilemma-like "game" is played once or many times. Indeed, in actual economic relationships in which opportunism on the part of one party is discovered, future relationships may be seriously jeopardized. For example, a producer who invests in specialized resources and is "held-up" by the consumer of those resources might be unwilling to contract with that consumer again.

Ethics and Efficient Contracting

Analogies to prisoner's dilemma games are instructive only up to a point, however. The rules of a prisoner's dilemma fit very few contracting relationships perfectly and some contracting relations quite imperfectly. In particular, parties to contracting relationships do not always have repeated, regular interactions. Some interactions are either unique or repeated on an intermittent or irregular basis. Further, contracting relationships, unlike the described game, need not always occur with the same partner or "opponent." In repeat play prisoner's dilemmas, one player can learn about the behavior of his or her opponent by experience; he or she need not face each round ignorant of the other player's prior behavior. If the identity of the other player changes, prior knowledge (of that player) is not available. (Of course, knowledge of prior players' behavior could, over time, induce optimism or pessimism about the focal player's behavior.) In addition, as Noreen (1988) pointed out, real-life agency situations are often characterized by considerable uncertainty regarding what the other player did on the prior round; learning about the opponent's behavior may be quite difficult at best. This lack of congruence between the game theoretic situation and real contracting relationships would, at minimum, suggest that stable, mutually cooperative, efficient solutions would be slow to evolve, even under conditions of enlightened self-interest. Impeding the development of such solutions is the specter of the opportunist deciding that the benefit of noncooperation outweighs the benefit of further cooperation. This problem becomes particularly acute when one or both players sense that the end of the sequence of plays is near.

Another solution to the opportunism-problem is suggested by Robert Frank in his book *Passions Within Reason: The Strategic Role of the Emotions*

(1988). Although his terminology is somewhat different than that used here (his "commitment problem" is similar to the opportunism problem), he argued that people who behave honestly, even when they could escape detection or at least get away with dishonest behavior, will often fare well in economic endeavors. His view, supported by ample evidence, is that narrow self-interest is often incompatible with productive and advantageous economic relationships. Conversely, "an honest person will benefit by being able to solve important commitment problems. He will be trustworthy in situations where the purely self-interested person would not, and will be much sought after as a partner in situations that require trust" (Frank, 1988: 18). A person's desirability as a contracting partner is based on his or her intrinsic trustworthiness, which is not dependent on a balance of interests and thus not subject to continuous reevaluation.

Frank's larger thesis, aptly reflected in the book's subtitle, is that emotions help solve the commitment problem by giving important clues about a person's true moral sentiments. Emotions help others to accurately judge a person's honesty and integrity and, hence, to engage (or refrain from engaging) in certain types of economic transactions in accordance with those judgments.

Essential to Frank's argument is the conclusion that moral sentiments are difficult to fake. He posits two "pathways" to judgments of the moral tendencies of other people: "sincere-manner" and reputation. Sincere manner consists of an assessment of a number of physical cues. Facial blushing, perspiration, mouth dryness, certain eye movements, voice pitch, voice cadence, imprecise hand movements, and facial gestures are often associated with deceit (Frank, 1988). Human beings can significantly improve the accuracy of their judgments of the honesty and integrity of other people by careful attention to these cues, although no claim is made that these cues are always detectable or even that they always exist. DePaulo, Zuckerman, and Rosenthal (1980) provided empirical evidence that people can detect deception significantly better than chance would suggest.

Similarly, reputation is a fairly reliable indicator of a propensity toward opportunism, Frank argued, because "dishonest persons tend to cheat in situations where the odds militate against cheating" (1988: 76). Drawing evidence from experimental psychology, he shows that a person who is merely prudent (i.e., cooperative for self-interested reasons) will be caught cheating with sufficient frequency that a reputation for honesty will be difficult to maintain. Because the rewards of opportunism are often immediate and the rewards of cooperation temporally distant, and because the value of rewards is often discounted in an irrational manner, prudent (as opposed to intrinsically moral) persons will often mistakenly opt for the quick payoff of opportunistic behavior. This tendency makes their getting caught more likely and increases the probability that the prudent person will lose his or her reputation for honesty. "Knowing this, we can infer that a person who has not been caught is probably something more than a merely prudent person" (Frank, 1988: 88). Honest, trust-worthy behavior is difficult to fake, even in the absence of face-to-face contact.

Much of this argument can be recast in ethical terms. The sentiments expressed by people who (a) are honest; (b) have personal integrity; (c) don't lie, cheat, or steal; and (d) honor their commitments are clearly moral in nature. People who have these sentiments are desirable partners for a large range of economic relationships. They will make good agents in principal/agent relationships because they will not require expensive monitoring by principals. They will make good sellers of resources in transaction cost situations because they will not opportunistically misrepresent the value of their resources, thereby reducing search and monitoring costs incurred by the buyer. Also, these persons, as buyers (consumers) of specialized resources in transaction cost situations, will not be inclined to "hold up" the sellers (producers) of such resources. Finally, people with the moral sentiments described above will make good team members in team production situations because they will not shirk or "free ride" on the work of others. Thus, Frank's argument can be adapted to reach a conclusion that good ethics, made manifest in the context of economic relationships with others, is also good business.

This conclusion, shortened to read "ethics pays," must be distinguished from the conclusion reached by Noreen (1988). Noreen argued that efficient contracting in agency relationships is best achieved through shared norms and ethical rules that reduce opportunism. His argument is utilitarian in nature; the economy (and hence society) will benefit from ethics in economic relationships. Frank (1988) took the argument a step further by concluding that not only is ethics good for us collectively, but it is also good for us individually. "[T]he modern presumption of a severe penalty for behaving morally is utterly without foundation" (Frank, 1988: xi); indeed, the ability to make credible commitments, "which springs from a failure to pursue self-interest, confers genuine advantage" (Frank, 1988: 5).

Corporate Morality

The benefits to individuals of good ethics in contracting relationships do not necessarily translate into similar benefits for corporations, however. To demonstrate that firms, like individuals, will benefit from moral behavior, it is necessary to show that the firm's behavior will, in general, reflect the moral sentiments of its top management and that stakeholders will be able to assess the moral sentiments of top management with reasonable accuracy. Because some stakeholders (employees and representatives of the company such as dealers, salespersons, purchasing agents, attorneys, and service personnel) are also agents of top management in their dealings with external stakeholders (e.g., customers, vendors, shareholders, and the neighboring community), these two arguments will be intertwined in the following paragraphs.

First, assume that the behavior of corporations with respect to moral issues ("corporate morality"), like individual morality, is detectable in two ways—through sincere manner and reputation—and further assume that corporate morality is reflected in the policies and decisions of the firm and in the nature of its direct dealings with corporate stakeholders. In addition, recall that company policies and decisions will be products of its top managers. Some of the firm's policies and decisions will be readily apparent to the stakeholders affected by them. For example, if a firm decides to lay off 10 percent of its salaried workforce in order to boost profits, the decision and its implications will be well known to salaried employees. If a company establishes a strict policy of "no returns" on merchandise, the policy will soon become known to dealers and certain customers. These decisions are "visible" to the affected stakeholders, and the company's reputation among its employees and customers, respectively, will be affected accordingly. Further, decisions and policies of this type are likely to influence the judgments of stakeholders other than those immediately affected. That is, the effect of these decisions and policies on the firm's reputation is likely to transcend the relationship between the firm and the immediately affected stakeholder group. For example, if the firm reneges on its pension obligations to company retirees, it will probably have difficulty maintaining the trust of its current (or potential) employees. Further, the firm's policies and decisions with respect to stakeholders are likely to have a cumulative effect on its reputation. If a single firm made all three of the decisions used as examples above, its reputation would reflect, in some measure, opportunistic policies toward employees, customers, and pensioners. Thus, the firm's reputation, and that of its top managers, will be partly a direct function of its policies and decisions.

Other facets of corporate morality will not be as readily detectable as will the policies and decisions described above. The effects of some managerial policies and decisions will be experienced by stakeholders only indirectly through the behavior of various company employees and representatives—dealers, salespersons, purchasing agents, service personnel, and so on. By what mechanism does the behavior of these individuals reflect the moral sentiments of top managers?

First, the morality of top managers will be reflected in the system of incentives and sanctions employed by the firm (i.e., the rewards and punishments that are given to or imposed on employees for various behaviors). These rules, both formal and informal, will reflect the values and, hence, the moral sentiments of top managers. Management's enforcement of these rules also will be a strong indicator of its values regarding moral issues. Top management also influences the corporate culture; the examples it sets through its behavior tend to be adopted by individuals at lower levels of the firm (Clinard, 1983).

Employees who are subordinates of the top executives will tend to adopt the "moral coloration" of the firm and its top managers (Jones & Quinn, 1993) through a process of social learning (Bandura, 1986). Evidence that moral clues from the organization play a role in individual morality is provided by Treviño and Youngblood (1990), who found that vicarious reward positively influenced ethical decision making indirectly through outcome expectancies, as predicted by social learning theory. Jones (1989) argued that language also plays a role in individual morality. Because human beings "make sense" of their environment through the language that they have available to interpret it, the ready availability of moral (or opportunistic) language within the organization's lexicon will lead individuals to make decisions along moral (or opportunistic) lines. Firms with opportunistic vocabularies will enhance the opportunistic tendencies of employees; firms with moral vocabularies will nurture the moral tendencies of employees.

Further, through a process of self-selection, moral people will tend to leave (Lee & Mitchell, 1994) or avoid opportunistic firms. According to image theory (Beach, 1990), such individuals will find the values of the firm incompatible with their value images (Lee & Mitchell, 1994). Similarly, the *value* images of opportunists will be incompatible with the values of moral firms. In addition, opportunists will tend to leave moral firms because they may become frustrated with "irrational" (moral) decision making and because the norms and incentives of such firms will make it difficult to capture the benefits of their opportunistic behavior. Further, moral firms will tend either to avoid opportunistic individuals (Clinard, 1983) or to dismiss them because their superiors find the behavior of these individuals morally objectionable and because these individuals may damage the firm's reputation and, thus, harm it economically.

In those cases in which opportunistic individuals remain in moral firms, they will be constrained from behaving opportunistically by the prospect of sanctions by the firm (unless, of course, the gains from opportunism outweigh the costs of sanctions). Further, it may not matter that the opportunist cleverly conceals his or her opportunism (self-interest with guile); as long as he or she intends to act in a moral manner (if only out of fear of corporate retribution), he or she need not be insincere, and, hence, need not reveal his or her opportunism through "insincere manner." That is, if insincerity can be thought of as the result of a person's intending to do something other than what he or she promises to do (real intent is not the same as declared intent), then sincerity consists of a match between real intent and declared intent. As long as the person truly intends to do what he or she says that he or she will do, it may not matter *why* he or she intends to do it. Morality "induced" by the firm's norms and rules may be functionally identical to intrinsic morality; an opportunistic person may appear sincere (and act morally) when acting as the agent of a moral firm.

In addition, in the relationships between internal stakeholders at adjacent levels of the firm's hierarchy, tests of sincere manner and reputation will be frequent due to the frequency of interaction. The moral sentiments of corporate employees will, therefore, be well known to those with whom they work closely. Similarly, employees who deal directly with external stakeholders (e.g., suppliers and customers) will be known for moral sentiments that are a function of external signals (e.g., complaints and litigation) in addition to signals from other employees. Thus, throughout the corporate hierarchy the moral sentiments of individual employees will be known to at least several of their co-workers.

Given the previous argument that individuals whose moral sentiments are incompatible with the values of the firm's top management will tend to avoid, leave, or be driven out of the company and the argument that the moral sentiments of firm employees will be fairly well known, it follows that a firm will tend to have a relatively homogeneous culture with respect to morality. Thus, even though the behavior of corporations regarding moral issues will not be simple extensions of the morality of their top managers, firms will tend to be populated by employees whose moral sentiments are compatible with the values of their top management.

It then follows that the behavior of lower level employees and representatives will have an effect on the company's reputation similar to that which is acquired directly through the decisions and policies of top management (as described previously). Further, in the frequent interactions between the corporation's employees and representatives and its external stakeholders, the firm's "morality" will be relatively accurately portrayed through the presence (or absence) of "sincere manner."

It should be noted that the cumulative reputation acquired by a firm may be ambiguous with respect to its moral behavior. Some firms may have relationships with some stakeholders (e.g., customers) based on high levels of trust and cooperation, but they may have wary, opportunistic relationships with other stakeholders (e.g., hourly workers). Additionally, a firm may hire a new CEO who is known for honesty and integrity in order to burnish a reputation for opportunistic dealings with some (or all) stakeholder groups. Further, it is likely that some firms, rather than having a single, unambiguous corporate morality, will have subcultures that have their own "subcorporate morality." Situations like these will be the result of inconsistent, changing, or ambiguous morality on the part of the company's top management.

Because the reputation of top managers is tested (a) periodically through policies and decisions that affect stakeholders directly and (b) frequently through indirect interactions with stakeholders through the behavior of their agents (employees and representatives), corporate morality should be well reflected in the company's reputation. Firm morality, like individual morality, is difficult to fake. It also follows that the benefits available to ethical individuals also should be available to ethical corporations. Such firms will be desirable, sought after partners in relationships in which opportunism is a problem. They will be in demand in situations that require agents who do not require expensive monitoring, sellers who do not misrepresent the value of their resources, buyers who do not "hold up" sellers of specialized resources, and team members who do not shirk on collective efforts. These firms will, in short, be offered opportunities unavailable to opportunistic firms; briefly stated, "corporate morality pays."

According to this formulation, firms do not signal their trustworthiness except by avoiding signals of opportunism. Recall that the relationships for which moral firms (and moral individuals) will be sought are those in which a high level of trustworthiness and cooperation is required. A firm that *usually* honors its contracts, *usually* cooperates in joint efforts, and *usually* delivers on time may not qualify as a desirable partner in such relationships. Thus, a reputation for trustworthiness is really a reputation for not being opportunistic. Although firms may attempt to enhance their reputations by advertising or by being visibly generous or altruistic, such acts do not form the foundation of a good reputation. A good reputation generally must be earned by avoiding behavior that discourages or dissipates trust. In contrast, the reputations of firms could be deliberately, even unfairly, tarnished by the acts or accusations of other firms, the media, or government agencies. Discussion of this latter set of possibilities is beyond the scope of this paper.

A Theory of Competitive Advantage

The explicit promise of this article was to develop an instrumental theory of stakeholder management. The instrumental theory presented here is simultaneously contingent, descriptive, and empirical. It is contingent on certain types of behavior. It describes the result (outcome) of the postulated behavior. It posits an empirically testable link between the behavior and the outcome. Recall that no behavioral assumption was made in the Assumptions section. I will now explain the reason for that omission. As Margolis (1984) and Etzioni (1988) demonstrated, human beings are capable of a wide range of behavior, particularly with respect to the extent that they are self-interested (or opportunistic) and rational. Etzioni's argument that people are rarely fully rational or totally unconcerned with the well-being of others underlies his call for a "socio-economics" to replace or supplement neoclassical economic theory. The instrumental theory presented here is a partial response to Etzioni's challenge; it claims that the manifestations of certain types of ethical behavior will result in competitive advantage.

The theory of competitive advantage, developed here, can be summarized as follows. Recall that (a) the firm is characterized by relationships with many stakeholders; (b) the contract metaphor applies to these relationships; (c) the firm, therefore, can be seen as a "nexus of contracts"; (d) corporate managers are the contracting agents for the firm; and (e) markets tend toward equilibrium and, in turn, produce a tendency toward efficient contracting. Given that the contracting process gives rise to agency problems, transaction cost problems, and team production problems (in general, commitment problems), efficient contracting will be profoundly affected by the costs of solving these commitment problems. Because these commitment problems (opportunism) abound, firms that solve commitment problems efficiently will have a competitive advantage over those that do not. Further, because ethical solutions to commitment problems are more efficient than mechanisms designed to curb opportunism, it follows that *firms that contract (through their managers) with their stakeholders on the basis of mutual trust and cooperation will have a competitive advantage over firms that do not.*

This source of competitive advantage does not, of course, mean that firms employing ethical contracting frameworks will always outperform firms in which contracting mechanisms are based on the assumption of opportunism. However, all else being equal, firms in the former group will have an advantage over firms in the latter group. They will experience reduced agency costs, transaction costs, and costs associated with team production. More specifically, monitoring costs, bonding costs, search costs, warranty costs, and residual losses will be reduced. The resources saved will benefit not only the firm employing ethical contracting but also the stakeholders with whom it contracts. In such cases, overall contracting costs are reduced, and the benefits are shared among the firm and its stakeholders.

It must be stressed that the emphasis in this summary statement of the theory is on *mutual* trust and cooperation. Nothing in the theory suggests that trustworthy, cooperative firms must also be trusting dupes.

No assumption is made that a moral firm will always have (or will be able to attract) equally trustworthy and cooperative stakeholders. A trustworthy, cooperative firm must (like all firms) reject relationships with prospective partners whose potential or revealed opportunism is not within limits that it can manage. For these moral companies, the threshold of manageable opportunism is likely to be quite low, however. Because the benefits of mutually trusting and cooperative economic relationships are realized through reduced contracting costs, the moral corporation must choose its partners carefully in order to ensure that the desired benefits are obtained. The competitive advantage that accrues to moral firms takes the form of substantially increased *eligibility* to take part in certain types of economic relationships and transactions that will be unavailable to opportunistic firms. It, like all firms, must be discriminating in its choice of contracting partners. Further, careful discrimination in the choice of contracting partners applies to terminating contracts with existing stakeholders who prove to be opportunistic, and rejecting contracts with prospective stakeholders who are potentially opportunistic. These addenda to the theory are analogous to Axelrod's (1984) "provocability" criterion in prisoner's dilemma situations and do not detract from the conclusion that trustworthy, cooperative firms will have a competitive advantage.

I should also note that the role of trust and cooperation in organizations has been addressed by other authors in organization theory and related fields. In addition to economists Adam Smith and Douglas North, organization scholars including Barnard (1938/1968), Simon (1945), Etzioni (1965), and Weick (1969) have focused on these issues. Ouchi also emphasized the importance of trust and cooperation in his discussion of clans (1980) and his development of "Theory Z" (1981). Hill, in a recent game theory analysis of transaction cost economics, argued that market forces favor "actors whose behaviors are biased toward cooperation" (1990: 501).

Research Propositions and Instrumental Implications

The focus of this instrumental theory of stakeholder management is the *contract* (i.e., a metaphor for the relationships between the firm and its various stakeholder groups). The firm will gain competitive advantage if it is able to develop relationships with its stakeholders based on mutual trust and cooperation. Implicit in this theory is the notion that the problems of opportunism and a lack of trust and cooperation are real problems in firm/stakeholder relations such that instrumental conclusions are appropriate. Thus, in addition to the formal research propositions that follow, all of which have instrumental implications, this section contains some examples of problems of potential opportunism for which formal propositions are inappropriate at present. The development of these examples into theoretically compelling empirical propositions is left to future researchers.

Shareholders are among the firm's important stakeholders. Several features of the law of corporations govern the relative power of managers and shareholders. Some of the legal options available to firms serve primarily to make hostile takeovers more difficult. Examples of such options are "poison pills," "shark repellents," dual-class stock, and incorporation in states (such as Delaware) in which corporation law favors broad management discretion. Researchers have used two theories to explain the emergence of such phenomena—the shareholder interest hypothesis and the management entrenchment hypothesis. According to the shareholder interest hypothesis (e.g., Grossman & Hart, 1980; Linn & McConnell, 1983), managers undertake such actions in order to protect and enhance the interests of shareholders. The management entrenchment hypothesis (DeAngelo & Rice, 1983) posits that such actions as these are motivated by the desire of managers to retain their employment and its associated perquisites. The difference between these two theories, in terms relevant to the theory developed in this article, is that the shareholder interest hypothesis assumes trustworthy behavior on the part of management, whereas the management entrenchment hypothesis assumes opportunistic behavior. Thus, empirical tests of these theories are relevant to instrumental stakeholder theory.

That managers are threatened by takeovers is an accepted fact. Furtado and Karan (1990), Martin and McConnell (1991), and Walsh and Ellwood (1991) found that incumbent managers are frequently fired soon after a change in control. That takeovers tend to benefit shareholders of target firms is also beyond question. Bid premiums in takeovers average 30 percent over pre-bid share prices (Jarrell, Brickley, & Netter, 1988). In addition, shareholders received $86 billion through takeovers and share repurchases, amounting to 68 percent of their total cash returns, between 1981 and 1986 (Bergsma, 1988). In order for antitakeover actions to benefit shareholders, they must either result in more bid offers being made or result in higher bid premiums overall. What does the evidence suggest?

Pound (1987) found that certain types of shark repellents (antitakeover charter amendments) substantially reduced the probability of a takeover bid. Frankforter (1991) also found shark repellents to have a deterrent effect on takeover bids. Neither author found significantly higher bid premiums for firms with shark repellents than for "defenseless" firms, leading both to conclude that shark repellents serve managerial, not shareholder, interests.

Shareholders also seem to be aware of the divergence of their interests and managerial interests with respect to shark repellents.

Institutional investors, likely to be among the most sophisticated shareholders, were far more likely than individual holders to vote against shark repellents in corporate proxy votes (Brickley, Lease, & Smith, 1988). In addition, DeAngelo and Rice (1983) and Jarrell and Poulsen (1987) found that shark repellents have a negative effect on shareholder wealth. Thus, in the case of shark repellents, the evidence offers support for the management entrenchment hypothesis and, hence, for the conclusion that management opportunism is at work. Thus, if the adoption of shark repellents signals managerial opportunism, instrumental stakeholder theory predicts that:

Proposition 1: Firms that do not adopt shark repellents will outperform firms that adopt these devices.

Poison pills (contingent securities that burden an acquiring firm with various obligations after takeovers) are also devices intended to deter hostile takeovers. Ryngaert (1988) and the SEC (1986) found that poison pills were effective in helping firms defeat unsolicited tender offers. "Event studies" of stock prices showed significant negative effects of the adoption of poison pills (Malatesta & Walkling, 1988; Ryngaert, 1988; SEC, 1986) and significant price increases when they were abandoned (Malatesta & Walkling, 1988) or declared by a court to be invalid (Ryngaert, 1988; SEC, 1986). Thus, poison pills, like shark repellents, signal managerial opportunism because they tend to protect managerial employment at the expense of shareholders, who are denied the potential windfall benefits of tender offers. Instrumental stakeholder theory predicts that:

Proposition 2: Firms that do not adopt poison pills will outperform firms that adopt these devices.

Research on (a) the effects of the issuance of dual-class stock, which places a disproportionate share of voting power in "management friendly" hands, or (b) the movement of the corporate charter to a state that allows management substantial discretion in its dealings with shareholders has been limited. (See Jarrell & Poulsen, 1988, and Karpoff & Malatesta, 1989, for exceptions.) Therefore, formal propositions relating these events to corporate performance are inappropriate at present. However, because these changes in corporate governance, undertaken under the law of corporations, seem to promote management entrenchment and not shareholder interest, they also seem to signal managerial opportunism and, hence, be relevant events in the application of instrumental stakeholder theory.

Control repurchases ("greenmail" in less formal parlance) are purchases of blocks of stock from potential "raiders" who pose a threat to the control of top management of a firm (Kosnik, 1990). Although raiders are usually paid a premium for their shares (often a substantial premium) (Bradley & Wakeman, 1983), other shareholders cannot take advantage of the offer (Kosnik, 1990). Although theory has been advanced to the effect that greenmail benefits nonparticipating shareholders (Macey & McChesney, 1985; Shleifer & Vishny, 1986), empirical evidence supports the conclusion that greenmail substantially harms shareholders (Bradley & Wakeman, 1983; Dann & DeAngelo, 1983; SEC, 1984). Thus, the payment of greenmail appears to be another manifestation of managerial opportunism and, hence, an event of relevance to instrumental stakeholder theory, which predicts that:

Proposition 3: Firms that do not pay greenmail will outperform firms that do pay greenmail.

The relationship between executive compensation and corporate financial performance has been the subject of substantial empirical scrutiny. Some researchers have found a positive link between CEO pay and stock returns (Coughlan & Schmidt, 1985; Deckop, 1988; Jensen & Murphy, 1990; Murphy, 1985, 1986). These authors are quick to praise the pay-for-performance plans implemented by many firms, because they tend to align the interests of managers with those of shareholders. Other authors, including Kerr and Bettis (1987), Benston (1985), and Boyd (1994), found no links between CEO pay and stock returns, leading them to conclude that managerial dominance of corporate boards (Berle & Means, 1932; Herman, 1981; Mace, 1971) alters the pay-performance relationship. The mixed nature of these results has led other authors to seek additional explanations for these disparate findings. Gomez-Mejia, Tosi, and Hinken (1987) and Tosi and Gomez-Mejia (1989), for example, explored the effect of ownership structure on the pay-performance link, whereas Hill and Phan (1991) examined the impact that CEO tenure had on the strength of the pay-performance relationship.

Instrumental stakeholder theory turns the (assumed) causal relationship between pay and performance around. This theory would predict a negative relationship, positing that disproportionately high executive pay is an example of inefficient contracting between the firm and its managers. Because top managers contract with stakeholders (including themselves, as previously argued) on behalf of the firm, excessive executive compensation can be seen as an abuse of trust and a symbol of a lack of trustworthiness on the part of top managers. The reputation earned by this type of behavior could cause inefficient contracting with other stakeholders and a decline in relative performance. Thus, rather than the theory postulated in prior studies that *high (low) performance causes high (low) pay*, instrumental stakeholder theory leads to the prediction that:

> *Proposition 4: Firms with disproportionately high levels of executive compensation will perform less well than firms without high levels of executive compensation.*

Suppliers also are important corporate stakeholders and the level of mutual trust and cooperation between a firm and its suppliers can affect the firm's cost structure significantly. Hill (In press) has explored the differences between Japanese and American auto firms in terms of their dealings with subcontractors. American firms, seeking to economize by inducing component part suppliers to invest in specific assets, settled on vertical integration, a relatively expensive solution because the costs of bureaucracy are high relative to those of the market (Monteverde & Teece, 1982). Japanese firms, in sharp contrast, entered into long-term "relational contracts" with their important (first-tier) suppliers. Aoki (1988) reported that Toyota and Nissan manufacture less than 30 percent of their components in house, whereas Ford and General Motors manufacture 50 percent and 70 percent of their components in house, respectively. The ability of Japanese firms to successfully employ such relationships is a function of the cultural institution of mutual trust and mutual obligation (Dore, 1987). The focal firm's long-term commitment to the subcontractor is matched by the subcontractor's obligation to conscientiously meet the focal firm's component manufacturing needs. Because such relationships facilitate investment in efficient specific assets, cost savings can be substantial (Hill, In press). If these arguments are expressed in terms of instrumental stakeholder theory, it appears that long-term relationships with a relatively small number of suppliers are indicative of cooperative, mutually trusting relationships.

A firm that keeps several suppliers "on line" competing for its business or that changes suppliers regularly is not indicating an interest in contracts built on mutual trust. Accordingly, its suppliers will not be able to achieve economies of scale in their operations and will not be willing to invest in assets specific to the production of the firm's needs. Therefore,

> *Proposition 5: Firms that have relatively few suppliers will outperform firms that have many suppliers.*

Proposition 6: Firms that have long-term relationships with their suppliers will outperform firms that have relatively brief relationships with their suppliers.

Employees also are important stakeholders, and mutually trusting, cooperative relationships between a firm and its employees should provide a competitive advantage. Pfeffer, in his book entitled *Competitive Advantage Through People* (1994), made this point well. He argued that employment relationships built on the assumptions about human behavior implicit (and explicit) in neoclassical economic models (i.e., agency theory and transaction cost economics) are antithetical to the kinds of relationships that firms need to create in order to compete effectively in the long run. The assumption of opportunism (self-interest with guile) leads to expensive control mechanisms that are ultimately dysfunctional because they substantially reduce the level of trust in the organization. He noted that the five top-performing firms (in terms of percentage return on stock price) from 1972 to 1992 differentiated themselves by the way they managed their workforces (Pfeffer, 1994). These firms emphasized the value of their human assets rather than the economic factors that have been commonly believed (largely as a result of the work of Michael Porter, 1985) to be decisive in achieving competitive advantage. More generally, empirical evidence regarding the favorable effect of good industrial relations on economic performance has been provided by Katz, Kochan, and Gobeille (1983).

These general conclusions can be used to derive some specific research propositions that link evidence of managerial opportunism to corporate performance. In recent years, many firms have begun to "contract out" work formerly done by employees (in some cases to the former employees themselves). According to Pfeffer (1994), these firms do so (a) to increase employment flexibility, (b) to save money, (c) to increase staff quickly, and (d) to inflate statistical measures of productivity (e.g., sales per employee). Such practices are hardly conducive to the trusting and cooperative relationships advocated by instrumental stakeholder theory, suggesting instead managerial opportunism. It follows that:

Proposition 7: Firms that contract out work formerly done by employees will perform less well than those that do not follow this practice.

Firms that hire only at the entry level and promote from within (internal labor markets) will enhance trusting relationships with their employees in contrast with those that rely heavily on labor markets external to the firm. Pfeffer touts the advantages of "promotion from within" (1994: 53), because such practices (a) bind workers to the firm and, thus, encourage training and skill development; (b) promote internal trust and, hence, facilitate delegation, participation, and decentralization; (c) promote informal relationships that make formal hierarchy less important; (d) provide a sense of justice and fairness, because loyal employees will not be passed over in favor of outside candidates for job openings; (e) offer better incentives for good performance; and (f) ensure that employees in key positions actually understand the business. Further, the firm will be able to count on the loyalty of internally developed employees, as opposed to "opportunists" who hop from job to job. Because internal labor markets promote trusting and cooperative relations between the firm and its employees, it can be predicted that:

Proposition 8: Firms with internal labor markets will outperform firms that rely on external labor markets.

Close monitoring and surveillance of employees is indicative of a lack of trust on the part of management. Such practices tend to (a) increase stress and physical ailments, (b) undermine intrinsic interest in work, and (c) produce distrust and alienation among employees (Pfeffer, 1994). Instrumental stakeholder theory predicts that:

Proposition 9: Firms that provide close monitoring of employees (perhaps including surveillance) will perform less well than firms that do not engage in such monitoring.

The relationships between firms and their employees are affected by other factors that are indicative of managerial opportunism or low levels of mutual trust and cooperation but for which theory and empirical work is as yet insufficient to warrant formal propositions. For example, firms that have undertaken major efforts to decertify unions might have trouble maintaining trusting and cooperative relations with their stakeholders and, hence, perform less well than those that have not taken such steps. Similarly, firms that undertake major downsizing efforts might perform less well than those that have not taken such actions, according to instrumental stakeholder theory. Of the current trend toward downsizing and similar activities in which people are viewed as short-term costs to be reduced, Noer says that "it represents a fundamental shift in the psychological covenant between the individual and the organization" (1993:16). Such "covenants" (contracts) are central elements in instrumental stakeholder theory.

Other firm-stakeholder relationships also may be characterized by evidence of opportunism or a lack of trust and cooperation. For example, firms with pension plans may not fully fund the plans, thereby jeopardizing the retirement security of employees. Firms may have "caveat emptor" policies with regard to the satisfaction and safety of those who buy and use their products. In view of the high cost of losing existing customers and the high sensitivity of profits to the retention of customers (Reichheld & Sasser, 1990), product return, warranty, and recall policies that are sensitive to customer satisfaction and safety would seem to confer competitive advantage on firms that adopt them. Management-led leveraged buyouts, common in the 1980s, often led to the enrichment of participating managers (and gains for shareholders) at the expense of bondholders, whose bonds dropped in value as firms took on new debt. Further, employees often lost their jobs as a result of these buyouts. The "contracts" between firms and local communities also are subject to opportunism. Firms can bargain for costly infrastructure or low tax rates in areas in which they want to locate a facility and then renege on their commitments once the infrastructure has been provided and/or the community has grown dependent on the jobs the firms provide. Likewise, communities can renege on promises to keep taxes low.

These specific relationships, about which research propositions could be developed, might be supplemented by a prospective relationship between the extent of a firm's legal activities and its economic performance. A firm's legal department handles (either directly or indirectly) much of its formal contracting with shareholders, suppliers, customers, employees, bondholders, and dealers. Attorneys also are involved in the negotiation and litigation that attend after-the-fact contracting disagreements. Thus, the extent of legal activity that a firm engages in reflects the general level of trust across the full spectrum of manager/stakeholder relations. In summary, opportunism can be a factor in the relationships between the firm and many of its stakeholders. Instrumental stakeholder theory implies that managers should eschew policies and decisions that reveal opportunism and avoid relationships with stakeholders (existing or potential) thought to be opportunistic.

Clearly, some of these formal propositions and suggested relationships will seem counterintuitive to some readers because they run counter to conventional economic wisdom. However, the point of instrumental stakeholder theory is exactly this: manifestations of opportunism *may not* lead to optimal economic performance. The theory is intended to explain why certain behaviors heretofore thought to be irrational or altruistic are, in fact, quite compatible with economic success. It is also intended to explain why these behaviors persist in economic relationships despite their presumed irrational or altruistic nature.

Further, a few empirical caveats are in order. First, these research propositions are intended to be illustrative of the relationships indicated by the theory. However, researchers may find that no single proposition is empirically "true"; it may be the case that a threshold of trusting and cooperative relationships between the firm and its stakeholders must be met before empirically significant differences in performance are found. Second, as in all empirical work, the assumption of "all else being equal" must be made; trusting relationships with its stakeholders may be irrelevant to the success of a firm that has obsolete products, inefficient production processes, or uninspired marketing plans.

Implications and Extensions of the Theory

The most important academic implication of this theory may be its impact on transaction cost economics. Transaction cost economists, most notably Williamson (1975), posited that reduction of transaction costs is a critical element in the choice between markets and hierarchies as coordinating mechanisms in the production process. Markets have been alleged to reduce certain types of opportunism, whereas hierarchies (corporate bureaucracies) have been alleged to reduce other types of opportunism. Hill (In press) suggests that cultural patterns in Japan (trust, obligation, cooperation) reduce transaction costs and result in a competitive advantage for Japanese firms. Similarly, moral sentiments that resemble cultural traits such as those found in Japan may render the debate over markets versus hierarchies less relevant with regard to international competition. Moral firms, like Japanese firms, may solve problems of opportunism in markets and in hierarchies better than do their less moral counterparts. Efficiency within organizations, often best described in agency theory or team production theory terms, and efficiency at organizational boundaries, well described by transaction cost economic theory, may both be better achieved through trust and cooperation than through mechanisms purporting to efficiently curb opportunism. Moral sentiments may transcend both markets and hierarchies as efficient contracting mechanisms.

Another area of academic interest that can be illuminated through applications of instrumental stakeholder theory is the relationship between corporate social performance and financial performance. Although several studies have examined this relationship (e.g., Alexander & Buchholz, 1978; Cochran & Wood, 1984; Sturdivant & Ginter, 1977), none has been based on credible theory, prompting Ullmann (1985) to call them "data in search of a theory." In view of the ideas advanced in this article, the theory under examination could be simply stated: Certain types of corporate social performance are manifestations of attempts to establish trusting, cooperative firm/stakeholder relationships and should be positively linked to a company's financial performance. Corporate social performance would then be defined in terms of the contracting relationship rather than particular behavior. Researchers would be compelled to correctly describe and categorize the nature of the contract involved and to link it to the form of social performance under examination, of course, but theory-based research would be possible under the proposed framework. The research propositions I have included suggest some of these relationships as well as some of the means of operationalizing the characteristics of contracts.

An interesting extension of this theory is related to predicted changes in the global economy of the future. According to Robert Reich, in his book *The Work of Nations: Preparing for 20th Century Capitalism* (1991), economic wealth in the future will not accrue to "national firms" but rather to national people," whose skills will be part of large and fluid global enterprise webs." Business tasks will be performed by those who can carry them out most efficiently, and most of the repetitive production tasks will be performed abroad where wage rates are low. The wealth of nations will be a function of the number of "symbolic analysts"—problem identifiers, problem solvers, and strategic brokers—the nation supplies to these enterprise webs. The United States has, according to Reich, a substantial head start on other nations in terms of the number and skills of its symbolic analysts, who should do quite well at performing the tasks of conceiving, brokering, and implementing the specialized, high-value, market-niche-oriented production of the future. What Reich overlooks, in view of instrumental stakeholder theory, is the competitive disadvantage that results from a cultural tradition of opportunism or of expensively constrained opportunism. If the economy of the future depends on the success of countless "deals," those who can consummate and deliver on those deals efficiently should be more successful than those who cannot or will not honor their commitments. American symbolic analysts, with their penchant for opportunism, and the American legal system, with its penchant for expensive before-the-fact legal contracting and after-the-fact litigation, may be unattractive elements in a system that would seem to rely heavily on trust and cooperation. America's head start in education and critical skills may be dissipated by its cultural tradition of self-interest.

Because public policy often affects firm/stakeholder relationships, the theory has implications for government policy as well. Frank (1988) suggested one such implication: the questionable value of "mobile" resources. Economists stress the virtue of resources (e.g., capital, labor) being moved to their most efficient use. Plant closings, job hopping, takeovers, and leveraged buyouts are manifestations of this credo. The theory I present suggests that the opposite might be true. The instability and insecurity resulting from mobile resources can seriously impair the development of the trusting, cooperative relationships upon which efficient contracting depends. Firms that move part of their production overseas can hardly expect trust and cooperation (beyond what they can command) on the part of their remaining employees. Companies that are constantly acquiring and/or "spinning off" subsidiaries or divisions cannot expect commitment from their stakeholders. In short, mobile resources may not be efficient because they signal opportunism and promote further opportunism. It follows that the economy and the larger society might be well served by government policies designed to stabilize the economic environment rather than by letting market forces prevail unhindered. Specific policies worthy of consideration in this context are trade protection and takeover protection for domestic corporations. Hostile takeovers in particular, thought by economists to promote efficiency (the "market for corporate control" at work), can be enormously destructive to the trust and cooperation needed for efficient contracting. The long-term benefits of stable corporate ownership and control may outweigh the benefits of active markets for corporate control. Public policy promoting such stability may be superior to that promoting mobile resources. Again, conventional economic wisdom is questioned by the new theory.

Conclusions

At this point, a brief overview of the article and a summary of its main points are in order. The theory advanced here is intended to strengthen the case for using the stakeholder model as a central paradigm for the business and society field. The theory is built on an integration of the stakeholder concept, economic concepts (agency theory, transaction cost economics, and team production theory), insights from behavioral science, and ethics. It focuses on the contracts (relationships) between the firm and its stakeholders and posits that trusting and cooperative relationships help solve problems related to opportunism. Because the costs of opportunism and of preventing or reducing opportunism are significant, firms that contract on the basis of trust and cooperation will have a competitive advantage over those that do not use such criteria. This instrumental theory of stakeholder management essentially turns the neoclassical theory of the firm upside down. It implies that behavior that is trusting, trustworthy, and cooperative, not opportunistic, will give the firm a competitive advantage. In the process, it may help explain why certain "irrational" or altruistic behaviors turn out to be productive and why firms that engage in these behaviors survive and often thrive.

Thomas M. Jones received his Ph.D. from the University of California at Berkeley. He is a professor of organization and environment at the University of Washington in Seattle. His current research interests include business and society paradigms, ethical decision-making models, and moral justifications for stakeholder management.

Dennis P. Quinn's help during the formative stages of this article is gratefully acknowledged. Tom Donaldson, Lee Preston, and four anonymous reviewers made helpful comments on earlier drafts of this article.

Akerlof. G. A. 1970. The market for lemons: Quality, uncertainty and the market mechanism. *Quarterly Journal of Economics,* 84: 488-500.

Alchian, A., & Demsetz, H. 1972. Production, information costs, and economic organization. *American Economic Review,* 62: 777-795.

Alexander, G. J., & Buchholz, R. A. 1978. Corporate social responsibility and stock market performance. *Academy of Management Journal.* 21: 479-486.

Angeles, P. A. 1992. *The HarperCollins dictionary of philosophy* (2nd ed.). New York: HarperCollins.

Aoki, M. 1988. *Information, incentives, and bargaining in the Japanese economy.* Cambridge, England: Cambridge University Press.

Aram, J. D. 1989. The paradox of interdependent relations in the field of social issues in management. *Academy of Management Review,* 14: 266-283.

Axelrod, R. 1984. *The evolution of cooperation.* New York: Basic Books.

Bandura, A. 1986. *Social foundations of thought and action: A social cognitive theory.* Englenwood Cliffs. NJ: Prentice Hall.

Bamard, C. I. 1968. *The functions of the executive.* (30th anniversary ed.). Cambridge, MA: Harvard University Press. (Original work published in 1938)

Beach, L. R. 1990. *Image theory: Decision making in personal and organizational contexts.* Chichester, England: Wiley.

Benston, G. 1. 1985. The self-serving management hypothesis: Some evidence. *Journal of Accounting and Economics,* 7: 67-84.

Bergsma, E. 1988. Do-it-yourself takeover curbs. *Wall Street Journal,* February 12: 12.

Berle, A. A., & Means, G. C. 1932. *The modern corporation and private property.* New York: Macmillan.

Boyd, B. K. 1994. Board control and CEO compensation. *Strategic Management Journal,* 15: 335-344.

Bradley, M. & Wakeman, L. M. 1983. The wealth effects of targeted share repurchases. *Journal of Financial Economics*, 11: 366-373.

Brenner, S. N., & Cochran, P. 1991. The stakeholder theory of the firm: Implications for business and society theory and research. In J. F. Mahon (Ed.), *International Association for Business and Society—1991 Proceedings*: 449-467.

Brickley, J. A., Lease, R. C., & Smith, C. W.. Jr. 1988. Ownership structure and voting on antitakeover amendments. *Journal of Financial Economics*, 20: 267-291.

Carroll, A. B. 1979. A three-dimensional conceptual model of corporate performance. *Academy of Management Review*, 4: 497-505.

Carroll, A. B. 1994. Social issues in management research: Experts' views, analysis and commentary. *Business and Society* (The Journal of the International Association for Business and Society), 33(1): 5-29.

Clarkson, M. B. E., Deck, M. C., & Shiner, N. J. 1992. *The stakeholder management model in practice.* Paper presented at the annual meeting of the Academy of Management, Las Vegas, NV.

Clinard, M. B. 1983. *Corporate ethics and crime: The role of middle management.* Beverly Hills, CA: Sage.

Coase, R. H. 1937. The nature of the firm. *Economica*, 4: 386-405.

Cochran, P. L., & Wood, R. A. 1984. Corporate social responsibility and financial performance. *Academy of Management Journal*, 27: 42-56.

Coughlan, A. T., & Schmidt, R. M. 1985. Executive compensation, managerial turnover, and firm performance. *Journal of Accounting and Economics*, 7: 43-66.

Dann, L. Y., & DeAngelo, H. 1983. Standstill agreements, privately negotiated stock purchases and the market for corporate control. *Journal of Financial Economics*, 11: 275-300.

DeAngelo, H., & Rice, E. M. 1983. Antitakeover charter amendments and stockholder wealth. *Journal of Financial Economics*. 11: 329-359.

Deckop, J. R. 1988. Determinants of chief executive officer compensation. *Industrial and Labor Relations Review*, 41: 215-226.

DePaulo, B. M., Zuckerman, M., & Rosenthal, R. 1980. Humans as lie detectors. *Journal of Communication*, 30(4): 129-139.

Domhoff, G. W. 1967. *Who rules America?* Englewood Cliffs. NJ: Prentice Hall.

Donaldson, T., & Preston, L. E. 1995. The stakeholder theory of the corporation: Concepts, evidence, and implications. *Academy of Management Review*, 20: 65-91.

Dore, R. 1987. *Taking Japan seriously.* Stanford. CA: Stanford University Press.

Dunfee, T. W. 1991. Business ethics and extant social contracts. *Business Ethics Quarterly*, 1: 23-51.

Eisenhardt, K. M. 1988. Agency—and institutional—theory explanations: The case of retail sales compensation. *Academy of Management Journal*. 31: 488-511.

Eisenhardt, K. M. 1989. Agency theory: An assessment and review. *Academy of Management Review*, 14: 57-74.

Etzioni, A. 1965. Organizational control structures. In J. G. March (Ed.), *Handbook of organizations*: 650-677. Chicago: Rand McNally.

Etzioni, A. 1988. *The moral dimension*. New York: Basic Books.

Evan, W. M., & Freeman, R. E. 1993. A stakeholder theory of the modem corporation: Kantian capitalism. In T. L. Beauchamp & N. E. Bowie (Eds.), *Ethical theory and business*: 75-84. Englewood Cliffs, NJ: Prentice Hall.

Frank, R. H. 1988. *Passions within reason: The strategic role of emotions*. New York: Norton.

Frankforter, S. A. 1991. *Antitakeover charter amendments: Entrenchment devices or serving the interests of shareholders?* Paper presented at the annual meeting of the Midwest Decision Science Institute, Indianapolis. IN.

Freeman, R. E. 1984. *Strategic management: A stakeholder approach*. Boston: Pitman.

Freeman, R. E., & Gilbert, D. R., Jr. 1987. Managing stakeholder relationships. In S. P. Sethi & C. M. Falbe (Eds.), *Business and society*: 397-423. Lexington, MA: Lexington Books.

Freeman, R. E.. & Reed, D. L. 1983. *Stockholders and stakeholders*: A new perspective on corporate governance. *California Management Review*, 25(3). 88-106.

Furtado, E. P. H., & Karan, V. 1990. Causes, consequences, and shareholder wealth effects of management turnover: A review of the empirical evidence. *Financial Management*, 19(2): 60-76.

Gomez-Mejia, L. R., Tosi, H., & Hinken, T. 1987. Managerial control, performance, and executive compensation. *Academy of Management Journal*, 30: 51-70.

Grossman, S. J., & Hart, O. D. 1980. Takeover bids, the free-rider problem, and the theory of the corporation. *Bell Journal of Economics*, 80: 42-64.

Hardin, G. 1968. The tragedy of the commons. *Science*. 162: 1243-1248.

Herman, E. S. 1981. *Corporate control. corporate power*. Cambridge, England: Cambridge University Press.

Hill, C. W. L. 1990. Cooperation, opportunism, and the invisible hand: Implications for transaction cost theory. *Academy of Management Review*, 15: 500-513.

Hill, C. W. L. In press. National institutional structures, transaction cost economizing and competitive advantage: The case of Japan. *Organization Science.*

Hill, C. W. L., & Jones, T. M. 1992. Stakeholder-agency theory. *Journal of Management Studies.* 29: 131-154.

Hill, C. W. L., & Phan, P. 1991. CEO tenure as a determinant of CEO pay. *Academy of Management Journal,* 34: 707-717.

Jacobson, R. 1992. The "Austrian" school of strategy. *Academy of Management Review,* 17: 782-807.

Jarrell, G. A., Brickley, J. A., & Netter, J. M. 1988. The market for corporate control: The empirical evidence since 1980. *Journal of Economic Perspectives,* 2(1): 49-68.

Jarrell, G. A., & Poulsen, A. B. 1987. Shark repellents and stock prices: The effects of antitakeover amendments since 1980. *Journal of Financial Economics,* 19: 127-168.

Jarrell, G. A., & Poulsen, A. B. 1988. Dual-class recapitalizations as antitakeover mechanisms: The recent evidence. *Journal of Financial Economics,* 20: 129-152.

Jensen, M. C., & Meckling, W. H. 1976. Theory of the firm: Managerial behavior, agency costs, and ownership structure. *Journal of Financial Economics.* 3: 305-360.

Jensen, M. C., & Murphy, K. J. 1990. Performance pay and top management incentives. *Journal of Political Economy,* 98: 225-264.

Jones, T. M. 1979. Corporate governance: Who controls the large corporation? *Hastings Law Journal.* 30: 1261-1286.

Jones, T. M. 1982. An integrating framework for research in business and society: A step toward the elusive paradigm? *Academy of Management Review,* 8: 559-564.

Jones, T. M. 1989. Ethics education in business: Theoretical considerations. *The Organizational Behavior Teaching Review,* 13(4): 1-18.

Jones, T. M., Hill, C. W. L., & Kelley, P. C. 1989. *A generalized theory of agency: A paradigm for business and society.* Paper presented at the annual meeting of the Academy of Management, Washington, DC.

Jones, T. M., & Quinn. D. P. 1993. Taking ethics seriously: The competitive advantage of intrinsic morality. *International Association for Business and Society Annual Meeting.* 1993 Proceedings: 262-266.

Karpoff, J. M., & Malatesta, P. A. 1989. The wealth effects of second-generation state takeover legislation. *Journal of Financial Economics,* 25: 291-322.

Katz, H. C., Kochan, T. A., & Gobeille, K. R. 1983. Industrial relations performance, economic performance, and QWL programs: An interplant analysis. *Industrial and Labor Relations Review,* 37: 3-17.

Kerr, J., & Bettis, R. A. 1987. Boards of directors, top management compensation, and shareholder returns. *Academy of Management Journal,* 30: 645-664.

Kirzner, I. M. 1979. *Perception, opportunity, and profit.* Chicago: University of Chicago Press.

Kosnik, R. D. 1990. Effects of board demography and directors' incentives on corporate greenmail decisions. *Academy of Management Journal.* 33: 129-150.

Larner, R. J. 1970. *Management control and the large corporation.* New York: Dunellen.

Lee, T. W., & Mitchell, T. R. 1994. An alternative approach: The unfolding model of voluntary employee turnover. *Academy of Management Review,* 19: 51-89.

Linn, S. C., & McConnell, J. J. 1983. An empirical investigation of the impact of antitakeover amendments on common stock prices. *Journal of Financial Economics,* 11: 361-399.

Mace, M. L. 1971. *Directors: Myth and reality.* Boston: Harvard University, Graduate School of Business Administration.

Macey, I. R., & McChesney, F. S. 1985. The theoretical analysis of corporate greenmail. *Yale Law Journal,* 95: 13-26.

Macneil, I. R. 1978. Contracts: Adjustments of long-term economic relations under classical, neoclassical, and relational contract law. *Northwestern University Law Review,* 72: 854-906.

Malatesta, P. H., & Walkling, R. A. 1988. Poison pill securities: Stockholder wealth, profitability, and ownership structure. *Journal of Financial Economics,* 20: 347-376.

Margolis, H. 1984. *Selfishness, altruism, and rationality: A theory of social choice.* Chicago: University of Chicago Press.

Martin, K. J., & McConnell, J. J. 1991. Corporate performance, corporate takeovers, and management turnover. *Journal of Finance.* 46: 671-688.

Mitnick, B. M. 1982. Regulation and the theory of agency. *Policy Studies Review,* 1: 442-453.

Monteverde, K., & Teece, D. 1. 1982. Supplier switching costs and vertical integration in the automobile industry. *Bell Journal of Economics,* 13: 203-213.

Murphy, K. 1985. Corporate performance and managerial remuneration. *Journal of Accounting and Economics,* 7: 11-42.

Murphy, K. 1986. Incentives, learning, and compensation: A theoretical and empirical investigation of managerial labor contracts. *Rand Journal of Economics*, 17: 59-76.

Noer, D. M. 1993. *Healing the wounds*. San Francisco: Jossey-Bass.

Noreen, E. 1988. The economics of ethics: A new perspective on agency theory. *Accounting, Organizations and Society*, 13: 359-369.

North, D. C. 1981. *Structure and change in economic history*. New York: Norton.

Olson, M. 1965. *The logic of collective action*. Cambridge, MA: Harvard University Press.

Ouchi, W. G. 1980. Markets, bureaucracies, and clans. *Administrative Science Quarterly*, 25: 129-141.

Ouchi, W. G. 1981. *Theory Z*. Reading, MA: Addison-Wesley.

Pfeffer, J. 1994. *Competitive advantage through people*. Boston: Harvard Business School Press.

Porter, M. E. 1985. *Competitive advantage*. New York: Free Press.

Pound, J. 1987. The effects of antitakeover amendments on takeover activity: Some direct evidence. *Journal of Law & Economics*, 30: 353-367.

Preston, L. E. 1975. Corporation and society: The search for a paradigm. *Journal of Economic Literature*. 13: 434-453.

Preston, L. E., & Sapienza, H. J. 1990. Stakeholder management and corporate performance. *Journal of Behavioral Economics*, 19: 361-375.

Pruitt, D. G., & Kimmel, M. J. 1977. Twenty years of experimental gaming: Critique, synthesis, and suggestions for the future. *Annual Review of Psychology*, 363-392.

Reich, R. B. 1991. *The work of nations*. New York: Knopf.

Reichheld, F. F., & Sasser, W. E., Jr. 1990. Zero defections: Quality comes to service. *Harvard Business Review*, 68(5): 105-111.

Ross, S. A. 1973. The economic theory of agency: The principal's problem. *American Economic Review*, 63:134-139.

Ryngaert, M. 1988. The effect of poison pill securities on shareholder wealth. *Journal of Financial Economics*. 20: 377-417.

Shleifer, A., & Vishny, R. W. 1986. Large shareholders and corporate control. *Journal of Political Economy*. 94: 461-488.

Securities and Exchange Commission. 1984. *The impact of targeted share repurchases on stock prices*. (Information Memorandum, 84-100). New York: SEC, Office of the Chief Economist.

Securities and Exchange Commission. 1986. *The effects of poison pills on the wealth of target shareholders*. Washington, DC: SEC, Office of the Chief Economist.

Simon, H. A. 1945. *Administrative behavior*. New York: Free Press.

Stone, C. D. 1975. *Where the law ends*. New York: Harper & Row.

Sturdivant, F. D.. & Ginter, J. L. 1977. Corporate social responsiveness: Management attitudes and economic performance. *California Management Review*, 19(3): 30-39.

Tosi, H. L., & Gomez-Mejia, L. 1989. The decoupling of pay and performance: An agency theory perspective. *Administrative Science Quarterly*. 34: 169-189.

Trevifio, L. K., & Youngblood, S. A. 1990. Bad apples in bad barrels: A causal analysis of ethical decision-making behavior. *Journal of Applied Psychology*, 75: 378-385.

Ullmann, A. A. 1985. Data in search of a theory: A critical examination of the relationships among social performance, social disclosure, and economic performance of U.S. firms. *Academy of Management Review*, 10: 540-557.

Walsh, J. P., & Ellwood, J. W. 1991. Mergers, acquisitions, and the pruning of managerial deadwood. *Strategic Management Journal*, 12: 201-217.

Wartick, S. L., & Cochran, P. L. 1985. The evolution of the corporate social performance model. *Academy of Management Review*, 10: 758-769.

Weick, K. E. 1969. *The social psychology of organizing*. Reading, MA Addison-Wesley.

Williamson, O. E. 1975. *Markets and hierarchies*. New York: Free Press.

Williamson, O. E. 1984. Corporate governance. *The Yale Law Journal*, 93: 1197-1230.

Williamson, O. E. 1985. *The economic institutions of capitalism*. New York: Free Press.

Wood, D. J. 1991a. Corporate social performance revisited. *Academy of Management Review*, 16: 691-718.

Wood, D. J. 1991b. Social issues in management: Theory and research in corporate social performance. *Journal of Management*. 17: 383-406.

Zeitlin, M. 1974. Corporate ownership and control: The large corporation and the capitalist class. *American Journal of Sociology*, 79: 1073-1119.

Copyright © *Academy of Management Review*, 1995.
Reprinted with permission from the Academy of Management.

A Stakeholder Framework for Analysing and Evaluating Corporate Social Performance

Max B.E. Clarkson, University of Toronto

This article presents conclusions from a 10-year research program, the purpose of which has been to develop a framework and methodology, grounded in the reality of corporate behavior, for analysing and evaluating corporate social performance. There are three principal sections: (a) a summary of the approaches, models, and methodologies used In conducting more than 70 field studies of corporate social performance from 1983-1993; (b) a discussion of the principal conclusions derived from the data that (1) corporations manage relationships with stakeholder groups rather than with society as a whole, (2) it is important to distinguish between social issues and stakeholder issues, and (3) it is necessary to identify the appropriate level of analysis in order to evaluate CSP; and (c) a discussion of propositions and areas for further research.

A fundamental problem in the field of business and society has been that there are no definitions of corporate social performance (CSP), corporate social responsibility (CSR_1), or corporate social responsiveness (CSR_2) that provide a framework or model for the systematic collection, organization, and analysis of corporate data relating to these important concepts. No theory has yet been developed that can provide such a framework or model, nor is there any general agreement about the meaning of these terms from an operational or a managerial viewpoint. Wood's (1991) concern that the "definition of corporate social performance (CSP) is not entirely satisfactory" is shared by many scholars and managers. CSP, together with CSR_1 and CSR_2, carry no clear meaning and remain elusive constructs. They have defied definition for reasons that are set forth in the second section.

I propose that corporate social performance can be analyzed and evaluated more effectively by using a framework based on the management of a corporation's relationships with its stakeholders than by using models and methodologies based on concepts concerning corporate social responsibilities and responsiveness. The stakeholder framework has been derived from data contained in more than 70 field studies of CSP, conducted from 1983-1993.

During this research program there have been three principal stages in the development of the methodologies for data collection, analysis, and evaluation: (a) 1983-1985: 30 field studies; (b) 1986-1988: 28 studies; and (c) 1989-1993: 20 studies.

A Research Program to Analyse and Evaluate CSP

Stage 1: 1983-1985

When this research and teaching program on CSR_1 was initiated in 1983, there had been only one significant empirical study of CSP in Canada, *Corporate Social Performance in Canada* (the Royal Commission on Corporate Concentration [RCCC], 1977). The situation in the United States was very much the same: "actual empirical research designed to test the multitude of definitions, propositions, concepts, and theories that have been advanced has been scarce" (Aupperle, Carroll, & Hatfield, 1985). To develop a methodology in 1975, the researchers in Canada had used the corporate social response matrix, which had been developed by Preston (1977), who was then the academic consultant to the group responsible for the research and writing of *Corporate Social Performance in Canada*. The focus of Preston's matrix or framework was the management of social issues by corporations. It was assumed that managers followed stages of a process identified as *corporate social involvement*. The stages of this process were defined by Preston as follows: (a) awareness or recognition of an issue, (b) analysis and planning, (c) response in terms of policy development, and (d) implementation.

This analytic framework was implemented using survey instruments and guidelines developed by Kelly and McTaggart (1979). These materials provided the basis for the methodology that was developed for use in 1983. The nine companies selected initially for study at that time had been among those studied seven years earlier, thus providing the opportunity for noting changes and trends in performance. (A more detailed description can be found in Clarkson, 1988.)

Preston's (1975) framework, however, provided no definition of what was, or was not, a social issue; nor was there guidance for a corporation's managers or researchers in determining whether a social issue was one about which the company should become concerned and involved. In

1983, at the beginning of the research program, several human resource issues were identified as important enough for most corporations to regard them as issues to be managed:

> communications with employees; training and development; career-planning; retirement and termination counseling; layoffs, redundancies and plant closings; stress and mental health; absenteeism and turnover; health and safety; employment equity and discrimination; women in management; performance appraisal; day care. (Clarkson, 1988: 52)

Because these are all issues, the assumption was made that they are also social issues. Consequently, the next assumption was made: Corporations and their managers should be concerned about, and responsive to, these *social* issues if they were to be evaluated as socially responsible. As researchers, we had introduced, without explicit acknowledgment or understanding, a set of normative assumptions about how corporations should behave and how their performance should be evaluated.

Stage 2: 1986-1988
The development of Carroll's (1979) original model represented an advance over Preston's (1975) framework and introduced a new conceptualization of CSP. Carroll was attempting to (a) reconcile the achievement of both corporate social and economic objectives, (b) to reconcile CSR_1 with CSR_2, and (c) to focus on the most important element, CSP.

Carroll's model was both comprehensive and integrative. The strength of its influence can best be judged by its longevity and that of its progeny. The model defined CSR_1 in terms of principles or categories and CSR_2 in terms of processes or strategies toward both social responsibilities and social issues. Social issues were defined by Carroll as consumerism, the environment, discrimination, and so on, and were used as surrogates for actual performance. It was plausible that corporations were expected to "do something" about these issues. But why they were expected to do something and what they were expected to do were not easily explained. Carroll's model, in the form of a three-dimensional cube, was complex and difficult to test. It did not lend itself to the development of a methodology that could be used in the field to collect, organize, and evaluate corporate data.

Wartick and Cochran (1985), building on Carroll's integrative view of CSP, also rejected earlier views that social responsibility, social responsiveness, and the management of social issues were separate, alternative corporate concerns. Their model, based on Carroll's, recognized and incorporated economic performance as the first among the dimensions or elements of social responsibility, without excluding the other responsibilities defined by Carroll: legal, ethical, and discretionary. Their model, again like Carroll's, was an attempt to show that there is an underlying and continuous interaction between and among the principles of social responsibility, the processes of social responsiveness, and the policies and programs developed to address social issues.

Models and frameworks are helpful for clarifying theories and abstract concepts or constructs. But to be useful in practice, a model or framework must be applicable to the conditions that it is attempting to describe, analyze, or predict. Empirical testing of a model is important to establish its validity. Whereas Preston's corporate social response matrix was limited to policies and programs responding to social issues, the Wartick and Cochran model, based on the Carroll construct, included the dimensions of corporate social responsibility and the processes of corporate social responsiveness. By the end of the third year of field research, 30 studies had been completed using the initial methodology based on Preston's matrix.

Changing methodologies is not done lightly, because data obtained previously must be reorganized to be useful. But because the Wartick and Cochran model appeared to be suitable for testing in the field and, in terms of the management of social issues, was compatible with Preston's approach, the decision was made to revise the methodology to use the new model for studies beginning in 1986. Details of the methodology developed for using and testing the model in the field have been described elsewhere (Clarkson, 1988). Only the most important conceptual difficulties and problems are discussed in the second section.

The principles of social responsibility

Under the heading of principles of social responsibility in the Wartick and Cochran model, the elements or dimensions of social responsibility are defined as economic, legal, ethical, and discretionary, following Carroll's original classification. Consequently, the methodology developed for the field studies required that data be gathered on each of these four dimensions.

Obtaining economic data presented few problems, with annual reports and data on industry profitability usually available. Being profitable for the preceding five years was established as the measure that a company had been fulfilling its economic responsibilities.

Databases of the financial press were checked to provide data about litigation and allegations of illegal corporate behavior. Government departments, unions, and municipalities in company towns were also checked to discover data about environmental or safety problems. If no evidence was found, the assumption was made that the company was fulfilling its legal responsibilities. This, of course, was an easy test to pass.

Ethical responsibilities were more difficult to define and test. There are no generally accepted ethical principles that can be cited or enforced as with accounting principles. The existence of a corporate code of conduct, practice, or ethics is certainly evidence that a company is aware of some responsibilities but does not tell the researcher how the code is being implemented or whether it is simply window dressing. Many company codes were primarily defensive, aimed at protecting the company and its property from its employees (Clarkson & Deck, 1993).

It was also difficult to define discretionary responsibilities, except in terms of the extent of the corporation's philanthropic activities and the nature of its involvement in the communities in which it did business. As Carroll (1979) noted, "discretionary responsibilities of business are volitional or philanthropic in nature, and, as such, are also difficult to ascertain and evaluate."

Given the four dimensions of corporate social responsibility defined by the model, the corporate studies provided little empirical data to show that a company was not socially responsible, unless there was a history of unprofitability, coupled with evidence of illegal or unethical corporate behavior. It developed that the model did not provide a satisfactory means by which the concept of social responsibility could be tested with reasonably accessible corporate data. Votaw's (1973) criticism of the term *corporate social responsibility* remained valid:

> The term is a brilliant one; it means something, but not always the same thing, to everybody. To some it conveys the idea of legal responsibility or liability; to others it means socially responsible behavior in an ethical sense; to still others, the meaning transmitted is that of "responsible for", in a causal mode; many simply equate it with a charitable contribution. (Votaw, 1973: 11)

The processes of social responsiveness
The processes of social responsiveness were defined by both models in terms of corporate strategy or posture toward social issues. Carroll (1979) identified these processes of response as being reactive, defensive, accommodative, or proactive. Wartick and Cochran's model (1985) used the same four categories of social responsiveness. As Wood (1991: 703) correctly observed: "These approaches may indeed characterize various organizational responses to social pressure, but they are not themselves processes." Consequently, the research question for the field studies became one of determining the types of behavior that could serve as reliable indicators of, or surrogates for, these differing characterizations of

corporate postures or strategies toward social responsiveness and social issues.

In an attempt, therefore, to describe a corporation's social responsiveness and analyze its elements, the methodology that was developed in 1986 included the following descriptions of the data to be gathered:

> A corporation's statement of mission or purpose, its code of conduct or ethics, and the structure of its processes for managing issues in such areas as environmental scanning and analysis, the integration of social issues into policy and planning, and the internal linkages in a corporation whereby strategic decisions about social issues are integrated into operations by means of objective setting, performance appraisal and rewards; and the extent of public policy involvement, either directly or through trade associations. (Clarkson, 1988)

When questions arose from student researchers and managers in the field, it became apparent that there was no logical explanation for the inclusion of statements about corporate mission or purpose, together with evidence of public policy involvement, under the heading of social responsiveness rather than under the management of social issues. It was not clear whether policies, programs, and performance data concerning codes of ethics, conduct, or practice should be included under the headings of ethical responsibilities or management of social issues.

The fundamental problem was, and remains, that no definition of social responsiveness provides a framework for the systematic collection, organization, and analysis of corporate data. The term *social responsiveness* carries no clear meaning for managers, students, or academic researchers and scholars. Consequently, much time, energy, and paper have been consumed in attempts to explain the term. But it remains an elusive construct, lacking both logic and rigor, which limits seriously its usefulness for empirical research.

Although the categories were confusing, the terms used by the model to describe a corporation's strategy or posture toward the management of issues were helpful in the field. Strategies, posture, and behavior that are reactive, defensive, accommodative, or proactive can be demonstrated by the presence or absence of policies and programs concerning relevant issues and by the corporation's performance in implementation. The following extract, from the field study of Canada's second largest bank in 1986, illustrates this point:

> A characterization of the company's attitude towards social responsiveness can be summed up by a couple of statements from

interviews with the Bank's representatives. The Manager of Media Relations said of the Bank: "We are not a government, we are a bank. We do not set social policy, we look to government for social policy." In another interview with a Vice President of Human Resources, it was said: "The government is into every nook and cranny of our business." These statements, and many others, indicate that the social orientation of the company, using the RDAP scale, is, at best, accommodative. (Vincent, Olliers, & Starasts, 1986: 6)

Performance and nonperformance are concrete, measurable criteria. If an issue is being managed, there will be data. The terms *reactive, defensive, accommodative,* and *proactive* have been incorporated into the RDAP scale, which was developed to evaluate corporate performance and is discussed in the second section.

Stage 3: A New Framework is Developed

From 1986-1988, researchers gathered case study data about 28 companies, using the new methodology. Data had now been collected from more than 50 corporations about policies, programs, and issues concerning the social and physical environments, public affairs and government relations, community relations and charitable donations, employee relations, and human resource management, as well as customer and shareholder relations. In short, the data that were being collected fit into categories that could be classified, as later became apparent, in terms of the management of a corporation's relationships with its stakeholder groups. The methodology, however, required that the data be organized to fit the Wartick and Cochran model, which was based on distinctions among the principles of corporate social responsibility, the processes of corporate social responsiveness, and the management of social issues. These distinctions, which had intuitive appeal on the printed page, failed the test of practicality.

Attempts were made to fit the data to the methodology, but finally it became clear that the categories of the model were not applicable to the data that were being gathered and that the classifications of the model were not grounded in the realities of corporate practice. As the volume of data and the number of studies grew, it became increasingly difficult to achieve consistency in the collection and classification of these data to conform with the methodology.

The model and, consequently, the methodology were at variance with the way in which corporations actually manage their relationships with employees, customers, shareholders, suppliers, governments, and the communities in which they operate. Although the term *stakeholder management* was not necessarily in use, it became clear that all the corporations being studied had relationships with various groups or constituencies, which could be defined as stakeholder groups, and that these relationships were either being managed, or not being managed, for better or worse. Whether these groups of customers, employees, shareholders, etc., were classified as internal or external stakeholders was irrelevant, just as it was irrelevant for the companies themselves whether these groups were described as stakeholders at all. What was relevant to the research program was that the data that had been collected and analyzed corresponded with the concepts and models of stakeholder management (Freeman, 1984). rather than with the concepts and models of corporate social responsibilities, responsiveness, and performance.

The data showed that, in the normal course of conducting their business, corporate managers do not think or act in terms of the concepts of corporate social responsibilities and responsiveness, nor of social issues and performance. The following statement from *Corporate Social Performance in Canada* illustrates this point and also provides an early example of the use of the term *stakeholder issues*.

> It is also worth pointing out that in many cases public affairs departments were not established to handle social responsibility issues as such but to help the organization respond more competently to a whole range of "stakeholder issues," including the company's relationships with employees, media, and with government. (RCCC, 1977: 81)

CSR_1 and CSR_2 are concepts that have been generated outside business. They have normative connotations lacking clarity and specificity and have the disadvantage of sounding like jargon. "Socially responsible to whom?", "Socially responsive about what?", "Social performance judged by whom and by what standards?": These are legitimate questions to which business people have not received satisfactory or meaningful responses. Understandably, they have resisted attempts to make them responsible for social issues that they do not perceive as corporate or business issues.

Managers are trained in the management of the processes of production, marketing, finance, accounting, and human resources. Managers understand the meaning of responsibility in the context of these functional disciplines, and they understand the meaning of accountability for the results of their decisions. Obligations and responsibilities to customers, shareholders, employees, and other important constituencies are defined by most companies, together with corresponding accountabilities. Consequently, there are data concerning the management of corporate relationships with these constituencies or stakeholder groups.

Managers do not find it difficult to understand the concepts and models of stakeholder management. They recognize that important issues of concern to groups of stakeholders may be identified as stakeholder issues as well as social issues. For example, occupational health and safety or employment equity and discrimination are issues of sufficient concern to society as a whole to result in legislation and regulation, but they are also issues of concern for all corporations in terms of their relationships with employee stakeholder groups and government. Similarly, the social issues of product safety or truth in advertising have also led to legislation and regulation, but from a corporate perspective, these are stakeholder issues involving obligations and responsibilities to both customers and governments. Social issues concerning environmental pollution are of concern to a variety of government regulatory agencies, as well as to the communities in which corporations have their operations, employees, and customers.

Research Design and Data Collection
From its beginning in 1983, the design of this research has been influenced by several factors. MBA students at the University of Toronto's Faculty of Management provided most of the necessary research time and effort, studying individual companies in groups of two or three and writing the case studies as their term project for a second-year elective course on corporate social responsibilities (Clarkson, 1988. 1991). To describe and evaluate a company's performance, the researchers had to gain the confidence of the relevant managers so as to be able to ask the right questions and obtain written material about policies and programs. Both researchers and managers needed a framework and guide to facilitate the provision, analysis, and evaluation of data. It was essential for such a framework and guide to be expressed in terms that would be understood in a corporation as well as in a classroom.

Proceeding from the conclusion that a "stakeholder management" model provided the most appropriate organizing principle, an inventory of representative stakeholder issues was developed from the data contained in the field studies. This inventory, or index, of approximately 50 issues is shown in Table 1. This index is described as "representative" because it lists the issues identified most frequently in the studies. It is reasonably comprehensive, but not exhaustive. It can serve as a stimulus to some managers to consider a wider range of stakeholder issues than has been their practice.

This index provides a uniform entry and coding system and is central to the organization of the data in each study for the computerized database. Information pertinent to each of the stakeholder issues is organized into four areas: description, performance data, evaluation, and analysis.

To facilitate data collection and comparisons, it was necessary to define clearly the issues identified in Table 1. It was also important to define the performance data that were being requested from the companies being studied. This guide for researchers and managers is illustrated in the appendix. Clarkson described the data as follows:

> The corporations are asked to provide the descriptive data covering the company itself and relevant stakeholder and social issues. This material is then edited and returned to the company with requests for the performance data identified in the guide. Interviews with appropriate executives are then held in order to check and explore the implications of the performance data that have, and have not, been supplied... Experience shows that corporations find this task worthwhile. Few have hitherto identified stakeholder and social issues so comprehensively. (1991: 344)

Sixty-five of the more than 70 corporations that have been studied are among the largest 250 companies in Canada, in terms of sales or assets, or are subsidiaries of companies listed in the *Fortune* 500. Ten of the 14 largest financial institutions in Canada have been studied, as well as the two largest transportation companies, the two largest steel companies, the three largest publishing companies, the three largest breweries, the largest electric and gas utilities, and the largest nickel, auto parts, pulp and paper, and telecommunications companies, together with four of the five largest integrated oil companies and six large retail companies. The universe of companies studied is large and diverse, containing companies with various forms of ownership: Canadian, U.S. and foreign, public and private. Most companies in the sample were large, but several small companies were studied as well.

Discussion of Conclusions From the research

The principal conclusions drawn from the research program are as follows:

1. It is necessary to distinguish between *stakeholder* issues and *social* issues because corporations and their managers manage relationships with their *stakeholders* and not with society.
2. It is necessary to conduct analysis at the appropriate level: institutional, organizational, or individual.
3. It is then possible to analyze and evaluate both the social performance of a corporation and the performance of its managers in managing the corporation's responsibilities to, and relationships with, its stakeholders.

Table 1: Typical corporate and stakeholder issues

1. **Company**
    1.1. Company history
    1.2. Industry background
    1.3. Organization structure
    1.4. Economic performance
    1.5. Competitive environment
    1.6 Mission or purpose
    1.7 Corporate codes
    1.8 Stakeholder and social issues management systems
2. **Employees**
    2.1. General policy
    2.2. Benefits
    2.3. Compensation and rewards
    2.4. Training and development
    2.5. Career planning
    2.6. Employee assistance program
    2.7. Health promotion
    2.8. Absenteeism and turnover
    2.9. Leaves of absence
    2.10. Relationships with unions
    2.11. Dismissal and appeal
    2.12. Termination, layoff, and redundancy
    2.13. Retirement and termination counseling
    2.14. Employment equity and discrimination
    2.15. Women in management and on the board
    2.16. Day care and family accommodation
    2.17. Employee communication
    2.18. Occupational health and safety
    2.19. Part-time, temporary, or contract employees
    2.20. Other employee or human resource issues
3. **Shareholders**
    3.1. General policy
    3.2. Shareholder communications and complaints
    3.3. Shareholder advocacy
    3.4. Shareholder rights
    3.5. Other shareholder issues

Table 1: Typical corporate and stakeholder issues (continued)

4.	**Customers**	
	4.1.	General policy
	4.2.	Customer communications
	4.3.	Product safety
	4.4.	Customer complaints
	4.5.	Special customer services
	4.6.	Other customer issues
5.	**Suppliers**	
	5.1.	General policy
	5.2.	Relative power
	5.3.	Other supplier issues
6.	**Public Stakeholders**	
	6.1.	Public health, safety, and protection
	6.2.	Conservation of energy and materials
	6.3.	Environmental assessment of capital projects
	6.4.	Other environmental issues
	6.5.	Public policy involvement
	6.6.	Community relations
	6.7.	Social investment and donations

Distinguishing Between Social Issues and Stakeholder Issues

A multitude of issues have been described as social issues in the CSP literature. Under the rubric of the Social Issues in Management division of the Academy of Management, an extraordinarily wide range of subjects pertaining to business and society is discussed at conferences and written about in journals. It has become difficult, if not impossible, to define what is, or what is not, a social issue. The difficulties that have been encountered in defining CSR_1, CSR_2, and CSP can be attributed in part to the broad and inclusive meaning of the word *social*. The connotation of social is society, a level of analysis that is both more inclusive, more ambiguous, and further up the ladder of abstraction than a corporation itself. Preston noted that

> corporate social performance was intended to suggest a broad concern with the impact of business behavior on society. The concern is with ultimate outcomes or results, not simply with policies or intentions; moreover there is some implication that these outcomes are to be evaluated, not simply described. (1988: xii)

There has been general agreement with this definition of CSP and the objective, but the underlying assumptions have not been questioned rigorously. It has been assumed that, because there is a "broad concern," it would therefore be possible to evaluate the impact of business on society. The impact of a business or corporation on society is a different matter from the impact of business in general on society as a whole. Wood (1991: 691) observed that "the concept of corporate social performance has received serious theoretical and empirical attention... but the concept's theoretical framework and impact have not moved significantly beyond Wartick and Cochran's (1985) articulation." The principal reason for this failure has been the lack of clarity about the appropriate level of analysis.

This failure, together with the confusion and misunderstanding about the definition and meaning of corporate social responsibility, corporate social responsiveness, and corporate social performance, is a direct result of the inclusive and vague meaning of the word *social*. Friedman (1970) took advantage of this ambiguity and semantic confusion in his criticism of "those who speak eloquently about the 'social responsibilities of business' in a free-enterprise system." He continued:

> The discussions of the "social responsibilities of business" are notable for their analytical looseness and lack of rigor ... The first step towards clarity in examining the doctrine of the social responsibility of business is to ask precisely what it implies for whom.

Friedman chose to interpret *social* issues and *social* responsibilities to mean nonbusiness issues and nonbusiness responsibilities. He, like so many neoclassical economists, separated business from society, which enabled him to maintain that "the business of business is business." By placing the two abstractions of business and society into separate compartments, Friedman (1970) was able to deny the necessity, or even the validity, of the concept of CSR, decrying it as "a fundamentally subversive doctrine":

> [Businessmen who believe that] business has a "social conscience" and takes seriously its responsibilities for providing employment, eliminating discrimination, avoiding pollution ... are preaching pure and unadulterated socialism.

The move from the innocuousness of social to the taint of socialism was made skillfully by this master of rhetoric.

Neither business in general nor specific corporations in particular can properly be made responsible for dealing with all social issues. Before responsibilities can be assigned and before corporations and their managers can be held accountable for the results of their actions, it is necessary to develop a systematic method of determining what is and what is not a social issue for a corporation.

From the data in the field studies of corporate performance, an inventory of issues was developed. These issues have been identified as typical *stakeholder* issues rather than as typical *social* issues. The reason for this distinction is that all these issues are of concern to one or more stakeholder groups, although these issues are not necessarily of concern to society as a whole. The positions being advanced here are:

1. A particular society (municipal, state, or national) determines, usually over an extended period of time, what is a *social* issue, and, when it is considered necessary, the relevant polity enacts legislation and regulation.
2. When there is no such legislation or regulation, an issue may be a *stakeholder* issue, but it is not necessarily a *social* issue. A test of whether an issue has become a social issue is the presence or absence of legislation or regulation.

In Table 1, 20 different issues are shown under the stakeholder heading of employees. Several, but by no means all, of these issues have been of sufficient concern to society as a whole, in the United States and Canada, that legislation and regulations have been enacted. Occupational health and safety and employment equity and discrimination are such *social* issues. (It is interesting to note in this context that some opposition to the North American free trade agreement [NAFTA] appears to have occurred because these are *not* social issues in Mexico.) No legislation has yet been enacted concerning the majority of the employee issues, such as employee assistance programs and career planning. But each can be identified as a stakeholder issue, when the level of analysis is the corporation itself.

Defining the appropriate level of analysis is important, as Wood (1991: 695) has shown:

> Once these three levels of analysis are distinguished (institutional, organizational, and individual) then several formerly competing concepts can be melded together to explain three corresponding principles of corporate social responsibility.

Using the same levels of analysis—institutional, organizational, and individual—Table 2 proposes a framework that is different from Wood's and is grounded in the data of the corporate case studies. The level of business and society is shown as the *institutional* level, the level that is appropriate for discussions of CSR_1 and CSR_2. The *organizational* level is identified as that of the corporation and its stakeholder groups, the level appropriate for analysis and evaluation of CSP. The *individual* level is shown as that of managers who manage stakeholder issues and relationships with stakeholders, the level appropriate for analysing and evaluating management performance.

Confusion arises when terms from one level are applied at another level. For example, whether the *stakeholder* issues of employee assistance plans and career planning are social issues is a question that should properly be discussed and answered at the level of society. Corporate managers certainly should be cognizant of such discussions and concerns in society, but the position being advanced here is that a particular society and its polity determine what is a social issue, and, when it is considered necessary, legislation and regulations are enacted.

By applying this analytic approach, it becomes evident that managers of a corporation cannot be expected to accept the claim that they have a *social* responsibility to institute an employee assistance plan or career planning or to provide day care, although an interesting discussion could take place about whether they have any responsibility to their stakeholders to implement such programs. Employee assistance plans, career planning, and day care are stakeholder issues at the corporate level of analysis and management issues at the level of stakeholder issues and relationships. It is the responsibility of the corporation's managers to determine whether policies and programs will be implemented to manage these issues. Whether these are social issues is not relevant in this context. This approach makes it clear that all social issues are not necessarily stakeholder issues, just as all stakeholder issues are not necessarily social issues.

Table 2:   Levels of analysis

Corporate social responsibility and responsiveness (CSR_1 and CSR_2)	Institutional	Business	Society
Corporate social performance (CSP)	Organizational	Corporations	Stakeholder groups
Stakeholder management	Individual	Managers	Issues/ relationships

A company and its management are free to decide the extent to which they will acknowledge, recognize, or pursue obligations and responsibilities to their stakeholders concerning the issues shown in Table 1, and, of course, any additional issues identified by the corporation or its stakeholders. Their performance can then be evaluated in terms of the RDAP Scale as reactive, defensive, accommodative, or proactive.

Clearly, there are legal requirements regarding certain social issues, as defined previously. *Social* issues, such as occupational health and safety, shareholder rights, and product safety, have generated significant regulation, but there are no legal requirements for a company to assume any responsibilities to its employees for training and development or career planning, or to its customers for communications and complaints.

An outside observer, a financial analyst, or an academic researcher might consider such programs to be socially desirable or socially responsible on the part of a corporation, but these are in fact matters of policy and choice for each corporation to decide. Such corporate decisions are usually made on the basis of market forces, for example, employee productivity or customer satisfaction, not necessarily because they are socially desirable. Managers are interested in results, first and foremost.

Performance is what counts. Performance can be measured and evaluated. Whether a corporation and its management are motivated by enlightened self-interest, common sense, or high standards of ethical behavior cannot be determined by the empirical methodologies available today. These are not questions that can be answered by economists, sociologists, psychologists, or any other kind of social scientist. They are interesting questions, but they are not relevant when it comes to evaluating a company's performance in managing its relationships with its stakeholder groups.

Defining Stakeholders and Stakeholder Groups

The definitions of stakeholders and primary and secondary stakeholders that are proposed here are straightforward. Freeman's (1984) landmark work provided a solid and lasting foundation for many continuing efforts to define and to build stakeholder models, frameworks, and theories. His account of the historical roots of the stakeholder approach gave credit to SRI International for its definition of stakeholders in 1963. Preston's (1990) account, however, is different. He traced the origins of the stakeholder approach, if not the actual use of the term, as having occurred some 30 years earlier, during the Depression, when the General Electric Company identified four major "stakeholder" groups: shareholders, employees, customers, and the general public. In 1947, Johnson & Johnson's president listed the company's "strictly business" stakeholders as customers, employees, managers, and shareholders. Using this approach, Robert Wood Johnson developed the well-known business credo of Johnson & Johnson. In 1950, General Robert Wood, who led Sears' rapid postwar growth, listed the "four parties to any business in the order of their importance" as "customers, employees, community, and stockholders" (Preston 1990: 362). He maintained that if the appropriate needs and interests of the first three groups were looked after effectively, the company's stockholders would be the beneficiaries. Profit, in General Wood's view, was a by-product of success in satisfying responsibly the legitimate needs and expectations of the corporation's primary stakeholder groups.

Stakeholders are persons or groups that have, or claim, ownership, rights, or interests in a corporation and its activities, past, present, or future. Such claimed rights or interests are the result of transactions with, or actions taken by, the corporation, and may be legal or moral, individual or collective. Stakeholders with similar interests, claims, or rights can be classified as belonging to the same group: employees, shareholders, customers, and so on.

A *primary* stakeholder group is one without whose continuing participation the corporation cannot survive as a going concern. Primary stakeholder groups typically are comprised of shareholders and investors, employees, customers, and suppliers, together with what is defined as the public stakeholder group: the governments and communities that provide infrastructures and markets, whose laws and regulations must be obeyed, and to whom taxes and other obligations may be due. There is a high level of interdependence between the corporation and its primary stakeholder groups.

If any primary stakeholder group, such as customers or suppliers, becomes dissatisfied and withdraws from the corporate system, in whole or in part, the corporation will be seriously damaged or unable to continue as a going concern. For example, the inability of Dow Corning in 1991 to keep its customer and public stakeholder groups satisfied with the safety of one of its products led to the collapse of the stakeholder system for that product and complete withdrawal of that division from its leading position in the breast implant market. The refusal of suppliers of capital to continue investing in Olympia and York's commercial paper in April 1992 resulted in its bankruptcy filing the following month. Earlier in the 1980s, the top managers of A. H. Robins and the Manville Corporation did not acknowledge that there were justifications for the health concerns and lawsuits of many of their customers. The disruption of their stakeholder systems and the ensuing bankruptcies were the consequences of their inability to manage satisfactorily their relationships with primary stakeholder groups. The breakup of AT&T can be attributed to this giant corporation's inability to satisfy two primary stakeholder groups, customers and the public, whose interests were represented by the Department of Justice.

From this perspective, the corporation itself can be defined as a system of primary stakeholder groups, a complex set of relationships between and among interest groups with different rights, objectives, expectations, and responsibilities. The corporation's survival and continuing success depend upon the ability of its managers to create sufficient wealth, value, or satisfaction for those who belong to each stakeholder group, so that each group continues as a part of the corporation's stakeholder system. Failure to retain the participation of a primary stakeholder group will result in the failure of that corporate system.

Secondary stakeholder groups are defined as those who influence or affect, or are influenced or affected by, the corporation, but they are not engaged in transactions with the corporation and are not essential for its survival. The media and a wide range of special interest groups are considered as secondary stakeholders under this definition. They have the capacity to mobilize public opinion in favor of, or in opposition to, a corporation's performance, as demonstrated in the cases of the recall of Tylenol by Johnson & Johnson (favorable) and the Exxon *Valdez* oil spill (unfavorable).

The corporation is not dependent for its survival on secondary stakeholder groups. Such groups, however, can cause significant damage to a corporation. As Freeman commented:

> Some groups may have as an objective simply to interfere with the smooth operations of our business. For instance, some corporations must count "terrorist groups" as stakeholders. As unsavory as it is to admit that such "illegitimate" groups have a stake in our business, from the standpoint of strategic management, it must be done. (1984: 53)

Secondary stakeholders may be opposed to the policies or programs that a corporation has adopted to fulfill its responsibilities to, or to satisfy the needs and expectations of, its primary stakeholder groups. For example, the issue of "red-lining" by banks and insurance companies to reduce exposure and losses often forced people living in urban ghettos into the role of secondary stakeholders, if they wanted to obtain a mortgage or property insurance. They could not become part of a bank's or an insurance company's primary stakeholder group of customers until legislation was enacted and enforced to require these companies to provide services for them.

Recently, the Federal Reserve Board shocked the banking world by denying Shawmut National Corp.'s application to acquire New Dartmouth Bank in Manchester, N.H., because of questions about its minority lending record ... Attorney General Janet Reno made clear that the mild [settlement] penalty recognizes that Shawmut has made considerable progress in seeking out potential minority borrowers and adjusting its lending procedures to help more applicants qualify for loans. Shawmut took these actions after 1990 data showed that black and Hispanic mortgage applicants were twice as likely to be turned down as whites. (*Wall Street Journal*, 1993: A2)

The cause of this shock to the banking world was the belated enforcement of the Community Reinvestment Act, a 1979 law that was meant to require banks to lend money in the areas in which they do business.

Evaluating Corporate Performance

The usefulness and value of a system of evaluation depends upon its validity. Although the use of the RDAP Scale obviously introduces qualitative terms such as *reactive* and *proactive*, such terms are appropriate for the purpose of characterizing a management's strategy or posture toward a particular stakeholder group concerning one or more stakeholder issues. Strategy or posture are made manifest as the data are analyzed.

As a consequence of shifting the level of analysis from business and society to the corporation and its stakeholders, as shown in Table 2, data gathering can be focused on a corporation's management of the stakeholder issues identified in Table 1. The heart of the problem of evaluating performance lies in obtaining the data, not in the use of a system or a scale to apportion rankings or values. Performance data describe what a company is actually doing or has done with reference to specific issues. The stakeholder management methodology that has been in use since 1989 in more than 20 studies includes a detailed guide to the descriptions and definitions of the stakeholder issues and the data that are required to demonstrate performance in the management of each issue (Clarkson, 1991: Appendix 2).

If data about an issue are not available, that fact in itself is important in evaluating a company's strategy or posture. When no data are available, that issue is not being managed. There may or may not be valid reasons. Performance data are available whenever a particular stakeholder issue is considered by a company to be of sufficient importance to justify being managed. The data also show the levels within a company at which reports are made. A factor in evaluating the posture of a company toward a stakeholder issue, such as employee safety, is to know if cumulative data about accidents are reported only to the first or second levels of management, senior levels, or the Board.

Wartick and Cochran (1985), following Carroll (1979), used the terms *reactive, defensive, accommodative,* and *proactive* to characterize corporate strategy or posture toward social responsiveness. This approach was converted into the RDAP Scale and is described by Clarkson (1988, 1991) and summarized in Table 3. This performance scale is based on the concepts identified by Carroll and Wartick and Cochran in their models of social performance. Further refinements were added by Starik, Pinkston, and Carroll (1989).

Table 3: The Reactive-Defensive-Accommodative-Proactive (RDAP) Scale

Rating	Posture or strategy	Performance
1. Reactive	Deny responsibility	Doing less than required
2. Defensive	Admit responsibility but fight it	Doing the least that is required
3. Accommodative	Accept responsibility	Doing all that is required
4. Proactive	Anticipate responsibility	Doing more than is required

To make this RDAP Scale more practical and useful in terms of the concepts of stakeholder relationships and responsibilities, another element, Posture or Strategy, has been added to the earlier scale. This addition provides a means of characterizing a company's posture or strategy toward the management of stakeholder issues. Posture thus becomes one of the two central elements in applying a measure to and evaluating the level of responsibility that a company demonstrates in its management of stakeholder relationships and issues. This managerial approach can also be expressed in the terms used by McAdam (1973) and quoted by Carroll (1979: 502):

1. Fight all the way   (Reactive)
2. Do only what is required (Defensive)
3. Be progressive   (Accommodative)
4. Lead the industry   (Proactive)

The second element, performance, applies a measure of stakeholder satisfaction by evaluating the data concerning the actions and record of the company with regard to the management, of particular stakeholder issues and the levels of responsibility that the company has assumed or defined. Details of the application of this approach to stakeholder satisfaction in the field are contained in Clarkson, Deck, and Shiner (1992). The concept of acceptance or rejection of responsibility for results and for effects on stakeholders is central to the characterization and evaluation of a company's strategy or posture.

Under performance, the phrase "doing less, or more, than is required" invites the question: "Required by whom?" In the example of Shawmut National Corporation's lending practices, the requirements are specified by legislation. Another form of requirement occurs when a company states specifically, in a code or by other means of communication such as advertising, that it undertakes certain responsibilities and obligations toward specific stakeholder groups. There are also obligations that occur as transactions are made with stakeholders. As well, there is the general requirement for a corporation to keep its principal stakeholder groups reasonably satisfied so that they continue as part of the corporate stakeholder system.

By characterizing and evaluating posture, the revised RDAP scale provides the means by which the concept of social responsiveness can be defined more clearly. The conceptual basis of Carroll's three-dimensional model of corporate social performance (1979) and of Wartick and Cochran's model (1985) was the interaction between and among (a) the categories of corporate social responsibility (economic, legal, ethical, and discretionary); (b) the philosophy, posture, or strategy of social responsiveness; and (c) the social issues involved. As a result of shifting to the appropriate level of analysis and examining the data about a corporation's policies and performance as they relate to its management of stakeholder relationships and issues, its philosophy, posture, or strategy of social responsiveness can now be characterized and evaluated by the use of the RDAP Scale.

When, for example, companies like Manville or A.H. Robins deny responsibility for the results of their actions toward employees or customers, their posture and performance would be rated as reactive, whereas the response of Johnson & Johnson's managers to the Tylenol crisis by accepting and anticipating responsibility to present and future customers would be characterized as proactive. As a recent news item reported, the Tylenol example of Johnson & Johnson's proactive posture and performance was not unique:

> **Family Friendly:** Many companies go farther than the law requires. Non-mandated work and family policies abound. Johnson & Johnson allows employees to bring children to work to get picked up and dropped off for camp during the summer. (*Wall Street Journal*, 1994: A1)

Propositions and Issues for Further Research

The stakeholder framework provides the basis for the following definition of the corporation and its purpose:

1. The corporation is a system of primary stakeholder groups.
2. The survival and continuing profitability of the corporation depend upon its ability to fulfill its economic and social purpose, which is to create and distribute wealth or value sufficient to ensure that each primary stakeholder group continues as part of the corporation's stakeholder system.
3. Failure to retain the participation of a primary stakeholder group will result in the failure of that corporate system and its inability to continue as a going concern.
4. Failure to retain the participation of a primary stakeholder group will be the result of
   a. the corporation's inability to create and distribute sufficient wealth or value to satisfy one or more primary stakeholder groups, or
   b. distribution by the corporation of increased wealth or value to one primary stakeholder group at the expense of one or more other primary stakeholder groups, causing their dissatisfaction and withdrawal from the system.
5. Failure, and success, may be lengthy processes. The stakeholder framework can be used to provide data, nonfinancial as well as financial, that can indicate whether stakeholder dissatisfaction has begun the process of failure, or whether stakeholder satisfaction is pointing toward success.

Based on the foregoing, the following three propositions are advanced for empirical testing:

Proposition 1: When a corporation has been unable to continue as a going concern or has sought bankruptcy protection, it will be shown that one or more primary stakeholder groups withdrew from participation in that corporate system.

This proposition can be addressed through a literature survey of large U.S. or Canadian corporations that have been unable to continue as going concerns or have sought bankruptcy protection, to determine whether their failure can be attributed to the complete or partial withdrawal of support by one or more primary stakeholder groups.

Proposition 2: A corporation whose profits have been above the average of its industry for the preceding live years or more will be shown to have created wealth or value for all its primary stakeholder groups.

Proposition 3: A corporation whose profits have been below the average in its industry for the preceding five years or more will be shown to have been unable to create sufficient wealth or value to satisfy one or more groups of primary stakeholders or to have distributed increased wealth or value to one group of stakeholders, causing dissatisfaction on the part of one or more of its other primary stakeholder groups.

In designing a research program to test Propositions 2 and 3, the following points should be borne in mind. Corporate performance is best evaluated on an industry-by-industry basis to reduce the number of variables when making comparisons. A bank's performance in terms of the management of its stakeholder relationships cannot reasonably be compared with that of an integrated oil company or a manufacturer of chemicals. The criteria of performance, profit, and stakeholder satisfaction should be appropriate to that industry. The measures of profit and other elements of performance will vary by industry and will include consideration of exogenous variables that may affect performance, such as market share and growth patterns in the industry and the economy.

Because, across the range of primary stakeholders, wealth and value are not necessarily and exclusively financial, it is suggested that "stakeholder satisfaction" be used as a common measure. One approach to the development of such a measure would be to survey representatives of primary stakeholder groups to determine their levels of satisfaction with the wealth and value creation of particular companies. Such surveys would provide for each firm an aggregate stakeholder satisfaction rating, together with satisfaction ratings for each primary stakeholder group. Multivariate statistical analysis could then be applied to isolate the relative importance of stakeholder satisfaction in assessing long-term profitability. Because there would be both time-series and cross-section data, panel data methods could be applied to the analysis.

Conclusion

The measurement of corporate success has traditionally been limited to the satisfaction of and creation of wealth for only one stakeholder, the shareholder. It has been demonstrated that the pursuit of this single measure is self-defeating (Clarkson, 1988). *Stakeholder* is not synonymous with *shareholder*. The economic and social purpose of the corporation is to create and distribute increased wealth and value to all its primary stakeholder groups, without favoring one group at the expense of others. Wealth and value are not defined adequately only in terms of increased share price, dividends, or profits.

Managers can no longer be held responsible for maximizing returns to shareholders at the expense of other primary stakeholder groups. Instead, managers are now accountable for fulfilling the firm's responsibilities to its primary stakeholder groups. This means that managers must resolve the inevitable conflicts between primary stakeholder groups over the distribution of the increased wealth and value created by the corporation. Resolving conflicting interests fairly requires ethical judgment and choices.

Fairness and balance in the distribution to its primary stakeholder groups of the increased wealth and value created by the firm are necessary to preserve the continuing participation of each primary group in the firm's stakeholder system and to avoid favoring one group unduly and at the expense of other groups. If any primary group perceives, over time, that it is not being treated fairly or adequately, whether it is the employee, customer, or shareholder group, it will seek alternatives and may ultimately withdraw from that firm's stakeholder system. If that withdrawal occurs, the firm's survival will be threatened.

The moment that corporations and their managers define and accept responsibilities and obligations to primary stakeholders, and recognize their claims and legitimacy, they have entered the domain of moral principles and ethical performance, whether they know it or not. So long as managers could maintain that shareholders and their profits were supreme, the claims of other stakeholders could be subordinated or ignored. There was no need for the manager to be concerned with fairness, justice, or even truth. The single-minded pursuit of profit justified any necessary means, so long as they were not illegal. But as managers make decisions and act in terms of stakeholder management in resolving inevitable conflicts of interest between stakeholder groups, they can no longer rely on "the invisible hand" to solve problems and, instead, must deal directly themselves with ethics and moral principles. When ethical judgments and choices may become issues of survival, the management of ethics and ethics programs in a corporation becomes a matter of strategic importance.

Max B. E. Clarkson is the founding Director of The Centre for Corporate Social Performance and Ethics and Professor Emeritus in the Faculty of Management at the University of Toronto. Formerly a business executive and Dean of the Faculty, his principal research interests are in the relationships among stakeholder management, ethical behavior, and effective corporate social and economic performance.

Aupperle, K. E., Carroll, A. B., & Hatfield, 1. D. 1985. An empirical examination of the relationship between corporate social responsibility and profitability. *Academy of Management Journal*, 28(2): 446-463.

Carroll, A. B. 1979. A three-dimensional conceptual model of corporate performance. *Academy of Management Review*, 4: 497-505.

Clarkson, M. B. E. 1988. Corporate social performance in Canada, 1976-86. In L. E. Preston (Ed.), *Research in corporate social performance and policy*, vol. 10: 241-265. Greenwich, CT: JAI Press.

Clarkson. M. B. E. 1991. Defining, evaluating, and managing corporate social performance: The stakeholder management model. In L. E. Preston (Ed.), *Research in corporate social performance and policy*, vol. 12: 331-358. Greenwich, CT: JAI Press.

Clarkson, M. B. E., & Deck, M. C. 1993. Applying the stakeholder management to the analysis and evaluation of corporate codes. In D. C. Ludwig (Ed.), *Business and society in a changing world order*: 55~76. New York: Mellen Press.

Clarkson, M. B. E., Deck, M. C., & Shiner, N. 1. 1992. *The stakeholder management model in practice.* Paper presented at the annual meeting of the Academy of Management, Las Vegas, NV.

Freeman, R. E. 1984. *Strategic management: A stakeholder approach.* Boston: Pitman/Ballinger.

Friedman, M. 1970. The social responsibility of business is to increase its profits. *New York Times Magazine*. Sept. 13.

Kelly, D., & McTaggart, T. 1979. *Research in corporate social performance and policy,* vol. 1. Greenwich, CT: JAI Press.

McAdam, T. W. 1973. How to put corporate responsibility into practice. *Business and Society Review/Innovation*, 6: 8-16.

Preston, L. E. (Ed.). 1988. *Research in corporate social performance and policy* (Vol. 10). Greenwich, CT: JAI Press.

Preston, L. E. 1990. Stakeholder management and corporate performance. *Journal of Behavioral Economics*, 19(4): 361-375.

The Royal Commission on Corporate Concentration (RCCC). 1977. *Corporate social performance in Canada* (Study No. 21). Ottawa: Ministry of Supply and Services.

Starik, M., Pinkston, T. S., & Carroll, A. B. 1989. *Evolutionary and performance aspects of performance management.* Unpublished paper, College of Business, University of Georgia, Athens.

Vincent, J., Olliers, I., & Starasts, J. 1986. *A social audit of Bank of Montreal.* Unpublished paper, Faculty of Management, University of Toronto.

Votaw, D. 1973. Genius becomes rare. In D. Votaw & S. P. Sethi (Eds.), *The corporate dilemma: Traditional values versus contemporary problems:* 11 - 45. Englewood Cliffs. NJ: Prentice Hall.

Wall Street Journal. 1993. Shawmut settles charges of bias in its lending. December 14: A2.
Wall Street Journal. 1994. Family friendly: Many companies go farther than the law requires. January 11: A1.
Wartick, S. L., & Cochran, P. L. 1985. The evolution of the corporate social performance model. *Academy of Management Review*, 4: 758-769.
Wood, D. 1991. Corporate social performance revisited. *Academy of Management Review*, 16: 691- 718.

Appendix: Guide to the description and performance data (excerpts)

2. Employees

2.1. General Policy
2.1.1. *Description*: General philosophy, objectives, code of practice, policies, and performance assessment process.
2.1.2. *Performance Data:* Data about employee attitudes, satisfaction, etc. Results of employee satisfaction surveys.

2.2. Benefits
2.2.1. *Description*: Employee benefits program.
2.2.2. *Performance Data:* Scope and scale relative to industry.

2.3. Compensation and Rewards
2.3.1. *Description:* Objectives of compensation/reward system; linkage to employee performance on social and stakeholder issues.
2.3.2. *Performance Data:* Level of compensation relative to industry group. Ethical neutrality of compensation reward system. Evidence of linkage to performance on social and stakeholder issues.

2.4. Training and Development
2.4.1. *Description:* Employee training and development, including job retraining, literacy.
2.4.2. *Performance Data:* Dollars spent per annum, number of employees involved/ annum, time spent/employee/annum.

2.5. Career Planning
2.5.1. *Description:* Career planning programs and policies including lateral transfers and internal promotion.
2.5.2. *Performance Data:* Utilization of programs. Percentage of lateral transfers and promotions that are internal.

2.6. Employee Assistance Program
2.6.1. *Description:* Services available.
2.6.2. *Performance Data:* Utilization rate, data on job-related cases.

2.7. Health Promotion
2.7.1. *Description:* General policy, including commitment of senior management to a balanced lifestyle for employees, and programs offered.
2.7.2. *Performance Data:* Budget allocated, utilization rate.

2.8. Absenteeism and Turnover
2.8.1. *Description:* Performance objectives, programs and policies. External and internal factors affecting absenteeism and turnover.
2.8.2. *Performance Data*: Absenteeism and turnover data. relative to industry group(s).

2.9. Leaves of Absence
2.9.1. *Description:* Policies on leaves of absence (e.g., childbirth, adoption, sabbatical, political office).
2.9.2. *Performance Data:* Utilization rates, comparison of policy to industry practice.

2.10. Relationships with Unions
2.10.1. *Description:* Specific policies regarding unions, historical experience, and traditional stance.
2.10.2. *Performance Data:* Comparison with industry practice. Record of complaints, frequency of job actions, legal proceedings, etc.

2.11. Dismissal and Appeal
2.11.1. *Description:* Policies and processes for dismissal and dismissal appeal.
2.11.2. *Performance Data*: Utilization rate for appeal process. Record of suits for wrongful dismissal.

2.12. Termination, Layoff, and Redundancy
2.12.1. *Description:* Policy and practice regarding terminations, layoffs, and plant closures, job security, retraining, job restructuring, early retirement. advance notice of closures.
2.12.2. *Performance Data:* Number of employees per annum terminated or laid off over the last five years. Layoff frequency. Industry comparisons.

2.13. Retirement and Termination Counseling
2.13.1. *Description:* Retirement and termination counseling programs.
2.13.2. *Performance Data:* Utilization rates, budget and staffing allocated.

2.14. Employment Equity and Discrimination
2.14.1. *Description:* Policies and programs in hiring and promotion. Policies regarding on-the-job discrimination, including sexual harassment.
2.14.2. *Performance Data:* Numbers of complaints, legal actions, citations for excellence, data from employee surveys.

2.15. Women in Management and on the Board
2.15.1. *Description:* Stated policies and objectives regarding women in management and on the board.
2.15.2. *Performance Data:* Recent data on numbers of women in management and on the board, including length of service and proportion by level and functional area.

2.16. Day Care and Family Accommodation
2.16.1. *Description:* Provision for day care and other responses to accommodate family needs.
2.16.2. *Performance Data:* Utilization rates, data from employee satisfaction surveys, commitment to funding programs.

2.17. Employee Communication
2.17.1. *Description*: Communication processes both to and from employees. Examples of communication from employees are: "open door" to management; employee suggestion process, including incentives; confidential reporting processes (e.g., an "ombudsman"); policy and process to encourage employees to raise ethical concerns, including "whistle-blowing" protection.
2.17.2. *Performance Data:* Utilization rates and patterns. Results of employee satisfaction surveys.

2.18. Occupational Health and Safety
2.18.1. *Description:* General philosophy, code of practice, policy and program, including employee training and performance appraisal, emergency response and monitoring or auditing procedures. Level to which assessment data are reported. Key issues and specific policies and programs of particular importance.
2.18.2. *Performance Data:* Details of awards; legal or other disciplinary actions against company, accidents and lost days data, workers compensation, industrial disease and injury data. Evidence that data are reported to levels specified. Rating by the International Safety Rating System, if applicable.

2.19. Part-time, Temporary, or Contract Employees
2.19.1. *Description* Policy: Access to programs and benefits.
2.19.2. *Performance Data:* Evidence of access.

6. Public Stakeholders

6.1. Public Health, Safety, and Protection
6.1.1. *Description:* Policies, code of practice, objectives, and programs including employee training and performance assessment. Extension of policies to suppliers, distributors, and customers, domestically and internationally. Description of emergency response plan, monitoring and auditing procedures for environmental protection. Level to which data are reported. Policy on disclosure of incidents and audits.
6.1.2. *Performance Data:* Evidence that data are reported to designated level. History of complaints and offenses. Legal proceedings. Effectiveness of follow-through on planned response to emergencies. Degree of government pressure required prior to policy change. Timing of decisions relative to public relations crises. Comparison with performance of competitors.

6.2. Conservation of Energy and Materials
6.2.1. *Description:* Policies, objectives, and programs, including employee training and performance assessment. Auditing process. Adoption of the reject-reduce-reuse-recycle hierarchy for energy and material use and waste management, and commitment to treatment before disposal for hazardous wastes. Extension of policies to suppliers, distributors, and customers.
6.2.2. *Performance Data:* Data on quantity of materials saved, changes in consumption, reduction in waste produced, etc. Comparison with performance of competitors. Related R&D expenditures.

6.3. Environmental Assessment of Capital Projects
6.3.1. *Description:* Process for incorporating environmental principles into capital project assessment (construction, operations, and closure). Performance assessment of the process.
6.3.2. *Performance Data:* History of success or complaints on capital projects. Congruence of accepted projects with stated values with respect to the environment.

6.5. Public Policy Involvement
6.5.1. *Description:* Direct or through industry associations. Policy and processes that give the company a role in the formation of public policy. The role of the Board of Directors.
6.5.2. *Performance Data:* Specific policy involvement and record of participation. Comparison with other companies in the industry.

6.6. Community Relations
6.6.1. *Description:* Community liaison and communications programs and policies, including stakeholder consultation on decisions which effect the community. Performance assessment process. Specific benefits and consideration of the local community (i.e., local hiring, business opportunities, emergency response programs, plant closings).
6.6.2. *Performance Data:* Record of stakeholder consultation. Value of benefits to community.

6.7. Social Investment and Donations
6.7.1. *Description:* Specific social investment policies and programs, including corporate donations (financial, "in-kind," and use of facilities) and the allocation formula for same; employee involvement in community service and expectations of same in job descriptions and performance appraisal; corporate sponsorship. Performance assessment process.
6.7.2. *Performance Data:* Awards, $s/annum and percentage of earnings allocated for donations and corporate sponsorship. time/employee/annum spent in community service. Performance relative to industry group(s).

Copyright © *Academy of Management Review*, 1995.
Reprinted with permission from the Academy of Management.

Toward a Theory of Stakeholder Identification and Salience: Defining the Principle of Who and What Really Counts

Ronald K. Mitchell, *University of Victoria*
Bradley R. Agle, *University of Pittsburgh*
Donna J. Wood, *University of Pittsburgh*

Stakeholder theory has been a popular heuristic for describing the management environment for years, but it has not attained full theoretical status. This paper builds toward a theory of stakeholder identification and salience based on stakeholder possession of one or more of three relationship attributes: power, legitimacy, and urgency. Combinations of these attributes result in a typology of stakeholders, propositions concerning their salience to managers of the firm, and research and management implications.

Since publication of Freeman's (1984) landmark book, the concept of "stakeholders" has become embedded in management scholarship and managers' thinking. Yet, as popular as the term has become, and as richly descriptive as it is, there is no agreement on what Freeman (1994) calls "The Principle of Who or What Really Counts"—that is, who (or what) are the stakeholders of the firm? And, to whom (or what) do managers pay attention? The first question calls for a *normative theory of stakeholder identification,* to explain logically why managers should consider certain classes of entities as stakeholders. The second question calls for a *descriptive theory of stakeholder salience,* to explain the conditions under which managers do consider certain classes of entities as stakeholders.

Stakeholder theory, reviewed in this paper, offers a maddening variety of signals on how questions of stakeholder identification might be answered. We will see stakeholders identified as primary or secondary, as owners and non owners of the firm, as owners of capital or owners of less tangible assets, as actors or acted upon, as existing in voluntary or involuntary relationship with the firm, as rights-holders or contractors or moral claimants, as resource providers to or dependents of the firm, as risk-takers or influencers, and as legal principals to whom agent-managers bear a fiduciary duty. In the stakeholder literature there are a few *broad* definitions, attempting to specify the empirical reality that virtually anyone can affect or be affected by an organization's actions. Needed is a theory of stakeholder identification that can reliably separate stakeholders from nonstakeholders.

Also in the stakeholder literature there are a number of *narrow* definitions, attempting to specify the pragmatic reality that managers simply cannot attend to all actual or potential claims, and proposing a variety of priorities for managerial attention. In this paper we suggest that the question of stakeholder salience—the degree to which managers give priority to competing stakeholder claims—goes beyond the question of stakeholder identification, because the dynamics inherent in each relationship involve complex considerations that are not readily explained by the stakeholder framework as it currently stands. Needed also, is a theory of stakeholder salience that can explain who and what managers actually pay attention to.

Throughout the various ways of identifying stakeholders, as well as in the agency, behavioral, ecological, institutional, resource dependence, and transaction cost theories of the firm, we have found no single attribute within a given theory that can reliably guide us on these issues. However, one can extract from these literatures the idea that just a few attributes can be used to identify different classes of stakeholders in a firm's environment. We begin our analysis with Freeman's (1984) definition of stakeholder—"Any group or individual who can affect or is affected by the achievement of the organization's objectives"—and develop a theory of stakeholder identification drawn from these various theoretical literatures. We start with a broad definition so that no stakeholders, potential or actual, are excluded from analysis arbitrarily or a priori. We then propose that classes of stakeholders can be identified by their possession or attributed possession of one, two, or all three of the following attributes: the stakeholder's *power* to influence the firm, the *legitimacy* of the stakeholder's relationship with the firm, and the *urgency* of the stakeholder's claim on the firm. This theory produces a comprehensive typology of stakeholders based on the normative assumption that these variables define the field of stakeholders, those entities to whom managers *should* pay attention.

Building upon this typology, we further propose a theory of stakeholder salience. In this theory we suggest a dynamic model based upon the identification typology, that permits the explicit recognition of situational uniqueness and managerial perception to explain how managers prioritize stakeholder relationships. We demonstrate how the identification typology allows predictions to be made about managerial behavior with respect to each class of stakeholder, as well as predictions about how stakeholders change from one class to another and what this means to managers. In the theory of stakeholder salience we do not argue that managers should pay attention to this class of stakeholders or that. Rather, we argue that, to achieve certain ends, or because of perceptual factors, managers do pay certain kinds of attention to certain kinds of stakeholders. Knowing what types of stakeholders actually exist, which our identification typology facilitates, and why managers respond to them the way they do, which our notion of salience clarifies, sets the stage for future work in stakeholder theory that specifies how and under what circumstances managers can and should respond to various stakeholder types.

The argument proceeds as follows. First, we review the stakeholder literature, laying out the various explicit and implicit positions on The Principle of Who or What Really Counts. Then, we present our defense of the three key attributes—power, legitimacy, and urgency—as identifiers of stakeholder classes, and briefly examine the major organizational theories to discern how they handle these three crucial variables. Next, we introduce managers and salience into the discussion, and present our analysis of the stakeholder classes that result from possession of one, two, or three of these attributes, with special attention to the managerial implications of the existence and salience of each stakeholder class. Finally, we further illustrate the theory's dynamic qualities by showing how stakeholders can shift from one class to another, with important consequences for managers and the firm itself, and we explore the research questions and directions that emerge from the theory.

Stakeholder Theory—State of the Art

For more than a decade, the stakeholder *approach* to understanding the firm in its environment has been a powerful heuristic device, intended to broaden management's vision of its roles and responsibilities beyond the profit maximization function to include interests and claims of non-stockholding groups. Stakeholder *theory*, in contrast, attempts to articulate a fundamental question in a systematic way: which groups are stakeholders deserving or requiring management attention, and which are not? In this section, we will examine how scholars have so far answered a few central questions: Who is a stakeholder, and what is a stake? What does stakeholder theory offer that is not found in other theories of the firm?

Who Is a Stakeholder, and What Is a Stake?
There is not much disagreement on *what kind of entity* can be a stakeholder. Persons, groups, neighborhoods, organizations, institutions, societies, and even the natural environment are generally thought to qualify as actual or potential stakeholders. We find that it is the view taken toward the existence and nature of the *stake* that presents an area of argument, because it is upon the basis of "stake" that "what counts" is ultimately decided.

Early Vagueness in Definition
In an early statement, Jones (1980:59-60) defines corporate social responsibility as "the notion that corporations have an obligation to constituent groups in society other than stockholders and beyond that prescribed by law or union contract, indicating that a slake may go beyond mere ownership." Then he asks the pragmatic questions stakeholder theory still seeks to answer: "What are these groups? How many of these groups must be served? Which of their interests are most important? How can their interests be balanced? How much corporate money should be allotted to serve these interests?" (1980:60).

These questions are still being explored in stakeholder literature and management thinking. Alkhafaji (1989:36), for example, defines stakeholders as "groups to whom the corporation is responsible." Thompson, Wartick & Smith (1991:209) define stakeholders as groups "in relationship with an organization." Most scholars, however, have attempted to specify a more concrete stakeholder definition, albeit with limited success.

Broad or Narrow View?
Windsor (1992) correctly points out that stakeholder theorists differ considerably on whether they take a broad or narrow view of a firm's stakeholder universe. Freeman & Reed (1983:91) recognize early on that there would be serious differences of opinion about broad vs. narrow definitions of "Who or What Really Counts." Their broad definition of a stakeholder as an individual or group who "can affect the achievement of an organization's objectives or who is affected by the achievement of an organization's objectives" is virtually identical to Freeman's (1984) definition. And their narrow definition reverted to the language of the Stanford Research Institute (1963), defining stakeholders as those groups "on which the organization is dependent for its continued survival."

Freeman's (1984:46) now-classic definition is this: "A stakeholder in an organization is (by definition) any group or individual who can affect or is affected by the achievement of the organization's objectives." This is certainly one of the broadest definitions in the literature, as it leaves, the notion of stake, and the field of possible stakeholders unambiguously open to include virtually anyone. In this definition, the basis of the stake can be unidirectional or bidirectional: "can affect or is affected by," and there is no implication or necessity of reciprocal impact, as definitions involving relationships, transactions, or contracts require. Excluded from having a stake are only those that cannot affect the firm (have no power) *and* are not affected by it (have no claim or relationship).

In contrast, Clarkson (1994:5) offers one of the narrower definitions of stakeholders as voluntary or involuntary risk-bearers: "Voluntary stakeholders bear some form of risk as a result of having invested some form of capital, human or financial, something of value, in a firm. Involuntary stakeholders are placed at risk as a result of a firm's activities. But without the element of risk there is no stake." A stake, in this sense, is only something that can be lost. The use of risk to denote stake appears to be a way to narrow the stakeholder field to those with *legitimate claims*, regardless of their power to influence the firm or the legitimacy of their relationship to the firm. This search for legitimacy, we will argue later, is necessary to fully understand a firm's stakeholder environment, but it can also be a powerful blinder to the real impact of stakeholder power and claim urgency. We will argue, in contrast to the position of all those who appear to focus primarily on legitimacy, that this narrower view captures only one key attribute of stakeholder salience to managers.

In between the broad and narrow are many other efforts to define what constitutes a stakeholder. The range of definitions as it has developed chronologically appears in Table 1.

Major Differences between Broad and Narrow Views
Narrow views of stakeholders are based on the practical reality of limited resources, limited time and attention, and limited patience of managers for dealing with external constraints. In general, narrow views of stakeholders attempt to define relevant groups in terms of their *direct relevance to the firm's core economic interests*. For example, several scholars define stakeholders in terms of their necessity for the firm's survival (Freeman & Reed, 1983; Bowie, 1988; Nasi, 1995); and as noted, Clarkson (1995) defines stakeholders as those who have placed something at risk in relationship with the firm; while Freeman & Evan (1990), Hill & Jones (1992), and Cornell & Shapiro (1987) speak of stakeholders as contractors or participants in exchange relationships.

A few scholars narrow the field of relevant groups in terms of their *moral claims,* arguing that the essence of stakeholder management should be the firm's participation in creating and sustaining moral relationships (Freeman, 1994. Wicks et al., 1994), or the firm's fulfilling its affirmative duty to stakeholders in terms of fairly distributing the harms and

Table 1: Who is a shareholder? A chronology

Source	Stake
Stanford memo, 1963	"those groups without whose support the organization would cease to exist." (cited in Freeman & Reed, 1983, and Freeman, 1984)
Rhenman, 1964	"...are depending on the firm in order to achieve their personal goals and on whom the firm is depending for its existence." (cited in Näsi, 1995)
Ahlstedt & Jahnukainen, 1971	"...driven by their own interests and goals are participants in a firm, and thus depending on it and whom for its sake the firm is depending." (cited in Näsi, 1995)
Freeman & Reed, 1983: 91	Wide: "...can affect the achievement of an organization's objectives or who is affected by the achievement of an organization's objectives." Narrow: "...on which the organization is dependant for its continued survival."
Freeman, 1984: 46	"...can affect or is affected by the achievement of the organization's objectives."
Freeman and Gilbert, 1987	"...can affect or is affected by business."
Cornell & Shapiro, 1987: 5	"claimants" who have "contracts."
Evan & Freeman, 1988: 75-76	"...have a stake in or claim on the firm."
Evan & Freeman, 1988: 79	"...benefit from or are harmed by, and whose rights are violated or respected by, corporate actions."
Bowie, 1988: 112, n. 2	"...without whose support the organization would cease to exist."
Alkhafaji, 1989: 36	'...groups to whom the corporation is responsible.'
Carroll, 1989	"...asserts to have one or more of these kinds of stakes"— "ranging form an interest to a right (legal or moral) to ownership or legal title to the company;s assets or property."
Freeman and Evans, 1990	contract holders
Thompson et al, 1991: 209	...in "relationship with an organization."
Savage et al., 1991: 61	"...have an interest in the actions of an organization and ... have the ability to influence it."

Table 1:   Who is a shareholder? A chronology (continued)

Source	Stake
Hill and Jones, 1992: 133	"...constituents who have a legitimate claim on the firm... established through the existence of an exchange relationship." They supply "the firm with critical resources (contributions) and in exchange each expects its interests to be satisfied (by inducements."
Brenner, 1993: 205	"...having some legitimate, non-trivial relationship with an organizations [such as] exchange transactions, action impacts, and moral responsibilities."
Carroll, 1993	"...asserts to have one or more of the kinds of stakes in business." May be affected or affect...
Freeman, 1994: 415	Participants in "the human process of joint value creation."
Wicks et al., 1994: 483	"...interact with and give meaning and definition to the corporation."
Langtry, 1994: 433	The firm is significantly responsible for their well-being, or they hold a moral or legal claim on the firm.
Starik, 1994: 90	"...can and are making their actual stakes known;" "...are or might be influenced by, or are or potentially are influencers of, some organization."
Clarkson, 1994: 5	"...bear some form of risk as a result of having invested some sort of capital, human or financial, something of value, in a firm," or "are placed at risk as a result of a firm's activities."
Clarkson, 1995: 106	"...have, or claim, ownership, rights, or interests in a corporation and its activities."
Näsi, 1995: 19	"...interact with the firm and thus make its operation possible."
Brenner, 1995: 76, n.1	"...are or which could impact or be impacted by the firm/organization."
Donaldson & Preston, 1995: 85	"...identified through the actual or potential harms and benefits that they experience or anticipate experiencing as a result of the firm's actions or inactions."

benefits of the firm's actions (Evan & Freeman, 1989; Langtry, 1994; Donaldson & Preston, 1995). In any case, we see those favoring a narrow definition of stakeholders as searching for a "normative core" of legitimacy so that managers can be advised to focus on the claims of a few legitimate stakeholders.

The broad view of stakeholders, in contrast, is based on the empirical reality that companies can indeed be vitally affected by, or can vitally affect, almost anyone. But it is bewilderingly complex for managers. The idea of comprehensively identifying stakeholder types, then, is to equip managers with the ability to recognize and respond effectively to a disparate, yet systematically comprehensible set of entities, who may or may not have legitimate claims, but who may be able to affect or are affected by the firm nonetheless, and thus affect the interests of those who do have legitimate claims.

The ultimate aim of stakeholder management practices, according to this view, could be firm-centered or system-centered; that is, managers might want to know about all their stakeholders for firm-centered purposes of survival, economic well-being, damage control, taking advantage of opportunities, "doing in" the competition, winning friends and influencing public policy, coalition-building, and so forth. Or, in contrast, managers might want an exhaustive list of all stakeholders in order to participate in a fair balancing of various claims and interests within the firm's social system. The former public affairs approach, and the latter social responsibility approach, both require broad knowledge of actual and potential actors and claimants in the firm's environment.

Claimants versus Influencers
In order to clarify the term "stake," it is necessary to differentiate between groups that have a legal, moral, or presumed claim on the firm, and groups that have an ability to influence the firm's behavior, direction, process, or outcomes. Savage, Nix, Whitehead, & Blair (1991) consider two attributes to be necessary to identify a stakeholder: a claim, and the ability to influence a firm. Brenner (1993) and Starik (1994), however, pose these attributes as either/or components of the definition of those with a stake.

In our view, this is a muddled set, confusing and contrasting two of the three criteria we see as important. Influencers have power over the firm, whether or not they have valid claims or any claims at all, and whether or not they wish to press their claims. Claimants may have legitimate claims or illegitimate ones, and they may or may not have any power to influence the firm. Power and legitimacy are different, sometimes overlapping dimensions, and each can exist without the other. A theory of stakeholder identification must accommodate these differences.

Actual versus Potential Relationship
Another crucial question leading to the comprehensibility of the term stake, is whether an entity can be a stakeholder without being in actual relationship with the firm. Some scholars (e.g. Ring, 1994) answer emphatically "no." We argue that, on the contrary, the *potential* relationship can be as relevant as the actual one. Clarkson's (1994) idea of involuntary stakeholders as those with something not wilfully placed at risk addresses the potentiality issue somewhat. Starik (1994) quite clearly includes potential when he refers to stakeholders as those who "are or might be influenced by, or are or potentially are influencers of, some organization." We suggest that a theory of stakeholder identification and salience must somehow account for *latent* stakeholders if it is to be both comprehensive and useful, because such identification can, at a minimum, help organizations to avoid problems, and perhaps even to enhance effectiveness.

Power, Dependence, and Reciprocity in Relationships
If the firm and a stakeholder are in relationship, what is the nature of that relationship? The literature offers a confusing jumble of answers to this question, but most answers use a power-dependence frame of some sort. As Table 2 shows, some definitions focus on the firm's dependency on stakeholders for its survival; some focus on the stakeholder's dependency on the firm for upholding its rights or minimizing harms or achieving its interest; and some focus on the mutuality of power-dependence relations (although, interestingly, we found no definition that emphasized mutual power, and only two from Scandinavia that emphasized mutual dependence).

As shown, a broad-view sorting of stakeholders along previously defined dimensions is still somewhat overwhelming.

Sorting Criteria
Thus, although Freeman's (1984) definition is widely cited in the literature, it is not universally accepted among scholars working in the stakeholder minefields. Narrowing the range of stakeholders requires applying some acceptable and justifiable sorting criteria to the field of possibilities. Some additional approaches are relationship-based, built on acknowledged transactional conditions such as the existence of a legal or implied contract, an exchange relationship, or an identifiable power-dependence relationship. Others are claim-based, citing the existence or attribution of a legal or moral right, or a real or attributed benefit or harm, or merely an interest.

Overall, the information in Table 2 suggests that scholars who attempt to narrow the definition of stakeholder emphasize the *claim's*

Table 2: A sorting of rationales for stakeholder identification

A relationship exists

The firm and stakeholder are in relationship:
Thompson et al, 1991: 209:... in "relationship with an organization."
Brenner, 1993: 205: "... having some legitimate, non-trivial relationship with an organization [such as]exchange transactions, action impacts, and moral responsibilities."
Freeman, 1994: 415: participants in "the human process of joint value creation."
Wicks et al., 1994: 483: "... interact with and give meaning and definition to the corporation."
The stakeholder exercises voice with respect to the firm:
Starik, 1994: 90: "...can and are making their actual stakes known;" "... are or might be influenced by, or are or potentially are influencers of, some organization."

Power-dependence: Stakeholder dominant

The firm is dependent on the stakeholder:
Stanford memo, 1963: "those groups without whose support the organization would cease to exist." (cited in Freeman & Reed, 1983, and Freeman, 1984)
Freeman & Reed, 1983: 91: Narrow: "... on which the organization is dependent for its continued survival."
Bowie, 1988: 112, n. 2: "...without whose support the organization would cease to exist."
Näsi, 1995: 19: "... interact with the firm and thus make its operation possible."

The stakeholder has power over the firm:
Freeman, 1984: 46: "...can affect or is affected by the achievement of the organization's objectives."
Freeman and Gilbert, 1987: "... can affect or is affected by a business."
Savage et al., 1991: 61: "... have an interest in the actions of an organization and... the ability to influence it."
Carroll, 1993: "asserts to have one or more of the kinds of stakes in business." May be affected or affect... Starik, 1994: 90: "...can and are making their actual stakes known.," "... are or might be influenced by, or are or potentially are influencers of, some organization."
Brenner, 1995: 76, n. 1: "... are or which could impact or be impacted by the firm/organization."

Power-dependence: Firm dominant

The stakeholder is dependent on the firm:
Langtry, 1994: 433: the firm is significantly responsible for their well-being, or they hold a moral or legal claim on the firm.

Table 2: A sorting of rationales for stakeholder identification (continued)

The firm has power over the stakeholder:

Freeman & Reed, 1983: 9 1: Wide: "... can affect the achievement of an organization's objectives or who is affected by the achievement of an organization's objectives."

Freeman, 1984: 46: "... can affect or is affected by the achievement of tile organization's objectives."

Freeman and Gilbert, 1987: "... can affect or is affected by a business."

Carroll, 1993: "asserts to have one or more of the kinds of stakes in business." May be affected or affect.... Starik, 1994: 90: "...can and are making their actual stakes known;" "... are or might be influenced by, or are or potentially are influencers of, some organization."

Brenner, 1995: 76, n. 1: "... are or which could impact or be impacted by the firm/organization."

Mutual power-dependence relationships

The firm and stakeholder are mutually dependent:

Rhenman, 1964: "... are depending on the firm in order to achieve their personal goals and on whom the firm is depending for its existence." (cited in N‰si, 1995)

Ahlstedt & Jahnukainen, 197 1: "... driven by their own interests and goals are participants in a firm, and thus depending on it and whom for its sake the firm is depending." (cited in Näsi, 1995)

Basis for legitimacy of relationship

The firm and stakeholder are in contractual relationship:

Cornell & Shapiro, 1987: 5: "claimants" who have "contracts."

Carroll, 1989: "... asserts to have one or more of these kinds of stakes"—"ranging from an interest to a right (legal or moral) to ownership or legal title to the company's assets or property."

Freeman and Evan, 1990: contract holders.

Hill and Jones, 1992: 133: "... constituents who have a legitimate claim on the firm... established through the existence of an exchange relationship." They supply "the firm with critical resources (contributions) and in exchange each expects its interests to be satisfied (by inducements)."

The stakeholder has a claim on the firm:

Evan & Freeman, 1988:75-76: "... have a stake in or claim on the firm."

Alkhafaji, 1989: 36: '... groups to whom the corporation is responsible'

Carroll, 1989: "... asserts to have one or more of these kinds of stakes"—"ranging from an interest to a right (legal or moral) to ownership or legal title to the company's assets or property."

Table 2: A sorting of rationales for stakeholder identification (continued)

Hill and Jones, 1992: 133: "... constituents who have a legitimate claim on the firm... established through the existence of an exchange relationship." They supply "the firm with critical resources (contributions) and in exchange each expects its interests to be satisfied (by inducements)."

Langtry, 1994: 433: the firm is significantly responsible for their well-being, or they hold a moral or legal claim on the firm.

Clarkson, 1995: 106: "... have, or claim, ownership, rights, or interests in a corporation and its activities."

The stakeholder has something at risk:

Clarkson, 1994: 5: "... bear some form of risk as a result of having invested some form of capital, human or financial, something of value, in a firm," or "are placed at risk as a result of a firm's activities."

The stakeholder has a moral claim on the firm:

Evan & Freeman, 1988:79: "... benefit from or are harmed by, and whose rights are violated or respected by, corporate actions."

Carroll, 1989: "... asserts to have one or more of these kinds of stakes"—"ranging from an interest to a right (legal or moral) to ownership or legal title to the company's assets or property."

Langtry, 1994: 433: the firm is significantly responsible for their well-being, or they hold a moral or legal claim on the firm.

Clarkson, 1995: 106: "... have, or claim, ownership, rights, or interests in a corporation and its activities."

Donaldson & Preston, 1995: 85: "... identified through the actual or potential harms and benefits that they experience or anticipate experiencing as a result of the firm's actions or inactions."

Stakeholder interests — legitimacy not implied

The stakeholder has an interest in the firm:

Carroll, 1989: "... asserts to have one or more of these kinds of stakes"—"ranging from an interest to a right (legal or moral) to ownership or legal title to the company's assets or property."

Savage et al., 1991: 61: "... have an interest in the actions of an organization and... have the ability to influence it."

Carroll, 1993: "... asserts to have one or more of the kinds of stakes in business." May be affected or affect...

Clarkson, 1995: 106: "... have, or claim, ownership, rights, or interests in a corporation and its activities."

legitimacy based upon contract, exchange, legal title, legal right, moral right, at-risk status, or moral interest in the harms and benefits generated by company actions. On the other hand, scholars who favor a broad definition emphasize the *stakeholder's power* to influence the firm's behavior, whether or not there are legitimate claims. As a bridging concept, we argue that the broad concept of stakeholder management must be better defined in order to serve the narrower interests of legitimate stakeholders. Otherwise, influencing groups with power over the firm can disrupt operations so severely that legitimate claims cannot be met and the firm may not survive. Yet, at the same time, it is important to recognize the legitimacy of some claims over others. Power and legitimacy, then, are necessarily core attributes of a comprehensive stakeholder identification model. We argue that when evaluated in light of the compelling demands of urgency, a systematic, comprehensible, and dynamic model is the result.

What Added Value Does a Theory of Stakeholder Identification Offer?

As we see from the preceding discussion of the stakeholder literature, one can extract just a few attributes to identify different classes of stakeholders that are salient to managers in certain respects. We can also see that stakeholder power and legitimacy of the claim are frequently treated as competing explanations of stakeholder status, when instead they are partially intersecting variables. Interestingly, this conceptual competition between power and legitimacy is reflected in virtually every major theory of the firm, particularly in agency, behavioral, institutional, population ecology, resource dependence, and transaction cost theories. This state-of-the-field provides an opportunity for a theory of stakeholder identification to move us forward by showing how power and legitimacy interact, and when combined with urgency, create different types of stakeholders with different expected behavioral patterns with respect to the firm.

Agency, resource dependence, and transaction cost theories are particularly helpful in explaining why power plays such an important role in the attention given by managers to stakeholders. The central problem that agency theory addresses is how principals can control the behavior of their agents to achieve their, rather than the agent's, interests. The power of agents to act in ways that diverge from the interests of principals may be limited through the use of incentives or monitoring (Jensen & Meckling, 1976), so that managers are expected to attend to those stakeholders who have the power to reward and/or punish them. Resource dependence theory suggests that power accrues to those who control resources needed by the organization, creating power differentials among parties (Pfeffer, 1981), and confirms that the possession of resource power would make a stakeholder important to managers. Transaction cost theory proposes that the power accruing to economic actors with small numbers bargaining advantages will affect the nature of firm governance and structure (Williamson, 1975, 1985). That is, stakeholders outside the firm boundary who participate in a very small competitive set can increase transaction costs to levels that justify their absorption into the firm, where the costs of hierarchy are lower than the transaction costs of market failure, a clear indication of their significance to managers (Jones & Hill, 1988).

These three organizational theories teach us why power is a crucial variable in a theory of stakeholder-manager relations. But as previously noted, power alone does not help us to fully understand salience in the stakeholder-manager relationship. There remain stakeholders who do not have power, but who nevertheless matter to firms and managers. Other means to identify "who or what really counts" are needed.

Organizational theories with an open-system orientation (Scott, 1987) including institutional and population ecology theories, help us to understand the crucial effects of the environment upon organizations, but they are less helpful when it comes to understanding power in stakeholder-manager relationships. Under both theories, organizational legitimacy is linked closely with its survival (see Meyer & Rowan, 1977, and Carroll & Hannan, 1989, respectively). In the socially constructed world within which managers engage stakeholders, these two theories suggest that "legitimate" stakeholders are the ones who "really count." Under institutional theory, "illegitimacy" results in isomorphic pressures on organizations that operate outside of accepted norms (DiMaggio & Powell, 1983). Under population ecology theory, the lack of legitimacy results in organizational mortality (Carroll & Hannan, 1989). According to these two theories, legitimacy figures heavily in helping us to identify stakeholders that merit managerial attention. However, emphasizing legitimacy and ignoring power leaves major gaps in a stakeholder identification scheme because some legitimate stakeholders have no influence.

A final attribute that profoundly influences managerial perception and attention, although it is not the primary feature of any particular organizational theory, is nevertheless implicit in each. Agency theory treats this attribute in terms of its contribution to cost, as does transaction cost theory. Behavioral theory (Cyert & March, 1963) treats it as a consequence of unmet "aspirations." Institutional, resource dependence, and population ecology theories treat it in terms of outside pressures on the firm. This attribute is *urgency*, or the degree to which stakeholder claims call for immediate attention. Whether dealing with the prevention of losses, the pursuit of goals, or with selection pressures; one constant in the stakeholder-manager relationship is the attention-getting capacity of the urgent claim. Urgency, as we discuss below, adds a catalytic component to a theory of stakeholder identification because urgency demands attention.

In summary, it is clear that no one organizational theory offers systematic answers to questions about stakeholder identification and salience, although most such theories have much to tell us about the role of power *or* legitimacy (but not both) in stakeholder-manager relations. Urgency, in contrast, is not a main focus of any organizational theory, but is nonetheless critical to any theory that purports to identify stakeholders and explain the degree of attention paid to them by managers. We thus suggest that for us to better understand the Principle of Who and What Really Counts, we need to systematically evaluate stakeholder-manager relationships, both actual and potential, in terms of the relative absence or presence of all or some of these three attributes: power, legitimacy, and/or urgency.

Defining Stakeholder Attributes

Power

Most current definitions of power derive, at least in part, from the early Weberian idea that power is "the probability that one actor within a social relationship would be in a position to carry out his own will despite resistance" (Weber, 1947). Pfeffer (1981:3) rephrases Dahl's (1957) definition of power as "a relationship among social actors in which one social actor, A, can get another social actor, B, to do something that B would not otherwise have done." Like Pfeffer and Weber, we concur that "power may be tricky to define, but it is not that difficult to recognize: '[It is] the ability of those who possess power to bring about the outcomes they desire' (Salancik & Pfeffer, 1974:3)." This leads to the question: How is power exercised? Or alternatively, what are the bases of power?

French and Raven's (1960) typology of power bases is one framework that is commonly cited in the organizational literature in answer to this question, but from a sociological perspective it is messy, because there is not a sorting logic at work to create the mutually exclusive and exhaustive categories that a true typology requires. Etzioni (1964:59) suggests a logic for the more precise categorization of power in the organizational setting, based on the type of resource used to exercise power: *coercive* power, based on physical resources of force, violence, or restraint; *utilitarian* power, based on material or financial resources; and *normative* power, based on symbolic resources.[1]

A party to a relationship has power, therefore, to the extent it has or can gain access to coercive, utilitarian, or normative means to impose its will in the relationship. We note, however, that this access to means is a variable, not a steady state, which is one reason why power is transitory—it can be acquired as well as lost.

Legitimacy
It is apparent from our analysis in Table 2 that narrow-definition scholars, particularly those seeking a "normative core" for stakeholder theory, are focused almost exclusively on defining the basis of stakeholder legitimacy. Whether that core of legitimacy is to be found in something "at risk," or in property rights, or in moral claims, or in some other construct, articulations of the Principle of Who or What Really Counts are generally legitimacy based.

However, the notion of legitimacy, loosely referring to socially accepted and expected structures or behaviors, is often implicitly coupled with that of power when evaluating the nature of relationships in society. Davis (1973:314), for example distinguishes legitimate from illegitimate use of power by declaring "...In the long run, those who do not use power in a manner which society considers responsible will tend to lose it." Many scholars seeking to define a firm's stakeholders narrowly also make an implicit assumption that legitimate stakeholders are necessarily powerful when this is not always the case (e.g. minority stockholders in a closely held company), and that powerful stakeholders are necessarily legitimate (e.g. corporate raiders in the eyes of current managers).

Despite this common linkage, we accept Weber's (1947) proposal that legitimacy and power are distinct attributes that can combine to create *authority* (defined by Weber as the legitimate use of power), but that can exist independently as well. An entity may have legitimate standing in society, or it may have a legitimate claim on the firm, but unless it has either power to enforce its will in the relationship, or a perception that its claim is urgent, it will not achieve salience for the firm's managers. For this reason, we argue that a comprehensive theory of stakeholder salience requires that separate attention be paid to legitimacy as an attribute of stakeholder-manager relations.

Recently, Suchman (1995) has worked to strengthen the conceptual moorings of the notion of legitimacy, building upon Weber's functionalism (1947), Parson's structural-functional theory (1960), "open systems" theory (Scott, 1987) and institutional theory (DiMaggio & Powell, 1983, 1991). The definition that Suchman suggests is broad-based, and recognizes the evaluative, cognitive, and socially constructed nature of legitimacy. He defines legitimacy as "...a generalized perception or assumption that the actions of an entity are desirable, proper, or appropriate within some socially constructed system of norms, values, beliefs, and definitions" (1995:574),

Although this definition is imprecise and difficult to operationalize, it is representative of sociologically-based definitions of legitimacy and contains several descriptions that are useful in our approach to stakeholder identification. Therefore, we accept and utilize Suchman's definition of legitimacy, recognizing that the social system within which legitimacy is attained is a system with multiple levels of analysis, the most common of which are the individual, organizational, and societal (Wood, 1991). This definition implies that legitimacy is a desirable social good, that it is something larger and more shared than a mere self-perception, and that it may be defined and negotiated differently at various levels of social organization.

Urgency

Viewing power and legitimacy as independent variables in stakeholder-manager relationships takes us some distance toward a theory of stakeholder identification and salience, but it does not capture the dynamics of stakeholder-manager interactions. We propose that adding the stakeholder attribute of urgency helps move it from a static to a dynamic model. Urgency, is defined by the Merriam-Webster Dictionary as "calling for immediate attention," or "pressing." We believe that urgency, with synonyms including compelling, driving, and imperative, only exists when two conditions are met; first, when a relationship or claim is of a time-sensitive nature, and second, when that relationship or claim is important or critical to the stakeholder. Thus, similar to Jones' (1993) description of moral intensity as a multidimensional construct, we argue that urgency is based on the following two attributes: 1) time sensitivity—the degree to which managerial delay in attending to the claim or relationship is unacceptable to the stakeholder, and 2) criticality—the importance of the claim or the relationship to the stakeholder. We define urgency as the degree to which stakeholder claims call for immediate attention.

While virtually ignored until now in any explicit sense in the stakeholder literature, the idea of paying attention to various stakeholder relationships in a timely fashion has been a focus of issues management (Wartick & Mahon, 1994) and crisis management literature for decades. Eyestone (1978) highlights the speed with which an issue can become salient to a firm, while Cobb & Elder (1 972:13 9), discuss the important role symbols play in creating time urgency: "Symbols such as 'Freedom Now' have an advantage because they connote a specific time commitment to action. If one is attempting to mobilize a public against some outside threat, one must emphasize the rapidity with which the opponent is gaining strength."

But although time sensitivity is necessary it is not sufficient to identify a stakeholder's claim or "manager relationship" as urgent. In addition, the stakeholder must view its claim on the firm or its relationship with the firm as critical, or highly important. Some examples of why a stakeholder would view its relationship with the firm as critical include

1) ownership—the stakeholder's possession of firm-specific assets, assets tied to a firm which cannot be used in a different way without loss of value (Williamson, 1985; Hill & Jones, 1992) that make it very costly for the stakeholder to exit the relationship; 2) sentiment—as in the case of easily traded stock which is held by generations of owners within a family regardless of the stock's performance; 3) expectation—the stakeholder's anticipation that the firm will continue providing it with something of great value, e.g. compensation and benefits in the case of employees; or 4) exposure—the importance the stakeholder attaches to that which is at risk in the relationship with the firm (Clarkson, 1994).

Our theory does not specify why stakeholders would assess their relationships with firms as critical. Furthermore, our theory does not attempt to predict the circumstances under which "time will be of the essence." Rather, when both factors are present, our theory captures the resulting multidimensional attribute as "urgency," juxtaposes it with the attributes of power and legitimacy, and proposes dynamism in the systematic identification of stakeholders.

Additional Features of Stakeholder Attributes
Table 3 summarizes the constructs, definitions, and origins of the concepts discussed thus far in the paper. To support a dynamic theory of stakeholder identification and salience, however, several additional implications of power, legitimacy, and urgency need to be considered. First, each attribute is a variable, not a steady state, and can change for any particular entity or stakeholder-manager relationship. Second, the existence (or degree present) of each attribute is a matter of multiple perceptions and is a constructed reality rather than an "objective" one. Third, an individual or entity may not be "conscious" of possessing the attribute, or, if conscious of possession, may not choose to enact any implied behaviors. These features of stakeholder attributes, summarized below, are important to the theory's dynamism; that is, they provide a preliminary framework for understanding how stakeholders can gain or lose salience to a firm's managers:

1. Stakeholder attributes are variable, not steady state.
2. Stakeholder attributes are socially constructed, not objective, reality.
3. Consciousness & willful exercise may or may not be present.

Thus, with respect to power, for example, access to the means of influencing another entity's behavior is a variable, with both discrete and continuous features. As we argued earlier, power may be coercive, utilitarian, or normative—qualitatively different types that may exist

Table 3: Key constructs in the theory of stakeholder identification and salience

Construct	Definition	Sources
Stakeholder	Any group or individual who can affect or is affected by the achievement of the organization's objectives.	Freeman, 1984 Jones 1995 Kreiner & Bhambri, 1988
Power	A relationship among social actors in which one social actor, A, can get another social actor, B, to do something that B would not otherwise have done.	Dahl, 1957 Weber, 1947 Pfeffer, 1981
Bases	Coercive - Force/Threat Utilitarian - Material/Incentives Normative - Symbolic Influences	Etzioni, 1964
Legitimacy	A generalized perception or assumption that the actions of an entity are desirable, proper or appropriate within some socially constructed system of norms, values, beliefs, definitions.	Suchman, 1995 Weber, 1947
Bases	Individual Organizational Societal	Wood, 1991
Urgency	The degree to which stakeholder claims call for immediate attention.	Original–Builds on the definition from the Merriam-Webster Dictionary
Bases	Time Sensitivity - the degree to which managerial delay in attending to the claim or relationship is unacceptable to the stakeholder	Eyestone, 1978 Wartick & Mahon, 1994
	Criticality - the importance of the claim or the relationship to the stakeholder	Original–Asset Specificity from Williamson, 1985 Hill & Jones, 1992
Salience	The degree to which managers give priority to competing stakeholder claims	Original–Builds on the definition from the Merriam-Webster Dictionary

independently or in combination. Each type of power may range from nonexistent to complete. Power is transitory—it can be acquired as well as lost. Further, possession of power does not necessarily imply its actual or intended use. Nor does possession of power imply consciousness of such possession by the possessor, or "correct" perception of objective reality by the perceivers. An entity may possess power to impose its will upon a firm, but unless it is aware of its power and willing to exercise it on the firm, it is not a stakeholder with high salience for managers. Rather, latent power exists in stakeholder relationships, and the exercise of stakeholder power is triggered by conditions that are manifest in the other two attributes of the relationship—legitimacy and urgency. That is, power by itself does not guarantee high salience in a stakeholder-manager relationship. Power gains authority through legitimacy, and it gains exercise through urgency.

Legitimacy, like power, is a variable rather than a steady state, a dynamic attribute of the stakeholder-manager relationship. It may be present or absent. If it is present, it is based upon a generalized virtue that is perceived for or attributed to a stakeholder at one or more social levels of analysis. Claimants may or may not correctly perceive the legitimacy of their claims, and likewise managers can have perceptions of stakeholder legitimacy that are at variance with the stakeholder's own perception. Also like the attribute of power, legitimacy's contribution to stakeholder salience depends upon interaction with the other two attributes: power and urgency. Legitimacy gains rights through power, and voice through urgency.

Finally, urgency is not a steady-state attribute but can vary across stakeholder-manager relationships or within a single relationship across time. As is true of power and legitimacy, urgency is a socially constructed perceptual phenomenon and may be correctly or falsely perceived by the stakeholder, the managers, or others in the firm's environment. For example, neighbors of a nuclear power plant that is about to meltdown have a serious claim on that plant, but they may not be aware of the time-pressure and criticality, and thus not act on their claim. Urgency by itself is not sufficient to guarantee high salience in the stakeholder-manager relationship. However, when combined with at least one of the other attributes, urgency will change the relationship and cause it to increase in salience to the firm's managers. Specifically, in combination with legitimacy, urgency promotes access to decision-making channels. In combination with power, it encourages one-sided stakeholder action. In combination with both, it triggers reciprocal acknowledgment and action between stakeholders and managers.

These three features of stakeholder attributes—variable status, perceptual quality, and variable consciousness and will—lay the groundwork for a future analysis of the dynamic nature of stakeholder-manager relations. The common "bicycle wheel" model of a firm's stakeholder environment does not begin to capture the ebb and flow of changes in stakeholder-manager relations or the fact that these relations are multilateral and often coalitional, not bilateral and independent. The dynamic possibilities of the theory of stakeholder salience will be explored briefly in the concluding section, but it seems clear that a great deal more paradigmatic development is now possible because of our ability to theoretically recognize that stakeholder-manager relations are not static but are in constant flux.

Managers' Role in the Theory

Cyert & March (1963) contribute to the management literature the notion of organizations as a coalition of individuals and organized "sub coalitions" (1963:27) with "disparate demands, changing foci of attention, and limited ability to attend to all problems simultaneously" (1963: 43) which under uncertainty must seek feedback from the environment (1963:12). Pfeffer & Salancik (1978) pick up the idea of organizations as coalitions of varying interests, and contribute the notion that organizations are "other-directed" (1978:257), being influenced by actors that control critical resources and have the attention of managers (1978:259-260). In developing their stakeholder-agency model, Hill and Jones (1992) employ the agency theory view of the firm as a nexus of contracts between stakeholders and managers at a central node, where managers' responsibility is to reconcile divergent interests by making strategic decisions and allocating strategic resources in a manner that is most consistent with the claims of the other stakeholder groups (1992:134). They write:

> Whatever the magnitude of their stake, each stakeholder is a part of the nexus of implicit and explicit contracts that constitutes the firm. However, as a group, managers are unique in this respect because of their position at the centre of the nexus of contracts. Managers are the only group of stakeholders who enter into a contractual relationship with all other stakeholders. Managers are also the only group of stakeholders with *direct* control over the decision-making apparatus of the firm [emphasis in original].

The idea that the organization is an environmentally dependent coalition of divergent interests, which depends upon gaining the attention of (making claims upon) managers at the center of the nexus to effect reconciliations among stakeholders, suggests that the perspective of managers might be vital. We propose that, although groups can be reliably identified as stakeholders based on their possession of power, legitimacy, and urgency in relationship to the firm, it is the firm's managers who determine which stakeholders are *salient* and therefore will receive management attention. In short, a firm's stakeholders can be identified based on attributes, but managers may or may not perceive the stakeholder field correctly. The stakeholders that win management's attention will only be those the managers perceive to be highly salient.[2]

Therefore, if managers are central to this theory, what role do their own characteristics play? The propositions presented later suggest that the manager's *perception* of a stakeholder's attributes is critical to the manager's view of stakeholder salience. Therefore, we suggest, although space prohibits systematic development here, that managerial characteristics are a moderator of the relationships presented in this paper. For example, managers vary greatly on their environmental scanning practices (Daft, Sormunen, & Park, 1988), and their values (Hambrick & Mason 1984). Differences in managerial values are illustrative of the moderating effects of management characteristics (Frederick, 1995). Greer and Downey (1982) find that managers' values relative to social regulation have a strong effect on how they react to stakeholders covered by these statutes. Another value suggested to be important in this relationship is management's sense of self-interest or self-sacrifice. While some theorists have suggested that all behavior is ultimately self-interested (Dawkins, 1976; Wilson, 1992), several social scientists have questioned the common assumption of self-interest and have suggested that people often act in ways that benefit others, even to their own detriment (see Granovetter, 1985; Etzioni, 1988; Perrow, 1986). Like Perrow (1986) and Brenner & Cochran (1991), we treat managerial characteristics as a variable and suggest that it will be an important moderator of the stakeholder-manager relationship.

Stakeholder Classes

To this point in the paper we have argued that a definition of the principle of Who or What Really Counts rests first, upon the assumption that managers who want to achieve certain ends pay particular kinds of attention to various classes of stakeholders; second, that managers' perceptions dictate stakeholder salience, and third, that the various classes of stakeholders might be identified based upon the possession, or the attributed possession, of one, two, or all three of the attributes: power, legitimacy, and urgency. We now proceed to our analysis of the stakeholder classes that result from the various combinations of these attributes, as shown in Figure 1.

Figure 1: Qualitative classes of stakeholders

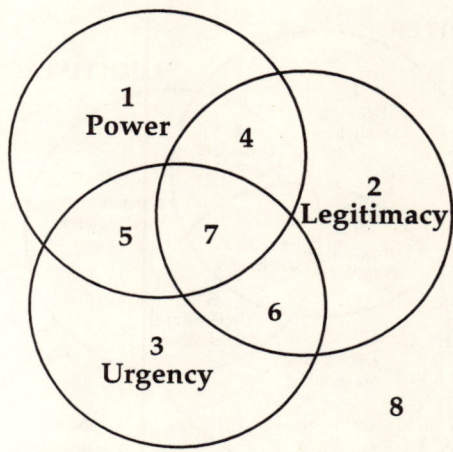

We first lay out the stakeholder types that emerge from various combinations of the attributes of power, legitimacy, and urgency. Logically and conceptually, seven types are examined, three possessing only one attribute, three possessing two attributes, and one possessing all three attributes. We propose that stakeholders' possession of these attributes, upon further methodological and empirical work, can be reliably measured. This analysis allows and justifies identification of entities that should be considered stakeholders of the firm, and also constitutes the set from which managers select those entities they perceive as salient. According to this model, then, entities with no power, legitimacy, or urgency in relation to the firm are not stakeholders and will be perceived as having no salience by the firm's managers.

In conjunction with the analysis of stakeholder types, and based on the assumption that managers' perceptions of stakeholders are the crucial variable in determining organizational resource allocation in response to stakeholder claims, we also present several propositions leading to a theory of stakeholder salience.

Therefore:

> PROPOSITION 1: *Stakeholder salience will be positively related to the cumulative number of stakeholder attributes—power, legitimacy, and urgency —perceived by managers to be present.*

Figure 2: Stakeholder typology: One, two or three attributes present

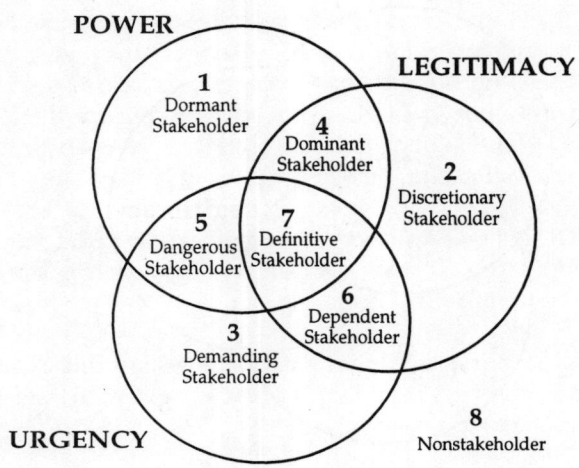

The low salience classes (areas 1, 2, and 3) which we term "latent" stakeholders, are identified by their possession or attributed possession of only one of the attributes. The moderately salient stakeholders (areas 4, 5, and 6) are identified by their possession or attributed possession of two of the attributes, and because they are stakeholders who "expect something," we call them "expectant" stakeholders. The combination of all three attributes (including the dynamic relations among them) is the defining feature of highly salient stakeholders (area 7).

In this section we present our analysis of the stakeholder classes that the theory identifies, with special attention to the managerial implications of the existence of each stakeholder class. We have given each class a descriptive name to facilitate discussion, recognizing that the names are less important than the theoretical types they represent. We invite the indulgence of the reader as we alliterate these descriptive names as a mnemonic device to promote recall, and as a further means to suggest a starting point for future dialogue

As Figure 2 illustrates, latent stakeholders are those possessing only one of the three attributes, and include dormant, discretionary, and demanding stakeholders. Expectant stakeholders are those possessing two attributes and include dominant, dependent, and dangerous stakeholders. Definitive stakeholders are those possessing all three attributes. Finally, individuals or entities possessing none of the attributes are non or potential stakeholders.

Latent Stakeholders
With limited time, energy, and other resources to track stakeholder behavior and to manage relationships, managers may well do nothing about stakeholders that they believe possess only one of the identifying attributes, and may not even go so far as to recognize their existence. Similarly, latent stakeholders are not likely to give any attention or acknowledgment to the firm. Hence:

> PROPOSITION 1a: *Stakeholder salience will be low where only one of the stakeholder attributes, power, legitimacy, and urgency, is perceived by managers to be present.*

In the next few paragraphs, the reasoning behind this expectation as it applies to each class of latent stakeholder is explained, and the implications for managers are discussed.

Dormant Stakeholders
The relevant attribute of a dormant stakeholder is power. Dormant stakeholders possess power to impose their will on a firm, but by not having legitimate relationship or an urgent claim, this power remains unused. Examples of dormant stakeholders are plentiful. For example, power is held by those who have a loaded gun (coercive), can spend a lot of money (utilitarian), or who can command the attention of the news media (symbolic), etc. Dormant stakeholders have little or no interaction with the firm. However, because of their potential to acquire a second attribute, management ought to remain cognizant of such stakeholders because the dynamic nature of the stakeholder-manager relationship suggests that dormant stakeholders will become more salient to managers if they acquire either urgency or legitimacy.

Though difficult, it is oftentimes possible to predict which dormant stakeholders may become salient. For example, while employees who have been fired or laid off from an organization could be considered to be dormant stakeholders by the firm, experience suggests that these stakeholders can seek to exercise their latent power. The multiple shootings at postal facilities by ex-U.S. mail employees (coercive), the filing of wrongful dismissal suits in the court system (utilitarian), and an increase in "speaking out" on talk radio (symbolic) are all evidence of such combinations.

Discretionary Stakeholders
Discretionary stakeholders possess the attribute of legitimacy, but have no power to influence the firm and no urgent claims. Discretionary stakeholders are a particularly interesting group for scholars of corporate social responsibility and performance (see Wood, 1991), for they are most likely to be recipients of what Carroll (1979) calls discretionary corporate social responsibility, which he later redefined as corporate philanthropy (Carroll, 1991). The key point regarding discretionary stakeholders is that in the absence of power and urgent claims, there is absolutely no pressure on managers to engage in an active relationship with such a stakeholder, although managers can choose to so actively engage.

Not all recipients of corporate philanthropy are discretionary stakeholders—only those with neither power over nor urgent claims on the firm. Examples of discretionary stakeholders include the beneficiaries of the Take-A-Taxi program in the Twin Cities, in which the Fingerhut company picks up the tab for anyone who feels they've consumed too much alcohol to drive; and non-profit organizations, such as schools, soup kitchens, and hospitals, who receive donations and volunteer labor from companies such as Rhino Records, Timberland, Honeywell, JustDesserts, and Levi-Strauss.

Demanding Stakeholders
Where the sole relevant attribute of the stakeholder-manager relationship is urgency, the stakeholder is described as demanding. Demanding stakeholders, those with urgent claims but neither power nor legitimacy, are the "mosquitoes buzzing in the ears" of managers: irksome but not dangerous, bothersome but not warranting more than passing management attention, if any at all. Where stakeholders are unable or unwilling to acquire either the power or the legitimacy necessary to move their claim into a more salient status, the "noise" of urgency is insufficient to project a stakeholder claim beyond latency. For example, a lone millenarian picketer who marches outside the headquarters with a sign that says, "The end of the world is corning! Acme chemical is the cause!" might be extremely irritating to Acme's managers, but the claims of the picketer remain largely unconsidered.

Expectant Stakeholders
As we consider the potential relationship between managers, and the group of stakeholders with two of the three identifying stakeholder attributes, we observe a qualitatively different zone of salience. In analysing the situations in which any two of the three attributes: power, legitimacy, and urgency, are present, we cannot help but notice the change in momentum that characterizes this condition. Whereas

"one-attribute" low-salience stakeholders are anticipated to have a latent relationship with managers, "two-attribute" moderate-salience stakeholders are seen as "expecting something" because the combination of two attributes leads the stakeholder to an active versus a passive stance, with a corresponding increase in firm responsiveness to the stakeholder's interests. —Thus, the level of engagement between managers and these "expectant" stakeholders is likely to be higher. Accordingly,

> PROPOSITION 1b: *Stakeholder salience will be moderate where two of the stakeholder attributes, power, legitimacy, and urgency, are perceived by managers to be present.*

The three expectant stakeholder classes (dominant, dependent, & dangerous) are described below.

Dominant Stakeholders
In the situation where stakeholders are both powerful and legitimate, their influence in the firm is assured, since by possessing power with legitimacy, they form the "dominant coalition" in the enterprise (Cyert & March, 1963). We characterize these stakeholders as dominant, in deference to the legitimate claims they have upon the firm and their ability to act on these claims (rather than as a forecast of their intentions with respect to the firm—they may or may not ever choose to act on their claims). It seems clear to us, at least, that the expectations of any stakeholders perceived by managers to have power and legitimacy will "matter" to managers.

Thus, we might expect that dominant stakeholders will have some formal mechanism in place which acknowledges the importance of their relationship with the firm. For example, corporate boards of directors generally include representatives of owners, significant creditors, and community leaders, and there is normally an investor relations office to handle ongoing relationships with investors. Most corporations have a human resources department which acknowledges the importance of the firm-employee relationship. Public affairs offices are common in firms that depend on maintaining good relationships with government. In addition, corporations produce reports to legitimate, powerful stakeholders including annual reports, proxy statements, and increasingly, environmental and social responsibility reports. Dominant stakeholders, in fact, are just those stakeholders that so many scholars are trying to establish as the only stakeholders of the firm. In our typology, dominant stakeholders expect and receive much of managers' attention, but are by no means the full set of stakeholders to whom managers should or do relate.

Dependent Stakeholders
We characterize stakeholders who lack power but who have urgent legitimate claims as dependent, because these stakeholders depend upon others (other stakeholders or the firm's managers) for the power necessary to carry out their will. Because power in this relationship is not reciprocal, its exercise is governed either through the advocacy or guardianship of other stakeholders, or through the guidance of internal management values.

Turning to the case of the giant oil spill from the Exxon Valdez in Prince William Sound as an example, several stakeholder groups had urgent and legitimate claims, but had little or no power to enforce their will in the relationship. To satisfy their claims, these stakeholders had to rely on the advocacy of other, powerful stakeholders, or on the benevolence and voluntarism of the firm's management. Included in this category were local residents, marine mammals and birds, and even the natural environment itself (Starik, 1993). For the claims of these dependent stakeholders to be satisfied, it was necessary for "dominant" stakeholders, the Alaska state government and the court system, to provide guardianship of the region's citizens, animals, and ecosystems. Here a dependent stakeholder moved into the most salient stakeholder class by having its urgent claims adopted by dominant stakeholders, illustrating the dynamism that can be effectively modeled using the theory and principles of stakeholder identification and salience suggested herein.

Dangerous Stakeholders
Where urgency and power characterize a stakeholder who lacks legitimacy, we suggest that this stakeholder will be coercive and possibly violent, making that stakeholder literally "dangerous" to the firm. Coercion is suggested as a descriptor because the use of coercive power often accompanies illegitimate status.

Examples of unlawful, yet common, attempts at using coercive means to advance stakeholder claims (which may or may not be legitimate) include wildcat strikes, employee sabotage, and terrorism. For example, in the 1970s, General Motors' employees in Lordstown, Ohio, welded pop cans to engine blocks to protest certain company policies. Other examples of stakeholders using coercive tactics include environmentalists' spiking trees in areas to be logged, and religious or political terrorists who use bombings, shootings, or kidnappings to call attention to their claims. The actions of these stakeholders are not only outside the bounds of legitimacy, they are dangerous, both to the stakeholder-manager relationship, and to the individuals and entities involved.

It is important for us to note that we, along with other responsible individuals, are very uncomfortable with the notion that those whose actions are dangerous both to stakeholder-manager relationships as well as to life and well-being, might be accorded some measure of legitimacy by virtue of the typology proposed in this analysis. Notwithstanding our discomfort, however, we are even more concerned that failure to identify dangerous stakeholders would result in missed opportunities for mitigating the dangers, and in lower levels of preparedness where no accommodation is possible. Further, to maintain the integrity of our approach to better define stakeholders, we feel bound to "identify" dangerous stakeholders without "acknowledging" them, for like most of our colleagues, we abhor their practices. We are fully aware that society's "refusal to acknowledge" after the "identification" of a dangerous stakeholder is an effective counteragent in the battle to maintain civility and civilization, by counteracting terror in all its forms. The identification of this class of stakeholder is undertaken with the support of this tactic in mind.

Definitive Stakeholders

We have previously defined "salience" as the degree to which managers give priority to competing stakeholder claims. Thus,

> PROPOSITION 1c: *Stakeholder salience will be high where all three of the stakeholder attributes, power, legitimacy, and urgency, are perceived by managers to be present.*

By definition, a stakeholder exhibiting both power and legitimacy will already be a member of a firm's dominant coalition. When such a stakeholder's claim is urgent, then managers have a clear and immediate mandate to attend to and give priority to that stakeholder's claim. The most common occurrence is likely to be the movement of a dominant stakeholder into the definitive category.

For example, in 1993, stockholders (dominant stakeholders) of IBM, General Motors, Kodak, Westinghouse, and American Express became active when they felt that their legitimate interests were not being served by the managers of these companies. A sense of urgency was engendered when these powerful, legitimate stakeholders saw their stock values plummet. And, because top managers did not respond sufficiently or appropriately to these "definitive" stakeholders, they were removed, thus demonstrating in a general way the importance of an accurate perception of power, legitimacy, and urgency, the necessity of acknowledgment and action that salience implies, and more specifically the consequences of the misperception of or inattention to the claims of definitive stakeholders.

Any expectant stakeholder can become a definitive stakeholder by acquiring the missing attribute. As we saw earlier, dependent Alaskan citizens became definitive stakeholders of Exxon by acquiring a powerful ally in government. Likewise, the dangerous African National Congress became a definitive stakeholder of South African companies when it acquired legitimacy by winning free national elections.

Research and Management Consequences of a Dynamic Theory of Stakeholder Identification

This analysis has proposed that stakeholders possess some combination of three critical attributes; power, legitimacy, and urgency. The salience of a particular stakeholder to the firm's management is predicted to be low if only one attribute is present, moderate if two attributes are present, and high if all three attributes are present.

Dynamism in Stakeholder-Manager Relations

As the earlier discussion demonstrates, latent stakeholders can increase their salience to managers and move into the "expectant stakeholder" category by acquiring just one of the missing attributes. If the stakeholder is particularly clever, for example, at coalition-building or political action or social construction of reality, it can move into the "definitive stakeholder" category, characterized by high salience to managers, starting from any position, latent, expectant, or potential.

Static maps of a firm's stakeholder environment are heuristically useful if the intent is to raise consciousness about Who or What Really Counts to managers, or to specify the stakeholder configuration at a particular time point. But even though most theorists might try for static clarity, managers should never forget that stakeholders will change in salience, requiring different degrees and types of attention depending on their attributed possession of power, legitimacy, and/or urgency, and that levels on these attributes (and thereby salience) can vary from issue to issue, from time to time.

An example of stakeholder dynamism can be observed in the recent events in South Africa. The African National Congress (ANC) began as a group with an urgent claim, but not a legitimate one given the ruling South African culture and government, and had no power. It was first a latent, demanding stakeholder. The ANC next moved into the dangerous category through the use of coercive power. However, this did not lead to definitive status. It was only through the acquisition of legitimacy while relinquishing the use of coercive power—Thus becoming a dependent stakeholder—that the road to definitive status, high salience and eventual success was achieved.

Thus, by moving the urgent claim into the world environment, the claim's legitimacy was established, and the ANC as well as the South

Africans it represented became an expectant, "dependent stakeholder" of the multinational enterprises (MNEs) located in South Africa. As a dependent stakeholder, they were able to acquire the protection, advocacy, and guardianship of more salient stakeholders (especially investors). With the powerful advocacy of these stakeholders, the ANC moved into the "definitive" zone of the stakeholder attribute model for South Africans. In fact, it is now widely acknowledged that the worldwide divestment/disinvestment movement, led by MNE stockholders, was a major force in the transformation of the South African system of government and the rise to political power of the ANC (see, e.g., Paul, 1992).

Another example of dynamism in stakeholder attributes is offered by Näsi, Näsi & Savage (1994). This case involving a business owner, workers, and the courts, illustrates how a dependent stakeholder worker group (one with a legitimate and urgent claim) can increase its salience to a firm's managers by aligning itself with other stakeholders (in this case, a union and the courts) who have power to impose their will upon a stubborn business owner.

Thus, using our identification typology, we are able to explain stakeholder salience and dynamism systematically. This new capability has implications for management, research, and for the future of the stakeholder framework.

Implications for Management, Research, and Future Directions

On the basis of the model developed in this paper, we can envision refinements in longstanding management techniques designed to assist managers in dealing with multiple stakeholders' interests. Presently, management techniques based on the stakeholder heuristic are being utilized to help managers deal effectively with multiple stakeholder relationships. Current methods include identification of stakeholder roles (e.g. employees, owners, communities, suppliers, customers, etc.), analysis of stakeholder interests, and evaluation of the type and level of stakeholder power (see current textbooks, e.g., Frederick, Post, Lawrence, & Weber, 1996; Wood, 1994).

The approach introduced in this paper has the potential to improve upon current practice. In addition to current techniques that emphasize power and interests, the model we suggest adds the vital dimensions of legitimacy and urgency. Further, this model enables a more systematic sorting by managers of stakeholder-manager relationships as these relationships attain and relinquish salience in the dynamics of ongoing business. In addition, this three dimensional model permits managers to map the legitimacy of stakeholders and so become sensitized to the moral implications of their actions with respect to each stakeholder. In this sense, our model supports and initiates normative thought in the managerial context. Thus, these refinements contribute to the potential effectiveness of managers as they deal with multiple stakeholder interests. And, as these refinements find their way into accepted practice, we can further envision subsequent rounds of inquiry, which test whether "new maps" result in "new methods."

Stakeholder theory, we believe, holds the key to more effective management and to a more useful, comprehensive theory of the firm in society. Focusing attention on salience in the manager-stakeholder relationships existing in a firm's environment appears to be a productive strategy for researchers and managers alike in realizing these aspirations. The stakeholder identification typology we have developed here is amenable to empirical operationalization and to the generation of testable hypotheses concerning, for example, predictions about the circumstances under which a stakeholder in one category might attempt to acquire a missing attribute and thus enhance its salience to a firm's managers. We have not developed such operational definitions and hypotheses here, for lack of space, but believe that such development is the next logical step in articulating completely the Principle of Who or What Really Counts.

Specifically, we call for empirical research that answers the questions: are present descriptions of stakeholder attributes adequate? Do the inferences we make herein hold when examining real stakeholder-manager relationships? Are there models of interrelationships among the variables identified here (and possible others), that reveal more subtle but perhaps more basic systematics? We realize that for these and other such questions to be addressed, item and scale development, demographic calibration, and second-order model-building, among other things, are a necessity.

In the process, we hope that additional clarity can be achieved at the conceptual level as well. We ask: what are the implications of this model and its subsequent tests for additional research on power, legitimacy, and urgency? And, more importantly, are power, legitimacy, and urgency really the correct and parsimonious set of variables in understanding stakeholder-manager relationships? We acknowledge that despite their level of emphasis in the second Toronto conference, and our logical and theoretical justification of their importance in developing a more inferential, and empirically-based stakeholder theory, other stakeholder attributes may also be well-suited to stakeholder analysis—and we call for the critical evaluation of our choices.

Finally, in attempting to build momentum in the development of stakeholder theory, we are acutely aware that we have necessarily made sweeping assumptions that—for the sake of clarity in a preliminary articulation—are passed over, with the implicit understanding that for the theory to hold, these must be revisited and assessed. For example, we assume and argue that power and legitimacy are distinct attributes. Some might cast one as a subset of the other. To build our identification typology we treat each attribute as "present or absent," when it is clear that each operates on a continuum or series of continua. Each of these issues, and others like them, point toward additional inquiry that can enrich the theory and adds to its usefulness.

Conclusion: The Search for Legitimacy in Stakeholder Theory

Many stakeholder scholars, in attempting to narrow the range of Who or What Really Counts in a firm's stakeholder environment, are searching for the bases of legitimacy in stakeholder-manager relationships. When scholars such as Freeman, Clarkson, Donaldson, Preston, and Dunfee argue that stakeholder theory must articulate a "normative core," they are looking for a compelling reason why some claims and some relationships are legitimate and worthy of management attention, and others are not. They discount the importance of power in stakeholder-manager relations, arguing that the important thing is whether the stakeholder has legitimate (e.g., moral, legal, property-based, etc.) claims.

The theory of stakeholder identification and salience developed in this paper in no way discredits this search for a legitimate normative core for stakeholder theory. It makes sense to articulate theoretically why certain groups will hold legitimate, possibly stable claims on managers and firm—these are the stakeholders who should "really count." Our aim, however, is to expand scholarly and management understanding beyond legitimacy to incorporate stakeholder power and urgency of a claim, because these attributes of entities in a firm's environment—and their dynamism over periods of time or variation in issues—will make a critical difference in managers' ability to meet legitimate claims and protect legitimate interests. We offer this preliminary theory as a way of understanding which stakeholders do "really count."

In 1976, William C. Frederick observed that business & society scholarship was in a transition from a moral focus on social responsibility (CSR_1) to an amoral focus on social responsiveness (CSR_2). When stakeholder theory focuses only on issues of legitimacy, it acquires the fuzzy moral flavor of CSR_1. Focusing only on stakeholder power, however, as several major organizational theories would lead us to do, yields the amorality and self-interested action focus of CSR_2. Instead, we propose a merger.

In sum, we argue that stakeholder theory must account for power and urgency as well as legitimacy, no matter how distasteful or unsettling the results. Managers *must* know about entities in their environment that hold power and have the intent to impose their will upon the firm; *power and urgency must be attended to if managers are to serve the legal and moral interests of legitimate stakeholders.*

We would like to thank the members of the Second Toronto Conference on Stakeholder Theory, sponsored by the Centre for Corporate Social Responsibility at the University of Toronto, where the centrality of these three attributes to a theory of stakeholder-manager relationships was first noted. We also recognize the contribution of various working groups in SIM and IABS. We are also grateful for the comments provided by A.R. Elangoven and Barry Mitnick, the intellectual and financial support of Fritz Faulhaber, and the valuable insights of the consulting editor and the anonymous reviewers.

---

[1] Etzioni explains these types of power as follows:

The use of a gun, a whip, or a lock is physical since it affects the body; the threat to use physical sanctions is viewed as physical because the effect on the subject is similar in kind, though not in intensity, to the actual use. Control based on application of physical means is ascribed as coercive power.

Material rewards consist of goods and services. The granting of symbols (e.g. money) which allow one to acquire goods and services is classified as material because the effect on the recipient is similar to that of material means. The use of material means for control purposes constitutes utilitarian power.

Pure symbols are those whose use does not constitute a physical threat or a claim on material rewards. These include normative symbols, those of prestige and esteem; and social symbols, those of love and acceptance. When physical contact is used to symbolize love, or material objects to symbolize prestige, such contacts or objects are viewed as symbols because their effect on the recipient is similar to that of "pure" symbols. The use of symbols for control purposes is referred to as normative, normative-social, or social power.

[2] We note, however, that Freeman & Evan (1990:342) view the firm "as a series of multilateral contracts among stakeholders" with no central role for managers. This implies a network theory solution to the problem of systematic description, in comparison with the cognitive approach that we take. We make no representations about a fully-networked, non-nexus approach. We merely suggest the sociology-organization theory approach as a logically developed "sorting system" for improving the descriptive capability of the stakeholder approach.

Ahlstedt, L. & Jahnukainen, I. 1971. *Yritysorganisaatio yhteistoiminnan ohjausjaerjesteimaenae*. Helsinki, Weilin + Goeoes.

Alkhafaji, A.F. 1989. A stakeholder approach to corporate governance: Managing in a dynamic environment. - Westport, CT: Quorum Books.

Bowie, N. 1988. The moral obligations of multinational corporations. Pp. 97-113 in S. Luper- Foy (ed.), *Problems of International Justice*. Boulder, CO: Westview Press.

Brenner, S.N., & Cochran, P.L. 1991. The stakeholder model of the firm: Implications for business and society theory and research. *Proceedings of the International Association for Business and Society*, 449-467.

Brenner, S.N. 1993. The stakeholder theory of the firm and organizational decision making: Some propositions and a model. *Proceedings of the International Association for Business and Society*, 205-210.

Brenner, S.N. 1995. Stakeholder theory of the firm: Its consistency with current management techniques. Pp. 75-96 in Juha Näsi (ed.), *Understanding Stakeholder Thinking*. Helsinki: LSR-Julkaisut Oy.

Carroll, A.B. 1979. A three-dimensional model of corporate performance. *Academy of Management Review*, 4: 497-505.

Carroll, A.B. 1991. The pyramid of corporate social responsibility-. Toward the moral management of organizational stakeholders. *Business Horizons*. July-Aug. 30-48.

Carroll, A.B. 1993. *Business and Society: Ethics and Stakeholder Management*. Cincinnati: South-Western.

Carroll, G.R., & Hannan, M.T. 1989. Density delay in the evolution of organizational populations: A model and five empirical tests. *Administrative Science Quarterly*, 34:411 430.

Clarkson, M. 1994. A risk based model of stakeholder theory. *Proceedings of the Second Toronto Conference on Stakeholder Theory*, University of Toronto, Centre for Corporate Social Performance & Ethics.

Clarkson, M.B.E. 1995. A Stakeholder Framework for Analyzing and Evaluating Corporate Social Performance. *Academy of Management Review* 20(1): 92-117,

Cobb, R.W. & Elder, C.D. 1972. *Participation in American politics: The dynamics of agenda-building*. Baltimore, MD: The Johns Hopkins University Press.

Comell, B. & Shapiro, A.C. 1987. Corporate stakeholders and corporate finance. *Financial Management* 16, 5-14.

Cyert, R. M., & March, J.G. 1963. *The behavioral theory of the firm*. Englewood Cliffs, NJ: Prentice-Hall.

Daft, R.L., Sormunen, J. & Parks, D. 1988. Chief executive scanning, environmental characteristics, and company performance: An empirical study. *Strategic Management Journal*, 9:123-139.

Dahl, R.A. 1957. The concept of power. *Behavioral Science*, 2:201-215.

Davis, K. 1973. The case for and against business assumption of social responsibility. *Academy of Management*, 16:2, 312-322.

Dawkins, R. 1976. *The selfish gene.* New York, NY: Oxford University Press

DiMaggio, P.J. & Powell, W.W. 1983. The iron cage revisited: Institutional isomorphism and collective rationality in organization fields. *American Sociological Review*, 46:147-160.

Donaldson, T. & Preston, L.E. 1995. The stakeholder theory of the corporation-. Concepts, evidence, and implications. *Academy of Management Review* 20:1, 65-91.

Etzioni, A. 1964. Modern organizations. Englewood Cliffs, NJ: Prentice-Hall.

Etzioni, A. 1988. *The moral dimension.* New York: Basic Books.

Evan, W.M., & Freeman, R.E. 1988. A stakeholder theory of the modem corporation: Kantian capitalism. In Tom L. Beauchamp and Norman Bowie (eds.,) *Ethical Theory and Business*, 3rd ed. Englewood Cliffs, NJ: Prentice Hall.

Eyestone, R. 1978. *From social issue to public policy.* New York: Wiley

Frederick, W.C. 1995. *Values, nature and culture in the American corporation.* New York, NY: Oxford University Press.

Frederick, W.C., Post, J.E., & Lawrence, A. & Weber, J. 1996. *Business and Society: Corporate Strategy, Publick Policy, Ethics*, Eighth Edition. New York, NY.: McGraw-Hill.

Freeman, R.E. 1984. *Strategic management: A stakeholder approach.* Boston: Pitman.

Freeman, R.E. 1994. The politics of stakeholder theory: Some future directions. *Business Ethics Quarterly* 4(4): 409-421,

Freeman, R.E. & Evan, W.M. 1990. Corporate governance: A stakeholder interpretation. *Journal of Behavioral Economics*, 337-359.

Freeman, R.E. & Gilbert, D.R. 1987. Managing stakeholder relationships. Pp. 397-423 in S.P. Sethi and C.M. Falbe (eds.), *Business and Society: Dimensions of Conflict and Cooperation*, Lexington, @: Lexington Books.

Freeman, R.E., & Reed, D.L. 1983. Stockholders and stakeholders: A new perspective on corporate governance. *California Management Review* 25(3): 93-94.

French, J.R.P. & Raven, B. 1960. The base of social power. In D. Cartwright and A.F. Zander (eds.), *Group dynamics* (2nd ed, pp 607-623). Evanston, IL: Row, Peterson.

Granovetter, M. 1985. Economic action and social structure: A theory of embeddedness. *American Journal of Sociology* 91 (3): 481-5 1 0.

Greer, C.R. & Downey, H.K. 1982. Industrial Compliance with social legislation: Investigations of Decision Rationales." *Academy of Management Review*, 7(3):488-498.

Hambrick, D.C. & Mason, P.A. 1984. Upper echelons: The organization as a reflection of its top managers. *Academy of Management Review*, 9:193-206.

Hill, C.W.L., & Jones, T.M. 1992. Stakeholder-agency theory. *Journal of Management Studies*, 29(2): 131-154.

Jensen, M.C. & Meckling, W.H. 1976. Theory of the firm: managerial behavior, agency costs, and ownership structure, *Journal of Financial Economics*, 3:305-360.

Jones, G.R. & Hill, C.W.L. 1988. Transaction cost analysis of strategy-structure choice. *Strategic Management Journal*, 9:159-172.

Jones, T.M. 1980. Corporate social responsibility revisited, redefined. *California Management Review* 22:2 (Spring): 59-67.

Jones, T.M. 1993. Ethical decision-making by individuals in organizations: An issue-contingent model. *Academy of Management Review* 16(2): 366-395.

Kreiner, P. & Bhambri, A. 1988. Influence and information in organization-stakeholder relationships. *Academy of Management Proceedings*, pp. 319-323.

Langtry, B. 1994. Stakeholders and the moral responsibilities of business. *Business Ethics Quarterly* 4(4): 431-443.

Merton, R.K. 1957. *Social theory and social structure*. Glencoe, Il: Free Press.

Meyer, J.W. & Rowan, B. 1977. Institutional organizations: Formal structures as myth and ceremony. American *Journal of Sociology*, 80:340-363.

Näsi, J. 1995. What is stakeholder thinking? A snapshot of a social theory of the firm. Pp. 1932 in Juha Näsi (ed.), *Understanding Stakeholder Thinking*. Helsinki: LSR-Julkaisut Oy.

Näsi, J., Näsi, S. & Savage, G.T. 1994. A stubborn entrepreneur under pressure of a union and the courts: An analysis of stakeholder strategies in a conflict process. In Wartick S. and Collins, D. (eds.) Proceedings of the Fifth Annual Meeting of the International Association for Business and Society, PP. 228-234.

Parsons, T. 1960. *Structure and process in modern societies*. New York: Free Press.

Paul, K. 1992. The impact of U.S. sanctions on Japanese business in South Africa: Further developments in the internationalization of social activism. Business & Society 31(1): 51-58.

Perrow, C. 1986. *Complex organizations: A critical essay.* New York: Random House.
Pfeffer, J. 198 1. *Power in organizations.* Marshfield, MA: Pitman.
Pfeffer, J., & Salancik, G. 1978. *The external control of corporations: A resource dependence perspective.* New York: Harper & Row.
Rhenman, E. 1964. *Foeretagsdemokrati och foeretagsorganisation.* Stockholm, Thule.
Ring, P. S. 1994. Fragile and resilient trust and their roles in cooperative interorganizational relationships. Proceedings of the International Association for Business and Society, pp. 107-113.
Salancik, G.R. & Pfeffer, J. 1974, The bases and use of power in organizational decision-making: The case of universities. *Administrative Science Quarterly,* 19:453-473.
Savage, G.T., Nix, T.H., Whitehead, C.J. & Blair, J.D. 1991. Strategies for assessing and managing organizational stakeholders. *Academy of Management Executive.* 5(2): 61-75.
Scott, W.R. 1987. *Organizations: Rational, natural, and open systems.* Englewood Cliffs, NJ: Prentice-Hall, Inc.
Starik, M. 1993. Is the environment an organizational stakeholder? Naturally! Paper presented at the 4th annual conference of the Inter-national Association for Business and Society, San Diego, CA.
Starik, M. 1994. Essay by Mark Starik. Pp. 89-95 of The Toronto conference: Reflections on stakeholder theory. *Business & Society* 33(1): 82-13 1.
Suchman, M.C. 1995. Managing legitimacy: Strategic and institutional approaches. *Academy of Management Review,* 20(3): 5 71-6 1 0.
Thompson, J.K., Wartick, S.L., & Smith, H.L. 1991. Integrating corporate social performance and stakeholder management: Implications for a research agenda in small business. *Research in Corporate Social Performance and Policy,* Vol. 12, 207-230
Wartick, S.L., & Mahon, J.M. 1994. Toward a substantive definition of the corporate issue construct: A review and synthesis of the literature. *Business & Society* 33(3): 293-311.
Weber, M. 1947. *The theory of social and economic organization.* New York: Free Press.
Wicks, A.C., Gilbert, D.R. Jr., & Freeman, R.E. 1994. A feminist reinterpretation of the stakeholder concept. *Business Ethics Quarterly* 4:4, 475-497.
Williamon, 1975. *Markets and hierarchies.* New York: Free Press.
Williamson, 1985. *The economic institutions of capitalism.* New York: Free Press.

Wilson, E.O. 1974. *Ecology, evolution and population biolboy, readings from Scientific American.* San Francisco, CA: W.H. Freeman.

Windsor, D. 1992. Stakeholder management in multinational enterprises. Proceedings of the International *Association for Business and Society,* 121-128.

Wood, D.J. 1991. "Corporate social performance revisited." *Academy of Management Review* 16:4, 691-718,

Wood, D.J. 1994. *Business and Society,* 2nd Edition. New York, NY.: HarperCollins.

Copyright © *Academy of Management Review,* 1997.
Reprinted with permission from the Academy of Management.

Stakeholder Mismatching: A Theoretical Problem in Empirical Research on Corporate Social Performance

Donna J. Wood
Raymond E. Jones
University of Pittsburgh

This paper uses a stakeholder framework to review the empirical literature on corporate social performance (CSP), focusing particularly on studies attempting to correlate social with financial performance. Results show first that most studies correlate measures of business performance that as yet have no theoretical relationship (for example, the level of corporate charitable giving with return on investment). To make sense of this body of research, CSP studies must be integrated with stakeholder theory. Multiple stakeholders (a) set expectations for corporate performance, (b) experience the effects of corporate behavior, and (c) evaluate the outcomes of corporate behaviors. However, we find that the empirical CSP literature mismatches variables in terms of which stakeholders are relevant to which kind of measure. Second, only the studies using market-based variables and theory show a consistent relationship between social and financial performance, particularly those showing a negative abnormal return to the stock price of companies experiencing product recalls. Although this paper shows that the CSP construct is not yet well-specified enough to produce stronger results, recent research suggests that much progress is being made both empirically and theoretically in developing valid and reliable measures of corporate social performance.

The literature on corporate social performance (CSP) has yet to develop an accepted depiction of what CSP is and what it should be. Previous research has provided a few of the pieces of the puzzle in terms of showing a variety of perspectives on the roles and responsibilities of business, how they are fulfilled, and how they can be measured. However, viewing this research as a true body of knowledge has been difficult in the absence of a broad and more integrative context. The CSP literature is still most accurately seen as a vast collection of disparate views of interpenetrating business and society relationships. We propose that stakeholder theory, despite its minimal development to date, is the most relevant theoretical framework for assessing corporate social performance. Most research in CSP, however, relies implicitly or explicitly on the neoclassical economic theory of the firm. In this paper we review the empirical literature in corporate social performance, arguing that this body of literature produces ambiguous results largely because the studies have not chosen variables and predicted relationships that would be appropriate within a stakeholder/CSP framework. In short, the theory and the methods have been incongruent; thus, not surprisingly, the results have been disappointingly thin.

Stakeholders and Corporate Social Performance

There is a decades-long debate concerning the roles and obligations of business in society. The neoclassical economic view stems from Friedman's (1962, 1970) contention that "the social responsibility of business is to make a profit." On the other hand, the social responsibility/performance view, represented by scholars in the field of business and society (or social issues in management, SIM), has focused on business's interdependencies with other elements of society and the responsibilities that arise because of these interrelationships. The development of the corporate social performance (CSP) model and two of its principal components, corporate social responsibility and corporate social responsiveness, has been documented elsewhere (see Frederick, 1994; Preston, 1986; Wood, 1991a, 1991b). Also published elsewhere (Wood & Jones, in press) is a review and analysis of empirical work deriving from the conceptual works of Carroll (1979), Preston and Post (1975), Wartick and Cochran (1985), and Wood (1991a). In this paper we will only review the stakeholder-related empirical CSP literature, using a modified version of Wood's (1991) definition of corporate social performance as principles, processes, and outcomes. The difference is in the "outcomes" portion of her model, which is originally given as "policies, programs, and outcomes," and which we redefine as "internal stakeholder effects, external stakeholder effects, and external institutional effects." We make this change to better assess the stakeholder implications of corporate social performance measures.

Most business and society scholars have attempted either openly or implicitly to remain within the neoclassical paradigm, although arguing to broaden its parameters and incorporate its externalities (Kang & Wood, in press). Scholars operating within this tradition have been quite concerned with demonstrating an empirical link between corporate social performance (variously defined and operationalized) and financial performance (using standard accounting or market-based measures). Lately, however, some scholars have begun to move toward a new theory of the firm—a stakeholder theory—that would permit a more complex analysis and understanding of company-society relationships (e.g., Brenner & Cochran, 1991; "Toronto," 1994; Mitchell, Agle & Wood, 1995; Clarkson, 1995; Donaldson & Preston, 1995; Swanson, 1994, 1995). We propose that stakeholder theory holds the key to understanding the structures and dimensions of business-and-society relationships, since it is the essential foundation for discerning the relationships among various indicators of corporate performance.

Stakeholders—groups and organizations that are affected by or can affect a company's operations (Freeman, 1984)—are the answer to the question, "To whom should the firm be responsible?" Eventually corporate social performance will be understood within a stakeholder-based theoretical perspective—not as a set of self-interested "strategic" acts, or as a way of muddling through environmental complexities, but as a framework within which firms can engage more fully in their societal relationships and duties. Stakeholders are not unitary entities which serve a single function for a firm; rather, they engage in many different behaviors with respect to the firm, while filling several critical roles. Consistent with Wood's (1991a) three-part corporate social performance model, we propose that stakeholders serve at least three roles with respect to corporate social performance:

1. Stakeholders are the *source of expectations* about what constitutes desirable and undesirable firm performance.
2. Stakeholders *experience the effects* of corporate behavior, that is, they are the recipients of corporate actions and output.
3. Stakeholders *evaluate* how well firms have met expectations and/or how firms' behaviors have affected the groups and organizations in their environment.

Otherwise put, as sources of expectations, stakeholders define the norms for corporate behavior; they fill with normative content Wood's structural principles of social responsibility. As those who experience the effects of corporate behavior, stakeholders are acted upon by firms and they act upon firms, via processes of social responsiveness (playing an active role with respect to a firm) as well as being the literal recipient of corporate action and outcome (playing an active or a passive role). This dimension of stakeholder relationship cuts across Wood's second and third categories. Finally, as evaluators, stakeholders make judgments about their experiences, the experiences of other stakeholders, and the degree to which expectations have been met by firm performance. They are intimately involved with assessing firm's outcomes (Wood's third category), and they provide feedback so that an iterative corporate social performance process is continually in play (see Epstein, 1987). In short, stakeholders define the norms for corporate behavior; they are acted upon by firms; and they make judgments about these experiences.

As we shall see, a great deal of research in CSP is implicitly oriented toward evaluating a firm's effectiveness in meeting certain needs and expectations of particular stakeholders. Despite this bottom-line approach, most of the empirical work in CSP displays a serious mismatch of variables which are mixed and correlated almost indiscriminately with a set of stakeholder-related performance variables that are not theoretically linked. In particular, this research has taken no account of the fact that different stakeholders might set expectations, experience the effects, and evaluate the outcomes for a particular measure of corporate performance; that is, multiple stakeholders can be involved in different ways in a single instance of firm behavior. Measures of CSP almost never take this stakeholder multiplicity into account. Furthermore, stakeholder theory has the potential to provide systematic predictions about relationships among variables representing these different stakeholders, if the notions could be dispelled that CSP can be defined by just about any available nonfinancial measure, and that CSP however defined should be related to any measure of financial performance. Our analysis demonstrates this theoretical and methodological incongruity and suggests ways to conduct CSP research in a manner that avoids the problem of stakeholder-variable mismatch.

Research Defining Corporate Social Performance

Early definitions of corporate social responsibility were too vague to rigorously guide theoretical development, nor could they be operationalized for research purposes. Some examples follow:

1. [CSR is] the firm's consideration of, and response to, issues beyond the narrow economic, technical, and legal requirements of the firm...[to] accomplish social benefits along with the traditional economic gains which the firm seeks. (Davis, 1973, pp. 312-313)

2. The fundamental idea of 'corporate social responsibility' is that business corporations have an obligation to work for social betterment. (Frederick, 1994, p. 150)

Scholars in the 1980s and 1990s built on the theoretical contributions of their predecessors by systematically integrating such topics as interpenetrating systems (Preston & Post, 1975), social betterment (Frederick, 1994), and responsiveness (Ackerman, 1975) into theories of corporate social *performance*. Wartick and Cochran (1985) made the initial effort to synthesize the various conceptual threads of SIM into a comprehensive model, building on Carroll's (1979) depiction of a three-dimensional model of corporate social performance. Wood (1991a, 1991b) continued the effort, constructing a model (slightly adapted in Figure 1) that currently organizes much of the research and thinking about corporate social performance today (Carroll, 1994). The intellectual development of the CSP concept, and research done at each stage of development, are discussed in this section.

Carroll's Four Domains
Carroll (1979) defined corporate social responsibility as encompassing "the economic, legal, ethical, and discretionary expectations that society has of organizations at a given point in time" (p. 500). In his CSP model, Carroll constructs a three-dimensional box, bounded by "economic, legal, ethical, and discretionary expectations" (p.499) on one axis, management philosophies on the second axis, and particular social issues on the third axis. This model, although intuitively appealing, has not been very helpful in guiding empirical research. There are something like ninety boxes in Carroll's own depiction, and it is not clear what exactly is supposed to be found within them. However, Carroll's easily operationalizable idea that businesses have *economic, legal, ethical,* and *discretionary* responsibilities has been used in empirical research by a number of SIM scholars.

Most research using Carroll's four-part description of CSR categories has sought to validate his contention that managers consider economic responsibilities to be fundamental, followed in order of magnitude by legal and ethical responsibilities, and then (if resources permit) discretionary (philanthropic) responsibilities. Aupperle (1984) constructed a survey instrument consisting of 20 items, each containing four statements (one for each of Carroll's four dimensions of CSR). Respondents (192 CEOs) were asked to allocate up to ten points across the statements for each item. Mean scores showed that CEOs did weight the dimensions as Carroll had proposed. Factor analysis, however, showed that the economic and ethical dimensions appeared to be opposing ends of a single factor rather than two distinct factors. Aupperle reported this finding but did not follow through in interpreting it, choosing instead to emphasize the mean-score distribution across the four dimensions of CSR and lending weight to Carroll's assertion that economic factors come first, then legal, ethical, and discretionary factors. Correlation analysis showed that the economic factor was negatively related to each of the other factors, which showed weak positive relationships among themselves.

Aupperle, Carroll, and Hatfield (1985) were unable to find a relationship between CEOs' "social orientation," using Aupperle's questionnaire described above (1984), and financial performance or profitability measures. Likewise, Pinkston and Carroll (1993) found no relationships between managers' CSR orientation (using the Aupperle scale) and organizational size. Attitudinal research using Aupperle's scaling of Carroll's four categories of social responsibility has produced few significant empirical results.

Although this remains a point of some confusion among scholars, Carroll's model does emphasize that the *fundamental* responsibility of business is economic. While his work is an attempt to extend the neoclassical paradigm to accommodate societal relationships and the effects of business operations, Carroll's main emphasis is that "the business of business is business."In practice, unfortunately, this view of business can mean that legal, ethical, and discretionary (charitable) responsibilities might be "put on hold" if business is bad or times are tough (see Kang & Wood, in press).

Development of the CSP Concept
The idea of social responsibility has its modern roots in the work of Berle and Means (1932), who documented a separation of control from ownership in large corporations. The purpose of the organization—the control function of the firm—was to maximize the firm's self-interest, which was ostensibly the interests of owners, but in practice overlapped to a large extent with the interests of managers. Early definitions of CSR were tied more to society's interests than to those of the firm. Preston and Post (1975) moved social responsibility closer to firm self-interest, albeit "enlightened self-interest" (see Keim, 1978a, 1978b), and opened the door to a new action-oriented way of thinking that came to be called "corporate social responsiveness" or, in Frederick's (1994) shorthand—CSR_2, defined as "the capacity of a corporation to respond to social pressures" (p. 154).

Ackerman (1975) was also an early proponent of the self-interested/public affairs approach to corporate social responsiveness. He argued that a company must act "responsibly" in meeting societal expectations about how a business should perform in order to increase its financial performance. The corollary was that a company might not improve financial performance by meeting "discretionary" responsibilities (those that went beyond what was expected of business by society). Ackerman's social responsiveness approach was similar to Preston and Post's public policy approach, in that "social performance" was seen as guided solely by the firm's self-interest. Morality, ethics, and "discretionary" or voluntaristic behaviors were not necessarily part of responsiveness.

Ackerman suggested that CEO involvement was crucial to the success of responsible/responsive programs, but some research has shown that corporate responsiveness need not be CEO-driven. In a comparative study of corporate responses to youth unemployment in (former) West Germany and Great Britain, Antal (1992) discovered that responsive innovations happen at many corporate levels, and can be communicated and supported in several directions, including middle-up, lateral, and middle-out (not just top-down). Nevertheless, there is widespread support for the idea that top management support for a company's charitable giving program—and likely other aspects of CSP as well—is essential. Miles (1987) took the view of responsiveness as a result of self-interest even further by emphasizing the "external affairs function" of business. Miles claimed that business needed to *appear* responsible, in addition to undertaking activities in society's best interests, in order to achieve greater profits. The external affairs function was viewed as an outcome of top management philosophy and business exposure (or industry variables). To Miles, responsibility was a means to the end of increasing financial performance.

This self-interested view of social responsibility and performance in some ways is stronger than ever in SIM literature. For example, observe the attention paid to cause-related marketing and strategic philanthropy (Burke, Logsdon, Mitchell, Reiner, and Vogel, 1986; Smith & Alcorn, 1991). In this literature, a firm's philanthropic activity is seen as a means of producing some benefit (financial or otherwise) for the firm as well as providing some benefit to society. This research reflects the assumption that the economists are right about self-interest as the "prime mover" in human and organizational affairs, even as business and society scholars strive to introduce other motives and incentives into the picture.

The development of this literature from the early days of Preston and Post (1975) up through the recent work on cause-related marketing and strategic philanthropy can be characterized by the simple idea that CSR/CSP would be supported by managers and their decision making processes if only it could be shown that companies can "do good and do well," or even better, that they can "do well by doing good." This literature, however, has provided little explanation of why companies undertake "discretionary" activities that may or may not produce benefits, which may or may not be measurable. Furthermore, this simplistic connection between "social" and "financial" performance has rarely received a serious challenge. The problem with blindly accepting this narrow view of CSP, however, is that only *owners are seen as having the right to evaluate corporate performance, and only that performance judged to be relevant to owners is an appropriate concern of management*. These suppositions are in clear violation of a stakeholder model of the firm, which would suggest that *all* stakeholders have certain rights in evaluating firm performance. Thus, a variety of measures of firm performance might be appropriate and desirable when measuring some aspect of corporate social performance, but few measures (and no extant measure) could accurately represent the CSP construct as a whole.

Wartick and Cochran's CSP Model
After the development of important concepts like interpenetrating systems, public responsibility and social responsiveness were articulated, scholars began to view the business and society relationship as a complex web that could not simply be explained by examining how business influences society. The recent literature on corporate social performance has advocated this broader view of business and society. Wartick and Cochran (1985) were the first to show how a corporate social performance model could move the SIM field beyond the basic pro-and-con debates on social responsibility, economic vs. social responsibility, and responsibility vs. responsiveness. Toward this objective, they incorporated three major "challenges" to corporate social responsibility (which they identify as economic responsibility, public responsibility, and social responsiveness) into their CSP model, which consisted of three segments: (1) principles of corporate social responsibility (using Carroll's categories of economic, legal, ethical, and discretionary responsibility as "principles"), (2) processes of corporate social responsiveness (reactive, defensive, accommodative, and interactive), and (3) issues management. They emphasized that CSP can *integrate* the various concerns of business and society thinking (for example, firms' social, economic, and public responsibilities), thus promoting more rigorous theory development in the field.

Extensive research to test the ideas of the Wartick and Cochran CSP model has been conducted by Clarkson and his colleagues, using a case-study database gathered on Canadian companies over a ten-year period. In early publications, Clarkson praised the Wartick and Cochran model for its ability to emphasize economic performance as business's primary responsibility, without excluding legal, ethical, and discretionary responsibilities. He saw the model as a means of connecting social responsibility and ethics with the firm's primary objective—profitability. Clarkson attempted to measure Wartick and Cochran's concept of social responsiveness by identifying companies that exemplified "best practices" in responding to changing values, issues, and conditions in the management of specific social issues (such as human relations, natural environment, community relations, and ethics policies). He analyzed the social responsiveness of 32 Canadian firms and found that the data confirmed Aupperle's (1984) study on the relationship between economic performance and the social performance orientations of managers. He provided some evidence for the contention that the more economically motivated a firm is, the less emphasis it will place on legal, ethical, and discretionary issues and responsibilities (Clarkson, 1988).

In his most recent work, however, Clarkson (1995) has declared that the Wartick and Cochran CSP model is *not effective* in guiding research on corporate social performance. He now believes that "a fundamental problem...has been that there are no definitions of...corporate social responsibility (CSR_1) or corporate social responsiveness (CSR_2) that provide a framework or model for the systematic collection, organization, and analysis of corporate data" (p.92). This shift in Clarkson's opinion of the construct validity of social responsiveness, as defined by Wartick and Cochran, came as a result of his increased exposure to and acceptance of stakeholder theory as a means of understanding CSP. Instead of focusing on the processes by which social responsiveness occurs, Clarkson is now interested in the relationship between stakeholder theory and ethical management in the workplace ("Toronto," 1994). Clarkson believes that the construct "social responsiveness" cannot effectively deal with multiple stakeholder interests; similarly, the Wartick and Cochran CSP model alone cannot push the theory of the firm away from its neoclassical roots toward a stakeholder approach.

Wood's CSP Model
Wood (1991a, 1991b) built on Wartick and Cochran (1985) to articulate structural principles of social responsibility, to show how processes of social responsiveness have defined much of the research in SIM, and to focus on outcomes of corporate behavior as indicators of "performance." In this model, corporate social performance is defined as a *business organization's configuration of principles of social responsibility, processes of social responsiveness, and observable outcomes as they relate to the firm's societal relationships* (Wood, 1991a, p.693). These three facets of CSP are interlinked and consist of subdimensions, including structural principles at the individual, organizational, and institutional levels; corporate processes of environmental assessment, stakeholder management, and issues management; and policies, processes, and stakeholder outcomes that result from organizational activities.

In his expert panel research, Carroll (1994) found that among recently published papers, Wood's CSP model was widely believed to be the most influential for the future of SIM research over the next decade. Collins (1992) attempted an explicit link between Wood's CSP model and stakeholder theory. Arguing that CSP could be defined only in relation to specific stakeholders, he constructed a matrix with Wood's CSP dimensions down the column and various critical stakeholder categories (customers, owners, employees, etc.) across the rows. In the cells of the matrix were to be ratings of corporate performance on each CSP dimension with respect to each stakeholder group. Despite the fact that Collins has not yet been able to work out a satisfactory rating system, this work is potentially fruitful.

Mallott (1993), attempting to test both Carroll's CSR hierarchy and Wood's CSR principles, interviewed middle-level and senior managers who related stories they considered to reflect corporate social responsibility and irresponsibility. She found that managers did not easily distinguish between legal and economic CSR, that ethical issues were seen as both personal and organizational in nature, and that discretionary CSR was a poorly understood concept. She also found that managers related well to the principle of public responsibility (Preston & Post, 1975), but did not grasp Wood's macrolevel principle of business legitimacy or the microlevel principle of managerial discretion. Mallott correctly observed that managers' failure to see these principles does not mean that they do not exist; but research to substantiate their existence still remains to be done. Key's (1995) dissertation research may shed some light on the question of managerial perceptions of the extent and nature of their CSP-related discretion.

Mitnick (1993, 1994) has applied general systems theory to Wood's CSP model to show how the various concepts involved in CSP—Carroll's social responsibility categories, Wood's social responsibility structural principles, Ackerman's responsive processes, Sethi's social responsiveness types, Preston and Post's interpenetrating systems, Freeman's stakeholders, Wartick and Cochran's issues management, and more—can be systematized and sorted according to their contribution to the guidance, implementation, or evaluation of a CSP "system." Although Mitnick does not go so far as to derive a theoretical logic for CSP, he does show how to use systems theory as a "sorting logic" for the various competitive concepts in CSP.

The development of the CSP concept shows no clear differentiation among the interests, expectations, experiences, or evaluations of corporate stakeholders. And yet such differentiation is essential if CSP theory is to continue to develop. In the next section, as we discuss the various ways corporate social performance has been measured in empirical research, we will show how an implicit stakeholder model is underlying most of these measures.

Measuring Corporate Social Performance

In addition to the conceptual development of corporate social performance, a great many studies have been done attempting to measure CSP and to relate it to firm financial performance. In this section, we review some of the more commonly-used CSP measures, before moving on in the next section to a stakeholder-based analysis of this literature.

While the theoretical development of CSP has shown the need to consider business and society in a broader framework, the empirical research on CSP has provided a number of interesting findings which suggest that it is possible to measure various dimensions of the complex business and society relationship. A vast array of measures has been used in empirical research on corporate social performance. Some measures indicate the results of company *responses* (either verbal or procedural) to particular social issues, such as minority or female workers or pollution abatement. Some measures merely indicate the company's *intent* to address social problems, for example, the existence of written policy statements on minority hiring or pollution control. Events such as factory explosions, plane crashes, oil spills, or product recalls have been used as negative indicators, or measures of corporate social irresponsibility (CSI). A company's objective record of criminal convictions or regulatory fines has been similarly used to indicate CSI. Some measures, such as the *Fortune* "most admired" ratings, are based on executives' own assessments of their and others' performance. The percent of pretax earnings donated to charity has been used as a CSP measure. Newer indices, such as the 1980s Sullivan Principles compliance scale or the 1990s KLD social investment scale, are crude rankings of company performance on several dimensions believed to be part of overall CSP. Because both the *Fortune* and KLD ratings are composite indices in current use, we will describe each of them briefly.

Every year *Fortune* magazine publishes its Corporate Reputation Survey, a list of America's most admired corporations. These "reputation" rankings are based on an opinion poll which measures the perceptions of large corporations among over 8,000 senior executives, outside directors, and financial analysts. More than 300 companies in 32 industries are included in the list. The *Fortune* index measures such subjective attributes as management quality, product quality, innovativeness, long-term investment value, financial soundness, ability to attract and retain talented people, responsibility to the community and environment, and wise use of corporate assets. Multiple regression analysis is applied to the data to obtain a reputation rating from 1 (low) to 10 (high). Not surprisingly, given the nature of the respondents, "quality of management" is typically considered the most important attribute of corporate reputation by those polled.

Although it is an interesting example of how various corporate managements are perceived by peers and "intimates," the *Fortune* ranking has questionable value and validity as a measure of CSP. Are companies "admired" simply because they have good financial performance? Perhaps good financial performance plus a strong public affairs focus gets a company to the top of the list (witness Philip Morris's top 5 position for several years). In fact, there does appear to be a "financial halo effect" which, when statistically removed, generates data that is a more reliable indicator of a firm's nonfinancial reputation (Brown & Perry, in press). More importantly, a firm can achieve an overall high score on "reputation," but still be very deficient in certain areas of social performance. Whose reputation is better: a firm with mediocre scores on all the measures or a firm with widely varying scores (say, very high financial performance and very low community performance)? Those who use these rankings as a CSP measure justify it with an "everybody thinks so" defense, which skirts the core CSP issue of what a company is actually doing and what its actual impacts are (see Thomas & Simerly, 1994). There is no theoretical basis for using the *Fortune* scale as a measure of corporate social performance, although it can certainly be used as an indicator of corporate reputation among executives and the financial community.

The KLD scale is a new composite indicator of corporate performance on a number of socially relevant dimensions. Kinder, Lydenberg & Domini (1993) is a social investment firm that specializes in "social choice" investing. Although the KLD ratings have been available for only a few years, they are already gaining wide acceptance as "social screens" among investors and investment analysts. The firm produces a social performance rating (KLD rating) on more than 800 publicly held firms based on performance on the following variables: product liability, community relations, South African involvement, nuclear power involvement, employee relations, environmental protection (pollution), women and minority issues, military contracting, and other CSP-relevant dimensions.

The Domini 400 Social Index (DSI) is an index of 400 common stocks of companies based on their performance on multiple applications of the KLD social performance screens. Aside from the social screens, this index mirrors the Standard & Poor 500. The DSI is predicated on the belief that customers and investors will choose products and companies that have favorable social performance ratings. Firms deemed to have an adequate score on these various screens, therefore, are portrayed in the investment community as "socially responsible firms" that are worthy candidates for social investing (Domini, 1994).

Although it is the best-researched and most comprehensive CSP measure currently available, there are a number of challenges that can be brought against the KLD ratings and the Domini Social Index. First, as a measure of corporate social performance, the numerical ratings are very crude (normally a 1-3 scale, and sometimes a 0-1 scale to indicate presence or absence of some trait) and are based on qualitative judgments about company performance, often taken from inadequate or self-reported information. Second, unweighted scores on the various screens are added to achieve an overall rating score for a company, even though there is no conceptual basis for believing that all screens carry equal importance. Third, and perhaps most conceptually limiting, no explanation is offered as to why these categories of activity are included and not others, or even why these categories are considered to indicate "social performance." There is an unfortunate "political correctness" factor in the KLD ratings, in that they are based on such high profile issues as South Africa and environmental protection. Other measures of CSP, such as the extent to which a company employs child labor, or presence in repressive countries other than South Africa, or political action activities, are not considered. Nevertheless, early comparisons show that *the Domini 400 has outperformed other lists* in terms of financial returns. In 1993, for example, the Domini 400 had a total return of 56.38 percent compared to the S&P 500's return of 46.54 percent (Brill & Reder, 1993). This does not prove the validity of the KLD rating or the Domini index (Sharfman, 1993), but it suggests that the idea of "doing well by doing good" may have some empirical basis.

Overall, the great disparity of CSP measures used has made it very difficult for research to cumulate. Measures are developed for certain purposes—say, to test for a statistical link between corporate crime and accounting measures such as ROI (see Baucus, 1989; Baucus & Near, 1991)—and they may not be readily transferrable to other purposes such as the development of a general theory of corporate social performance. In the remainder of this paper, we will examine the empirical research in CSP, represented by 65 separate studies, to see what we can learn about CSP and the emerging stakeholder theory of the firm.

To Whom Does Corporate Social Performance Make a Difference?

The most challenging and potentially fruitful question which has been addressed by the vast empirical research in CSP is this: "Who benefits from corporate social performance?" The various attempts to ask and answer this question have provided a great deal of interesting evidence suggesting that CSP does in fact influence business's performance and its relationships with stakeholders in society. In the neoclassical economic theory of the firm, CSP would be a viable concept only if it increased shareholder value. Friedman (1970) objected to the idea of corporate social responsibility (with an assumption that CSR was costly) on the grounds that managers had no right to spend owners' money on unprofitable aims and interests. So, the search has been on for many years to link CSP with firm financial performance and to show that CSP is not unprofitable. At worst, such a theory would show that CSP was benign; at best, CSP would be shown to be in the firm's best economic interests. "Enlightened self-interest" would stand as the ultimate justification for CSP.

Arlow and Gannon's (1982) review of research in CSP drew no conclusions about the relationship between firm social and financial performance. Ullmann (1985) surveyed the literature on social and financial performance and reported very mixed results. There were no consistent or accepted measures of CSR or CSP, and even worse, there was no sound theoretical reason why CSR/CSP *should* be related to financial performance. Ullmann's title, "Data in Search of a Theory," hints that, like a Pirandello play, the search for such a relationship might belong in the theatre of the absurd. Yet, although the idea of stakeholder theory has been in the literature and represents a potentially powerful theoretical vehicle for making these links, it has been too undeveloped to be a candidate for supplanting the traditional neoclassical economic view. Thus, researchers have been locked into at least an implicit acceptance of the neoclassical position that CSP is only justifiable as "enlightened self-interest," even though intimations of a more complex stakeholder approach have long existed.

Frooman (1994) has updated and gone beyond Ullmann's work, using the statistical techniques of meta-analysis, to produce the most comprehensive and interesting discussion of social-financial performance links currently in existence. Frooman groups studies according to the type of measure used to indicate economic performance. He finds that, regardless of the CSP measure used, mixed and ambiguous results are obtained in the aggregate from studies that use accounting measures, market share or sales measures, investor return measures, or risk measures as indicators of economic performance. However, of the nine event studies that correlated abnormal stock returns with the announcement of a socially irresponsible event, eight of them showed significant negative returns following the event announcement. In addition, we discovered two more studies showing negative stock price results following announcement of corporate criminal involvement (Randall & Neuman, 1979; Weir, 1983), bringing the consistency finding to ten of eleven studies; that is, *it appears that the stock market does indeed punish firms for socially irresponsible behavior.* Among the studies showing negative returns, CSP indicators included product recalls, accusations of criminal misconduct, and the publication of pollution indices. (The one insignificant finding used airplane crashes as the CSI indicator, suggesting that crashes may be seen as uncontrollable tragedies rather than corporate irresponsibility.)

Finance colleagues may not see what all the shouting is about. In fact, most of these event studies have been conducted by finance scholars who do not see the CSP or stakeholder implications of their findings. Product recalls are expensive and hurt profitability; criminal misconduct is expensive and may hurt profitability; a bad pollution rating means expensive clean-up operations and possible loss of good will, resulting in lower profit potential. Of course owners and their broker-agents will take these future cost possibilities into account when valuing the firm's worth and establishing a price for its stock! But for our purposes, the overlooked point is that in these event studies, the *dependent and independent variables are appropriately matched in terms of stakeholder relevance.* Stockholders will experience harm from the costs incurred by irresponsible firm behavior; stockholders will feel their *expectations* to be violated; stockholders will negatively *evaluate* such firm behavior and will punish it.

What if event studies were conducted using the same independent variable, but with a dependent variable relating to *another* stakeholder's interest in the event? Imagine, for example, the event of a product recall and its effect on *customers*. Do they lose or retain or gain trust in the company? Do they stop buying the type of product recalled, or do they switch brands? Do they share their knowledge of the recall with others in their social network (cooperative/communal behavior), or keep the news to themselves (hostile/competitive behavior)? Next, imagine relating a product recall to its effect on *distributors*. Do they experience unjust harms and loss of customer trust based on a faulty product from a supplier? Are they involved in litigation over the product, either as injured parties or as perpetrators of customer injury? Do they demand expensive and cumbersome contractual guarantees from future suppliers, based on their recall experience? Next, in the same way, imagine relating a product recall to its effect on any other stakeholder group that would be affected by it (say, regulators, employees, or competitors), and one begins to see why Frooman's research brings very exciting news to scholars of CSP and stakeholder theory.

The question, "to whom does corporate social performance make a difference?" necessarily involves stakeholders. These groups and organizations in the firm's environment that can affect or are affected by the firm's operations are the missing link in empirical studies of CSP and in our theoretical understanding of the firm in society. There is no theory to explain why stockholders would or would not prefer a company that gives one percent of pretax earnings to charity, or that hires and develops minority or women workers, or that ranks higher in pollution control indices. Yet most CSP research assumes that such preferences will exist, and that stockholders are the most (or only) appropriate stakeholder group for assessing the results of CSP, regardless of how it has been measured. Ullmann (1985) pointed out that a positive relationship between the two "could indicate that a company's management is dealing effectively with the firm's external stakeholders and their multiple demands" (p. 541). However, such an overall relationship cannot be asserted until the strands that make it up—the links among stakeholder expectations, effects, evaluations, and behaviors with respect to a firm—have been delineated.

McGuire, Sundgren, and Schneeweiss (1988) do not propose a coherent theory that would explain a relationship between firm social and financial performance, but they do briefly review a number of theoretical perspectives on such a relationship. In this context, they discuss stakeholder theory and its relevance to corporate social performance as follows:

> modern corporate stakeholder theory (Cornell & Shapiro, 1987) contends that the value of the firm depends on the cost not only of explicit claims but also of implicit claims. From this viewpoint, the set of claimants on a firm's resources goes beyond the stockholders and bondholders to include stakeholders who have explicit claims on the firm like wage contracts and others with whom the firm has made implicit contracts, involving, for instance, quality service and social responsibility. If a firm does not act in a socially responsible manner, parties to implicit contracts concerning the social responsibility of the firm may attempt to transform those implicit agreements into explicit agreements that will be more costly to it. For example, if a firm fails to meet promises to government officials in regard to actions that affect the environment (dumping, etc.), government agencies may find it necessary to pass more stringent regulations, constituting explicit contracts, to force the firm to act in a socially responsible manner. Moreover, socially, irresponsible actions may spill over to other implicit stakeholders, who may doubt whether the firm would honor their claims. Thus, firms with an image of high corporate social responsibility may find that they have more low-cost implicit claims than other firms and thus have higher financial performance (McGuire, Sundgren, & Schneeweiss, 1988, p. 856).

It should not be difficult to see, through all this economic talk of contracts implicit and explicit (see also Donaldson & Preston, 1995), that the key variable is the degree of *trust* in the stakeholder relationship (Calton & Lad, 1994; Calton & Ring, 1994). Boal and Peery (1985), in their research on the "cognitive structure" of CSR, claim that a "stakeholder perspective" is not supported by their data, yet they did find that their subjects differentiated the interests of owners, employees, customers, and society at large and appeared to understand that balancing of these interests was a necessary management task. Based on their findings, they offer these guidelines for socially responsible management decision making: "an acceptable decision outcome should be economically worthwhile, should justly affect stakeholders, and should either protect or promote the rights of those affected" (p. 80).

In a stakeholder theory, the question, "to whom does CSP make a difference?" would be broadened to include *stakeholders* in addition to stockholders. Understanding the empirical literature on CSP in a stakeholder context would require a better grasp of what dimensions of corporate-stakeholder relationships are most salient and how they are represented in empirical measures. Based upon their particular interests and levels of involvement in a company, stakeholders may:

1. *establish expectations* (which may be explicit or implicit, and which may or may not be communicated) about corporate performance,
2. *experience the effects* of corporate behaviors (with or without awareness of their source),
3. *evaluate the effects* or potential effects of corporate behaviors on their interests, or the fit of corporate behaviors with their expectations, and
4. *act* upon their interests, expectations, experiences, and/or evaluations.

Empirical research in CSP and stakeholder relationships must be concerned with (1) which stakeholder is setting the expectations that are relevant to the CSP measure being used, (2) which stakeholder experiences the effects of company behavior, (3) which stakeholder is evaluating the company's performance (and on what basis does the stakeholder evaluate performance), and (4) which stakeholder(s) are acting with respect to the firm.

For example, consider a hypothetical study that attempts to relate corporate charitable giving with stockholder returns. *Expectations* are set by industry (as in the 5 or 2 Percent Clubs), by government (which sets tax-deductible limits on corporate charitable giving), and by community group recipients (which argue for gifts based on the essential services they provide). The stakeholders *experiencing the effects* of corporate giving would include communities, agencies, and their clients. However, the *evaluative* stakeholder in such a study is only the owner group; neither the stakeholders setting expectations nor those experiencing effects are judging the outcomes of corporate performance. And, it is conceivable that no stakeholder at all is acting with respect to the firm's behavior in this case. Thus, in order for all these variables to be logically related, there would have to be a theory about how owners would evaluate information about charitable giving with respect to *their own* interests. The neoclassical argument about enlightened self-interest and charitable giving tends to be seen for what it is—a weak and easily defeated stance for "doing good... just because."

Stakeholders and CSP: An Analysis of Empirical Research

In order to push toward a stakeholder theory of corporate social performance, we conducted a meta-analysis of empirical studies of CSP. We assumed that CSP measures could be said to represent the interests and/or expectations of one or more stakeholder groups, and we grouped the studies according to the stakeholder(s) represented in the CSP measure. Space limitations prevent a full exposition here, but some of the data tables are shown below.

Community/Charity Studies

Table 1 shows a summary of CSP studies that use community involvement or charitable giving as a measure of CSP. The far righthand column of the table (and also Tables 2 through 5) provides brief summaries of the empirical relationships found between the CSP measure and other measures used in the studies.

Two findings shown in this table confirm what we already know about corporate charitable giving from regular Conference Board reports: larger firms give more money in absolute terms (Levy & Shatto, 1980), but larger firms give a lower proportion of their pretax earnings (Kedia & Kuntz, 1981). Also, Wokutch and Spencer (1987) tell us that companies giving a larger amount to charity are more likely to be highly ranked on this dimension in the *Fortune* reputation ratings; that is, their benevolent generosity is noted by executives and financial analysts.

Many of the findings concerning community involvement or charitable giving as a measure of CSP are ambiguous. Virtually all studies of CSP defined as community involvement or charitable giving present only descriptive statistics or correlations with company or industry structural characteristics. The implicit assumption seems to be that it is something about the company itself—its size, its product base, its ownership structure—that drives the company's community relations patterns. However, these results are very difficult to interpret. What do we know, for example, when we have seen that firms with highly concentrated ownership give a lower proportion of their earnings to charity? The direction of causality, if any is implied, is not clear. For example, do firms giving a larger proportion to charity therefore earn higher returns for owners, or do firms earning higher returns therefore give a larger proportion to charity? These questions arise from the implicit "enlightened self-interest"

Table 1: CSP studies relating to the community

Source	Year	CSP Measure	Direction of Findings*	Variables Related to CSP Measure
Cohn	1970	donations (financial or industrial)	+	industry type
Eilbert & Parket	1973	alphabetical list of 15 socially responsive behaviors		descriptive statistics show educational donations, minority employment, and pollution as high-involvement issues.
Corson & Steiner	1974	modified Eilbert & Parket scale of corporate involvement using the CED issues list		descriptive statistics show minority employment, donations, and pollution control as high-involvement issues.
Buehler & Shetty	1975	modified Eilbert & Parket scale of corporate involvement in 15 social issues		descriptive statistics show minority employment, urban renewal, and donations as high-involvement issues.
Holmes	1977	modified CED issues list		descriptive statistics show charitable contributions, education assistance, minority hiring/development, and community affairs as top 5 social issues, with some industry variance.
Ingram	1978	community donations & involvement disclosure		Uninterpretable relationships.
Keim	1978	"social effort" (philanthropy)	+ −	increasing smaller size increasing larger size

*Note: The "Direction of Findings" column briefly shows the statistical relationships of the CSP measure to other variables used in the study. "+" indicates a positive relationship, "−" a negative relationship, and "ns" a nonsignificant relationship with the variable listed in the last column, "Variables Relating to CSP Measure."

Table 1: CSP studies relating to the community (continued)

Source	Year	CSP Measure	Direction of Findings*	Variables Related to CSP Measure
Levy & Shatto	1980	charitable contributions	+	size of customer service expenditure
			+	size of advertising expenditure
			+	firm size (book value of equity)
			ns	firm income
			ns	regulatory agency posture on charitable giving
Kedia & Kuntz	1981	% charitable contributions	-	firm charter (state or federal regulation)
			-	ownership concentration
			-	corporate market share
			-	firm size
			-	firm income
Wokutch & Spencer	1987	philanthropic donations	+	high rating on Fortune "most admired" Item 8: "responsiveness to community and environment."
Morris, Rehbein, Hosseini, & Armacost	1990	sponsorship of community activities	+	organizational size
			+	long-term profitability
Pinkston & Carroll	1993	importance ranking of organizational stakeholders	ns	size. However, owners, consumers, & employees were ranked higher than communities and government.

*Note: The "Direction of Findings" column briefly shows the statistical relationships of the CSP measure to other variables used in the study. "+" indicates a positive relationship, "-" a negative relationship, and "ns" a nonsignificant relationship with the variable listed in the last column, "Variables Relating to CSP Measure."

underpinnings of most of these studies, but the studies simply do not address the questions of whose interests are served by firm charitable contributions, and what are the effects on the firm of those contributions?

Employee Studies

Very few significant results have been obtained when employees are used as the relevant stakeholder group for measuring CSP. From Pinkston and Carroll (1993) we get the descriptive information that managers consider employees to be important stakeholders and employee health and safety issues to be important to the firm. The limited statistical findings available show that larger firms are more likely to have a mandatory retirement policy (considered with little discussion to be negative CSP; Copperman, 1981), that companies with an employee newsletter have better long-term profitability (Morris Rehbein, Hosseini, & Armacost, 1990), and that diversified firms are more likely to have OSHA violations (Hill, Kelley, & Agle, 1990). Roman and Blum (1987) show that companies with managers that have more socially responsible attitudes are more likely to have Employee Assistance Programs (but one might wonder why employees of those companies are so overstressed as to need EAPs).

We suggest that this poverty of findings results from a mismatch of stakeholder measures. We would like to see a study that correlates data on treatment of employees (e.g., the existence of employee-friendly programs and policies) and variables such as placement on "the 100 best companies to work for," union organization, strike data, average wage and benefits rates compared to industry averages, and health and safety records. Such a study would not accept the idea that it is solely the responsibility of owners to evaluate how a company treats employees, as is the case with studies correlating employee variables with profits or stock price.

Social Justice/EEO Studies

Seven studies were categorized as relating to social justice and in particular, equal employment opportunity (EEO), using some measure of the treatment of minorities and women by corporations (Cohn, 1970; Eilbert & Parket, 1973; Corson & Steiner, 1974; Buehler & Shetty, 1976; Holmes, 1977; Ingram, 1978; Kedia & Kuntz, 1981). Most of these studies have to do with minorities and women as employees; a handful are concerned with minorities as customers. Kedia and Kuntz (1981) provide the best descriptive findings, showing that companies with larger proportions of minority employees tend to be larger, have more market share, and have facilities in neighborhoods with large minority populations. The same study found that the proportion of women officers was *negatively* related to these same organizational variables. Other studies in this set are so methodologically flawed that no reliable conclusions can be drawn from them.

Customer and Consumer Studies

When customers (buyers) or consumers (users) are the relevant *affected* CSP stakeholder, and the *evaluation* of CSP is being conducted by either customers or owners, a great many significant statistical relationships appear. Voluntary disclosure of product safety information yielded no interpretable results in Ingram's (1978) study, but most studies display statistically significant findings, as we see in Table 2.

Interestingly, two studies show *positive* relationships between product recalls and sales. Sales data are often used as a surrogate for organizational size, which would suggest that larger companies experience more product recalls. This result could be interpreted as merely a descriptive relationship; large companies sell more things and so would be expected to have more product recalls by the laws of probability. *Proportionally*, however, we do not know if larger (or higher sales) companies have more problems with product recalls; this would be interesting information about CSP.

The remainder of the studies using customers as a relevant stakeholder group are event studies that display an astonishing consistency in results, consistent with Frooman's (1994) finding regarding CSP studies using this methodology. Product recall announcements result in negative and permanent abnormal stock returns, in that investors calculate the future costs of bad product decisions and operationalize this calculation through the price they are willing to pay for a stock.

Finance and economics scholars have asserted for many years that their models work, that they can explain large amounts of variance in the variables they use, that their relationships are highly significant statistically, and that their theories are predictive. The problem is, from a CSP perspective, *they appear to be right*—given their theory, data, methods, and interpretive models. But in the context of broad intertwining stakeholder relationships and responsibilities, *they cannot be right*. Table 2, showing results of studies using customers as the affected stakeholder of CSP and owners as the evaluative stakeholder, demonstrates this dilemma and also points to a hopeful interpretation for CSP scholars. Consider that the 25-year search for a relationship between corporate social and financial performance has met with practically no success *except* when variables are chosen that represent stakeholders acting within *market* mechanisms. Markets are taking notice of irresponsible firm behavior because such behavior results in additional costs for the firm and, by extension, its owners. This finding should not be taken to mean that the economic model of the firm is correct after all, but that CSP scholars can learn something from the power of this model—when applied by its own rules— and then go beyond it toward a stakeholder theory of the firm in society. Independent and dependent measures must be correlated only within a cogent theory of their relationship.

Table 2: CSP studies relating to the customers or consumers

Source	Year	CSP Measure	Direction of Findings*	Variables Related to CSP Measure
Wynn & Hoffer	1976	product recalls	ns	market share
Ingram	1978	product safety/improvement disclosure		Uninterpretable relationships
Crafton, Hoffer, & Reilly	1981	product recalls	+	sales
Reilly & Hoffer	1983	product recalls	+	sales growth
Jarrell & Peltzman	1985	product recalls		Negative returns (event study)
Pruitt & Peterson	1986	product recalls		Negative returns (event study)
Davidson, Chandy, & Cross	1987	airplane crashes		No significant abnormal returns (event study)
Hoffer, Pruitt, & Reilly	1988	product recalls		Negative returns (event study)
Bromiley & Marcus	1989	product recalls		Negative returns (event study)
Davidson & Worrell	1992	product recalls		Negative returns (event study)
Pinkston & Carroll	1993	importance ranking of organizational	ns	size, but owners, consumers, stakeholders and employees were ranked higher than communities and government.

*Note: The "Direction of Findings" column briefly shows the statistical relationships of the CSP measure to other variables used in the study. "+" indicates a positive relationship, "–" a negative relationship, and "n.s." a nonsignificant relationship with the variable listed in the last column, "Variables Relating to CSP Measure."

Natural Environment Studies

To illustrate how we might proceed to build such a cogent theory, Table 3 shows results of CSP studies using the natural environment as the primary stakeholder affected by corporate behavior. Market-based studies are the only ones to show significant results. Spicer (1978a) found positive relationships between better pollution performance and several accounting measures of profitability, and in a second study (1978b) showed that higher risk factors correlated with worse pollution performance. Holman, New, and Singer (1985) correlated two accounting measures and find a negative relationship between federal pollution compliance liability costs and total rate of return. Higher costs/lower return is a simple market relationship that is not muddied by involvement of other stakeholders. Similarly, Shane and Spicer (1983) correlated the CEP pollution performance index with stock price and found negative abnormal returns for poor pollution performance (that is, a positive relationship between the variables but demonstrated only in a downward direction). Owners are apparently concerned with the idea that poor pollution performance may result in future fines, clean-up costs, technology upgrades, and additional costly regulation, and they adjust polluting stocks downward accordingly.

Most other studies concerning pollution performance, however, show no significant relationships among the variables used. We suggest again that stakeholder mismatches are responsible. Why would one expect pollution rankings to be correlated with accounting measures of financial performance (an indicator of customer evaluations of the firm), unless there were some organized, large-scale, systematic effort to boycott high-polluting firms and purchase from cleaner ones? Why would a company's disclosure of its pollution performance in the annual report (used largely by *owners* or potential investors) have any effect on profitability (again, an indicator of *customer* expectations, effects, and evaluations)? One wants instead to see studies correlating pollution ratings of companies *by environmental interest groups* and, as a surrogate for the environment itself, measures of actual pollution performance in absolute and relative terms. Also, studies relating pollution performance to corporate political action on environmental matters, as well as differential regulatory rulemaking and compliance efforts of the government, would be very interesting and would provide a much better match of stakeholder involvements.

Corporate Reputation Studies

Reputational indices include the early ones produced by Moskowitz (1972), the annual reputation rankings by *Fortune*, and more recently the KLD (Kinder Lydenberg Domini) scale. These indices have occasionally

Table 3: CSP studies relating to the natural environment

Source	Year	CSP Measure	Direction of Findings*	Variables Related to CSP Measure
Bragdon & Marlin	1972	CEP pollution index	+	return on equity
Eilbert & Parket	1973	alphabetical list of 15 socially responsive behaviors		descriptive statistics show educational donations, minority employment, and pollution as high-involvement issues.
Corson & Steiner	1974	modified Eilbert & Parket of corporate involvement using CED issues		descriptive statistics show minority employment, scale donations, and pollution list as high-involvement issues.
Fogler & Nutt	1975	Government pollution indices	ns ns ns	price/earnings ratio mutual fund purchases common stock price
Belkaoui	1976	pollution disclosure in annual reports	+	monthly average residuals (but result was temporary)
Ingram	1978	environmental disclosure in annual report		Uninterpretable relationships.
Spicer	1978a	CEP pollution performance index	+	return on equity, price/earnings ratio, total risk, and beta for three periods, 1968-1973
Spicer	1978b	CEP pollution performance index	-	risk
Ingram & Frazier	1980	CEP pollution performance index	ns	pollution disclosure in annual reports

*Note: The "Direction of Findings" column briefly shows the statistical relationships of the CSP measure to other variables used in the study. "+" indicates a positive relationship, "-" a negative relationship, and "ns" a nonsignificant relationship with the variable listed in the last column, "Variables Relating to CSP Measure."

Table 3: CSP studies relating to the natural environment (continued)

Source	Year	CSP Measure	Direction of Findings*	Variables Related to CSP Measure
Chen & Metcalf	1980	CEP pollution performance index	+	financial return variables but this relationship is spurious and due to size).
Freedman & Jaggi	1982	CEP pollution performance index	ns	social disclosure in annual report
Wiseman	1982	CEP pollution performance index	ns	social disclosure in annual report
Shane & Spicer	1983	CEP pollution performance index	-	stock price (event study)
Holman, New, & Singer	1985	Federal pollution compliance liability costs	-	total rate of return
Rockness, Schlachter, & Rockness	1986	pollution performance		ambiguous results w/ 12 accounting ratios
Pinkston & Carroll	1993	prioritization of social issues	ns	size, but employee health & safety, regulatory compliance liability costs & environmental protection rated high across all organizational sizes.

*Note: The "Direction of Findings" column briefly shows the statistical relationships of the CSP measure to other variables used in the study. "+" indicates a positive relationship, "-" a negative relationship, and "ns" a nonsignificant relationship with the variable listed in the last column, "Variables Relating to CSP Measure."

been used as a measure (or better, a surrogate) for corporate social performance on the assumption that companies with better reputations would be better social performers. Table 4 summarizes studies using these CSP indicators.

The stakeholder groups represented by reputational ratings are somewhat ambiguous. The Moskowitz ratings, for example, merely represent one person's judgment about how well a company is or is not meeting its social responsibilities. Given the nature of respondents, using the *Fortune* ratings as an indicator of social performance could be seen as similar to asking the foxes how well they keep guard over the henhouses. The KLD ratings, although more specifically targeted than the others at corporate social involvements, and ranging across a broader field of behaviors, are still crude and subjective indicators of company performance on a small set of questionable social responsibility dimensions. Are these measures good surrogates for overall societal views of firms? The answer is probably "no," although better measures are not yet available.

However, it can be argued that the ratings are a somewhat accurate representation of "corporate image" (and it can be argued that to some extent this is true—especially for the Fortune ratings). McGuire, Sundgren, and Schneeweis (1988) purported to show a significant relationship between CSP and financial performance. But in fact, what they showed was a relationship between financial performance and companies' reputations in the eyes of peers—other executives and financial analysts. Finally, the KLD database is new and will require further study before conclusions can be drawn about it as a CSP measure.

Information Disclosure Studies

Twelve studies used some measure of CSP information disclosure and related this disclosure to company financial performance. Many of these studies use the Social Involvement Disclosure Scale developed by Ernst & Ernst, a scale of the number of social involvement disclosures in company annual reports. A few studies did independent content analysis of annual reports for their CSP disclosure measure. One study (Kohls, 1985) used a process-oriented scale rather than a disclosure-oriented one.

Some studies find positive relationships between CSP disclosure and earnings (Fry & Hock, 1976; Preston, 1978; Bowman, 1978; Anderson & Frankle, 1980); two find negative relationships (Ingram & Frazier, 1983; Holman, New & Singer, 1985); one study reports a U-shaped curve (Bowman & Haire, 1975); and others find no relationship at all (Abbott & Monsen, 1979; Freedman & Jaggi, 1982). Kohls (1985) reports positive relationships between CSR disclosure in annual reports and the existence of responsive processes in the firm.

Table 4: CSP studies relating to corporate reputation

Source	Year	CSP Measure	Direction of Findings*	Variables Related to CSP Measure
Moskowitz	1972	apparently, author's perception of CSR (social responsibility)		Socially responsible firms outperform the Dow-Jones average
Parket & Eilbert	1975	response to their earlier survey = CSR	+	profit margin, return on equity, and earnings per share
Vance	1975	CSR company list from *Business & Society Review* (Moskowitz scale)	-	stock price increases
Fry & Hock	1976	Students' evaluation of industry reputation	-	CSP disclosure in annual report (worse reputation, more disclosure)
Heinze	1976	CSR company list from *Business & Society Review* (Moskowitz scale)	+	return on equity
Sturdivant & Ginter	1977	28 high-CSR firms from *Business & Society Review*	+	10-year growth in earnings per share
Alexander & Buchholz	1978	high-CSR firms from *Business & Society Review*	ns	2-year & 5-year stock price increases

*Note: The "Direction of Findings" column briefly shows the statistical relationships of the CSP measure to other variables used in the study. "+" indicates a positive relationship, "-" indicates a negative relationship, and "ns" a nonsignificant relationship with the variable listed in the last column, "Variables Relating to CSP Measure."

Table 4: CSP studies relating to corporate reputation *(continued)*

Source	Year	CSP Measure	Direction of Findings*	Variables Related to CSP Measure
Preston	1978	Moskowitz reputational scales	ns	Ernst & Ernst social disclosure scale
Cochran & Wood	1984	Moskowitz ratings: best, honorable mention, worst CSP	+	operating earnings/sales
			ns	operating earnings/assets
			+	asset age (measure of inefficiency)
McGuire, Sundgren, & Schneeweis	1988	*Fortune* reputation ratings	+	return on assets
			+	asset growth in one period
			-	debt/asset ratio
			ns	total assets
			ns	income
			ns	sales growth
			ns	total return
Cottrill & Faust	1991	*Fortune* reputation ratings	-	foreign sales
			-	foreign sales as % of total sales
Graves & Waddock	1994	KLD scale/ smart management	+	number of institutional investors
			+	percent of shares owned by institutional investors

*Note: The "Direction of Findings" column briefly shows the statistical relationships of the CSP measure to other variables used in the study. "+" indicates a positive relationship, "-" indicates a negative relationship, and "ns" a nonsignificant relationship with the variable listed in the last column, "Variables Relating to CSP Measure."

In this set of studies, the theoretical problem of stakeholder mismatching is apparent. Disclosure of information in annual reports might be assumed to have some effect on stock prices if owners or potential owners actually evaluate such information in relation to the firm's assumed financial worth as they make their investment decisions. But why would CSR disclosure have any impact on, or any relationship with, accounting measures of financial performance, which are more accurately seen as results of customer evaluations than of stockholder valuations? What stakeholders are involved in setting expectations, experiencing effects, or evaluating results? These unclear research findings reflect the lack of theoretical clarity in relating corporate social performance to stakeholder dimensions.

Responsiveness Studies

It is easier to make a theoretical argument about why a company's social responsiveness structures and processes might have an impact on profitability or stock price than it is to make the same argument about social responsibility. In Wood's (1991a) CSP model, processes of social responsiveness refer to how the firm manages information, people and organizations, and issues in its environment. These management questions can easily be tied to a firm's financial performance. For example, it makes sense to hypothesize that companies undertaking extensive systematic environmental assessment will be more profitable than companies without such assessment. Such companies would have the early advantage in spotting new market trends, juggling variations in resource flows, and grappling with political issues before they become detrimental. Similarly, it makes sense to hypothesize that companies with systematic stakeholder management processes—for example, public affairs offices for government and community relations, ethics ombudsmen for employees and external critics, and well-staffed customer and investor relations departments—would be more profitable. Such companies pay attention to the many demands and expectations placed upon them, are better situated to gather information about stakeholder interests and activities, and can better respond to stakeholders, thus creating positive alliances among stakeholders and warding off negative effects of stakeholder actions. Indeed, stakeholder management processes seem likely to hold the key to understanding corporate social performance from a stakeholder perspective.

Seven studies of CSP using indicators of responsiveness were included in our analysis. The results, however, do not tell us very much. Not surprisingly, some studies show that the existence of responsive mechanisms such as integrating social issues into strategic planning (Aupperle, 1984) or the existence of a public affairs unit (Sonnenfeld, 1982) correlates with a greater awareness of social problems. We do not learn, however, whether this greater awareness has any payoffs for the firm or its stakeholders. Newgren Rasher, LaRoe, and Szabo (1985) found a positive relationship between a company's use of environmental analysis and one measure of financial performance—the price/earnings ratio (but why?), and Morris et al. (1990) show a relationship between the existence of a public affairs office and long-term profitability. Otherwise, relationships between responsive structures and financial performance have been statistically insignificant (Mitchell, 1983; Aupperle, Carroll & Hatfield, 1985) or uninterpretable (Holmes, 1978).

Governance Studies
Very little quantitative research has been conducted on the governance aspects of CSP. Aupperle, Carroll, and Hatfield (1985) found no relationship between the existence of a social responsibility committee on the board of directors and firm financial performance (and indeed, why would there be such a relationship?). Kohls (1985) found that companies with a higher proportion of outside directors scored *lower* on his responsive process scale (a negative relationship), but the existence of a public policy or CSR committee of the board of directors was positively correlated with the existence of responsive processes. Since no other studies were discovered in this category, little can be said regarding the validity of corporate governance indicators as measures of CSP.

A stakeholder theory of CSP might suggest that CSP-supporting governance structures might serve as moderating or mediating variables in a relationship between, say, top management values and behaviors, and firm financial performance, because of the board's responsibility to oversee and direct basic management policy and direction. This hypothesis has yet to be tested empirically.

Studies of Managers' Values
Miles (1987) suggested that the philosophy of the top management team was a critical factor in the degree to which a company exhibited social responsiveness. Carroll (1979) also emphasized this factor in his model of corporate social performance. The studies that have attempted to use managers' values as a CSP indicator have all been based upon Carroll's four categories of CSR (economic, legal, ethical, and discretionary/philanthropic responsibilities), and use some variant of Aupperle's forced-choice measurement instrument. Aupperle (1984) found a positive relationship between his measure of "concern for economic performance" (vs. "concern for society") and a firm's total risk, but did not obtain significant results when correlating his "concern" measure with any financial performance variables, firm size, or industrial sector. Aupperle,

Table 5: *CSP studies relating to legal, illegal or regulatory behaviors*

Source	Year	CSP Measure	Direction of Findings*	Variables Related to CSP Measure
Randall & Neuman	1979	prosecution for antitrust violations		Decline in stock prices in the week following announcement of prosecution
Strachan, Smith, & Beedles	1983	accusations of criminal misconduct		Negative returns (event study)
Weir	1983	conviction for illegal acquisition or merger		Negative returns (event study)
Wokutch & Spencer	1987	criminal behavior criminal behavior + low charitable contributions	ns - -	Fortune rating on "community/environment" return on assets return on equity
Davidson & Worrell	1988	accusations of criminal misconduct		Negative returns (event study)
Baucus	1989	conviction for illegal behavior (antitrust, product liability, discrimination, other)	+ + - ns ns ns ns	environmental dynamism organizational size environmental scarcity organizational slack declining financial performance return on equity sales

*Note: The "Direction of Findings" column briefly shows the statistical relationships of the CSP measure to other variables used in the study. "+" indicates a positive relationship, "–" a negative relationship, and "ns" a nonsignificant relationship with the variable listed in the last column, "Variables Relating to CSP Measure."

Table 5: CSP studies relating to legal, illegal or regulatory behaviors (continued)

Source	Year	CSP Measure	Direction of Findings*	Variables Related to CSP Measure
Hill, Kelley, & Agle	1990	OSHA violations	ns + ns ns	organizational size degree of diversification decentralization poor financial performance
Pinkston & Carroll	1993	importance ranking of organizational stakeholders	ns	size, but owners, consumers, & employees were ranked higher than communities and government.
Pinkston & Carroll	1993	prioritization of social issues	ns	size, but employee health & safety, regulatory compliance, & environmental protection rated high across all organizational sizes.

*Note: The "Direction of Findings" column briefly shows the statistical relationships of the CSP measure to other variables used in the study. "+" indicates a positive relationship, "–" a negative relationship, and "ns" a nonsignificant relationship with the variable listed in the last column, "Variables Relating to CSP Measure."

Carroll, and Hatfield (1985) obtained similar results while showing that total risk was negatively correlated with "concern for society." Pinkston and Carroll (1993) found no relationship between organizational size and managers' social responsibility orientation (e.g., economic, legal, ethical, or philanthropic). Results have not been impressive, but this is understandable when one considers that the studies have not drawn explicit empirical links between managers' expressed values (or more accurately, preferences among four CSR categories) and their behaviors. In addition, they have not considered the interests and involvements of the stakeholders who are setting expectations, experiencing impacts, and evaluating results.

Legal/Regulatory Behavior Studies

Finally, in Table 5, studies examining CSP from a legal or regulatory compliance aspect are summarized. The event studies, showing that investors negatively evaluate the announcement of criminal accusation or conviction, are consistent in their findings of negative abnormal returns to stock prices following news of criminal conduct—alleged or demonstrated. Wokutch and Spencer (1987) show that companies with criminal convictions and low rates of charitable giving tend to have lower financial performance as measured by return on assets and return on sales. The other studies in this set, however, are either impossible to interpret or report no significant findings.

Again, as has been the case in so many other studies, a theoretical mismatch of stakeholder involvements may be to blame for these inconclusive results. For example, imagine if Baucus were to extend her data into a longitudinal study of corporate crime and its effects, showing eventually that criminal companies are more closely monitored by government, are less likely to get what they want from the public policy process, and over time have much higher regulatory compliance and legal defense costs than do noncriminal companies. Such a study would examine the consequences of lawbreaking from the point of view of a stakeholder—government—that is more intimately involved than owners. Or, imagine if Hill, Kelley, and Agle correlated OSHA violations with long-term OSHA compliance requirements (suggesting, perhaps, that government is a legitimate evaluator of regulatory compliance, and that firms might choose not to violate the law because of the likelihood of incurring higher future transaction costs). Or, OSHA violations could readily be correlated with unionization and union activity such as strikes or slowdowns, or even more relevant, contract negotiation demands concerning health and safety conditions (thus recognizing that employees are relevant evaluators of a CSP factor that affects them directly).

Toward A Stakeholder Theory of Corporate Social Performance

Some interesting findings appear when studying these tables of empirical work in CSP, grouped by the stakeholders of interest. First, it is apparent that Preston and Post's (1975) idea of corporate public responsibility existing in the areas of the firm's primary involvements with society is confirmed again and again. Companies commit to different kinds of social programs, policies, projects, and involvements, depending on the nature of their industry and their business exposure.

Second, it appears that consistent findings arise when *market measures* and market-oriented stakeholders are matched in the same study. Frooman's (1994) finding that event studies produce a consistent relationship between irresponsible acts and negative stock returns reflects a good theoretical match between measures. It makes sense, in market terms, that owners would evaluate the long-term financial implications (liability payouts and litigation costs, future cost of insurance, additional regulatory constraints, possible consumer boycotts, etc.) and adjust the price of the stock accordingly.

Third and we believe most interesting, a great many of the empirical studies we have reviewed exhibit a *mismatch of variables* when seen within the context of stakeholder theory. For example, ROE, ROI, and similar profitability accounting measures of profitability *do not indicate owners' evaluation of a firm's social performance.* Although they provide information that can then be used in decision making by anyone with an interest in buying, selling, or retaining stock, they are too narrowly focused to tell us much about how a company's stakeholder set is evaluating, and consequently acting upon, the firm's social performance. In fact, we could suggest that these studies use these measures not because *owners* use them, but because *managers* do. Thus, managers represent the great hidden stakeholder in corporate life and in corporate social performance.

Neoclassical economic theory insists that managers are agents of owners and are obliged to act as fiduciaries for owner's limited financial interests in the firm's performance. Berle and Means (1932) argued, however, that managers of large publicly owned companies are rarely subjected to direct owner control. Cyert and March's (1963) behavioral theory of the firm emphasizes that managers respond to a great many incentives, including their own self-interest. Agency theory and transaction costs economics place a great deal of emphasis on the problems of controlling agents who are far removed from principals, or who exhibit behavior that is very costly for principals to monitor and correct. In the field of business and society, we have already seen the effects of the dramatic conceptual shift in the 1970s from responsibility (which put managers too much in the spotlight and on the hook) to responsiveness (which allowed aggressive corporate political action to supplant moral

Table 6: Shareholders and corporate social performance

CSP Factor	Who sets expectations?	Who experiences the effects?	Who evaluates outcomes?
Product Safety	*Customers*— through demand	Customers and consumers— injuries and other harms.	Customers Consumer protection advocates Market analysts Government
	Government— through regulation	Customers— as above. Government-lobbying, Congressional oversight of regulation, etc. Insurance firms—through liability claims Stockholders — through effects on profitability and stock price	Government Public and electorate Courts Customers
Environmental Pollution	*Government*— through regulation	Natural environment Employees & families Communities Future generations	Government Public and electorate Activist groups Scientists
	Customers— through demand	Natural environment Employees & families Communities Future generations	Government Activist groups Economists Financial analysts Stockholders

Table 6: Shareholders and corporate social performance (continued)

CSP Factor	Who sets expectations?	Who experiences the effects?	Who evaluates outcomes?
Charitable Giving	*Communities*—through fund drives, moral suasion, etc.	Communities The least well-off The arts Educational organizations and their students	Communities The poor, sick, and disadvantaged, and helping agencies. Arts patrons & donors, arts organizations. Schools, parents, boards of education, and government.
	Government—through tax laws	same as above, plus taxpayers	same as above, plus tax bureaus and taxpayers.
	Industry—through benchmarking	same as above, plus competitors	same as above, plus competitors and industry associations.

responsibility). Does anyone wonder why Philip Morris, purveyor of tobacco and political action, consistently makes *Fortune's* top-five most admired companies list?

Mismatching of variables in CSP studies reflects our general scholarly confusion about what companies are about and who should be evaluating them. Our contention is simple, although the theoretical implications are complex: Expectations, effects, and evaluations need to be better matched in terms of the stakeholder(s) involved. Several examples of how one might think about matching appropriate stakeholders with events or CSP measures are shown in Table 6. On the issue of product safety, for example, expectations are set for the most part by *customers*—through market demand for safety features, safety testing, and price vs. safety tradeoffs; and by *government*, through regulation and adjudication. Customers and consumers (differentiating buyers from users) are the principal stakeholders who experience the effects of corporate product safety decisions and their own market choices. These outcomes, however, are evaluated by a variety of stakeholders, including customers, activist groups, market analysts who watch for stockholder effects, and government agents who watch for legal or regulatory needs. The other two issues illustrated in the table, environmental protection and charitable giving, can be thought about it the same way: different stakeholders may set expectations, experience effects, and evaluate outcomes.

This way of conceptualizing complex stakeholder involvements in a firm's activities provides more depth for understanding how relationships between stakeholders and a firm (and among stakeholders themselves) arise and are nurtured (or not), change and grow, explode into controversy or merge in warm alliances, and die. Measures will need to be developed that take into account the different stakeholders that are setting expectations, experiencing effects, and evaluating outcomes on any particular social performance issue or dimension.

Wood ("Toronto," 1994) has pointed out the difference between the bicycle-wheel model of stakeholder management (viewing stakeholders as things to be managed, see Carroll & Horton, 1994), and an interactive model of stakeholders in the environment (viewing stakeholders as members of relationships that are mutually driven and not completely controlled by on party or the other). The bicycle wheel approach results in a self-interested view of stakeholder management, while the interactive approach yields eventually to a social justice model of the firm in society (Kang, 1995).

The needs and interests of all the various stakeholders who will affect and be affected by corporate actions must be considered in any comprehensive approach to corporate social performance. The bicycle spoke model of stakeholders simply does not have the capability to look beyond corporate self-interest in "managing" these troublesome relationships.

A more systematic treatment of CSP will be achieved in future research by examining such questions as:

1. the type of power over resources that each stakeholder has with respect to the firm (e.g., symbolic, material, or coercive power),
2. the nature (number, complexity, type) of the issues involved in the relationship,
3. the ways in which stakeholders express their expectations and evaluations,
4. the ways in which the company receives and interprets those expectations and evaluations, and acts upon them.

Corporate Social Performance and Stakeholder Theory: Tentative Conclusions

The benefit of having a large body of empirical research available for review is that some findings are confirmed (as in the event studies showing market attention to corporate irresponsibility), some findings suggest directions for replication or extension, and some point to entirely new areas for research. A few tentative conclusions can be made from this paper's analysis of CSP research:

Conclusion 1: The performance of a business firm has no simple set of antecedents, and no simple consequences. Causality is complex.

Conclusion 2: Businesses do involve themselves, as Preston and Post predicted, in social responsibility activities related to their primary areas of involvement with society.

Conclusion 3: The relationship between corporate social performance and financial/economic performance is still ambiguous because (a) there is still no theory to clarify how these two should be related, although we are moving closer to such a theory by considering the importance of stakeholders to CSP, (b) there is no comprehensive, valid measure of CSP, (c) most studies are lacking in methodological rigor and are therefore of uncertain validity, reliability, and generalizability, and (d) there is confusion about which stakeholders are represented by which measures.

Conclusion 4: Event studies consistently show a relationship between news of social irresponsibility and abnormal negative stock returns. This is the only methodology that has produced such consistent results. We conclude that it is not the methodology per se that is so powerful, but the appropriate match of variables within a cogent theory that this methodology demands. Market measures, used within market-based theory and illustrating market processes, *do show a relationship between social and financial performance.* However, the demonstrated relationship is expressed negatively—bad social performance hurts the company financially—whereas we would prefer to have a theory and set of results expressing a positive relationship—good social performance helps the company financially.

Conclusion 5: An extrapolated finding, not directly addressed in any of these studies but implicit in the "grand view" of them as a body of literature, is this: The social control of business occurs through business's relationships with stakeholders. *Public policy controls* (law, regulation, litigation, public agendas), *market controls* (consumer, owner, employee, supplier, and competitor expectations and behaviors), and *normative controls* (moral suasion, symbols, references to values, or reputation) do exist. These controls can be related to the nature of stakeholder expectations, experiences, and evaluations of firm behavior, and so can inform a stakeholder theory of corporate social performance. This is a fruitful area for future research.

How corporate social performance is viewed is often a matter of what measurement tool is selected. Although the measures that have been used so far have focused on particular areas of CSP, and although many of them have value, they have limited use in depicting how and why specific stakeholder relationships occur and develop. Many of these measures have no underlying logic that explains why the variables being measured and correlated are supposed to produce meaningful results. The empirical rigor and mathematics of CSP theory are not just underdeveloped, but missing. CSP theory at present needs to be better integrated with stakeholder theory. Many scholars in the field are working toward such an integration, and great progress is being made. We hope to have contributed to these advances with this paper, and we look forward with excitement to continued developments in this area.

Donna J. Wood
Katz Graduate School of Business
University of Pittsburgh
Pittsburgh, PA 15260
Phone/Fax: 412-648-1547/1693
E-mail: djwood@vms.cis.pitt.edu.

Dr. Wood is Professor of Business Administration at the Katz Graduate School of Business, University of Pittsburgh. She is a founder and executive officer of the International Association for Business and Society (IABS), and has served as Chair of the Social Issues in Management Division of the Academy of Management. Currently she is editor is the IABS journal, Business & Society. Dr. Wood's research interests focus on corporate social performance and stakeholder theory, international dimensions of business and society relationships, collaborative social problem solving, business ethics, and business-government relations.

Raymond E. Jones is a doctoral student at the Katz Graduate School of Business, University of Pittsburgh. His research interests include corporate social performance, stakeholder theory, and business ethics.

Abbott, W. F., & Monsen, J. R. (1979). On the measurement of corporate social responsibility. *Academy of Management Journal*, 22, 501-515

Ackerman, R. W. (1975). *The social challenge to business.* Cambridge, MA: Harvard University Press.

Alexander, G. J., & Buchholz, R. A. (1978). Corporate social responsibility and stock market performance. *Academy of Management Journal*, 21, 479-486.

Anderson, J. C., & Frankle, A. W. (1980). Voluntary social reporting: An iso-beta portfolio analysis. *Accounting Review*, 55, 467-479.

Antal, A. B. (1992). *Corporate social performance: Rediscovering actors in their organizational contexts.* Frankfurt am Main: Campus Verlag.

Arlow, P., & Gannon, M. J. (1982). Social responsiveness, corporate structure, and economic performance. *Academy of Management Review*, 7, 235-241.

Aupperle, K. E. (1984). An empirical measure of corporate social orientation. In L. E. Preston (Ed.), *Research in corporate social performance and policy* (Vol. 6, pp. 27-54). Greenwich, CT: JAI Press.

Aupperle, K. E., Carroll, A. B., & Hatfield, J. D. (1985). An empirical examination of the relationship between corporate social responsibility and profitability. *Academy of Management Journal*, 28, 446-463.

Baucus, M. S. (1989). Why firms do it and what happens to them: A reexamination of the theory of illegal corporate behavior. In J. E. Post (Ed.), *Research in corporate social performance and policy* (Vol. 11, pp. 93-118). Greenwich, CT: JAI Press.

Baucus, M. S., & Near, J. P. (1991). Can illegal corporate behavior be predicted? An event history analysis. *Academy of Management Journal, 34,* 9-36.

Belkaoui, A. (1976). The impact of the disclosure of the environmental effects of organizational behavior on the market. *Financial Management,* 5 (1), 26-31.

Berle, A. A., & Means, G. C. (1932). *The modern corporation and private property.* New York: Macmillan.

Boal, K. B., & Peery, N. (1985). The cognitive structure of corporate social responsibility. *Journal of Management,* 11, 71-82.

Bowen, H. R. (1953). Social responsibilities of the businessman. New York: Harper.

Bowman, E. H. (1978). Strategy, annual reports, and alchemy. *California Management Review,* 20 (1), 64-71.

Bowman, E. H., & Haire, M. (1975). A strategic posture toward corporate social responsibility. *California Management Review,* 18 (1), 49-58

Bragdon, J. H., & Marlin, J. T. (1972). Is pollution profitable? *Risk Management,* 19 (1), 9-18.

Brenner, S. N., & Cochran, P.L. (1991). The stakeholder theory of the firm: Implications for business and society theory and research. *IABS Proceedings,* 449-467.

Brill, J., & Reder, A. (1993). Profit from your principles. *Financial Executive,* 9 (1), 54-56.

Bromiley, P., & Marcus, A. A. (1989). The deterrent to dubious corporate behavior: Profitability, probability, and safety recalls. *Strategic Management Journal,* 10, 233-250.

Brown, B., & Perry, S. (in press). Halo-removed residuals of Fortune's "responsibility to the community and environment:" A decade of data. *Business & Society,* 34.

Buehler, V. M., & Shetty, Y. K. (1975). Managing corporate social responsibility. *Management Review,* 64 (1), 4-17.

Burke, L., Logsdon, J. M., Mitchell, W., Reiner, M., & Vogel, D. (1986). Corporate community involvement in the San Francisco Bay area. *California Management Review,* 28 (3), 122-141.

Calton, J. M. (1992). What is at stake in the stakeholder model? *IABS Proceedings,* 205-214.

Calton, J. M., & Lad, L. J. (1995). Social contracting as a trust-building process of network governance. *Business Ethics Quarterly,* 5, 271-296.

Calton, J. M., & Ring, P.S. (1994). Symposium: Trust and trust building processes. *IABS Proceedings*, 233-239.

Carroll, A. B. (1979). A three-dimensional conceptual model of corporate social performance. *Academy of Management Review*, 4, 497-505.

Carroll, A. B. (1994). Social issues in management research: Experts' views, analysis, and commentary. *Business & Society*, 33, 5-29.

Carroll, A. B., & Horton, G. T. (1994). Do joint corporate social responsibility programs work? *Business and Society Review*, 90, 24-28.

Chen, K. H., & Metcalf, R. W. (1980). The relationship between pollution control record and financial indicators revisited. *Accounting Review*, 55 (1), 168-177.

Clarkson, M. B. E. (1988). Corporate social performance in Canada, 1976-86. In L. E. Preston (Ed.), *Research in corporate social performance and policy* (Vol. 10, pp. 241-265). Greenwich, CT: JAI Press.

Clarkson, M. B. E. (1995). A stakeholder framework for analysing and evaluating corporate social performance. *Academy of Management Review*, 20, 92-117.

Cochran, P. L., & Wood, R. A. (1984). Corporate social responsibility and financial performance. *Academy of Management Journal*, 27, 42-56.

Cohn, J. (1970). Is business meeting the challenge of urban affairs? *Harvard Business Review*, 48 (2), 68-82.

Collins, D. (1992, August). *An organization performance matrix: A framework for broad-based performance measurements*. Paper presented at the annual meeting of the Academy of Management, Las Vegas, NV.

Copperman, L. F. (1981). Employer policies and the older worker. In L. E. Preston (Ed.), *Research in corporate social performance and policy* (Vol. 3, pp. 175-201). Greenwich, CT: JAI Press.

Cornell, B., & Shapiro, A. (1987). Corporate stakeholders and corporate finance. *Financial Management*, 16 (1), 5-14.

Corson, J. J., & Steiner, G. A. (1974). *Measuring business' social performance: The corporate social audit*. New York: Committee for Economic Development.

Cottrill, M., & Faust, B. (1991). Corporate social performance and foreign sales exposure. *IABS Proceedings*, 354-360.

Council on Economic Priorities. (1977). *The pollution audit*. New York: C=EP.

Crafton, S. M., Hoffer, G. E. & Reilly, R. J. (1981). Testing the impact of recalls on the demand for automobiles. *Economic Inquiry*, 19, 694-703.

Cyert, R. M., & March, J. G. (1963). *A behavioral theory of the firm*. Englewood Cliffs, NJ: Prentice Hall.

Dalton, D. A., & Cosier, R. A. (1982). The four faces of social responsibility. *Business Horizons*, 25 (3), 19-27.

Davidson, W. N. III, Chandy, P. R., & Cross, M. (1987). Large losses, risk management and stock returns in the airline industry. *Journal of Risk and Insurance,* 54 (1), 162-172.

Davidson, W. N. III, & Worrell, D. L. (1988). The impact of announcements of corporate illegalities on shareholder returns. *Academy of Management Journal,* 31, 195-200.

Davidson, W. N. III, & Worrell, D. L. (1992). Research notes and communications: The effect of product recall announcements on shareholder wealth. *Strategic Management Journal,* 13, 467-473.

Davis, K. (1973). The case for and against business assumption of social responsibilities. *Academy of Management Journal,* 16, 312-322.

Domini, A. (1994, October). *Social responsibility research: Why we need it.* Paper presented at the annual meeting of Business for Social Responsibility, Boston, MA.

Donaldson, T., & Preston, L. E. (1995). The stakeholder theory of the corporation: Concepts, evidence, and implications. *Academy of Management Review,* 20, 65-91.

Eilbert, H., & Parket, R. J. (1973). The practice of business: The current status of corporate social responsibility. *Business Horizons,* 16 (2), 5-14.

Epstein, E. M. (1987). The corporate social policy process: Beyond business ethics, corporate social responsibility, and corporate social responsiveness. *California Management Review* 29 (3), 99-114.

Ernst & Ernst. (1978). *Social responsibility disclosure—1978 survey.* Cleveland, OH: Ernst & Ernst.

Fogler, H. R. & Nutt, F. (1975). A note on social responsibility and stock valuation. *Academy of Management Journal,* 18, 155-160.

Frederick, W. C. (1994). 1978 Classic Paper: From CSR1 to CSR2: The maturing of business-and-society thought. *Business & Society,* 33, 150-164.

Freedman, M., & Jaggi, B. (1982). Pollution disclosures, pollution performance and economic performance. *Omega,* 10 (3), 167-176.

Freedman, M., & Jaggi, B. (1986). An analysis of the impact of corporate pollution disclosures included in annual financial statements on investors' decisions. Advances in Public Interest Accounting, 1, 193-212.

Freeman, R. E. (1984). *Strategic management: A stakeholder approach.* Boston: Pitman.

Friedman, M. (1962). *Capitalism and freedom.* Chicago: University of Chicago Press.

Friedman, M. (1970, September 13). The social responsibility of business is to increase its profits. *New York Times Magazine,* pp. 32-33, 122-126.

Frooman, J. S. (1994). Does the market penalize firms for socially irresponsible behavior? *IABS Proceedings,* 112-119.

Fry, F., & Hock, R. J. (1976). Who claims corporate responsibility? The biggest and the worst. *Business & Society Review/Innovation*, 18, 62-65.

Graves, S. B., & Waddock, S. A. (1994). Institutional ownership and corporate social performance. *Academy of Management Journal*, 37, 1034-1046.

Heinze, D. C. (1976). Financial correlates of a social measure. *Akron Business and Economic Review*, 7 (1), 48-51.

Hill, C. W. L., Kelley, P. C., & Agle, B. R. (1990). An empirical examination of the determinants of OSHA violations. *IABS Proceedings*, 402-412.

Hoffer, G. E., Pruitt, S. W., & Reilly, R. J. (1988). The impact of product recalls on the wealth of sellers: A reexamination. *Journal of Political Economy*, 96, 663-670.

Holman, W. R., New, J. R., & Singer, D. (1985). The impact of corporate social responsiveness on shareholder wealth. In L. E. Preston (Ed.), *Research in corporate social performance and policy* (Vol. 7, pp. 137-152). Greenwich, CT: JAI Press.

Holmes, S. L. (1977). Corporate social performance: Past and present areas of commitment. *Academy of Management Journal*, 20, 433-438.

Holmes, S. L. (1978). Adapting corporate structure for social responsiveness. *California Management Review*, 21 (1), 47-54.

Ingram, R. W. (1978). An investigation of the information content of (certain) social responsibility disclosures. *Journal of Accounting Research*, 16, 270-285.

Ingram, R. W., & Frazier, K. B. (1980). Environmental performance and corporate disclosure. *Journal of Accounting Research*, 18, 614-622.

Ingram, R. W., & Frazier, K. B. (1983). Narrative disclosures in annual reports. *Journal of Business Research*, 11 (1), 49-60.

Jarrell, G., & Peltzman, S. (1985). The impact of product recalls on the wealth of sellers. *Journal of Political Economy*, 93, 663-670.

Jones, T. M. (1980). Corporate social responsibility revisited, redefined. *California Management Review*, 22 (2), 59-67.

Kang, Y. C. (1995). *Before-profit corporate social responsibility and stakeholder management systems*. Unpublished doctoral dissertation, University of Pittsburgh.

Kang, Y. C., & Wood, D. J. (1995). Before-profit corporate social responsibility: Turning the economic paradigm upside-down. *IABS Proceedings*.

Kedia, B. L., & Kuntz, E. C. (1981). The context of social performance: An empirical study of Texas banks. In L. E. Preston, (Ed.), *Research in corporate social performance and policy* (Vol. 3, pp. 133-154). Greenwich, CT: JAI Press.

Keim, G. D. (1978). Managerial behavior and the social responsibility debate: Goals vs. constraints. *Academy of Management Journal*, 21, 57-68.

Keim, G. (1978). Corporate social responsibility: An assessment of the enlightened self-interest model. *Academy of Management Review*, 3, 32-39.

Key, S. K. (1995). *Do managers matter? The role of managerial discretion in corporate social responsibility decisions.* Unpublished doctoral dissertation, University of Pittsburgh.

Kinder, P. D., Lydenberg, S. D., & Domini, A. L. (1993). *Investing for good: Making money while being socially responsible.* New York: HarperBusiness.

Kohls, J. (1985). Corporate board structure, social reporting and social performance. In L. E. Preston (Ed.), *Research in corporate social performance and policy* (Vol. 7, pp. 165-189). Greenwich, CT: JAI Press.

Levy, F. K., & Shatto, G. M. (1980). Social responsibility in large electric utility firms: The case for philanthropy. In L. E. Preston (Ed.), *Research in corporate social performance and policy* (Vol. 2, pp. 237-249). Greenwich, CT: JAI Press.

Mallott, M. J. (1993). *Operationalizing corporate social performance.* Doctoral dissertation, University of Pittsburgh.

McGuire, J. B., Sundgren, A., & Schneeweis, T. (1988). Corporate social responsibility and firm financial performance. *Academy of Management Journal*, 31, 854-872.

Miles, R. A. (1987). *Managing the corporate social environment: A grounded theory.* Englewood Cliffs, NJ: Prentice-Hall.

Mitchell, N. (1983). Ownership, control, and social policy. In L. E. Preston (Ed.), *Research in corporate social performance and policy* (Vol. 5, pp. 205-230). Greenwich, CT: JAI Press.

Mitchell, R. N., Agle, B. R., & Wood, D. J. (in press). *Stakeholder attributes and firm responsibilities and responses.* Paper presented at the annual meeting of the Academy of Management, Vancouver, Canada.

Mitnick, B. M. (1993). Organizing research in corporate social performance: The CSP system as core paradigm. *IABS Proceedings*, 2-15.

Mitnick, B. M. (1994). Systematics and CSP: The theory and processes of normative referencing. *Business & Society*, 34, 5-33.

Morris, S. A., Rehbein, K. A., Hosseini, J. C., & Armacost, R. L. (1990). Building a current profile of socially responsive firms. *IABS Proceedings*, 297-303.

Morris, S. A., Armacost, R. L., Hosseini, J. C., & Rehbein, K. A. (1991). Organizational misconduct: A test of three competing explanations. *IABS Proceedings*, 367-381.

Moskowitz, M. (1972). Choosing socially responsible stocks. *Business and Society Review*, 1, 71-75.

Newgren, K. E., Rasher, A. A., LaRoe, M. E., & Szabo, M. R. (1985). Environmental assessment and corporate performance: A longitudinal analysis using a market-determined performance measure. In L. E. Preston (Ed.), *Research in corporate social performance and policy* (Vol. 7, pp. 153-164). Greenwich, CT: JAI Press.

Parket, R., & Eilbert, H. (1975). Social responsibility: The underlying factors. *Business Horizons*, 18 (3), 5-10.

Pinkston, T. S., & Carroll, A. B. (1993). An investigation of the relationship between organizational size and corporate social performance. *IABS Proceedings*, 109-114.

Preston, L. E. (1978). Analyzing corporate social performance: Methods and results. *Journal of Contemporary Business*, 7 (2), 135-149.

Preston, L. E. (1986). Social issues in management: An evolutionary perspective. In D. A. Wren & J. A. Pearce II (Eds.), *Papers Dedicated to the Development of Modern Management: Celebrating 100 Years of Modern Management: 50th Anniversary of the Academy of Management* (pp. 52-57). Academy of Management.

Preston, L. E., & Post, J. E. (1975). *Private management and public policy: The principle of public responsibility*. Englewood Cliffs, NJ: Prentice-Hall.

Pruitt, S. W., & Peterson, D. R. (1986). Security price reactions around product recall announcements. *Journal of Financial Research*, 9 (2), 113-122.

Randall, N. H., & Neuman, W. L. (1979). *The impact of government sanctions on the large corporation: The cost of antitrust law violation*. Unpublished manuscript, Nashville, TN: Vanderbilt University.

Reilly, R. J., & Hoffer, G. E. (1983). Will retarding the information flow on automobile recalls affect consumer demand? *Economic Inquiry*, 21, 444-447.

Rockness, J., Schlachter, P., & Rockness, H. O. (1986). Hazardous waste disposal, corporate disclosure, and financial performance in the chemical industry. *Advances in Public Interest Accounting*, 1, 167-191.

Roman, P. M., & Blum, T. C. (1987). The relation of employee assistance programs to corporate social responsibility attitudes: An empirical study. In L. E. Preston (Ed.), *Research in corporate social performance and policy* (Vol. 9, pp. 213-235). Greenwich, CT: JAI Press.

Sethi, S. P. (1979). A conceptual framework for environmental analysis of social issues and evaluation of business response patterns. *Academy of Management Review*, 4, 63-74.

Shane, P. B., & Spicer, B. H. (1983). Market response to environmental information produced outside the firm. *Accounting Review*, 58, 521-538.

Sharfman, M. (1993). A concurrent validity study of the KLD social performance ratings data. *IABS Proceedings*, 551-556.

Smith, S. M., & Alcorn, D. S. (1991). Cause marketing. *Journal of Consumer Marketing*, 8 (3), 19-35.

Sonnenfeld, J. A. (1982). Structure, culture and performance in public affairs: A study of the forest products industry. In L. E. Preston (Ed.), *Research in corporate social performance and policy* (Vol. 4, pp. 105-127). Greenwich, CT: JAI Press.

Spicer, B. H. (1978a). Investors, corporate social performance and information disclosure: An empirical study. *Accounting Review*, 53 (1), 94-111.

Spicer, B. H. (1978b). Market risk, accounting data and companies' pollution control records. *Journal of Business, Finance and Accounting*, 5 (1), 67-83.

Spicer, B. H. (1980). The relationship between pollution control record and financial indicators revisited: Further comment. *Accounting Review*, 55 (1), 178-185.

Strachan, J. L., Smith, D. B., & Beedles, W. L. (1983). The price reaction to (alleged) corporate crime. *Financial Review*, 18 (2), 121-132.

Sturdivant, F. D., & Ginter, J. L. (1977). Corporate social responsiveness: Management attitudes and economic performance. *California Management Review*, 19 (1), 30-39.

Swanson, D. (1994). The CSP field divided: Irreconciled economic and deontological perspectives. *IABS Proceedings*, 412-423.

Swanson, D. (1995). Addressing a theoretical problem by reorienting the corporate social performance model. *Academy of Management Review*, 20, 43-64.

Thomas, A. S., & Simerly, R. L. (1994). The chief executive officer and corporate social performance: An interdisciplinary examination. *Journal of Business Ethics*, 13, 959-968.

Toronto conference: Reflections on stakeholder theory. (1994). *Business & Society*, 33, 82-131.

Ullmann, A. (1985). Data in search of a theory: A critical examination of the relationships among social performance, social disclosure, and economic performance. *Academy of Management Review*, 10, 540-577.

Vance, S. C. (1975). Are socially responsible corporations good investment risks? *Management Review*, 64 (1), 19-24.

Wartick, S. L., & Cochran, P. L. (1985). The evolution of the corporate social performance model. *Academy of Management Review*, 10, 758-769.

Weir, P. (1983). The costs of antimerger lawsuits. *Journal of Financial Economics*, 11, 207-224.

Wiseman, J. (1982). An evaluation of environmental disclosures made in corporate annual reports. *Accounting, Organizations, and Society,* 7 (1), 53-63.

Wokutch, R. E., & Spencer, B. A. (1987). Corporate saints and sinners: The effects of philanthropic and illegal activity on organizational performance. *California Management Review,* 29 (1), 62-77.

Wood, D. J. (1991a). Corporate social performance revisited. *Academy of Management Review,* 16, 691-718.

Wood, D. J. (1991b). Social issues in management: Research and theory in corporate social performance. *Journal of Management,* 17, 383-406.

Wood, D. J. (1991c). Toward improving corporate social performance. *Business Horizons,* 34 (4), 66-72.

Wood, D. J., & Jones, R. A. (in press). Research in corporate social performance: What have we learned? In D. Burlingame and D. R. Young (Eds.), *Corporate philanthropy at the crossroads.* Bloomington, IN: Indiana University Press.

Wynn, J. A., & Hoffer, G. E. (1976). Auto recalls: Do they affect market share? *Applied Economics,* 8 (2), 157-163.

Reprinted with the permission of the Centre for Advanced Studies in Management, Bowling Green, Kentucky.